Advisor-Consultants

Vincent J. Altamuro
Assistant Principal,
Thomas Jefferson School
Queens, New York

Sandra Pryor Clarkson
Associate Professor
of Mathematical Sciences
Hunter College of CUNY
New York, New York

Jeanette Gann
Mathematics and Science
Coordinator, High Point
Public Schools
High Point, North Carolina

Zelda Gold
Mathematics Advisor,
Los Angeles Unified
School District
Los Angeles, California

Dorothy Keane
Professor of Education
California State University,
Los Angeles
Los Angeles, California

Joel Levin
Teacher, Chicago Public Schools
Chicago, Illinois

Gail Lowe
Principal, Conejo Valley
Unified School District
Thousand Oaks, California

Kozo Nishifue
Administrator of Mathematics,
Oakland Unified School District
Oakland, California

James A. Peters, Jr.
Elementary Mathematics
Resource Teacher,
Samuel Powel School
Philadelphia, Pennsylvania

Andria P. Troutman
Professor, University
of South Florida
Tampa, Florida

LAIDLAW
Mathematics

LAIDLAW BROTHERS · PUBLISHERS
A Division of Doubleday & Company, Inc.

RIVER FOREST, ILLINOIS
Sacramento, California • Chamblee, Georgia • Dallas, Texas • Toronto, Canada

Acknowledgments

Developed by Kirchoff/Wohlberg, Inc.,
in cooperation with Laidlaw Brothers, Publishers

Editorial Director   Mary Jane Martin

Laidlaw Editorial Staff

Editorial Manager   David B. Spangler

Editor/Consultant   Barbara J. Huffman

Editors   Robert C. Mudd, Judith A. Witt

Educator/Reviewers

Deborah Abbott, Carole Bauer, Lynn Cohn, Cynthia Frederick,
Patricia A. Schwartz, Helene Silverman, Larry A. Tagle,
Josephine Wraith

TABLE OF CONTENTS

CHAPTER 1 USING MATHEMATICS

Using Mathematics 2
What Is Mathematics? 4
Number Skills: Getting Started 6
Measurement: Getting Started 8
Geometry: Getting Started 9
Patterns and Functions: Getting Started 10
Statistics and Probability: Getting Started 11
Logic: Getting Started 12
Algebra: Getting Started 13
Using This Book 14

CHAPTER 2 PLACE VALUE

Formulating Problems 16
Place Value to Billions 18
Place Value to Ten Billions 20
Application: Using Numeration 21
Problem Solving: Using the Five-Step Plan 22
Round Whole Numbers to Nearest Billion 24
Round Whole Numbers to Nearest Billion 26
Application: Using Measurement 27
Math in Sports: Soccer 28
Looking Back: Reviewing and Testing Chapter 2 30
Looking Ahead: Preparing for New Skills for Chapter 3 31

CHAPTER 3 PLACE VALUE AND EXPONENTS

Formulating Problems 32
Read, Write, and Compare Numbers to Ten Billions 34
Read, Write, and Compare Numbers to Ten Billions 36
Application: Using Statistics 37
Application: Problem Solving–Evaluating Information 37
Exponents: Write Numbers Using Bases Other Than Ten 38
Exponents: Write Numbers Using Bases Other Than Ten 40
Application: Using Numbers 41
Math in Architecture: The Shape of a Building 42
Looking Back: Reviewing and Testing Chapter 3 44
Looking Ahead: Preparing for New Skills for Chapter 4 45

CHAPTER 4   SIMPLE EQUATIONS

Formulating Problems 46
Algebra: Order of Operations 48
Algebra: Order of Operations 50
Application: Using Algebra 51
Algebra: Using Inverse Operations 52
Algebra: Using Inverse Operations 54
Application: Problem Solving–Evaluating Information 55
Math in Social Studies: Pyramids of Egypt 56
Looking Back: Reviewing and Testing Chapter 4 58
Looking Ahead: Preparing for New Skills for Chapter 5 59

CHAPTER 5   ADDITION AND SUBTRACTION

Formulating Problems 60
Addition: Whole Numbers..62
Addition: Whole Numbers Using Estimation 64
Application: Using Number Properties of Addition 65
Problem Solving: Evaluating Information......................................66
Subtraction: Whole Numbers..68
Subtraction: Whole Numbers With Zeros....................................70
Application: Using Estimation 71
Math in Cartography: Building Plans..72
Looking Back: Reviewing and Testing Chapter 5 74
Looking Ahead: Preparing for New Skills for Chapter 6 75

CHAPTER 6   NUMBER THEORY

Formulating Problems 76
Number Skills: Prime and Composite Numbers..............................78
Number Skills: Prime and Composite Numbers..............................80
Application: Using Prime Numbers 81
Application: Exploring With a Calculator 81
Prime Factorization: Using a Factor Tree......................................82
Prime Factorization: Using a Factor Tree......................................84
Application: Using Twin Primes..85
Application: Problem Solving–Evaluating Information 85
Math in Technology: What Is Computer Programming? 86
Looking Back: Reviewing and Testing Chapter 6 88
Looking Ahead: Preparing for New Skills for Chapter 7 89

CHAPTER 7   MULTIPLICATION AND DIVISION

Formulating Problems 90
Multiplication of Whole Numbers: By 1- or 2-Digit Numbers 92
Multiplication of Whole Numbers: By 1-, 2-, or 3-Digit
    Numbers 94
Application: Using Algebra 95
Division of Whole Numbers: By 1- or 2-Digit Numbers 96
Division of Whole Numbers: By 1- or 2-Digit Numbers 98
Application: Using Logic and Number Skills 99
Math in Space Cartography: Point of View 100
Looking Back: Reviewing and Testing Chapter 7 102
Looking Ahead: Preparing for New Skills for Chapter 8 103

CHAPTER 8   MULTIPLICATION AND DIVISION OF LARGER WHOLE NUMBERS

Formulating Problems 104
Multiplication of Whole Numbers: By 1-, 2-, 3-, or 4-Digit
    Numbers 106
Multiplication of Whole Numbers: Patterns in Multiplication 108
Application: Using Multiplication Properties.................................... 109
Division of Whole Numbers: By 1-, 2-, or 3-Digit Numbers 110
Division of Whole Numbers: Remainders in Division........................ 112
Application: Using Patterns 113
Math in Games: The Game of Nim 114
Looking Back: Reviewing and Testing Chapter 8 116
Looking Ahead: Preparing for New Skills for Chapter 9 117

Quarterly Review/Test 118

CHAPTER 9   NUMBER THEORY

Formulating Problems 120
Number Skills: Greatest Common Factor 122
Greatest Common Factor: Simplify Fractions 124
Application: Using Patterns 125
Problem Solving: Solving Multi-Step Problems 126
Number Skills: Least Common Multiple 128
Least Common Multiple: Using Prime Factorization 130
Application: Solving Problems 131
Application: Problem Solving–Solving Multi-Step Problems 132
Math in Art: Tessellations... 132
Looking Back: Reviewing and Testing Chapter 9 134
Looking Ahead: Preparing for New Skills for Chapter 10 135

CHAPTER 10 MEANING OF FRACTIONS

Formulating Problems 136
Equivalent Fractions: Using Cross Products................................ 138
Equivalent Fractions: Using Cross Products................................ 140
Application: Problem Solving–Solving Multi-Step Problems 141
Fractions: Compare and Order... 142
Fractions: Compare and Order... 144
Application: Using Number Skills.. 145
History of Math: Ancient Numbers.. 146
Looking Back: Reviewing and Testing Chapter 10.......................... 148
Looking Ahead: Preparing for New Skills for Chapter 11 149

CHAPTER 11 ADDITION AND SUBTRACTION OF FRACTIONS AND MIXED NUMBERS

Formulating Problems 150
Addition of Fractions and Mixed Numbers With Regrouping............. 152
Addition of Fractions and Mixed Numbers With Regrouping............. 154
Application: Solving Problems 155
Problem Solving: Using a Diagram.. 156
Subtraction of Fractions and Mixed Numbers With Regrouping......... 158
Subtraction of Fractions and Mixed Numbers With Regrouping......... 160
Application: Using Geometry 161
Math in Science: Gravity 162
Looking Back: Reviewing and Testing Chapter 11.......................... 164
Looking Ahead: Preparing for New Skills for Chapter 12 165

CHAPTER 12 GEOMETRY: AREA OF POLYGONS

Formulating Problems 166
Area: Finding the Area of a Rectangle 168
Area: Finding the Area of a Triangle 170
Application: Using Measurement... 171
Area: Finding Areas of Parallelograms 172
Area: Rectangles, Triangles, and Parallelograms 174
Application: Using Measurement... 175
Math in Technology: Writing an Algorithm 176
Looking Back: Reviewing and Testing Chapter 12.......................... 178
Looking Ahead: Preparing for New Skills for Chapter 13 179

CHAPTER 13   GEOMETRY: TRIANGLES AND QUADRILATERALS

Formulating Problems 180
Geometry: Angles and Triangles 182
Geometry: Sides of Triangles... 184
Application: Using Geometry 185
Geometry: Angles of Quadrilaterals 186
Geometry: Angles of Polygons... 188
Application: Using Geometry 189
Math in Consumer Education: Buying in Quantity...................... 190
Looking Back: Reviewing and Testing Chapter 13...................... 192
Looking Ahead: Preparing for New Skills for Chapter 14.................. 193

CHAPTER 14   STATISTICS

Formulating Problems 194
Data: Finding Mean, Median, Range, and Mode 196
Data: Finding Mean, Median, Range, and Mode 198
Application: Using Statistics... 199
Problem Solving: Finding a Pattern 200
Frequency Tables: Using Range and Mode............................... 202
Frequency Tables: Using Range and Mode............................... 204
Application: Using Statistics... 205
Math in Social Studies: The Parthenon................................... 206
Looking Back: Reviewing and Testing Chapter 14...................... 208
Looking Ahead: Preparing for New Skills for Chapter 15.................. 209

CHAPTER 15   MULTIPLICATION AND DIVISION OF FRACTIONS

Formulating Problems 210
Multiplication of Fractions: Multiplying a Fraction by a Fraction 212
Multiplication of Fractions: Reciprocals 214
Application: Using Estimation 215
Application: Using Number Skills... 215
Division: Fractions and Whole Numbers................................. 216
Division of Fractions: Dividing a Fraction by a Fraction 218
Application: Solving Problems 219
Math in Technology: Using an Algorithm 220
Looking Back: Reviewing and Testing Chapter 15...................... 222
Looking Ahead: Preparing for New Skills for Chapter 16.................. 223

CHAPTER 16 MULTIPLICATION AND DIVISION OF FRACTIONS AND MIXED NUMBERS

Formulating Problems 224
Multiplication: Fractions and Mixed Numbers.............................. 226
Multiplication: Fractions and Mixed Numbers.............................. 228
Application: Using Patterns 229
Division: Fractions and Mixed Numbers..................................... 230
Division: Fractions and Mixed Numbers..................................... 232
Application: Using Logic.. 233
Math in Games: The Tangram Puzzle......................... 234
Looking Back: Reviewing and Testing Chapter 16.......................... 236
Looking Ahead: Preparing for New Skills for Chapter 17.................. 237

Quarterly Review/Test.. 238
Midterm Review/Test 240

CHAPTER 17 FRACTIONS AND DECIMALS

Formulating Problems 242
Fractions and Decimals: Changing Fractions to Decimals 244
Mixed Numbers and Decimals: Changing Mixed Numbers to
    Decimals 246
Application: Using Measurement.. 247
Problem Solving: Making a List.. 248
Fractions, Mixed Numbers, and Decimals: Changing Decimals
    to Fractions and Mixed Numbers....................................... 250
Fractions and Decimals: Common Equivalents 252
Application: Using a Calculator.. 253
Math in Science: Energy Conservation....................................... 254
Looking Back: Reviewing and Testing Chapter 17.......................... 256
Looking Ahead: Preparing for New Skills for Chapter 18.................. 257

CHAPTER 18 MEANING OF DECIMALS

Formulating Problems 258
Round Decimals to the Nearest Hundredth or Thousandth 260
Round Decimals to the Nearest Hundredth or Thousandth 262
Application: Using a Calculator.. 263
Compare and Order Decimals to Ten-Thousandths 264
Compare and Order Decimals to Ten-Thousandths 266
Application: Round, Compare, and Order Money.......................... 267
Math in Technology: How Do Computers Print Messages? 268
Looking Back: Reviewing and Testing Chapter 18.......................... 270
Looking Ahead: Preparing for New Skills for Chapter 19.................. 271

CHAPTER 19 ADDITION AND SUBTRACTION OF DECIMALS

Formulating Problems 272
Addition of Decimals to Thousandths.......................... 274
Addition of Decimals to Thousandths.......................... 276
Application: Using Consumer Skills 277
Subtraction of Decimals to Thousandths...................... 278
Subtraction of Decimals to Thousandths...................... 280
Application: Using Consumer Skills 281
Math in Games: The Soma Cube................................... 281
Looking Back: Reviewing and Testing Chapter 19 284
Looking Ahead: Preparing for New Skills for Chapter 20 285

CHAPTER 20 MULTIPLICATION AND DIVISION OF DECIMALS

Formulating Problems 286
Multiplication of Decimals by 10, 100, or 1,000............. 288
Multiplication of Decimals: Estimating Products 290
Application: Using Measurement.................................. 291
Application: Using Mental Arithmetic.......................... 291
Problem Solving: Using a Formula............................... 292
Division of Decimals by 10, 100, or 1,000..................... 294
Division of Decimals: Estimating Quotients.................. 296
Application: Using Mental Arithmetic.......................... 297
Application: Using Mental Arithmetic.......................... 297
Math in Science: The Metric System............................. 298
Looking Back: Reviewing and Testing Chapter 20 300
Looking Ahead: Preparing for New Skills for Chapter 21 301

CHAPTER 21 METRIC MEASUREMENT

Formulating Problems 302
Metric Measures of Length 304
Metric Measures of Area 306
Application: Solving Problems 307
Metric Measures of Capacity and Mass 308
Metric Measures of Capacity and Mass 310
Application: Using Measurement–Volume 311
Math in Technology: Using the Order of Operations 312
Looking Back: Reviewing and Testing Chapter 21 314
Looking Ahead: Preparing for New Skills for Chapter 22 315

CHAPTER 22   MULTIPLICATION AND DIVISION OF DECIMALS

Formulating Problems 316
Multiplication of Decimals by a Decimal.................................... 318
Multiplication of Decimals by 0.1, 0.01, and 0.001 320
Application: Using Patterns 321
Division of Decimals by Whole Numbers.................................... 322
Division of Decimals: Dividing by a Decimal 324
Application: Using Measurement.. 325
Math in Music: The Metronome 326
Looking Back: Reviewing and Testing Chapter 22.......................... 328
Looking Ahead: Preparing for New Skills for Chapter 23 329

CHAPTER 23   RATIO AND PROPORTION

Formulating Problems 330
Ratio and Proportion: Writing Ratios and Proportions.................... 332
Ratio and Proportion: Solving Proportions 334
Application: Using Measurement.. 335
Problem Solving: Using Guess and Test 336
Ratio and Proportion: Using Proportions to Solve Problems.............. 338
Ratio and Proportion: Using Proportions to Solve Problems.............. 340
Application: Using Customary Units 341
History of Math: Ancient Time-keeping 342
Looking Back: Reviewing and Testing Chapter 23.......................... 344
Looking Ahead: Preparing for New Skills for Chapter 24 345

CHAPTER 24   PROBABILITY

Formulating Problems 346
Probability: Outcomes 348
Probability: Outcomes 350
Application: Using Ratio and Proportion 351
Probability: Sample Space... 352
Probability: Sample Space... 354
Application: Using Probability 355
Math in Technology: Writing a BASIC Program............................. 356
Looking Back: Reviewing and Testing Chapter 24.......................... 358
Looking Ahead: Preparing for New Skills for Chapter 25 359

Quarterly Review/Test... 360

CHAPTER 25   GEOMETRY: CIRCLES

Formulating Problems 362
Circles: Identify Parts of a Circle 364
Circles: Finding the Circumference of a Circle............................ 366
Application: Using Geometry 367
Circles: Finding the Area of a Circle.. 368
Circles: Finding the Area of a Circle.. 370
Application: Using Symmetry.. 371
Math in Consumer Education: Banking....................................... 372
Looking Back: Reviewing and Testing Chapter 25......................... 374
Looking Ahead: Preparing for New Skills for Chapter 26................. 375

CHAPTER 26   PERCENT

Formulating Problems 376
Percent: Ratios, Fractions, and Percents 378
Percent: Fractions, Decimals, and Percents................................. 380
Application: Using Statistics... 381
Problem Solving: Using Logic... 382
Percent: Finding a Percent of a Number 384
Percent: Finding a Percent of a Number 386
Application: Using a Calculator... 387
Math in Geography: Computing Distances................................... 388
Looking Back: Reviewing and Testing Chapter 26......................... 390
Looking Ahead: Preparing for New Skills for Chapter 27................. 391

CHAPTER 27   PERCENT

Formulating Problems 392
Percent: Finding What Percent One Number Is of Another 394
Percent: Finding What Percent One Number Is of Another 396
Application: Using Statistics... 397
Percent: Finding a Number When a Percent of It Is Known.............. 398
Percent: Finding a Number When a Percent of It Is Known.............. 400
Application: Solving Problems 401
Math in Music: Chance and Music... 402
Looking Back: Reviewing and Testing Chapter 27......................... 404
Looking Ahead: Preparing for New Skills for Chapter 28................. 405

CHAPTER 28 ADDITION OF INTEGERS

Formulating Problems 406
Integers: Comparing and Ordering 408
Integers: Comparing and Ordering 410
Application: Using Algebra 411
Addition of Integers With Like Signs........................ 412
Addition of Integers With Like Signs........................ 414
Application: Using Algebra 415
Math in Health: Heart Rate....................................... 416
Looking Back: Reviewing and Testing Chapter 28 418
Looking Ahead: Preparing for New Skills for Chapter 29 419

CHAPTER 29 ADDITION AND SUBTRACTION OF INTEGERS

Formulating Problems 420
Addition of Integers With Unlike Signs..................... 422
Addition of Integers With Unlike Signs..................... 424
Application: Using Algebra 425
Problem Solving: Choosing Strategies 426
Subtraction of Integers With Like Signs..................... 428
Subtraction of Integers With Like and Unlike Signs........ 430
Application: Using Algebra 431
Math in Geography: Numbers That Show Direction 432
Looking Back: Reviewing and Testing Chapter 29 434
Looking Ahead: Preparing for New Skills for Chapter 30 435

CHAPTER 30 MULTIPLICATION AND DIVISION OF INTEGERS

Formulating Problems 436
Multiplication of Integers With Like and Unlike Signs...... 438
Multiplication of Integers With Like and Unlike Signs...... 440
Application: Using Patterns and Functions.................. 441
Division of Integers With Like and Unlike Signs............ 442
Division of Integers With Like and Unlike Signs............ 444
Application: Using Front-End Estimation–Sums and Differences 445
Math in Technology: Programming Computers 446
Looking Back: Reviewing and Testing Chapter 30 448
Looking Ahead: Preparing for New Skills for Chapter 31 449

FOCUS

CHAPTER 31   EXPRESSIONS AND EQUATIONS

Formulating Problems 450
Algebra: Expressions.. 452
Algebra: Expressions.. 454
Application: Using Measurement.............................. 455
Algebra: Writing Equations and Inequalities 456
Algebra: Writing Equations and Inequalities 458
Application: Using Front-End Estimation–Products and Quotients 459
Math in Sports: Baseball.. 460
Looking Back: Reviewing and Testing Chapter 31 462
Looking Ahead: Preparing for New Skills for Chapter 32 463

CHAPTER 32   GEOMETRIC CONSTRUCTIONS

Formulating Problems 464
Geometry: Constructing Line Segments and Angles 466
Geometry: Constructing Line Segments and Angles 468
Application: Using Geometry 469
Geometry: Constructing Congruent Triangles 470
Geometry: Constructing Congruent Triangles 472
Application: Using Statistics..................................... 473
Math in Technology: How Does the Computer Deal With Fractions? ... 474
Looking Back: Reviewing and Testing Chapter 32 476
Looking Ahead: Preparing for Next Year 477

Quarterly Review/Test.. 478
Final Review/Test.. 480

Extra Practice 482
Data Bank 496
Glossary 502
Index 508

Use mathematics.

CHAPTER 1

Using Mathematics

The people in these photographs prepared for many years to do their jobs. Many of the skills required for each profession took years to acquire, but some of those necessary skills were learned at your age.

Pediatricians use logic to consider the symptoms of a patient and diagnose illnesses. They use measurement to find a patient's body weight, blood pressure, height, and other vital data. Statistics plays an important role as well. It is very important to keep accurate records on each patient in order to administer proper treatment.

The store owner uses statistics to determine projected sales for each month. Measurement and geometry are used to calculate the total of each sale, the commission earned by each salesperson, and even the amount of profit.

To measure how long and steep a course is, marathon runners use measurement and geometry. They use statistics to compare their past performances on a particular course or similar courses, with other runners' past performances.

The aerobics teacher uses number skills and measurement to plan the number and types of exercises, as well as to determine the "safe accelerated pulse rate" of each student. The teacher also uses number skills to help students plan a diet by calculating their caloric intake and energy output.

In what other ways can each of these people make use of math skills?

The people in these pictures use mathematics in their daily lives. Mathematics plays a much more important role than you would think, in not only these activities but every activity you could imagine doing! How might each of these people use math skills?

Mathematics is more than adding, subtracting, multiplying, and dividing. Studying mathematics can be compared to weaving a beautiful tapestry of many different colors. Each strand of color adds to the richness and strength of the tapestry. In this book we will show that mathematics is, like the tapestry, made up of many different strands. Each strand that we study adds richness and strength to our understanding of mathematics.

1. NUMBER SKILLS When you calculate using addition, subtraction, multiplication, or division, you are using number skills. Your calculations may involve whole numbers, fractions, decimals, and integers.

2. MEASUREMENT When you use rulers or straightedges, protractors, compasses, scales, and clocks you are using measurement skills. When you find the mass or weight of an object, or the perimeter or area of a figure you are also using measurement skills.

3. GEOMETRY When you study objects, compare their sizes and shapes, identify lines, rays, angles, and parts of a circle you are using geometry skills.

4. PATTERNS AND FUNCTIONS When you find the next term of a sequence by studying the previous term you are using pattern skills. When you find a rule that describes the relationship between two numbers you are using function skills.

5. STATISTICS AND PROBABILITY When you compile and analyze information you are using statistical skills. When you consider the likelihood of an event to occur you are using probability skills.

6. LOGIC When you draw conclusions from facts you are using logical reasoning skills.

7. ALGEBRA When you use symbols to represent numbers and when you write and solve phrases using these symbols you are using algebra skills.

NUMBER SKILLS

Getting Started

When you add, subtract, multiply or divide you are using number skills.

Perform the indicated operations. Each answer found in Column I will correspond to an answer found in Column II. Copy the row of numbers below the columns and place the appropriate letters from Column II over the corresponding numbers from Column I. You may use the same letter more than once. Then solve the riddle: What did the rider hope the horse had plenty of?

I

1. Find the sum of 225 and 132.

2. Compute: 301 − 253.

3. Subtract 42 from the sum of 385 and 157.

4. Divide: 888 ÷ 4.

5. Subtract 332 from 534.

6. Solve: 49 + ■ = 71

7. 9 tens + five ones

II

E. Divide: 15)‾3030

R. Round 485 to the nearest hundred.

H. Multiply: 119 × 3.

O. Number of eggs in four dozen

E. Divide: 12)‾264.

S. Number of minutes in 3 hours, 42 minutes

N. Add: 33 + 26 + 11 + 18 + 7.

■	■	■	■	■		■	■	■	■	■
1	2	3	4	5		4	6	7	4	6

Round each of the following numbers to the nearest hundred and to the nearest thousand.

8. 1,250   **9.** 1,306   **10.** 12,543   **11.** 512

12. 1,450   **13.** 4,049   **14.** 1,075   **15.** 76,697

Add, subtract, multiply, or divide.

16. $\begin{array}{r} 247 \\ +\ 66 \end{array}$ **17.** $\begin{array}{r} 768 \\ +\ 491 \end{array}$ **18.** $\begin{array}{r} 5{,}076 \\ +\ 6{,}631 \end{array}$ **19.** $\begin{array}{r} 2{,}794 \\ 19 \\ +\ \ 321 \end{array}$ **20.** $\begin{array}{r} 6{,}066 \\ 372 \\ +\ \ 459 \end{array}$

21. $\begin{array}{r} 593 \\ -\ 43 \end{array}$ **22.** $\begin{array}{r} 272 \\ -\ 57 \end{array}$ **23.** $\begin{array}{r} 7{,}608 \\ -\ 3{,}259 \end{array}$ **24.** $\begin{array}{r} 10{,}000 \\ -\ 1{,}725 \end{array}$ **25.** $\begin{array}{r} 24{,}000 \\ -\ 1{,}973 \end{array}$

26. $\begin{array}{r} 509 \\ \times\ \ 9 \end{array}$ **27.** $\begin{array}{r} 327 \\ \times\ 15 \end{array}$ **28.** $\begin{array}{r} 58 \\ \times\ 27 \end{array}$ **29.** $\begin{array}{r} 302 \\ \times\ 100 \end{array}$ **30.** $\begin{array}{r} 4{,}636 \\ \times\ \ 29 \end{array}$

31. $7\overline{)427}$ **32.** $16\overline{)576}$ **33.** $35\overline{)2{,}345}$ **34.** $24\overline{)12{,}720}$ **35.** $19\overline{)11{,}628}$

Estimate each answer. Then solve each problem. (To review estimation strategies, see page 497 in the Data Bank.)

36. Jose bought 3 apples at $0.49 each, 2 bunches of grapes at $0.89 each, and a can of juice for $0.65. How much did he spend? How much change did he get from a five-dollar bill?

37. Alexis' test scores this term are 86, 92, 100, 88, and 94. Find the sum of her test grades. Then find her average grade. (The average is often called the *mean*.)

38. Samantha invested $2,837 in stocks. Five years later, she sold the stocks for $7,502. How much profit did she make from this sale?

39. The Footware Outlet store bought 78 pairs of shoes for $936. If each shoe cost the same amount, how much did they pay for each pair of shoes?

40. Adam types an average of 49 words per minute. How many words can he type in 45 minutes at this rate?

41. If twenty-five yards of carpeting cost $350, how much does each yard of this carpeting cost?

MEASUREMENT
Getting Started

Almost every person uses some form of measurement in their daily activities. Bicyclists and drivers use speedometers, grocers use scales, and doctors use thermometers. These represent just a few of the activities that involve measurement.

Choose the best unit of measure.

1. distance between Denver and Miami

centimeter   meter   kilometer

2. length and width of a classroom

inch   foot   mile

3. capacity of a large fishtank

cup   quart   gallon

4. mass of a large garbage can

milligram   gram   kilogram

5. weight of a quarter

ounce   pound   ton

6. volume of a shoebox

cm^3 m^3 km^3

Use your centimeter ruler to measure each side of the figures below.

7.    **8.**    **9.**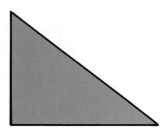

10. Find the perimeter of each figure above.

11. Find the area of each figure above.

Use the cube at the right to answer the following.

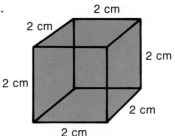

12. Find the perimeter of each face.

13. Find the surface area of each face.

14. Find the number of faces and edges.

15. Find the volume.

FOCUS | Review MEASUREMENT.

8

GEOMETRY
Getting Started

The world we live in is made up of many geometric shapes and patterns. Geometry is the study of these shapes. In this section, you will review lines, angles, and shapes.

Select one word which best describes each figure.

sphere   circle   pentagon   pyramid   cube
square   rectangle   rectangular solid   triangle
hexagon   octagon   isosceles triangle   equilateral triangle

16.

17.

18.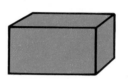

19.

20.

21.

22.

23.

24. Use the figure at the right to name four angles.

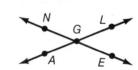

Use your protractor to find the measures of each angle.

25. m∠ABC

26. m∠CBD

27. m∠CBE

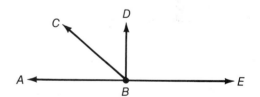

Use the circle to name each of the following.

28. a chord   **29.** a radius

30. a diameter   **31.** an arc

32. If the length of the radius is 3 cm, find the diameter.

33. Name the midpoint of the diameter.

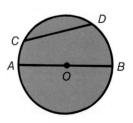

Review GEOMETRY.

PATTERNS AND FUNCTIONS

Getting Started

When you find the common relationship in a list of numbers you are finding a pattern.

Study the table at the right. Notice that each number in column 2 is 3 times the number in column 1. Use the rule to complete the table.

Rule: $n \times 3$

1	3
2	6
4	12
5	15
6	18
7	21
8	

Find the rule. Then copy and complete each table.

1. Rule: ■

3	6
1	2
	4
5	
7	
12	24
	100

2. Rule: ■

1	4
2	5
	8
11	
20	23
57	
	100

3. Rule: ■

9	3
15	
21	7
27	
	12
	20
99	

4. Rule: ■

6	5
18	
	32
50	49
72	
	86
100	99

5. Rule: ■

1	4
3	12
6	
	20
9	
25	100
	8

6. Rule: ■

25	5
100	
300	60
	30
5	1
20	
	2

Find the rule. Then copy and complete each pattern.

7. 1, 3, 5, 7, 9, ■, ■.

8. Z, Y, X, W, ■, ■.

9. 12, 10, 8, 6, 4, ■, ■.

10. 1, 5, 9, 13, 17, ■, ■.

11. A, C, E, G, ■, ■.

12. 0.1, 0.3, 0.5, 0.7, 0.9, ■, ■.

13. $\frac{1}{2}$, 1, $1\frac{1}{2}$, 2, $2\frac{1}{2}$, ■, ■.

14. $\frac{1}{3}$, $\frac{2}{3}$, 1, $1\frac{1}{3}$, $1\frac{2}{3}$, ■, ■.

15. 0.02, 0.2, 2, 20, 200, ■, ■.

16. 18, 15, 12, 9, 6, ■, ■.

FOCUS   Review PATTERNS and FUNCTIONS.

STATISTICS AND PROBABILITY
Getting Started

When you discuss the likelihood of an event taking place, you are considering the **probability** that such an event will take place. When you compile and analyze data relating to an event, you are using **statistics**.

The probability of an event is defined as follows:

$$P(\text{event}) = \frac{\text{number of successful outcomes}}{\text{total number of outcomes}}$$

Experiment: You spin the spinner once. What is the probability of the spinner stopping on

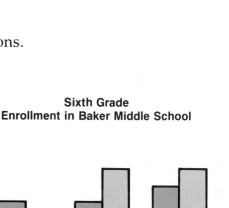

17. red?

18. yellow?

19. blue?

20. green?

21. red or yellow?

22. blue or green?

Now find the probability that the spinner will stop on a color that

23. is not blue.

24. is neither green nor blue.

25. is not red.

26. is neither yellow nor red.

Use the bar graph to answer the following questions.

27. How many boys are there in 6–2?

28. How many students are there in the sixth grade?

29. How many students are there in 6–1?

30. Which class has the largest enrollment?

31. What is the ratio of girls to boys in class 6–3?

32. Which two classes have the same number of girls?

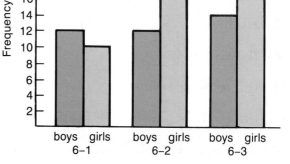

Review STATISTICS and PROBABILITY.

LOGIC

Getting Started

When you reason from facts you already know, you are using deductive reasoning. Use deductive reasoning to solve the following puzzle.

Use the facts below to find the subject that each student prefers. Read the clues. Copy the chart. Use a √ for yes or an x for no in each box as it is appropriate. Good Luck.

FACTS

1. No 2 people prefer the same subject.

2. Either Marla prefers science or Samson prefers music.

3. The subject Marla prefers deals with history.

4. The subject Mercedes prefers begins with the first initial of her name.

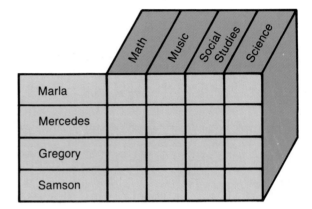

Use the figures at the right to answer the following questions.

Find the sum of the numbers in

5. the triangle.

6. the triangle but not the circle.

7. both the triangle and the circle.

8. the rectangle or in the triangle.

9. all three.

10. the rectangle.

11. the rectangle *only*.

12. the circle but *not* in the triangle.

13. the circle or the rectangle or the triangle.

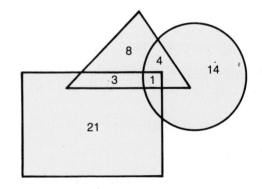

FOCUS | Review LOGIC.

ALGEBRA

Getting Started

When you use symbols or letters to represent numbers, you are using algebra.

In this section you will review some skills that you have already learned.

Use the proper order of operations to evaluate each of the following expressions.

14. $3 + 4 \times 5$ **15.** $6 + 7 \times 2$ **16.** $15 - 5 + 6$ **17.** $24 \div 6 + 2$

18. $(13 + 2) \div 5$ **19.** $5 \times 6 + 4$ **20.** $(37 - 2) \div 5$ **21.** $4 \times 6 + 18 \div 2$

22. $9 \times 5 + 20 \div 4$ **23.** $5 \times 5 \div 5$ **24.** $9 + 9 \div 9$ **25.** $10 \times 10 - 10$

Find the value of n that makes each sentence true.

26. $13 + n = 20$ **27.** $n + 6 = 18$ **28.** $n - 9 = 28$

29. $n + 25 = 39$ **30.** $20 \div n = 4$ **31.** $8 \times n = 48$

32. $n \div 7 = 98$ **33.** $n - 20 = 45$ **34.** $100 - n = 72$

Write in algebraic notation.

35. The sum of 4 and 3

36. The product of 5 and 2

37. The difference between 20 and 5

38. The quotient of 25 divided by 5

Find the letter that corresponds to each ordered pair and discover the name of the mathematician who developed much of the graphing we study today.

39. (4,3) **40.** (1,5,)

41. (1,2) **42.** (2,0)

43. (8,4) **44.** (7,1)

45. (5,6)

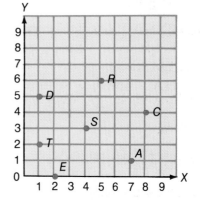

$$\overline{40} \quad \overline{42} \quad \overline{39} \quad \overline{43} \quad \overline{44} \quad \overline{45} \quad \overline{41} \quad \overline{42} \quad \overline{39}$$

Review ALGEBRA.

Understanding the Book's Organization

This book has been organized so that you will always know what kind of lesson you are doing—and the purpose of the lesson. Titles above the lines tell the general topic or strand used in the lesson. Titles below the lines tell more specifically what the lesson is about. The FOCUS tells the objective of the lesson.

Each chapter begins with a two-page FORMULATING PROBLEMS lesson. These lessons give you experience in thinking about and forming problems using real-life data.

NEW SKILLS lessons are organized this way:

1. First you are given a model of a new skill and then shown how to work through it.
2. Next you do some GUIDED PRACTICE to see if you understand the new skill.
3. Then PRACTICE exercises are provided to help you master the skill.
4. The MIXED PRACTICE that comes next helps you keep previously learned skills sharp.
5. A CHALLENGE section offers another way to use and apply your new skill.

The next two pages give you time to PRACTICE the skill you are learning.

1. First you have a quick review or an extension of the new skill.
2. PRACTICE exercises help you master the skill.

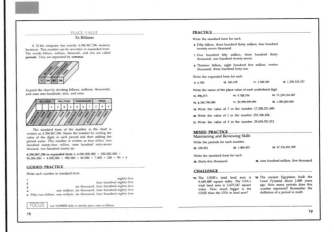

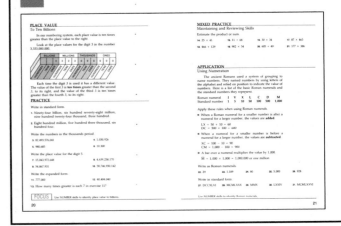

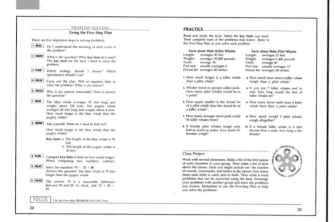

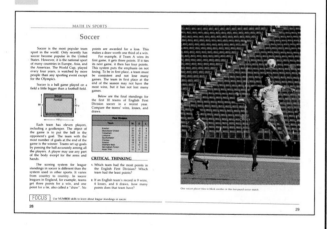

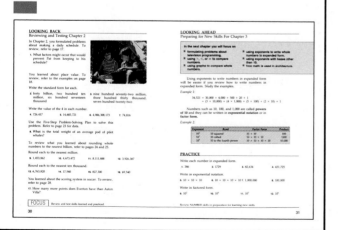

3. These are followed by MIXED PRACTICE exercises.
4. The next part of this lesson provides an APPLICATION of a new skill. You may use the skill with another math strand. Sometimes you apply the skill using ESTIMATION, MENTAL ARITHMETIC, or CALCULATORS.

PROBLEM-SOLVING lessons use the five steps—READ, KNOW, PLAN, SOLVE, and CHECK—to help you solve problems. You will also apply various strategies, like Using a Diagram and Using Guess and Test, to help you solve problems.

In MATH IN CONTENT you will learn how math is used in science, art, music, or geography. TECHNOLOGY lessons give you information about using computers.

In LOOKING BACK you will review or be tested on the skills you have just learned. By completing this review, you will know which skills you still need to work on and which skills you have mastered.

A LOOKING AHEAD page, at the end of every chapter, previews skills you will learn in the next chapter.

The DATA BANK (beginning on page 496) provides important information for you to use. A GLOSSARY (beginning on page 502) defines important math terms.

FOCUS   Formulate problems using photo, data, and text.

2

Place Value and Rounding Whole Numbers

9:00 AM–9:45 AM	Dress; breakfast
9:45 AM–10:30 AM	Yard work
11:00 AM–1:00 PM	Swim team
1:30 PM–2:00 PM	Lunch
2:00 PM–3:00 PM	Piano practice
3:00 PM–6:00 PM	Free time
6:00 PM–7:00 PM	Dinner
7:00 PM–7:30 PM	Do dishes
7:30 PM–9:30 PM	Free time
9:30 PM–10:30 PM	Shower; bed

School Year

7:00 AM–7:45 AM	Dress; breakfast
8:00 AM–8:25 AM	Bus ride to school
8:30 AM–11:45 AM	Classes
11:45 AM–1:00 PM	Lunch
1:00 PM–3:00 PM	Classes
3:00 PM–10:00 PM	To be scheduled

Pat wants to do many things during the coming school year. She still plans to participate on the swim team. Swimming practice, however, will only be half the time per day that it was during the summer. Pat and her friend want to divide a paper route. They each have agreed to deliver papers for forty-five minutes a day. Piano practice will take the same time during the school year as it did in the summer.

In order to be well prepared for class, Pat needs to allow enough time for homework. Pat's family expects some help around the house, too. But Pat also wants some free time.

Look at the data, which shows Pat's time plan for Monday through Friday. As you can see, the schedule for the school year is not completed.

What problems do you think Pat will have scheduling her time for the school year? Predict the activities Pat will do every weekday. Discuss reasons for your ideas.

To Billions

A 32-bit computer has exactly 4,294,967,296 memory locations. This number can be rewritten in expanded form. The words *billions*, *millions*, *thousands*, and *ones* are called **periods**. They are separated by **commas**.

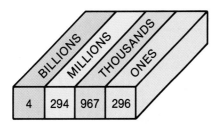

Expand the chart by dividing billions, millions, thousands, and ones into hundreds, tens, and ones.

	BILLIONS			MILLIONS			THOUSANDS			ONES	
		4	2	9	4	9	6	7	2	9	6
HUNDREDS	TENS	ONES	HUNDREDS	TENS	ONES	HUNDREDS	TENS	ONES	HUNDREDS	TENS	ONES

The standard form of the number in the chart is written as 4,294,967,296. Name the number by writing the value of the digits in each period and then adding the period name. This number is written as four *billion*, two hundred ninety-four *million*, nine hundred sixty-seven *thousand*, two hundred ninety-six.

4,294,967,296 in expanded form is 4,000,000,000 + 200,000,000 + 90,000,000 + 4,000,000 + 900,000 + 60,000 + 7,000 + 200 + 90 + 6

GUIDED PRACTICE

Write each number in standard form.

1. eighty-five
2. four hundred eighty-five
3. six thousand, four hundred eighty-five
4. one million, six thousand, four hundred eighty-five
5. Fifty-two billion, one million, six thousand, four hundred eighty-five

FOCUS | Use NUMBER skills to identify place value to billions.

PRACTICE

Write the standard form for each.

6. Fifty billion, three hundred thirty million, four hundred twenty-seven thousand.

7. Five hundred fifty million, three hundred thirty thousand, one hundred twenty-seven.

8. Thirteen billion, eight hundred five million, twelve thousand, three hundred forty-one.

Write the expanded form for each.

9. 6,500   10. 345,678   11. 2,500,505   12. 1,250,335,317

Write the name of the place value of each underlined digit.

13. 896,875   14. 9,748,536   15. 15,130,216,047

16. 4,240,700,000   17. 99,999,999,999   18. 1,000,000,000

19. Write the value of 7 in the number 17,200,021,649.

20. Write the value of 1 in the number 352,106,436.

21. Write the value of 3 in the number 29,634,921,011.

MIXED PRACTICE
Maintaining and Reviewing Skills

Write the periods for each number.

22. 238,852   23. 1,860,492   24. 47,256,831,999

Write the standard form for each.

25. thirty-five thousand   26. nine hundred million, five thousand

CHALLENGE

*27. The USSR's total land area is 8,649,489 square miles. The USA's total land area is 3,675,547 square miles. How much bigger is the USSR than the USA in land area?

*28. The ancient Egyptians built the Great Pyramid about 2,800 years ago. How many periods does this number represent? Remember the definition of a period in math.

PLACE VALUE
To Ten Billions

In our numbering system, each place value is ten times greater than the place value to the right.

Look at the place values for the digit 3 in the number 3,333,000,000.

BILLIONS			MILLIONS			THOUSANDS			ONES		
		3	3	3	3	0	0	0	0	0	0
HUNDREDS	TENS	ONES	HUNDREDS	TENS	ONES	HUNDREDS	TENS	ONES	HUNDREDS	TENS	ONES

Each time the digit 3 is used it has a different value. The value of the first 3 is **ten times** greater than the second 3, to its right, and the value of the third 3 is ten times greater than the fourth 3, to its right.

PRACTICE

Write in standard form.

1. Ninety-four billion, six hundred seventy-eight million, nine hundred twenty-four thousand, three hundred.

2. Eight hundred million, five hundred three thousand, six hundred four.

Write the numbers in the thousands period.

3. 82,493,576,041

4. 1,030,926

5. 980,685

6. 10,300

Write the place value for the digit 5.

7. 15,043,972,648

8. 4,639,258,170

9. 54,867,931

10. 58,746,930,142

Write the expanded form.

11. 777,000

12. 40,404,040

*13. How many times greater is each 7 in exercise 11?

MIXED PRACTICE
Maintaining and Reviewing Skills

Estimate the product or sum.

14. 25×41 **15.** $11 + 68$ **16.** 30×34 **17.** 87×463

18. $466 + 129$ **19.** 902×54 **20.** $605 + 49$ **21.** 177×386

APPLICATION
Using Numeration

The ancient Romans used a system of grouping to name numbers. They named numbers by using letters of the alphabet and relied on position to indicate the value of numbers. Here is a list of the basic Roman numerals and the standard numbers they represent.

Roman numeral	I	V	X	L	C	D	M
Standard number	1	5	10	50	100	500	1,000

Apply these rules when using Roman numerals.

- When a Roman numeral for a smaller number is after a numeral for a larger number, the values are **added**.

  LX = 50 + 10 = 60
  DC = 500 + 100 = 600

- When a numeral for a smaller number is before a numeral for a larger number, the values are **subtracted**.

  XC = 100 − 10 = 90
  CM = 1,000 − 100 = 900

- A bar over a numeral multiplies the value by 1,000.

  $\overline{\text{M}}$ = 1,000 × 1,000 = 1,000,000 or one million

Write as Roman numerals.

22. 29   **23.** 1,109   **24.** 80   **25.** 5,000   **26.** 928

Write in standard form.

27. DCCXLVI   **28.** MCMLXXX   **29.** MMX   **30.** LXXIV   **31.** MCMLXXVI

Use NUMBER skills to identify Roman numerals.

Using the Five–Step Plan

There are five important steps to solving problems.

1. READ	Do I understand the meaning of each word in the problem?
2. KNOW	What is the question? What **key facts** do I need? The **key facts** are the facts I need to solve the problem.
3. PLAN	Which strategy should I choose? Which operation(s) should I use?
4. SOLVE	Carry out the plan. Will an equation help to solve the problem? What is my answer?
5. CHECK	Why is my answer reasonable? Does it answer the question?

1. READ The blue whale averages 95 feet long and weighs about 150 tons. The pygmy whale averages 20 feet long and weighs about 4 tons. How much longer is the blue whale than the pygmy whale?

2. KNOW Ask yourself: What do I need to find out?

How much longer is the blue whale than the pygmy whale?

Key facts: a. The length of the blue whale is 95 feet.
b. The length of the pygmy whale is 20 feet.

3. PLAN Compare **key facts** to find out how much longer. When comparing two numbers, subtract.

4. SOLVE Solve the equation: $95 - 20 = $ ■
Answer the question: The blue whale is 75 feet longer than the pygmy whale.

5. CHECK The answer 75 is a reasonable difference between 95 and 20. To check, add: $75 + 20 = 95$.

FOCUS	Use the Five–Step PROBLEM–SOLVING Plan.

PRACTICE

Read and study the facts. Select the **key facts** you need.
Then complete each of the problems that follow. Refer to
the Five-Step Plan as you solve each problem.

Facts about Male Killer Whales
Length: averages 30 feet
Weight: averages 18,000 pounds
Teeth: average 36
Pod size: usually averages 6
Dorsal fin: averages 68 inches

Facts about Male Pilot Whales
Length: averages 21 feet
Weight: averages 6,400 pounds
Teeth: average 40
Pod size: usually averages 15
Dorsal fin: averages 30 inches

1. How much longer is a killer whale than a pilot whale?

2. How much more does a killer whale weigh than a pilot whale?

3. Whales travel in groups called pods. How many pilot whales would be in 5 pods?

4. If you put 7 killer whales end to end, how long would the line of killer whales be?

5. How much smaller is the dorsal fin of a pilot whale than the dorsal fin of a killer whale?

6. How many fewer teeth does a killer whale have than a pilot whale?

7. How many average–sized pods could 36 killer whales form?

8. How much would 3 pilot whales weigh altogether?

9. If female pilot whales weigh only half as much as males, how much do females weigh?

10. If a female killer whale is 6 feet shorter than a male, how long is the female?

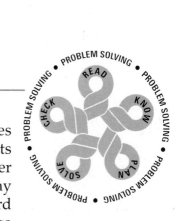

Class Project

Work with several classmates. Make a list of the first names
of each classmate in your group. Then make a list of facts
about the names. Facts you might include are: the number
of vowels, consonants, and letters in the names; how many
times each letter is used; and so forth. Then write 4 word
problems that can be answered using the facts. Exchange
your problems with another group and solve the problems
you receive. Remember to use the Five-Step Plan to help
you solve the problems.

To the Nearest Billion

Imagine that you scored record points at ZAPPO, the latest video game. Your score was 6,895,326,725. Instead of repeating this exact number each time you tell a friend, you would round your score to the nearest billion.

To round to the nearest billion, look at the first digit to the right of the billions digit. This is the hundred millions digit.

hundred millions

6,895,326,725

 billions

Since the digit 8 is 5 or greater, you add 1 to the billions digit. Your rounded number is 7,000,000,000, or seven billion.

If you wanted to compare your new record quickly with the old record of 5,225,573,075, you would first round the old record to the nearest billion.

5,225,573,075

Look at the first digit to the right of the billions digit. Since the digit 2 is less than 5, the billions digit stays the same.

The old record is rounded to 5,000,000,000 or five billion.

GUIDED PRACTICE

Use the questions below to round 621,458,670 to the nearest hundred million.

1. What is the first digit to the right of the hundred millions digit?

2. Is it greater than or less than 5?

3. Do you add one to the hundred millions digit or does it stay the same?

4. What does 621,458,670 round to?

FOCUS | Use NUMBER skills to round to the nearest billion.

PRACTICE

Round to the nearest thousand.

5. 1,156   **6.** 1,675   **7.** 973   **8.** 3,425   **9.** 963   **10.** 730

Round to the nearest ten thousand.

11. 15,326   **12.** 9,768   **13.** 43,628   **14.** 72,595   **15.** 19,321   **16.** 33,608

Round to the nearest million.

17. 1,365,315   **18.** 5,438,156   **19.** 6,849,728   **20.** 1,324,895   **21.** 2,953,619   **22.** 7,130,799

Round to the nearest hundred million.

23. 103,847,145   **24.** 245,792,436   **25.** 598,697,526   **26.** 657,954,862

Round to the nearest billion.

27. 1,238,725,643   **28.** 922,635,210   **29.** 6,315,572,850   **30.** 998,327,876

MIXED PRACTICE
Maintaining and Reviewing Skills

Write all of the digits in the millions period.

31. 45,678,859,304   **32.** 4,586,746,300   **33.** 6,003,587,890

Write all of the digits in the billions period.

34. 18,465,709,471   **35.** 10,202,789,456   **36.** 42,897,087,567

Write in standard form.

37. 13 billion, 202 million, 9 thousand, 808

38. 20 billion, 14 million, 233 thousand, 12

CHALLENGE

Tell why each is often rounded to the nearest billion.

*39. The population of the earth.

*40. The distances between stars and planets.

*41. The age of the earth.

ROUND WHOLE NUMBERS

To the Nearest Billion

Follow these steps to round whole numbers:

- Look at the digit to the *right* of the place value to which you are rounding.
- If the digit is *less than 5,* round *down* and make all the digits to the right zeros.
- If the digit is *5 or more,* round *up* and make all the digits to the right zeros.

To round to the nearest 10, look at the ones digit.

4 1 2 , 6 [1] 4   4 1 2 , 9 [6] 8

4 1 2 , 6 1 0   4 1 2 , 9 7 0

To round to the nearest thousand, look at the hundreds digit.

4 1 [8] , 6 1 2   4 6 [9] , 2 6 8

4 1 9 , 0 0 0   4 6 9 , 0 0 0

To round to the nearest hundred thousand, look at the ten thousands digit.

[4] 1 2 , 6 1 4   [4] 6 2 , 9 6 8

4 0 0 , 0 0 0   5 0 0 , 0 0 0

PRACTICE

Complete the chart by rounding each number.

	Number Being Rounded	Round to Nearest Hundred Thousand	Round to Nearest Ten Million	Round to Nearest Billion
1.	16,267,342,900	16,267,300,000	16,270,000,000	16,000,000,000
2.	21,143,621,000			
3.	42,653,481,202			
4.	75,879,621,421			
5.	34,220,166,434			
6.	66,874,341,600			
7.	59,195,590,195			

FOCUS | Use NUMBER skills to round whole numbers to nearest billion.

MIXED PRACTICE
Maintaining and Reviewing Skills

Estimate the difference or quotient.

8. $40 - 29$ **9.** $81 - 19$ **10.** $81 \div 12$ **11.** $49 \div 25$

12. $170 \div 8$ **13.** $66 - 24$ **14.** $200 \div 45$ **15.** $384 - 79$

APPLICATION
Using Mental Arithmetic

It is very helpful to be able to do arithmetic mentally. Use these steps to help you add, subtract, multiply or divide in your head.

To add $40 + 23$, think of 23 as $20 + 3$.

$$40 + 20 = 60$$
$$60 + 3 = 63$$

To subtract $74 - 38$, think of 38 as $30 + 8$.

$$74 - 30 = 44$$
$$44 - 8 = 36$$

To multiply 5×86, think of 86 as $80 + 6$.

$$5 \times 80 = 400$$
$$5 \times 6 = 30$$
$$400 + 30 = 430$$

Add, subtract, or multiply mentally. Write only your answer.

16. $10 + 24$ **17.** $6 + 77$ **18.** $29 - 16$

19. 2×41 **20.** $30 + 45$ **21.** $76 - 50$

22. 9×85 **23.** $95 - 45$ **24.** 6×452

25. 5×138 **26.** 7×630 **27.** $207 + 65$

28. $750 - 290$ **29.** $58 + 28$ **30.** 25×8

31. Write 3 ways mental arithmetic is helpful for you.

Use NUMBER skills and MENTAL ARITHMETIC to estimate differences or quotients and add, subtract, or multiply mentally.

Soccer

Soccer is the most popular team sport in the world. Only recently has soccer become popular in the United States. However, it is the national sport of many countries in Europe, Asia, and the Americas. The World Cup, played every four years, is watched by more people than any sporting event except for the Olympics.

Soccer is a ball game played on a field a little bigger than a football field.

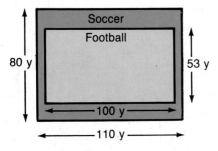

Each team has eleven players, including a goalkeeper. The object of the game is to put the ball in the opponent's goal. The team with the most number of goals at the end of the game is the winner. Teams set up goals by passing the ball accurately among all the players. A player may use any part of the body except for the arms and hands.

The scoring system for league standings in soccer is different than the system used in other sports. It varies from country to country. In soccer leagues in England, for example, teams get three points for a win, and one point for a tie, also called a "draw". No points are awarded for a loss. This makes a draw worth one third of a win.

For example, if Team A wins its first game, it gets three points. If it ties its next game, it then has four points. This system puts the emphasis on not losing. To be in first place, a team must be consistent and not lose many games. The team in first place at the end of the season may not have the most wins, but it has not lost many games.

Below are the final standings for the first 10 teams of English First Division soccer in a recent year. Compare the teams' wins, losses, and draws.

First Division			
Team	W	D	L
Everton	27	6	6
Manchester United	22	10	9
Tottenham	21	8	11
Liverpool	20	10	8
Southampton	19	10	12
Chelsea	18	12	11
Arsenal	19	9	14
Sheffield Wed	17	14	10
Nottingham Forest	19	7	15
Aston Villa	15	11	16

CRITICAL THINKING

1. Which team had the most points in the English First Division? Which team had the least points?

2. If an English team's record is 9 wins, 4 losses, and 6 draws, how many points does that team have?

FOCUS — Use NUMBER skills to learn about league standings in soccer.

One soccer player tries to block another in this fast-paced soccer match.

LOOKING BACK
Reviewing and Testing Chapter 2

In Chapter 2, you formulated problems about making a daily schedule. To review, refer to page 17.

1. What factors might occur that would prevent Pat from keeping to her schedule?

You learned about place value. To review, refer to the examples on page 18.

Write the standard form for each.

2. forty billion, two hundred ten million, six hundred seventeen thousand

3. nine hundred seventy-two million, three hundred thirty thousand, seven hundred twenty-two

Write the place value of the 4 in each number.

4. 726,417   5. 14,683,721   6. 4,986,308,173   7. 74,816

Use the Five-Step Problem-Solving Plan to solve this problem. Refer to page 23 for data.

8. What is the total weight of an average pod of pilot whales?

To review what you learned about rounding whole numbers to the nearest billion, refer to pages 24 and 25.

Round each to the nearest million.

9. 1,453,862   10. 4,673,472   11. 8,111,888   12. 3,926,387

Round each to the nearest ten thousand.

13. 6,763,820   14. 17,540   15. 827,300   16. 69,540

You learned about the scoring system in soccer. To review, refer to page 28.

17. How many more points does Everton have than Aston Villa?

| FOCUS | Review and test skills learned and practiced. |

LOOKING AHEAD
Preparing for New Skills For Chapter 3

In the next chapter you will focus on

- **formulating problems about television programming.**
- **using >, <, or = to compare numbers.**
- **using graphs to compare whole numbers.**
- **using exponents to write whole numbers in expanded form.**
- **using exponents with bases other than 10.**
- **how math is used in architecture.**

Using exponents to write numbers in expanded form will be easier if you review how to write numbers in expanded form. Study the examples.

Example 1:

$$34,521 = 30,000 + 4,000 + 500 + 20 + 1$$
$$= (3 \times 10,000) + (4 \times 1,000) + (5 \times 100) + (2 \times 10) + 1$$

Numbers such as 10, 100, and 1,000 are called **powers of 10** and they can be written in **exponential notation** or in **factor form.**

Example 2:

Exponent	Read	Factor Form	Product
10^2	10 squared	10×10	100
10^3	10 cubed	$10 \times 10 \times 10$	1000
10^4	10 to the fourth power	$10 \times 10 \times 10 \times 10$	10,000

PRACTICE

Write each number in expanded form.

1. 386
2. 1729
3. 82,634
4. 431,725

Write in exponential notation.

5. $10 \times 10 \times 10$
6. $10 \times 10 \times 10 \times 10$
7. 1,000,000
8. 100,000

Write in factored form.

9. 10^2
10. 10^4
11. 10^5
12. 10^6

Review NUMBER skills in preparation for learning new skills.

FOCUS Formulate problems using photo, data, and text.

CHAPTER 3

Place Value and Exponents

DATA

Monday Night Viewing

7:00	(1)	News
	(3)	News
	(6)	News
	(8)	Circus
7:15	(3)	Sports
7:30	(1)	Sports
	(6)	Sports
7:55	(3)	Weather
8:00	(1)	Mystery Movie
	(8)	Detective Movie
8:15	(6)	Romantic Movie
8:25	(3)	Dramatic Movie
10:00	(1)	Soap Opera
	(3)	Space Opera
	(6)	Horse Opera
	(8)	Verdi Opera
11:00	(1)	News
	(3)	News
	(6)	News
	(8)	Comedy

Newspapers often list each day's television viewing schedule.

The data shows a sample evening schedule which starts at 7:00 P.M. and lists programs through 11:00 P.M. The channel is given in parentheses, and a brief description of the program follows. Compare this listing with one from a newspaper.

Certain times are usually reserved for certain types of programs. Programs during prime time, 8:00 P.M. to 11:00 P.M., come usually from a television network with many stations across the country. Programs before and after prime time are usually local programs.

Television channels, particularly the networks, are very competitive. Each network wants everyone to watch their programs all evening. Therefore each channel tries to make its programs as appealing as possible.

News programs tend to be scheduled at the same time. Why? How could the Monday night schedule here be better organized? What problems might arise from such a reorganization?

To Ten Billions

Ten baseball teams each sold three million tickets. How many tickets were sold?

$$3,000,000 \times 10 = 30,000,000 \text{ (thirty million)}$$

If records were kept for 1,000 years, how many tickets would be sold by ten teams at that rate?

$$30,000,000 \times 1,000 = 30,000,000,000 \text{ (thirty billion)}$$

Compare the numbers in the place-value chart.

Period	BILLIONS			MILLIONS			THOUSANDS			ONES			
Number		3	0	0	0	0	0	0	0	0	0	0	Read as thirty billion
					3	0	0	0	0	0	0	0	Read as thirty million
						3	0	0	0	0	0	0	Read as three million
Place	HUNDREDS	TENS	ONES	HUNDREDS	TENS	ONES	HUNDREDS	TENS	ONES	HUNDREDS	TENS	ONES	

Read the numbers from left to right to *compare* them.

30,000,000,000 has digits through the **ten billions** place.
30,000,000 is greater than 3,000,000 since it has digits through the **ten millions** place.
3,000,000 has digits through the **one million** place.

The symbol < is used to say *is less than.*
The symbol > is used to say *is greater than.*

Numbers are written in order from least to greatest by first comparing the place value of the digits starting at the left.

$$3,000,000 < 30,000,000 < 30,000,000,000$$

GUIDED PRACTICE

Write which place value makes one number larger than the other.

1. 42   41
2. 590   690
3. 8,790,243   8,780,243

4. 81,659,700   82,659,700
5. 62,413,597,052   52,413,597,052

| FOCUS | Use NUMBER skills to read, write, and compare whole numbers. |

PRACTICE

Write each number.

6. Seven hundred and twenty-five million, nine hundred thirty-eight thousand, six hundred seventy-four.

7. Fifty-one billion, six hundred thirty-seven million, four hundred twenty-eight thousand, one hundred forty-two.

What is the place value of each underlined digit?

8. 2̲4,365

9. 786,4̲52,391

10. 9̲1,687,542,865

11. 6,3̲25,498,740

12. 58,74̲2,401

13. 2,706,3̲30

List the numbers in each row from least to greatest.

14. 117,650   57,150   24,000,000

15. 61,400   85,000   16,300

Place the symbol > or < between each pair of numbers.

16. 9 ● 5

17. 87 ● 78

18. 59 ● 95

19. 246 ● 264

20. 1,072 ● 1,100

21. 327 ● 326

22. 8,347 ● 9,049

23. 20,435 ● 2,998

24. 7,896 ● 7,986

25. 374,921 ● 374,291

26. 628,762 ● 682,762

27. 52,725 ● 52,752

MIXED PRACTICE
Maintaining and Reviewing Skills

Write the periods in each number.

28. 91,824,735

29. 875,489,362

30. 4,687

31. 985

32. 2,430,000,016

33. 50,000,284,539

CHALLENGE

*34. Using only the numbers from 1 to 9, find the 5-digit number whose second digit is three times the first; whose third digit is the second plus one; whose fourth digit is the first times 4; and whose fifth digit is one and one half times the second.

READ, WRITE, AND COMPARE NUMBERS
To Ten Billions

Light travels through 300 000 000 meters of space in one second. The number 300 000 000 is separated into the *millions*, *thousands*, and *ones* periods. It is read "three hundred million."

In 10 seconds light can travel 3 000 000 000 m. This number is read as "three billion."

In 100 seconds light can travel 30 000 000 000 m. This number is read as "thirty billion."

The numbers are written in order from greatest to least using the symbols > for greater than and < for less than.
30 000 000 000 > 3 000 000 000 > 300 000 000

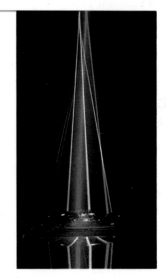

PRACTICE

Place the symbols > or < between each pair of numbers.

1. 62,579 ● 48,371

2. 16,616,000 ● 16,661,000

3. 712,272,000 ● 712,227,000

4. 90,901 ● 90,910

List in order from least to greatest.

5. 7,011   1,701   1,107   7,107

6. 8,075   875   7,805   5,087

7. 53,553   35,533   35,335

8. 434,343   434,434   434,334

Use the symbols >, <, or = to make each expression true.

9. 67 + 12 ● 95 − 21

10. 1 + 4 ● 3 + 2

11. 112 + 16 ● 85 + 43

12. 112 − 16 ● 85 − 43

MIXED PRACTICE
Maintaining and Reviewing Skills

Round to the nearest hundred thousand.

13. 636,490

14. 252,252

15. 777,707

16. 242,226

Round to the nearest ten million.

17. 81,433,340

18. 63,799,200

19. 48,200,718

20. 27,359,264

| FOCUS | Use NUMBER skills to read, write, and compare whole numbers. |

APPLICATION
Using Statistics

Graphs are used to show and compare information. The **bar graph** below shows the number of bound volumes in public libraries. The scale of numbers increases in equal units starting from zero.

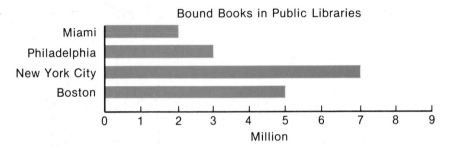

Bound Books in Public Libraries

Use the bar graph above to answer the following questions.

21. Are there more books in Philadelphia or Boston?

22. Which library had the most bound books? the least?

23. About how many books do the libraries have in all?

24. About how many more books does New York City have than Philadelphia?

Problem Solving: Evaluating Information

Sometimes you may not have enough data or information to solve a problem. You must reread the problem and determine what data you need to solve the problem. Here is a checklist to help you solve problems.

- Study the problem.
- Review the data.
- Decide what data you **need to know** to solve the problem.

Tell what information is needed to solve each problem.

25. Randi has a roll of film in her camera. She has taken 8 pictures. How many pictures are left on the roll?

26. Frameworld is having a 20% discount on all of their frames. Jay bought one frame. How much did he save?

Use STATISTICS to read and interpret bar graphs and evaluate information and apply the Five-Step PROBLEM-SOLVING Plan.

Write Numbers Using Bases Other Than Ten

Numbers may be used as factors many times.

$$2 \times 2 \times 2 = 8$$

The number 2 is used as a factor 3 times. The product is 8.

$$2 \times 2 \times 2 = 2^3 \longleftarrow \text{exponent}$$

base

repeated factors

Use **exponential notation** to write numbers which have repeated factors. An **exponent** shows how many times a number is used as a factor. The number is called the **base**.

$$2^3 = 8$$

2^3 is read as "two cubed" or "two to the third power."

The chart shows more examples.

	READ	FACTOR FORM	PRODUCT
2^2	2 squared	2×2	4
4^3	4 cubed	$4 \times 4 \times 4$	64
5^4	5 to the fourth power	$5 \times 5 \times 5 \times 5$	625

Any number, other than zero, to the zero power is 1.

$$2^0 = 1 \qquad 4^0 = 1 \qquad 5^0 = 1 \qquad 10^0 = 1$$

Any number to the first power is that number.

$$2^1 = 2 \qquad 4^1 = 4 \qquad 5^1 = 5 \qquad 10^1 = 10$$

GUIDED PRACTICE

Name the base and the exponent for each.

1. 4^3 **2.** 6^7 **3.** 2^4 **4.** 9^5 **5.** 6^3

Write each in exponential notation.   Write in standard form.

6. six cubed   **7.** $8 \times 8 \times 8 \times 8$ **8.** 12^0 **9.** 2^5 **10.** 9^1

FOCUS | Use NUMBER skills to write numbers in exponential notation.

PRACTICE

Write in exponential notation.

11. $3 \times 3 \times 3$

12. $8 \times 8 \times 8 \times 8 \times 8$

13. $2 \times 2 \times 2 \times 2 \times 6 \times 6$

14. $7 \times 7 \times 7 \times 7$

15. $4 \times 4 \times 4 \times 4 \times 4 \times 4$

16. 9 to the second power

17. 12 to the first power

18. $5 \times 5 \times 2 \times 2 \times 2$

19. 6 to the tenth power

Write in standard form.

20. 5^2

21. 2^5

22. 11^2

23. 10^0

24. 8^3

25. 4^4

26. 3^4

27. 19^1

28. 6^6

29. 2×6^2

30. 2×3^0

31. $4 + 5^3$

32. 7×3^5

33. 5×6^2

34. 4×4^3

35. 5×5^2

MIXED PRACTICE
Maintaining and Reviewing Skills

In what place is the underlined digit?

36. 33,421,662

37. 452,338

38. 61,661,261,415

Round to the nearest 10,000.

39. 66,204

40. 9912

41. 81,465

42. 47,222

Round to the nearest 100,000,000.

43. 777,373,616

44. 409,620,900

45. 929,778,982

46. 582,900,211

Choose the greater number.

47. 456,789
456,798

48. 45,687,089
45,678,098

49. 667,767
676,776

50. 33,989,593
33,989,953

CHALLENGE

Copy and complete each exercise.

*51. $1 + 3 = 4 = 2^{\blacksquare}$

*52. $1 + 3 + 5 = \blacksquare = \blacksquare^{\blacksquare}$

*53. $1 + 3 + 5 + 7 = \blacksquare = \blacksquare^{\blacksquare}$

EXPONENTS
Write Numbers Using Bases Other Than Ten

An **exponent** shows how many times the base is used as a factor.

The number 5 is used as a factor 3 times. This expression is read as "5 to the third power" or "5 cubed."

$$5^3 = 5 \times 5 \times 5$$
$$5^3 = 125$$

The number 2 is used as a factor 4 times. The number 5 is used as a factor 2 times. It is read as "2 to the fourth power times 5 squared" or "5 to the second power."

$$2^4 \times 5^2 = 2 \times 2 \times 2 \times 2 \times 5 \times 5$$
$$2^4 \times 5^2 = 400$$

PRACTICE

Write in exponential notation.

1. 27
2. 32
3. 36

4. $6 \times 6 \times 6 \times 6$
5. $5 \times 5 \times 5 \times 5 \times 5$
6. $3 \times 3 \times 3 \times 3 \times 3 \times 3$

7. $8 \times 8 \times 4 \times 4 \times 4$
8. $2 \times 2 \times 2 \times 2 \times 7$
9. $4 \times 4 \times 4 \times 4 \times 2 \times 2$

Write in factor form.

10. 5^3
11. 6^4
12. 9^6
13. 9 squared

Write the number.

14. $3^2 + 4^2$
15. $5^2 - 4$
16. $2^4 \times 8$

17. $2^3 \times 3^3$
18. $7^3 - 6$
19. $3^3 \times 5^2$

MIXED PRACTICE
Maintaining and Reviewing Skills

Write in expanded form.

20. 7,044
21. 29,138,000
22. 703,904,200
23. 39,220

Write the number.

24. $500,000 + 900 + 2$
25. $8,000 + 600 + 60 + 1$
26. $600,000 + 30,000 + 2,000$

27. $2,000 + 600 + 20 + 4$
28. $20,000 + 70 + 2$
29. $70,000 + 2,000 + 400 + 10$

FOCUS | Use NUMBER skills to write numbers using exponential notation.

APPLICATION
Using Numbers

Our place-value system is based on powers of ten. The binary or base two number system is based on the powers of two, using ones, twos, fours, eights, sixteens, and so on for its place values.

BASE 10 PLACE-VALUE CHART   **BASE 2 PLACE-VALUE CHART**

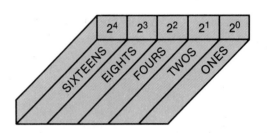

To indicate place value, the binary system uses only the digits 0 and 1. The values are added according to the place value to give the standard numeral in base ten.

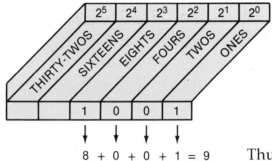

$$8 + 0 + 0 + 1 = 9 \qquad \text{Thus } 9_{ten} = 1\,001_{two}.$$

Look at the base 2 chart above. The digits 1 001 represent *1* in the *eights* place, *zero* in the *fours* and *twos* places, and *1* in the *ones* place. The added values equal the standard number 9 in base ten.

Write the standard number for each binary number.

30. 1 100   **31.** 10 100   **32.** 111   **33.** 11 101

34. 1 101   **35.** 100 010   **36.** 10 111   **37.** 11 111

Write the binary number for each standard number.

38. 32   **39.** 27   **40.** 17   **41.** 20

42. 25   **43.** 6   **44.** 14   **45.** 30

Use NUMBER skills to write numbers in Base Two.

The Shape of a Building

An architect is someone who designs buildings for a living. Before construction on a building can be started, an architect must plan it right down to the last detail.

One of the first decisions an architect must make is about how the building will look. First, the architect must map out a design on paper, in the form of plans and blueprints. This design shows the basic shapes that will make the finished building look as it does.

How does the architect decide on which shapes to use? One of the most important factors is the *purpose* of the building. Suppose an architect were designing a football stadium. It would be necessary to shape the stadium so as to allow the greatest number of people to see the game well. An oval-shaped stadium, like the Astrodome in Houston, allows for the best viewing.

Another important factor is the *appearance* of the building. Look at the photo of the Gateway Arch in St. Louis on the next page. The arc shape was chosen not only because it looks like a gateway, but also because it is beautiful. This amazing structure symbolizes St. Louis as "the gateway to the West."

An architect must plan the shape for a building's floor space, like the oval shape in the stadium. The shape of the walls, or the structure itself, like the arc shape of the Gateway Arch must be planned. Whether it is to make a building useful or beautiful, to design the floors or the walls, an architect must start with basic geometric shapes.

CRITICAL THINKING

1. What factors are important to an architect in designing a building?

2. Why is an oval the best shape for a football stadium? In what ways would a round or square stadium be less useful?

3. The Gateway Arch is shaped to remind people of a gateway. What other shapes might the architect have chosen? Draw one that you think might look attractive. Will you use angles or curves?

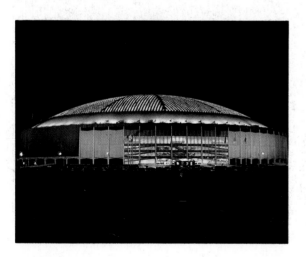

| FOCUS | Use GEOMETRY in architecture. |

The Gateway Arch was designed by Eero Saarinen in 1948 and completed in 1964.

LOOKING BACK
Reviewing and Testing Chapter 3

In Chapter 3 you formulated problems about making a television schedule. To review, refer to page 33.

1. What factors should be considered before scheduling a movie for the prime time slot?

You learned about reading, writing, and comparing whole numbers. To review, refer to page 34.

Place the symbol $<$ or $>$ between each pair of numbers.

2. 14,623 ● 16,794
3. 7,892 ● 6,742
4. 376,721 ● 7,383,916

5. 472,300 ● 427,308
6. 5,690,759 ● 5,960,759
7. 18,281,828 ● 18,281,882

8. 16,877,400 ● 3,922,817
9. 874,938 ● 97,000
10. 9,777,622 ● 9,843,700

To review what you learned about exponential notation, refer to pages 38 and 39.

Write in exponential notation.

11. $4 \times 4 \times 4$
12. $3 \times 3 \times 3 \times 5$
13. $2 \times 2 \times 2 \times 2 \times 2 \times 2$

14. $6 \times 6 \times 5 \times 5$
15. $5 \times 5 \times 5 \times 2 \times 2$
16. $8 \times 8 \times 7 \times 7 \times 7$

Write in standard form.

17. $4^2 + 2^2$
18. $3^3 \times 2^3$
19. $5^3 - 4^3$
20. $4^3 - 2^4$

21. $2^4 \times 2^4$
22. $8 + 6 + 3^2$
23. $4^2 - 2^3$
24. $5^2 + 2^5$

25. $5^4 + 2^3$
26. $6^3 - 2^5$
27. $9 + 3 + 4^3$
28. $3^4 - 27$

You learned about using geometric shapes when designing a building. Refer to page 42 to review how to use geometric shapes in architecture.

29. What would a bridge made up of angles and curves look like? Draw a diagram.

FOCUS | Review and test skills learned and practiced.

LOOKING AHEAD
Preparing for New Skills for Chapter 4

In the next chapter you will focus on

- **formulating problems about a relay race.**
- **using order of operations.**
- **solving equations with exponents and parentheses.**

- **using inverse operations.**
- **solving problems by selecting important facts.**
- **how math is used in social studies.**

In order to solve equations, you should review how to simplify exponential expressions. Study the examples.

Example 1:

$3^2 = 3 \times 3 = 9$

Example 2:

$5^4 = 5 \times 5 \times 5 \times 5 = 625$

Example 3:

$7^3 = 7 \times 7 \times 7 = 343$

Sometimes inverse operations can be used to solve equations. Study the examples.

Example 4:

$$\text{Solve: } n \div 3 = 4$$
$$n = 12$$

$$4 \times 3 = n$$
$$n = 12$$

Multiplication and division are inverse or opposite operations.

Example 5:

$$\text{Solve: } n - 5 = 8$$
$$n = 13$$

$$8 + 5 = n$$
$$n = 13$$

Addition and subtraction are inverse or opposite operations.

PRACTICE

Find each value.

1. 6^3 **2.** 10^5 **3.** 15^2 **4.** 8^4

Write a sentence using the inverse operation. Then solve.

5. $2 + n = 5$ **6.** $4 \times n = 8$ **7.** $n - 4 = 4$ **8.** $n \div 10 = 2$

Review NUMBER skills in preparation for learning new skills.

FOCUS   Formulate problems using photo, data, and text.

CHAPTER 4

Equations

DATA

Marlboro Milers' tryout times

Name	Time for the mile	Rank
Willa	6.05 min	1
Josef	6.08 min	2
Isa	6.80 min	3
Hawk	6.82 min	4
Jo Wen	7.00 min	5

Average tryout time   6.55 min

Milers after 6 months

Name	Time for the mile	Rank
Willa	4.90 min	1
Hawk	5.00 min	2
Josef	5.08 min	3
Isa	5.09 min	4
Jo Wen	5.90 min	5

Average after
6 months   5.194 min

Coastal Coasters
Best average time   4.88 min

To compute average, add the figures for the times given. Then divide the sum by the number of figures added. For example, to find the average of 8, 7, 5, and 4, add these numbers. Then divide the sum, 24, by 4 ($24 \div 4 = 6$). The average is 6.

The Marlboro Milers were pretty fast when they tried out for the track team. But after six months of training, the team's average time for the mile has improved by more than one minute.

In just two more weeks, the Milers are to compete in a five-mile relay against the Coastal Coasters. The Coasters are fast. Their best average time for the mile is better than that of the Milers.

Some of the Milers are expecting to lose, but Willa is optimistic. "We've all gotten better," she says. "In two weeks we can get even better. Nothing is impossible."

It took six months for the Milers to get as good as they are. To get even better in only two weeks will be hard. But Willa is certain that her team can win. Is this possible? What could the Milers do to win? Can just one Miler change the outcome? Give reasons to support your predictions.

Order of Operations

In an expression with more than one operation, use the **Rules of Order of Operations**. First multiply and divide in order from left to right. Then add and subtract in order from left to right.

$$45 + 6 \times 4 \div 2 - 7 = n$$ First multiply and divide in order from left to right.

$$45 + \quad 24 \quad \div 2 - 7 = n$$

$$45 + \quad\quad 12 \quad - 7 = n$$ Then add and subtract in order from left to right.

$$57 \quad\quad - 7 = 50$$

$$45 + 6 \times 4 \div 2 - 7 = 50$$

Sometimes expressions have parentheses. Do any computations *inside* the parentheses first.

$$(5 \times 3) + 4 = n \qquad\qquad (54 - 42) \div 6 = c$$
$$15 \quad + 4 = 19 \qquad\qquad\quad 12 \quad \div 6 = 2$$

When sentences have exponents, evaluate the powers first. If the sentence has both parentheses and exponents, do the computation inside the parentheses first, then evalute the powers.

$$5^2 \times 20 - 16 = x \qquad\qquad (2 + 1)^3 + (6 - 4)^2 = z$$
$$25 \times 20 - 16 = x \qquad\qquad\quad 3^3 \quad + \quad 2^2 \quad = z$$
$$500 - 16 = 484 \qquad\qquad\quad 27 \quad + \quad 4 \quad = 31$$

GUIDED PRACTICE

Solve.

1. $7 + (4 \times 6) = x$
   $\blacksquare + \quad 24 \quad = x$
     $\blacksquare \quad = x$

2. $(8 - 3) + 6^2 = w$
   $\blacksquare + 6^2 = w$
     $\blacksquare = w$

3. $20 + (6 - 1)^2 = h$
   $\blacksquare + \quad 5^2 \quad = h$
     $\blacksquare \quad = h$

FOCUS | Use ALGEBRA to solve equations.

PRACTICE

Solve.

4. $42 \div 6 - 1 \times 3 = r$ **5.** $6 + (10 \times 3) \div 5 = d$ **6.** $28 \div 2^2 \times 3 = l$

7. $7 + (3 \times 2) = n$ **8.** $(10 - 6) + 12 = c$ **9.** $(8 \times 5) \div 2 = b$

10. $5^2 \div (7 - 2) = w$ **11.** $2^2 + (30 - 2) = k$ **12.** $(100 \div 10) - 10 = c$

13. $(6 + 2) \times (10 + 5) = n$ **14.** $(10 - 8)^2 \div (8 - 6) = h$ **15.** $(3 + 2) \times (5 + 4) = y$

16. $(5 + 1)^2 \times 2 - 5^2 = h$ **17.** $(49 \div 7) - (6 \times 1) = s$ **18.** $9^2 - (6 \times 7) = t$

19. $8 + 9 \times 2 - 3 = f$ **20.** $4 \times 6 \times 8 \div 2 = h$ **21.** $35 - 8 \times 3 + 2 = c$

22. $6^3 + 4^3 = g$ **23.** $163 - 8^2 = y$ **24.** $(81 \div 9)^4 = d$

25. $3^3 \times 4^2 = h$ **26.** $(48 \div 8)^3 = c$ **27.** $52 \times 10^3 = j$

28. $3^2 + 7^3 = x$ **29.** $5^4 + (2 + 1)^2 = w$ **30.** $(2 \times 3)^3 \times (4 - 2)^2 = n$

31. $100 - 6^2 + 3 = e$ **32.** $(8 - 3)^2 - 4 \times 4 = b$ **33.** $8 - (16 \times 4) \div 4^2 = b$

MIXED PRACTICE
Maintaining and Reviewing Skills

Give the value of each underlined digit.

34. 3,5<u>4</u>1   **35.** 6,78<u>9</u>   **36.** <u>5</u>,073

37. <u>2</u>4,692   **38.** 78,<u>5</u>13   **39.** 6<u>0</u>,420

40. 363,6<u>3</u>6   **41.** 268,40<u>0</u>   **42.** 951,6<u>8</u>9

43. <u>5</u>,230,721   **44.** 38,4<u>2</u>6,131   **45.** 542,6<u>8</u>3,217

CHALLENGE

This sentence is **true**. $25 \times 37 = 925$
This sentence is **false**. $84 \div 12 = 9$
This sentence is **open**. $a + 78 = 463$

Tell whether each is *true*, *false*, or *open*.

*46. $9 + 6 = 15$ ***47.** $5 \times 8 = 40$ ***48.** $9 \div 3 = 3$

*49. $d - 56 = 97$ ***50.** $(6 \times 3) - 4 = x$ ***51.** $17 - 4 \times 4 = 52$

ALGEBRA
Order of Operations

Complete Rules for Order of Operations

1. Do any computations inside the parentheses first.

2. Then evaluate the powers.

3. Do the multiplication and division next, in order from left to right.

4. Do the addition and subtraction next, in order from left to right.

$$75 + (2 \times 4) - 9 = c \qquad (55 - 50)^3 \times 3 = m$$
$$75 + 8 - 9 = c \qquad 5^3 \times 3 = m$$
$$83 - 9 = c \qquad 125 \times 3 = m$$
$$74 = c \qquad 375 = m$$

PRACTICE

Solve.

1. $7 \times (4 - 3) = n$

2. $64 - (5 \times 2) = w$

3. $(49 \div 7) \times 1 = c$

4. $6 + 3 \times 2 + 7 = d$

5. $8 \times 9 + 2 - 1 = n$

6. $15 + 4 \times 6 = e$

7. $7^2 + 5 \times 6 = f$

8. $(15 - 9) + 4^3 = k$

9. $24 \div 3 \times 2 = h$

10. $2^3 \times 4 + 5 = m$

11. $18 - 9 + 3 = r$

12. $5^3 - 4^2 = t$

13. $10^4 \times 3 \times 2 = a$

14. $225 - 25 \times 4 = p$

15. $6 \times 5 + 4 \times 8 = j$

16. $5 + 4 \times 9 + 3 = c$

17. $8 + 15 \times 4 = w$

18. $7 \times 5 \times 6 + 2 = y$

19. $75 \div 5 \times 3 = z$

20. $50 \div (2 + 3)^2 = q$

21. $50 \div 2 + 3^2 = h$

MIXED PRACTICE
Maintaining and Reviewing Skills

Round to the nearest ten.

22. 723   **23.** 945   **24.** 677   **25.** 542   **26.** 916

Round to the nearest thousand.

27. 9,305   **28.** 12,777   **29.** 25,621   **30.** 89,005   **31.** 90,119

| FOCUS | Use ALGEBRA to solve equations. |

APPLICATION
Using Algebra

A mathematical sentence is **open** when it contains a variable, an unknown.

$$7 \times a = 35 \qquad \text{open}$$

A number must be substituted for the variable before a sentence becomes **true** or **false**.

$$7 \times 5 = 35 \qquad \text{true}$$
$$7 \times 6 = 35 \qquad \text{false}$$

Tell whether each sentence is *true* or *false*.
Let $a = 5$.

32. $3 \times a = 25$

33. $a \times 9 = 45$

34. $26 - a = 21$

35. $(a \times 2) + (a \times 3) = 35$

36. $50 \div a = 10$

37. $25 \div 6 = a$

38. $(17 \times a) - 80 = a$

39. $(27 - a) - a = 19$

40. $(a + 6) \times a = 55$

41. $(a \times a) + a = 30$

42. $(a - a) \times a = 0$

43. $(a \div a) \times a = 0$

Solve.
Let $x = 12$.

44. $x + 5 + x$
$12 + 5 + 12 = \blacksquare$

45. $(24 \div x) + x$
$(24 \div \blacksquare) + \blacksquare = \blacksquare$

46. $(x + x) \times 3$
$(\blacksquare + \blacksquare) \times 3 = \blacksquare$

Let $n = 7$.

47. $56 \div n$

48. $n \times 4 + 8$

49. $n \times n + n$

50. $(3 \times n) - n$

51. $125 - (n \times n)$

52. $(n \div 1)^n$

Let $c = 6$.

53. $3 \times c + c$

54. $(c \times c) + 14$

55. $c^2 + c$

56. $(c \times 4) - (c \times 2)$

57. $c^4 - (c \times c)$

58. $25 - (c \times 2)$

Let $t = 25$.

59. $(t + 4) \times (5 + t)$

60. $(t + 5) \times 50$

61. $15 \times (t \div 5)$

62. $(1{,}250 \div t) \times t$

63. $75 - t \times 3$

64. $t^4 - (t \div t)$

Using Inverse Operations

Inverse, or opposite, operations are those operations that "undo" each other. Inverse operations can be used to check one another.

Addition and subtraction are inverse operations. Addition can be "undone" by using subtraction.

$16 + 8 = 24$	$24 - 8 = 16$
$8 + 16 = 24$	$24 - 16 = 8$

Multiplication and division are inverse operations. Multiplication can be "undone" by using division.

$6 \times 7 = 42$	$42 \div 7 = 6$
$7 \times 6 = 42$	$42 \div 6 = 7$

You can use inverse operations to solve for n, an unknown.

$8 + n = 15$

$n = 15 - 8$

$n = 7$

Think: What is the inverse operation of addition? Subtraction undoes addition.

$6 \times n = 30$

$n = 30 \div 6$

$n = 5$

Think: What is the inverse operation of multiplication? Division undoes multiplication.

Check: Substitute the value of n in the addition equation.

$8 + n = 15 \longrightarrow 8 + 7 = 15$

Check: Substitute the value of n in the multiplication equation.

$6 \times n = 30 \longrightarrow 6 \times 5 = 30$

GUIDED PRACTICE

Write two inverse equations for each.

1. $16 + 5 = 21$

$21 - \blacksquare = 16$
$21 - \blacksquare = 5$

2. $5 \times 3 = 15$

$15 \div \blacksquare = 3$
$15 \div \blacksquare = 5$

3. $19 - 7 = 12$

$12 + \blacksquare = 19$
$7 + \blacksquare = 19$

4. $20 \div 2 = 10$

$10 \times \blacksquare = 20$
$2 \times \blacksquare = 20$

Write an inverse equation. Then solve.

5. $n - 16 = 2$
$n = 16 + 2$
$n = \blacksquare$

6. $n \times 4 = 24$
$n = 24 \div 4$
$n = \blacksquare$

7. $n + 9 = 17$
$n = 17 - \blacksquare$
$n = \blacksquare$

8. $n \div 4 = 9$
$n = \blacksquare \times \blacksquare$
$n = \blacksquare$

FOCUS | Use ALGEBRA to solve equations with inverse operations.

APPLICATION
Problem Solving: Evaluating Information

In order to solve a word problem you must evaluate the information given to see if you have enough information. Find the **key facts** and then use the Five-Step Problem Solving plan to solve the problem.

The following problems contain some facts that do not pertain to the solution. Find the key facts. Then solve.

37. Annie, who is 12 years old, and Tim, who is 14 years old, went to visit their grandmother who lives 125 miles away. They bought two bus tickets for $7.95 each. The bus left at 9:00 A.M. How much did it cost them to travel to their grandmother's town?

38. Susie and her three sisters drove from Boston to Washington, D.C., in 6 hours. They made a stop to buy gas and had to pay $1.57 a gallon. The car needed 24 gallons. If Susie and her three sisters left Boston at 7:00 A.M., what time did they arrive in Washington, D.C.?

39. John flew from New York to Los Angeles on a jumbo jet that held 369 passengers. The plane cruised at an altitude of 42,000 feet. During the flight, the plane made one stop in Chicago and another stop in Denver. If John paid $450 for his round-trip ticket, how much did it cost to fly one way?

40. Mark leaves his home at 7:55 A.M. every weekday morning so that he will arrive at school at 8:15 A.M. He has six classes every day and a lunch period. The lunch period is 35 minutes long. Each of Mark's classes is 43 minutes. How long does it take Mark to get to school every morning?

41. Tom baked some rolls for the family dinner on Thursday. He had to make enough rolls for 8 people. He used 2 cups of flour and 2 eggs. He added a teaspoon of salt and glazed them with a pat of butter. If Tom baked 24 rolls, how many rolls did each guest get?

42. Gina planted 60 tulip bulbs. The bulbs had to be planted 12″ apart and at least 6″ deep. It took Gina over 4 hours to plant all the bulbs. The bulbs came in many colors. If Gina paid $5 a dozen for the bulbs, how much did it cost to buy all the bulbs she planted?

43. There are 60 seconds in a minute, 60 minutes in an hour, 24 hours in a day, 7 days in a week, and 52 weeks in a year. How many days are there in 3 weeks?

44. There are 10 pennies in a dime, 10 dimes in a dollar, 20 nickels in a dollar, 5 pennies in a nickel, and 5 nickels in a quarter. How many pennies are there in a quarter?

Evalute Information and apply the Five-Step PROBLEM–SOLVING Plan.

Pyramids of Egypt

In ancient Egypt, when a king died his people felt that it was important to place him in a tomb suitable for his life after death.

For hundreds of years, kings were buried in square brick buildings. Beginning around 2700 BC, the king's burial chamber was in the form of a regular pyramid.

Geometrically, a regular pyramid is a solid. The base is a regular polygon, and the sides are isosceles triangles which meet at a point called the vertex.

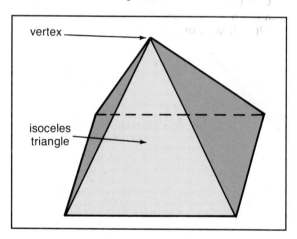

The earliest Egyptian pyramids were step pyramids. The step pyramids were really square tombs placed on top of each other. Each square was smaller than the one under it.

The first step pyramid was built for a king named Zoser. It was called "the king's stairway to Heaven." The architect who designed the pyramid, Imhotep, is well thought of today.

A hundred years after the death of Zoser, a king named Khufu ordered a pyramid to be built. By this time, the step pyramid had developed into a true pyramid, which has a square base and four smooth, triangular sides.

Khufu's pyramid, known as the Great Pyramid shown in the opposite photograph, is located at Gizeh in Upper Egypt. It took 20 years and thousands of laborers to build.

The Great Pyramid has a 755-foot base and is 481 feet high. It is estimated that 2,300,000 blocks of stone weighing 5,750,000 tons were needed to construct the Great Pyramid.

It has been said that the pyramid was a symbol of the sun's rays shining through the clouds. The Egyptians believed that through the pyramid a king could transport himself to the heavenly kingdom of the sun.

CRITICAL THINKING

1. What changes occurred in the construction of Egyptian tombs?

2. What is the average weight of a block of stone in the Great Pyramid?

3. Write a paragraph from the point of view of the builder of a true pyramid. Describe the problems you might have getting the stone blocks to the top.

FOCUS | Use GEOMETRY to learn about pyramids of Egypt.

The Step Pyramid at Sakkarah is composed of six *mastabas*, square tombs made of mud bricks.

The Great Pyramid at Giza, the largest stone structure in the world, was so accurately measured that on the 13 acre site the southeast corner is only a half inch taller than the northwest corner today.

Reviewing and Testing Chapter 4

In Chapter 4 you formulated problems about decreasing tryout time. Refer to pages 46 and 47.

1. What factors can help Willa achieve her best tryout time?

To review what you learned about the rules of order of operations, refer to pages 48 and 50.

Solve.

2. $9 + 2 \times 6 \div 4 = k$ **3.** $6 + 2 \times 4 = a$ **4.** $(3 \times 4) \times (6 \times 2) = c$

5. $8 + (4 + 3) = x$ **6.** $(3 + 2)^3 = z$ **7.** $(72 \div 8) - (5 - 2) = b$

8. $50 - (3 \times 8) = y$ **9.** $(27 \times 3) - (4 - 1)^4 = r$ **10.** $3^3 + (3 + 1)^2 = m$

You learned about substituting values for a variable to solve expressions. To review, refer to page 51.

Solve. Let $x = 8$.

11. $56 \div x$ **12.** $7 + x + 14$ **13.** $11 \times x$ **14.** $5 + (3 + x)$

15. $50 \times (x + x)$ **16.** $72 \div x$ **17.** $(x \times 2) - 7$ **18.** $(14 - x) + (x + 11)$

To review inverse equations, refer to pages 52 and 54.

Write an inverse equation. Then solve.

19. $n - 7 = 4$ **20.** $s - 9 = 3$ **21.** $4 \times t = 32$ **22.** $k \times 3 = 27$

23. $p - 8 = 8$ **24.** $5 + h = 14$ **25.** $m + 7 = 9$ **26.** $r \div 6 = 5$

Refer to page 56 to review how the Egyptians used different shapes to build pyramids.

27. What geometric shapes are used in a step pyramid?

FOCUS | Review and test skills learned and practiced.

LOOKING AHEAD

Preparing for New Skills for Chapter 5

In the next chapter you will focus on

- formulating problems about airport procedures.
- adding whole numbers.
- estimating sums.
- using properties of addition.
- using a problem solving strategy.
- subtracting whole numbers.
- estimating differences.
- how math is used in cartography.

When estimating, you will need to be able to round whole numbers. Study the examples.

Remember, to round a whole number to a given place, look at the digit to the right of that place.

- If the digit is 5 or more, add 1 to the digit in the place to which you are rounding. Replace the digits to the right with zeros.

- If the digit is less than 5, do not change the digit in the place to which you are rounding. Replace the digits to the right with zeros.

Example 1:

468,923 rounded to the nearest thousand

468,923
      —— 5 or greater
469,000   Round up

Example 2:

3,367,612 rounded to the nearest million

3,367,612
      —— less than 5
3,000,000   Round down.

PRACTICE

Round each number to the nearest thousand.

1. 7,892   **2.** 46,351   **3.** 240,342   **4.** 1,298,520

Round each number to the nearest ten thousand.

5. 58,743   **6.** 127,319   **7.** 406,519   **8.** 38,270,335

Round each number to the nearest million.

9. 8,154,263   **10.** 5,671,042   **11.** 27,946,023   **12.** 140,832,115

Review NUMBER skills in preparation for learning new skills.

FOCUS | Formulate problems using photo, data, and text.

5

Addition and Subtraction

DATA

Flight 517 to Oklahoma City
   Gate 19
   Departure   5:05 P.M.
   Arrival   6:50 P.M.
   Weather in Oklahoma City:
     cloudy

Flight 161 to Phoenix
   Gate 21
   Departure   6:10 P.M.
   Arrival   7:10 P.M.
   Weather in Phoenix: clear

Flight 626 to Denver
   Gate 15
   Departure   4:25 P.M.
   Arrival   5:00 P.M.
   Weather in Denver:
     thunderstorms

Flight 810 to Cheyenne
   Gate 8
   Departure   5:15 P.M.
   Arrival   6:45 P.M.
   Weather in Cheyenne: snow

An airport is a busy and exciting place to be. There are always many things that passengers have to do at the terminal before boarding a flight. Passengers may have to buy a ticket or confirm a reservation if the ticket has already been purchased. They may have to check their baggage and leave time for finding the gate before the flight. Then, at the gate, passengers may have to get a boarding pass. All passengers must wait for the boarding announcement before boarding the plane.

How long would it take to travel from Santa Fe to each of the cities in the data? Include the time it takes to get to the airport. Remember that the traffic around airports is often congested. Also, allowances must be made for all the things that must be done at the airport terminal.

What can be done to save time? What problems might air travelers face? Make a complete schedule for getting from home to the airport.

Whole Numbers

Grade six students collected 4,786 cans for a recycling project. Grade seven students collected 4,576 cans. How many cans were collected in all for the recycling project?

Add ones.	**Add tens.**	**Add hundreds.**	**Add thousands.**
Th|H|T|O	Th|H|T|O	Th|H|T|O	Th|H|T|O
1	1　1	1　1　1	1　1　1
4|7|8|6	4|7|8|6	4|7|8|6	4|7|8|6
+4|5|7|6	+4|5|7|6	+4|5|7|6	+4|5|7|6
2	6|2	3|6|2	9|3|6|2

12 ones = 1 ten and 2 ones
16 tens = 1 hundred and 6 tens
13 hundreds = 1 thousand and 3 hundreds

The students collected 9,362 cans in all.
You can check your answer by addition.

$$4{,}786 \\ +\ 4{,}576 \\ \overline{9{,}362}$$ Check. Add up.

One sixth grader was absent. She later brought in 508 cans. What was the new total for grade six?

Remember to line up numbers in the proper columns.

Add ones.	**Add tens.**	**Add hundreds.**	**Add thousands.**
1	1	1　1	1　1
4,786	4,786	4,786	4,786
+ 508	+ 508	+ 508	+ 508
4	94	294	5,294

The sixth graders collected 5,294 cans in all. You can check your answer by addition.

$$4{,}786 \\ +\ \ 508 \\ \overline{5{,}294}$$ Check. Add up.

GUIDED PRACTICE

Add. Remember to line up numbers properly.

	1.	2.	3.	4.	5.
		1 11	1 11	11 11	111 11
	3,261	5,638	8,976	36,845	179,426
	+ 5,427	+ 3,764	+ 988	+ 29,756	+ 368,799

FOCUS	Use NUMBER skills to add whole numbers through hundred millions with regrouping.

PRACTICE

Add.

6. 22
+ 7

7. 46
+ 13

8. 52
+ 29

9. 60
+ 39

10. $78
+ 54

11. 435
+ 64

12. 538
+ 347

13. 609
+ 36

14. 986
+ 735

15. $974
+ 86

16. 5,624
+ 3,175

17. 8,547
+ 439

18. 5,688
+ 3,006

19. 9,762
+ 979

20. $7,453
+ 958

21. 25,364
+ 51,415

22. 36,853
+ 2,498

23. 57,986
+ 8,347

24. 79,407
+ 62,943

25. $98,752
+ 73,688

26. 18,251
+ 363

27. 42,269
+ 5,743

28. 63,014
+ 29,722

29. 35,817
+ 929

30. 62,199
+ 14,381

31. 358,634
+ 863,079

32. 12,683,746
+ 56,983,297

33. 502,689,738
+ 896,705,397

34. $698,357,682
+ 211,569,781

*35. 876,239,067 + 9,856,776

*36. 568,437,996 + 784,693,357

*37. 296,045,188 + 22,616,055

*38. 298,401,622 + 371,987,622

MIXED PRACTICE
Maintaining and Reviewing Skills

Add.

39. 2,004
+ 4,763

40. 48,390
+ 872

41. 437
+6,718

42. 909
+ 888

43. 4,651
+ 9,987

44. 17,070
+ 5,591

45. 438
+ 697

46. 7,208
+ 468

47. 7,926
+ 2,784

48. 785
+ 94,317

CHALLENGE

*49. What is the total land area of these six islands in the
West Indies?

The Bahamas: 13 935 km^2 Barbados: 431 km^2 Puerto Rico: 8 891 km^2
Cuba: 114 524 km^2 Haiti: 27 750 km^2 Jamaica: 10 991 km^2

ADDITION
Whole Numbers Using Estimation

On Friday, 1,718 people visited the county fair. On Saturday, 3,278 people came. On Sunday, 5,124 people were counted. How many people visited the fair in all?

Estimate the answer.
Round to the nearest thousand.

$$
\begin{array}{rcl}
1\;\boxed{7}\;18 & \longrightarrow & 2{,}000 \\
3\;\boxed{2}\;78 & \longrightarrow & 3{,}000 \\
5\;\boxed{1}\;24 & \longrightarrow & +\,5{,}000 \\
& & 10{,}000
\end{array}
$$

Add to find the exact sum.

Add the ones.	**Add the tens.**	**Add the hundreds.**	**Add the thousands.**

Th	H	T	O		Th	H	T	O		Th	H	T	O		Th	H	T	O
			2				1	2		1	1	2			1	1	2	
1	7	1	8		1	7	1	8		1	7	1	8		1	7	1	8
3	2	7	8		3	2	7	8		3	2	7	8		3	2	7	8
+5	1	2	4		+5	1	2	4		+5	1	2	4		+5	1	2	4
			0				2	0			1	2	0		10	1	2	0

A total of 10,120 people visited the fair. The estimate of 10,000 people is reasonable.

PRACTICE

Find the exact sum. Estimate first.

1. 379
    248
  + 502

2. 645
     63
  + 250

3. 7,468
    3,921
  + 1,006

4. 4,518
      367
  + 1,350

5. 6,601
      190
  + 2,487

6. 346
    224
    698
  + 300

7. 541
    932
    307
  + 764

8. 7,639
    9,326
    5,410
  + 2,789

9. 4,345
    5,304
    9,149
  + 2,644

10. 3,799
     6,257
     4,681
   + 5,963

11. $3,835 + $5,514 + $7,351

12. 3,077 + 4,299 + 1,006 + 4,178

13. 3,433 + 4,662 + 7,346 + 2,266

14. $2,609 + $6,938 + $6,166 + $1,492

FOCUS	Use ESTIMATION to add whole numbers.

MIXED PRACTICE
Maintaining and Reviewing Skills

Regroup.

15. 14 tens = 13 tens ■ ones

16. 14 tens and 3 ones = ■ tens 13 ones

17. 6 hundreds and 1 ten = ■ hundreds 11 tens

18. 8 hundreds and 8 tens = 7 hundreds ■ tens

APPLICATION
Using Number Properties of Addition

In addition, groups can be joined in different ways.

Commutative Property

When you add two numbers in either order, the sum is always the same.

$$a + b = b + a \qquad 2 + 3 = 3 + 2$$

Associative Property

When you group addends differently, the sum is always the same. (Parentheses show what to do first.)

$$(a + b) + c = a + (b + c) \qquad (2 + 3) + 4 = 2 + (3 + 4)$$

Write whether each is the commutative or associative property.

19. $26 + 43 = 43 + 26$ **20.** $(22 + 33) + 68 = 22 + (33 + 68)$

21. $(R + S) + T = R + (S + T)$ **22.** $E + F = F + E$

Write two number sentences to show the commutative property.

23. The Gleasons harvested 338 bushels of corn. The Parkers harvested 265 bushels. How much corn was harvested in all?

Write two number sentences to show the associative property.

24. The Talber family drove 362 miles on Friday, 418 miles on Saturday, and 253 miles on Sunday. How many miles were driven in 3 days?

Use NUMBER skills to identify the commutative and associative properties of addition.

Evaluating Information: Too Much/Too Little

The five important steps to solving problems are READ, KNOW, PLAN, SOLVE, and CHECK. Evaluating information, to determine if there is too much or too little, can help you KNOW and PLAN the problem. When there is too much information, select only the **key facts** you need. When there is too little information, supply the information that is missing.

1. READ In 1896, the first modern Olympic Games were held in Athens, Greece. At these games 13 nations were represented by 311 competitors. 70,000 spectators attended the opening ceremonies.

At the 1984 Olympic Games in Los Angeles, California, more than 12,000 competitors represented 140 nations. Exactly 92,604 spectators attended the opening ceremonies.

How many more spectators attended the 1984 opening ceremonies than attended the 1896 opening ceremonies?

2. KNOW Ask yourself: What do I need to find out?

Facts:	1896	1984
	70,000 attend	92,604 attend
	13 nations	140 nations
	311 competitors	12,000 competitors

Key facts: 70,000 people attend in 1896
92,604 people attend in 1984

3. PLAN Subtract the number of people in 1896 from the number of people in 1984.

4. SOLVE 92,604 − 70,000 = 22,604
At the 1984 opening ceremony, 22,604 more people attended than at the 1896 opening ceremonies.

5. CHECK Reread the question and check your steps. Ask yourself: Why is the answer reasonable? Check by adding 70,000 and 22,604.

FOCUS	Evaluate information as part of the Five–Step PROBLEM–SOLVING Plan.

PRACTICE

Decide if there is too much or too little information to solve the problems. If there is too much information, write the **key facts** and solve the problem. If there is too little information, tell what information is missing.

1. There were 311 competitors in the 1896 Olympic Games, representing 13 nations. There were 12,000 competitors in the 1984 Games, representing 140 nations. How many more competitors were in the 1984 Games than were in the 1896 Games?

2. The United States participated in the 1896 Olympic Games. It participated in most of the Games through 1984, missing only a few. In how many Olympic Games has the United States competed in all?

3. In 1932 the ninth Olympiad was held. In 1984 the 20th Olympiad was held. If the Olympics are held every 4 years, how many Games should have occurred after 1932 and through 1984?

4. List the years the Olympic Games should have taken place between 1932 and 1984. Circle the years in which the Olympic Games didn't occur?

5. The 1984 Olympic Games were held at the Los Angeles Coliseum. There were 92,604 spectators at the opening ceremonies in which almost 12,000 competitors took part. How many more seats would have been needed if there were 100,000 spectators?

6. In the 1896 Olympic Games, 13 nations sent 311 competitors. In the 1984 Olympic Games, 140 nations sent about 12,000 competitors. How many more nations competed in the 1984 Games than competed in the 1896 Games?

7. Two Olympic Games were played in Los Angeles. The first was in 1932. The second was in 1984. They were both held in the Los Angeles Coliseum. How many years were there between the two Games?

8. There were 92,604 spectators at the opening ceremonies of the 1984 Olympic Games. Were there more or fewer spectators at the opening ceremonies of 1932 Olympic Games?

Class Project

Women first began to compete seriously in track and field events in the 1928 Olympic Games. Form a small group and make a list of the men's and women's Olympic track and field records. Determine how much improvement was made by both groups since 1928.

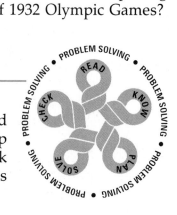

Whole Numbers

One Saturday 4,653 fans attended a football game. The next Saturday only 2,715 fans attended. What was the difference in attendance between the two Saturdays?

Subtract the ones.

Th	H	T	O
		4	13
4	6	5̶	3̶
− 2	7	1	5
			8

Regroup 5 tens and 3 ones as 4 tens and 13 ones.

Subtract the tens.

Th	H	T	O
		4	13
4	6	5̶	3̶
− 2	7	1	5
		3	8

Subtract the hundreds.

Th	H	T	O
3	16	4	13
4̶	6̶	5̶	3̶
− 2	7	1	5
	9	3	8

Regroup 4 thousands and 6 hundreds as 3 thousands and 16 hundreds.

Subtract the thousands.

Th	H	T	O
3	16	4	13
4̶	6̶	5̶	3̶
− 2	7	1	5
1	9	3	8

Check.

```
  1,938
+ 2,715
  4,653
```

There were 1,938 more fans the first Saturday. You can check your answer by addition.

When one number has more digits than the other number, be sure to line up numbers in the proper columns.

Subtract: 26,542 − 1,728.

TTh	Th	H	T	O
	5	15	3	12
2	6̶	5̶	4̶	2̶
−	1	7	2	8
2	4	8	1	4

Check.

```
  24,814
+  1,728
  26,542
```

GUIDED PRACTICE

Subtract. Remember to line up numbers properly.

1. 9,762 − 4,328 = 4	**2.** 8,931 − 3,850 = 81	**3.** 56,475 − 24,807 = 668	**4.** 758,354 − 236,736	**5.** 952,345 − 674,576
6. 7,682 − 4,198	**7.** 2,753 − 1,867	**8.** 95,316 − 77,688	**9.** 297,531 − 144,444	**10.** 598,766 − 135,355
11. 5,981 − 1,907	**12.** 4,735 − 1,462	**13.** 8,658 − 3,469	**14.** 725,641 − 456,791	**15.** 773,181 − 494,944

FOCUS Use NUMBER skills to subtract whole numbers through hundred millions with regrouping.

PRACTICE

Subtract.

16. 96 − 32	**17.** 83 − 47	**18.** 674 − 452	**19.** 572 − 254	**20.** 743 − 585
21. 6,495 − 2,374	**22.** 8,493 − 7,168	**23.** 6,522 − 4,375	**24.** 7,372 − 434	**25.** 34,689 − 23,457
26. 56,528 − 4,319	**27.** 47,346 − 23,758	**28.** 69,421 − 53,928	**29.** 34,623 − 3,975	**30.** 359,682 − 125,371
31. 576,439 − 357,319	**32.** 7,468,326 − 3,729,517	**33.** 9,314,526 − 582,978	**34.** 89,674,392 − 36,508,217	
35. 543,261,478 − 215,735,893	**36.** 834,527,312 − 527,618,402	**37.** 536,821,516 − 425,951,637	**38.** 874,212,753 − 67,204,875	

39. 546,324,215 − 79,859,637

40. 752,416,323 − 47,637,435

MIXED PRACTICE
Maintaining and Reviewing Skills

Add or subtract.

41. 6,079 + 2,783	**42.** 16,549 − 6,291	**43.** 929 + 412	**44.** 1,425 − 997	**45.** 47,138 + 6,937
46. 786 − 64	**47.** 4,692 − 3,984	**48.** 9,477 − 2,899	**49.** 4,296 + 9,732	**50.** 793,548 + 5,975

51. 407,013 + 9,498

52. 527,618 − 483,929

CHALLENGE

Replace A, B, C, and D with numbers that will correctly complete the exercise.

*53.
```
  D 3 B 1 4 9 7 D A
− 3 8 1 0 C B 3 2 4
  1 5 C 0 8 A 4 A 8
```

SUBTRACTION
Whole Numbers with Zeros

May has 500 stamps in her collection. Of these, 364 are European stamps. How many are not European stamps?

Regroup 5 hundreds as 4 hundreds and 10 tens.

```
  4 10
  5 0̸ 0
- 3 6 4
```

Regroup 10 tens as 9 tens and 10 ones.

```
      9
  4 1̸0 10
  5̸ 0̸ 0̸
- 3  6  4
```

Subtract.

```
      9
  4 1̸0 10
  5̸ 0̸ 0̸
- 3  6  4
  1  3  6
```

Check.

```
  136
+ 364
  500
```

May has 136 stamps that are not European. You can check your answer by addition.

PRACTICE

Subtract.

1. 80 − 56	**2.** 70 − 8	**3.** 350 − 125	**4.** 900 − 357	**5.** $850 − 375
6. 704 − 363	**7.** $905 − 377	**8.** 2,508 − 1,375	**9.** 8,403 − 5,734	**10.** 9,002 − 7,681
11. 54,069 − 32,549	**12.** 30,506 − 19,079	**13.** 300,406 − 190,370	**14.** 700,000 − 643,987	**15.** $800,000 − 76,053

16. 50,725 − 39,416

17. 40,080 − 26,019

18. 300,604 − 187,009

19. $900,000 − $842,763

MIXED PRACTICE
Maintaining and Reviewing Skills

Add or subtract.

20. 64,087 − 9,796	**21.** 438 + 20,997	**22.** 92,776 + 34,872	**23.** 3,567 − 1,794	**24.** 6,008 − 4,289

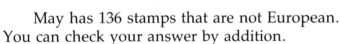

FOCUS Use NUMBER skills to subtract from numbers with zeros.

70

APPLICATION
Using Estimation

The Humber Bridge in Britain has a main span of 4,626 ft. The Brooklyn Bridge in New York has a main span of 1,595 ft. How much longer is the main span of the Humber Bridge?

Round to the nearest hundred. Estimate the difference.

Estimate		Exact
4,600		4,626
− 1,600		− 1,595
3,000 ⟵— Compare —⟶		3,031

The main span of the Humber Bridge is 3,031 feet longer.

Estimate the difference. Round to the nearest hundred.

25.	4,846 − 2,324	**26.**	6,704 − 4,476	**27.**	5,248 − 3,725	**28.**	6,052 − 1,738	**29.**	3,692 − 1,927
30.	72,695 − 38,426	**31.**	32,645 − 17,800	**32.**	57,650 − 35,242	**33.**	32,754 − 14,563	**34.**	25,762 − 19,426

Estimate the difference. Round to the nearest hundred. Then calculate the exact difference.

35. The air distance from Boston to Denver is 1,769 miles. From Boston to Dallas it is 1,551 miles. How much farther is it to Dallas?

36. Jet engine A has a cruise speed of 722 mph. Jet engine B has a cruise speed of 608 mph. How much faster does engine A cruise?

37. Martina made 2 476 kilograms of bread in her bakery. She sold 2 398 kilograms. How many kilograms does she have left?

38. Arturo bought 796 yards of wool for his tailor shop. He used 508 yards to make jackets. How many yards does he have left?

39. In a local election, Mr. Holtz received 8,324 votes and Mrs. Davis received 7,842 votes. How many more votes did Mr. Holtz receive?

40. On Friday, 437 books were borrowed from the book mobile. On Saturday, 673 books were borrowed. How many more books were borrowed on Saturday?

Use ESTIMATION to solve problems.

Building Plans

When we think of maps, we often think of road maps or maps of countries. Some maps show details of smaller areas, such as single buildings. We call maps of single buildings **plans**.

Architects, construction workers, and archaeologists use building plans.

House plans usually follow a standard pattern. They show the size of the house. This is a measure of floor space given in square feet. If the living area is made up of more than one level, the area of each level will be given. There is a wide range in the areas of houses of different sizes, from several hundred square feet to several thousand square feet.

All kinds of map makers use special symbols in their work. The types of symbols used on building plans vary, but some are very common.

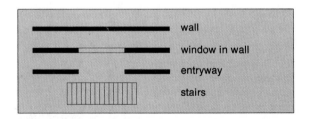

Thick black lines stand for walls, while breaks in those lines stand for doors or entranceways. Breaks in outside walls that are enclosed in thin black lines stand for windows. Stairs are shown by rectangles filled with parallel lines.

Furniture is not shown on plans, but built-in features like sinks, tubs and showers, cabinets and closets are.

Abbreviations are used on the plan. Each room is named. The measurements for the width and length of each room are in feet (') and inches (") as 13'6" × 19'3". This is read as "thirteen feet six inches by nineteen feet three inches." The notation $13^6 \times 19^3$ is also used to refer to the same measurement.

The dimensions of the entire house are shown along lines outside the drawing of the house itself.

CRITICAL THINKING

Look at the top plan on the opposite page, and answer these questions.

1. What do these abbreviations stand for? MBR, BR, B, K, DR, LR, G.

2. What might LC and REF stand for?

3. Which bedroom has the greatest area?

Now look at the bottom plan on the opposite page.

4. Compute the area of the house, using the outside dimensions.

5. Compare the areas of the rooms. Which rooms have the same area?

FOCUS   Use GEOMETRY and map skills to understand house plans.

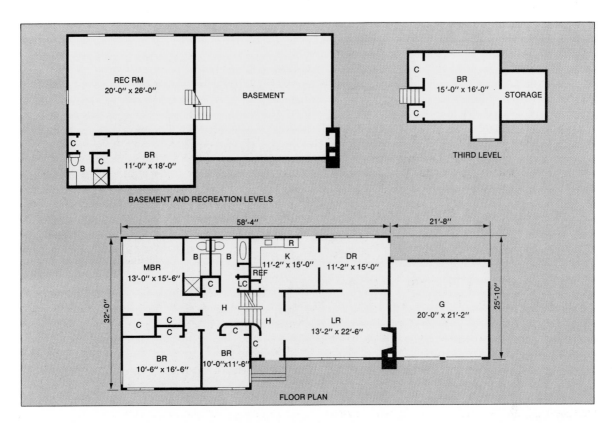

REC RM
20'-0'' x 26'-0''

BASEMENT

C

B   C

BR
11'-0'' x 18'-0''

BASEMENT AND RECREATION LEVELS

C

BR
15'-0'' x 16'-0''

STORAGE

C

THIRD LEVEL

58'-4''   21'-8''

32'-0''

B

B

R

K
11'-2'' x 15'-0''

DR
11'-2'' x 15'-0''

MBR
13'-0'' x 15'-6''

C

REF

LC

G
20'-0'' x 21'-2''

25'-10''

C

C
C

H

C

H

LR
13'-2'' x 22'-6''

C

C

BR
10'-6'' x 16'-6''

BR
10'-0''x11'-6''

FLOOR PLAN

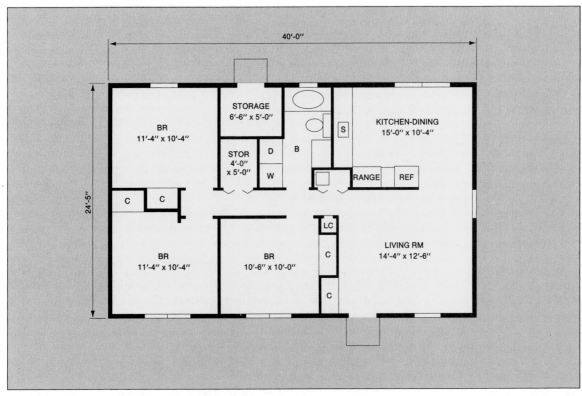

40'-0''

24'-5''

BR
11'-4'' x 10'-4''

STORAGE
6'-6'' x 5'-0''

S

KITCHEN-DINING
15'-0'' x 10'-4''

STOR
4'-0''
x 5'-0''

D

B

W

C   C

RANGE   REF

BR
11'-4'' x 10'-4''

BR
10'-6'' x 10'-0''

LC

C

LIVING RM
14'-4'' x 12'-6''

C

LOOKING BACK
Reviewing and Testing Chapter 5

In Chapter 5, you formulated problems about scheduling flights. To review, look at page 61.

1. Which of the scheduled flights will most likely depart on time? Which will most likely be the latest to depart?

To review addition of whole numbers and estimation, refer to pages 62 and 64.

Estimate to the nearest thousand. Then solve.

2. 3,553
   + 5,324

3. 5,786
   + 4,875

4. 76,824
    39,600
   + 9,807

5. 16,721
     3,243
   + 26,850

6. 24,326
    15,780
   + 38,975

Use the Five–Step Problem–Solving Plan to solve this problem. Refer to page 66

7. At the twenty-third Summer Olympics the United States won 83 gold medals, 61 silver medals and 30 bronze medals. Canada won 10 gold medals, 18 silver medals, and 16 bronze medals. How many medals altogether did the United States win?

To review subtraction of whole numbers, refer to pages 68 and 70.

Estimate to the nearest thousand. Then solve.

8. 3,974
   − 2,658

9. 5,631
   − 2,785

10. 25,690
    − 17,957

11. 500,602
    − 153,954

12. 673,920
    − 84,540

13. The art museum sold 1,309 posters during the month of June and 4,988 posters during the month of July. How many more posters were sold in July?

14. In one month the Artmar Corporation received 6,381 orders for a calendar. The next month they received 4,997 orders. How many calendars were ordered altogether?

You learned about dimensions on a floor plan. Refer to page 72 to review how floor plans are used.

15. Draw a complete floor plan of your classroom.

FOCUS | Review and test skills learned and practiced.

Preparing for New Skills for Chapter 6

In the next chapter you will focus on

- **formulating problems about fuel economy.**
- **deciding if a number is prime or composite.**
- **using a factor tree to find factors.**

- **finding prime factorizations.**
- **determining if a problem has enough information to solve.**
- **how math is used in technology.**

It will be helpful in working with prime and composite numbers if you can use exponents to simplify a product.

Example 1:

4 factors

$3 \times 3 \times 3 \times 3 = 3^4$

number used as a factor

Example 2:

3 factors

$7 \times 7 \times 7 = 7^3$

number used as a factor

Sometimes one number can be written as a power of another number.

Example 3:

$8 = 2 \times 2 \times 2 = 2^3$
8 is written as a power of 2.

Example 4:

$81 = 3 \times 3 \times 3 \times 3 = 3^4$
81 is written as a power of 3.

PRACTICE

Write each product using exponents.

1. $5 \times 5 \times 5 \times 5$ **2.** 16×16 **3.** $9 \times 9 \times 9$

4. $8 \times 8 \times 8 \times 8 \times 8$ **5.** $3 \times 3 \times 3 \times 3 \times 3 \times 3$ **6.** $4 \times 4 \times 4 \times 4 \times 4 \times 4$

7. $2 \times 2 \times 3 \times 3$ **8.** $3 \times 3 \times 3 \times 4 \times 4$ **9.** $5 \times 5 \times 5 \times 5 \times 8 \times 8$

Write each number as a power of another number.

10. 27 **11.** 4 **12.** 16 **13.** 25

14. 64 **15.** 36 **16.** 125 **17.** 1,000

Review NUMBER skills in preparation for learning new skills.

Formulate problems using photo, data, and text.

Prime Numbers, Composite Numbers, and Factoring Into Primes

DATA

Traffic Department Vehicles

Vehicle	Number of vehicles used	Miles per gallon
Motorscooters	48	60
Official city agency cars	18	34
Police cruisers	32	23
Ambulances	12	17
City buses	28	11
Fire trucks	11	7

Mayor Davis was campaigning for the new economic drive she had begun in her administration. She announced the fuel economy figures for six new models of vehicles used by the city over the past year. She proudly pointed to the figures in the data. "We're getting better mileage from our city vehicles than ever before. Looking at the mileage rates for the first three vehicles," she added, "we see that we are getting twenty-three miles or better per gallon."

"Mayor Davis is playing with figures," said her election opponent, Council Member Costas. "We all know that these new vehicles are expensive. With prices of gas and diesel fuel probably going up, her claims of 'economical government' don't mean much."

What other data might Mayor Davis and Mr. Costas need to intelligently judge fuel economy in city motor vehicles? What problems will they have to face in the upcoming election?

Prime and Composite Numbers

The **factors** of a number are whole numbers that divide it exactly. The number 13 has 2 factors.

$$1 \times 13 = 13$$

factor

The factors of 13 are 1 and 13.

A **prime number** has exactly two factors, 1 and the number itself.

$$1 \times 2 = 2 \qquad 1 \times 3 = 3 \qquad 1 \times 5 = 5$$

So, 2, 3, 5, and 13 are prime numbers.

The number 12 has several factors.

$$1 \times 12 = 12 \qquad 3 \times 4 = 12 \qquad 2 \times 6 = 12$$

factor   factor   factor

The factors of 12 are 1, 2, 3, 4, 6, and 12.

A **composite number** has more than two factors.

$$1 \times 4 = 4 \qquad 1 \times 6 = 6 \qquad 1 \times 9 = 9$$
$$2 \times 2 = 4 \qquad 2 \times 3 = 6 \qquad 3 \times 3 = 9$$

So, 4, 6, 9, and 12 are composite numbers.

Only nonzero numbers are called prime or composite. Therefore 0 is neither prime nor composite. The number 1 has only one factor. It too is neither prime nor composite.

GUIDED PRACTICE

1. What are the factors of 17? 1 and ■

2. Is 17 a prime or composite number? ■

3. What are the factors of 10? 1, 2, ■, and ■

4. Is 10 a prime or composite number? ■

FOCUS   Use NUMBER skills to determine prime and composite numbers.

PRACTICE

Find all the factors for each number.

5. 4   **6.** 8   **7.** 5   **8.** 45   **9.** 6

10. 7   **11.** 9   **12.** 14   **13.** 23   **14.** 36

15. 48   **16.** 53   **17.** 60   **18.** 75   **19.** 100

Write *prime* or *composite* for each number.

20. 5   **21.** 7   **22.** 9   **23.** 14   **24.** 21

25. 28   **26.** 33   **27.** 45   **28.** 53   **29.** 61

30. 67   **31.** 87   **32.** 369   **33.** 2,560   **34.** 3,725

MIXED PRACTICE
Maintaining and Reviewing Skills

Add or subtract.

35.
$$436 + 37{,}921 + 4{,}837$$

36.
$$43{,}208 + 88{,}711 + 739{,}726$$

37.
$$92{,}401 + 63{,}076 + 4{,}355$$

38.
$$73{,}928 + 8{,}169 + 754$$

39.
$$6{,}421 + 582{,}907 + 37{,}642$$

40.
$$30{,}044 - 29{,}776$$

41.
$$54{,}067 - 2{,}989$$

42.
$$33{,}972 - 8{,}682$$

43.
$$74{,}711 - 41{,}182$$

44.
$$97{,}002 - 7{,}954$$

45. $4{,}399 + 42 + 16{,}077$

46. $2{,}077 - 859$

47. $62{,}074 - 9{,}813$

48. $338{,}291 + 342 + 4{,}972$

CHALLENGE

Leap years occur in years exactly divisible by 4 except for years ending in 00, which must be divisible by 400 to be leap years.

*49. Choose all the leap years.

    1600   1900   2000   2100   2200

*50. List four leap years between 2001 and 2050.

NUMBER SKILLS
Prime and Composite Numbers

Every whole number greater than 1 is either a **prime** or a **composite** number. The numbers 0 and 1 are neither prime nor composite.

Prime numbers are those numbers with exactly two factors, 1 and the number itself.

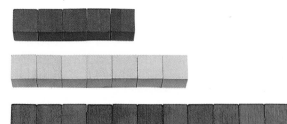

$$1 \times 5 = 5 \qquad 1 \times 7 = 7 \qquad 1 \times 11 = 11$$

Composite numbers are numbers with more than two factors.

$$1 \times 8 = 8$$
$$2 \times 4 = 8$$

$$1 \times 9 = 9$$
$$3 \times 3 = 9$$

PRACTICE

List all the factors of each number and tell whether it is prime or composite.

1. 56   **2.** 21   **3.** 41   **4.** 49

5. 38   **6.** 18   **7.** 23   **8.** 30

Choose all the prime numbers in each row.

9. 2   4   9   13   19   22   23

10. 11   39   41   47   52   53   60

11. 0   1   4   11   17   38   56

12. 8   15   22   29   32   39   71

MIXED PRACTICE
Maintaining and Reviewing Skills

Compare. Use > or <.

13. 476,144 ● 467,144   **14.** 81,372 ● 81,327   **15.** 19,566 ● 19,565

16. 68,661 ● 68,616   **17.** 521,413 ● 521,143   **18.** 7,051 ● 7,501

19. 74,474 ● 74,744   **20.** 3,403 ● 3,430   **21.** 3,663 ● 3,636

FOCUS   Use NUMBER skills to determine prime and composite numbers.

APPLICATION
Using Prime Numbers

Here is a way to find all prime numbers less than 100.

Write all the numbers from 1 to 100 as shown in the chart at right.

Follow these directions:

22. First cross out 1, since it is neither prime nor composite.

23. Circle 2, a prime. Cross out all the numbers that have 2 as a factor.

24. Circle 3, a prime. Cross out all the numbers that have 3 as a factor.

25. Continue in this manner until all numbers are either circled or crossed out. All circled numbers are prime.

1	2	3	4	5	6	7	8	9	10
11	12	13	14	15	16	17	18	19	20
21	22	23	24	25	26	27	28	29	30
31	32	33	34	35	36	37	38	39	40
41	42	43	44	45	46	47	48	49	50
51	52	53	54	55	56	57	58	59	60
61	62	63	64	65	66	67	68	69	70
71	72	73	74	75	76	77	78	79	80
81	82	83	84	85	86	87	88	89	90
91	92	93	94	95	96	97	98	99	100

26. List all the numbers in the chart that have not been crossed out.

27. Are these numbers prime or composite?

Exploring With a Calculator

Use your calculator to find out if one number is a factor of another.

Here is how to find out if 5 is a factor of 6,398.
Enter 6398 ÷ 5   Display 1279.6

The calculator shows a decimal number. Therefore 5 is not a factor of 6,398.

Next try the number 7.
Enter 6398 ÷ 7   Display 914

The calculator shows a whole number, not a decimal number. Therefore 7 is a factor of 6,398.

Use a calculator to find a factor. Enter each number and divide by any number other than 1 and the number itself. Divide until the display shows a whole number.

28. 316   29. 105   30. 143   31. 3,904   32. 6,470

Use NUMBER skills and a calculator to determine prime and composite numbers.

PRIME FACTORIZATION
Using a Factor Tree

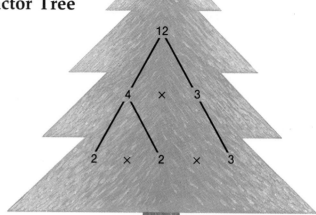

Every composite number can be expressed as a product of prime numbers. This is the **prime factorization** of the number.

The prime factorization of 12 is:

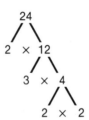

$$4 \times 3 = 12$$
$$2 \times 2 \times 3 = 12$$
$$2^2 \times 3 = 12$$

When a prime number is a factor more than once, exponents are used. This is called **exponential form.**

A **factor tree** can help you find the prime factorization of a number. Here is how a factor tree works.

Find any two factors of a number. If the factor is a composite, find any two factors of that number. Continue with each factor until you reach a prime number.

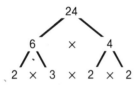

The prime factorization of 24 is $2 \times 2 \times 2 \times 3$ or $2^3 \times 3$.

No matter which factors are used to start a factor tree, the final row of the tree will contain only prime numbers.

GUIDED PRACTICE

Complete each factor tree to find the prime factorization.

1.   16
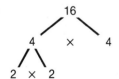
4 × 4
2 × 2

2.   28
4 × 7

3.   64
8 × 8
2 × 4

4.   27
3 ×

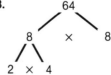

5. 48   **6.** 60   **7.** 36   **8.** 44

PRACTICE

Write *yes* or *no* to identify whether each
is a prime factorization.

9. $3 \times 2 \times 5$ **10.** $2 \times 3 \times 6$ **11.** 13×4

12. $7 \times 9 \times 2$ **13.** $2 \times 3 \times 5 \times 9$ **14.** $5 \times 7 \times 5$

15. $3 \times 3 \times 5 \times 5$ **16.** $13 \times 11 \times 3$ **17.** $3 \times 3 \times 2 \times 2 \times 5$

Complete each prime factorization.
Then express each answer in exponential form.

18. $90 = 2 \times 3 \times 3 \times \blacksquare$ **19.** $18 = 2 \times 3 \times \blacksquare$

20. $32 = 2 \times 2 \times 2 \times \blacksquare \times \blacksquare$ **21.** $63 = 3 \times 3 \times \blacksquare$

22. $81 = 3 \times 3 \times \blacksquare \times \blacksquare$ ***23.** $3{,}465 = 3 \times 3 \times 5 \times 7 \times \blacksquare$

Draw factor trees to find each prime factorization. Express
each answer in exponential form.

24. 54   **25.** 72   **26.** 96   **27.** 144   **28.** 210

MIXED PRACTICE
Maintaining and Reviewing Skills

Round each number to the nearest hundred.
Estimate each sum or difference.

29. $488 + 132$ **30.** $424 - 231$ **31.** $872 - 649$

32. $535 - 372$ **33.** $621 + 574$ **34.** $847 + 481$

35. $922 - 267$ **36.** $359 + 750$ **37.** $261 - 149$

CHALLENGE

*38. Use a calculator to find a
path through the maze to
the number 598,752.
Start at ENTER.
Move through the maze. Multiply
the number on your display by each
number along the path. The final
display must be 598,752.

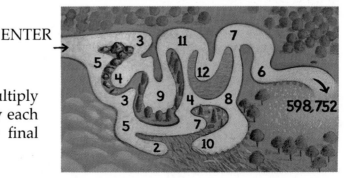

PRIME FACTORIZATION
Using a Factor Tree

When a composite number is written as a product of prime numbers, this is called the **prime factorization** of that number.

When writing the prime factorization of a number, a multiplication dot (•) is often used in place of a "times" sign.

Exponents are used when a prime number is a factor more than once.

The prime factorization of 45 is 5 • 3 • 3 or 5 • 3^2.

5 • 3 • 3

PRACTICE

Copy and complete the chart.

	Whole Number	Prime Factorization	Exponential Form
1.	80	2 • 2 • 2 • 2 • 5	
2.	216	3 • 3 • 3 • 2 • 2 • 2	
3.			2^3 • 5^2
4.		2 • 2 • 2 • 2 • 3 • 3	2^4 • 3^2
5.	296		
6.	64		
7.	180		2^2 • 3^2 • 5
8.		2 • 2 • 3 • 7	

MIXED PRACTICE
Maintaining and Reviewing Skills

Add or subtract.

9.	5,872 − 3,981	**10.**	6,466 + 7,982	**11.**	5,194 + 7,332	**12.**	4,672 − 2,748
13.	9,318 − 3,529	**14.**	8,846 − 2,710	**15.**	7,017 + 1,592	**16.**	3,549 + 6,916
17.	2,878 + 5,944	**18.**	1,492 + 6,269	**19.**	3,048 − 1,769	**20.**	4,679 + 3,903

FOCUS   Use NUMBER skills to determine prime factorization.

APPLICATION
Using Twin Primes

Twin primes are two prime numbers that differ by 2.

Here are the first 10 prime numbers.

The numbers 3 and 5 are twin primes. Their difference is 2.

21. List the 8 pairs of twin primes less than 100.

Problem Solving: Evaluating Information

An important step in problem solving is to choose the operation by evaluating the given information.

Read the word problem below and decide which operation you would use to solve the problem.

Stan wants to paint the kitchen. He bought 2 cans of paint. He spent $12 for each can. How much did he spend in all?

- **The key facts are:** Stan bought 2 cans of paint. Each can cost $12.
- **You need to find:** The total cost of the paint.

To find the total, you can add or multiply. Since each can costs the same and we know the price for one can, we multiply to find the total cost.

Write which operation you would use to solve each problem below.

22. The tiles that Ellen wants to buy for her bathroom cost $2.20 each. Ellen needs 40 tiles. Find the total cost.

23. Barry is putting shelf paper in the closets of his kitchen. He has $10.50 to spend on 3 rolls. How much does each roll cost?

24. It took 3 movers several hours to move Bert into his new home. The total cost for moving was $300. If it took 6 hours to move, how much per hour was Bert charged?

25. Tod plans to cover his kitchen counter with a vinyl covering. The vinyl covering is $16.75 per roll. Tod bought 4 rolls. What was the total cost?

Use NUMBER skills to find twin primes and evaluate information as part of the Five-Step PROBLEM-SOLVING Plan.

What is Computer Programming About?

Computer programming is an interesting career. The following exercise will illustrate the stages that take place in programming a computer.

You will need a piece of paper and a pen in order to do this activity. First read and memorize the instructions. Then follow the instructions each time you see the word GO.

Instructions:
1. On your piece of paper write this phrase.

   5 4 3 2 1   blast off!
2. Put your pen down.
3. This ends the instructions.

GO
GO
GO
GO

How many times did you write "5 4 3 2 1 blast off!"? If you wrote it only once, you did not follow the instructions correctly! Remember, you were supposed to follow all the instructions each time the word GO appeared. You should have written the phrase four times.

As simple as it seems, this exercise has a real purpose. In fact, it outlines the four stages of computer programming. Let us look at these four stages, and see how the exercise involves each one.

FOUR STAGES OF PROGRAMMING

Stage 1: *THE PLAN.*

In order to solve a problem, you must develop a plan *before* using the computer. The plan usually consists of a list of steps to follow in order to find the solution. In the exercise, we wanted you to learn what happens in computer programming.

Stage 2: *THE PROGRAM.*

Once the plan has been developed, it must be rewritten in a language the computer can understand, such as BASIC, FORTRAN, Pascal, COBOL, or Logo. This rewritten plan is called a **program**. It is a series of step-by-step instructions that tells the computer exactly what to do.

Stage 3: *ENTERING THE PROGRAM.*

Your instructions, in the form of a program, must be entered into the computer, which then stores them in a place called the **memory**.

Stage 4: *EXECUTING THE PROGRAM.*

Once the instructions are stored in the memory, the computer can follow them every time it is given a special command (RUN, for example).

CRITICAL THINKING

1. Why must instructions be stored in the computer's memory?

2. Why must you have a plan before going to a computer?

FOCUS | Use LOGIC to understand the four stages of programming a computer.

The Four Stages of Programming

1. THE PLAN

The plan can be presented in a flowchart such as the one below. A **flowchart** is a drawing that uses different symbols for each step in the program.

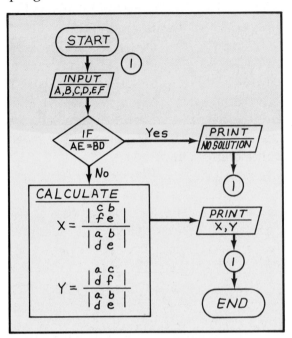

2. THE PROGRAM

The set of instructions written in computer language is called a **program**. Below is an example of a program written in BASIC language.

```
10 PRINT "AX + BY = C" : PRINT
    "DX + EY = F"
20 PRINT : PRINT
30 INPUT A, B, C, D, E, F
40 IF A*E = B*D THEN GOTO 90
50 X = (C*E - B*F)/(A*E - B*D)
60 Y = (A*F - C*D)/(A*E - B*D)
70 PRINT "X ="; X, "Y ="; Y
80 GOTO 20
90 PRINT "NO SOLUTION"
100 GOTO 20
110 END
```

3. ENTERING THE PROGRAM

This screen shows how the program looks after it has been entered.

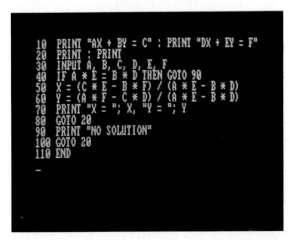

4. EXECUTING THE PROGRAM

After getting the RUN command, this computer followed the instructions.

87

Reviewing and Testing Chapter 6

In Chapter 6 you formulated problems about fuel economy. Refer to pages 76 and 77.

1. How might each of the candidates best support his or her arguments?

To review what you learned about prime and composite numbers, refer to page 78.

Write all the factors for each number.

2. 19   **3.** 50   **4.** 27   **5.** 36

6. 11   **7.** 29   **8.** 42   **9.** 62

Write *prime* or *composite* for each number.

10. 9   **11.** 17   **12.** 50   **13.** 67

14. 19   **15.** 91   **16.** 45   **17.** 15

To review prime factorization, refer to pages 82 and 84.

Complete each factor tree to find the prime factorization.

18.   **19.** 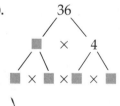   **20.**   **21.**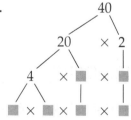

You learned about programming a computer. To review, refer to pages 86 and 87.

22. Which stage of programming are you in if you are putting your plan into computer language?

LOOKING AHEAD
Preparing for New Skills for Chapter 7

In the next chapter you will focus on

- formulating problems about deep-sea diving.
- multiplying whole numbers.
- using properties of multiplication.
- dividing whole numbers.
- using logic in magic squares.
- how math is used in cartography.

Multiplying and dividing with whole numbers will be easier if you review the order of operations. Study the examples.

When simplifying an expression, use the following rules for the order of operations.

- Do the operations inside the parentheses first.

- Next multiply and divide in order from left to right.

- Then add and subtract in order from left to right.

Example 1:

$$8 \times 7 + 4 \div 2$$
$$56 + 2 = 58$$

Example 2:

$$(3 + 5) - (16 \div 8)$$
$$8 - 2 = 6$$

Example 3:

$$15 - 6 \div 3$$
$$15 - 2 = 13$$

Example 4:

$$(15 - 6) \div 3$$
$$9 \div 3 = 3$$

PRACTICE

Simplify each expression.

1. $21 \div 3 - 2 \times 3$

2. $(8 + 7) \div 3$

3. $4 + 6 \times 2$

4. $(9 - 3) \div (2 \times 3)$

5. $8 \times (6 + 3) - 4$

6. $8 + 8 \div 4 - 1$

7. $12 - 6 \times 2$

8. $(12 - 6) \times 2$

9. $8 \times (4 + 3) - (18 \div 3)$

Review NUMBER skills in preparation for learning new skills.

FOCUS Formulate problems using photo, data, and text.

Multiplication and Division With Whole Numbers

DATA

Depth of wreck	8 fathoms*
Cargo	500 silver ingots
Number of divers	4
Number of sharks sighted	1
Nautical miles from port	43
Top speed of craft	18 knots**
Weather	storm warning
Time before storm	4 to 6 h
Number of ingots found	7
Number of ingots raised	2
Value of one ingot	$20,000
Time to raise ingot	45 min

*One fathom is a depth of 6 feet.
**A knot is one nautical mile
  per hour.

Scuba divers from the pleasure craft *Seabreeze* have found the wreck of the Spanish galleon *Santa Lucia.* The ship went down in a storm in 1632 with its cargo of silver ingots. The *Seabreeze* is not a salvage ship, but the divers have managed to raise two of the silver ingots.

A shark has been sighted. The captain has just heard on the radio that a storm warning has been issued by the weather service. The wind has picked up noticeably. The divers are reluctant to leave because they may never be able to relocate the *Santa Lucia.*

Consider the situation. What problems may the divers from the *Seabreeze* face? Predict the decisions that might be made and what will happen as a result.

By 1- or 2-Digit Numbers

Mrs. Arimoto ordered 6 boxes of pencils for the school bookstore. If each box contained 145 pencils, how many pencils did she order in all?

Multiply: 6 × 145.   6 × 145 = 870

factors   product

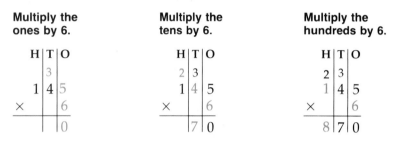

Multiply the ones by 6.

Multiply the tens by 6.

Multiply the hundreds by 6.

Mrs. Arimoto ordered 870 pencils.

She also ordered 12 packages of colored art paper. If each package contained 150 sheets, how many sheets of art paper did she order in all?

Multiply: 12 × 150.

Multiply 150 by 2.

Th	H	T	O
	1		
	1	5	0
×		1	2
3	0	0	

Multiply 150 by 10.

Th	H	T	O
	1		
	1	5	0
×		1	2
	3	0	0
1	5	0	0

Add the products.

Th	H	T	O
	1	5	0
×		1	2
	3	0	0
1	5	0	0
1	8	0	0

Mrs. Arimoto ordered 1,800 sheets of art paper.

GUIDED PRACTICE

Multiply. Remember to line up numbers properly.

1. 236
   × 3
   ▉08

2. 3,245
   ×   6
   ▉▉,▉70

3. 458
   × 23
   1374
   ▉▉60

4. 3,415
   ×   54

5. 4,206
   ×   70

FOCUS   Use NUMBER skills to multiply whole numbers.

PRACTICE

Multiply.

6. 34
× 2

7. 43
× 4

8. 513
× 3

9. 524
× 4

10. 2,342
× 4

11. 4,062
× 5

12. 3,216
× 4

13. 28
× 12

14. 72
× 53

15. 421
× 32

16. 567
× 40

17. 297
× 38

18. 8,219
× 23

19. 5,109
× 46

20. 9,504
× 58

21. 7,239
× 45

22. 8,305
× 57

23. 8,619
× 76

24. 7,609
× 85

25. 9,708
× 98

26. 4,300
× 69

27. 7,328
× 94

28. 8,940
× 77

29. 3,694
× 87

30. 9,347
× 85

31. $15 \times 6{,}297$ **32.** $56 \times 5{,}201$ **33.** $21 \times 3{,}808$ **34.** $90 \times 6{,}311$ **35.** $58 \times 7{,}007$

MIXED PRACTICE
Maintaining and Reviewing Skills

Solve.

36. $245 - s = 123$ **37.** $t + 58 = 207$ **38.** $48 \div n = 8$

39. $6 \times w = 54$ **40.** $r \div 9 = 7$ **41.** $a - 59 = 60$

42. $56{,}289 + 24{,}351 = n$ **43.** $84{,}072 + 7{,}638 = a$ **44.** $94{,}100 + 23{,}649 = x$

45. $256{,}891 + 37{,}624 = t$ **46.** $64{,}938 - 23{,}042 = s$ **47.** $570{,}629 - 326{,}042 = m$

48. $846{,}000 - 35{,}246 = c$ **49.** $78{,}621 - 75{,}037 = d$ **50.** $683{,}704 - 520{,}600 = k$

CHALLENGE

Find the pattern. Give the next three numbers.

*51. 1, 2, 4, 7, 11, ■, ■, ■

*52. 3, 8, 13, 18, 23, ■, ■, ■

*53. 1, 4, 9, 16, 25, ■, ■, ■

*54. 97, 96, 94, 91, 87, ■, ■, ■

*55. Write a paragraph explaining how you determined the pattern in each set of numbers.

MULTIPLICATION OF WHOLE NUMBERS
By 1-, 2-, or 3-Digit Numbers

A gas station pumped an average of 2,143 gallons of gasoline a day. How many gallons of gasoline did it pump in one year?

Multiply 2,143 by 365.

Multiply 2,143 by 5.

TTh	Th	H	T	O
	2	1	4	3
×		3	6	5
1	0	7	1	5

Multiply 2,143 by 60.

HTh	TTh	Th	H	T	O
		2	1	4	3
	×		3	6	5
	1	0	7	1	5
1	2	8	5	8	0

Multiply 2,143 by 300.

HTh	TTh	Th	H	T	O
		2	1	4	3
	×		3	6	5
	1	0	7	1	5
1	2	8	5	8	0
6	4	2	9	0	0

Add the products.

HTh	TTh	Th	H	T	O
		2	1	4	3
	×		3	6	5
	1	0	7	1	5
1	2	8	5	8	0
6	4	2	9	0	0
7	8	2	1	9	5

The station pumped 782,195 gallons.

PRACTICE

Multiply.
Remember to line up numbers properly.

1. 315
   × 124

2. 432
   × 312

3. 6,208
   × 215

4. 2,143
   × 345

5. 3,618
   × 307

6. 8,921
   × 456

7. 5,703
   × 514

8. 9,083
   × 674

9. 7,602
   × 393

10. 8,769
    × 798

11. 6,984
    × 356

12. 8,257
    × 763

13. 9,057
    × 666

*14. 2,405
    × 3,174

*15. 4,002
    × 1,136

MIXED PRACTICE
Maintaining and Reviewing Skills

Add or subtract.

16. 4,526
    + 3,104

17. 38,127
    + 24,075

18. 846,923
    + 215,046

19. 82,914
    + 25,078

20. 52,006
    + 43,458

21. 7,643
    − 2,132

22. 8,965
    − 4,798

23. 27,694
    − 14,735

24. 86,070
    − 35,290

25. 98,000
    − 72,065

FOCUS | Use NUMBER skills to multiply whole numbers.

APPLICATION

Using Algebra

Does changing the order of factors change the product?

$$3 \times 4 = 4 \times 3 \qquad 2 \times 5 = 5 \times 2 \qquad 10 \times 25 = 25 \times 10$$
$$12 = 12 \qquad\quad 10 = 10 \qquad\qquad 250 = 250$$

$$25 \times 8 = 8 \times 25 \qquad 45 \times 82 = 82 \times 45 \qquad 375 \times 218 = 218 \times 375$$
$$200 = 200 \qquad\quad 3,690 = 3,690 \qquad\quad 81,750 = 81,750$$

Changing the **order** of factors does not change the product.

This is called the **commutative property of multiplication.**

Complete. Use the commutative property.

26. $8 \times 9 = 9 \times \blacksquare$ **27.** $13 \times 17 = \blacksquare \times 13$ **28.** $52 \times 64 = \blacksquare \times 52$

29. $26 \times 84 = \blacksquare \times 26$ **30.** $279 \times 643 = 643 \times \blacksquare$ **31.** $574 \times 832 = \blacksquare \times 574$

32. $300 \times 200 = 200 \times \blacksquare$ **33.** $756 \times 89 = \blacksquare \times 756$ **34.** $100 \times 1,000 = 1,000 \times \blacksquare$

Does changing the grouping of factors change the product? Perform the operations inside the ( ) first.

$$(3 \times 4) \times 5 = 3 \times (4 \times 5) \qquad 12 \times (3 \times 8) = (12 \times 3) \times 8$$
$$12 \times 5 = 3 \times 20 \qquad\qquad 12 \times 24 = 36 \times 8$$
$$60 = 60 \qquad\qquad\qquad 288 = 288$$

Changing the **grouping** of factors does not change the product.

This is called the **associative property of multiplication**.

Complete. Use the associative property.

35. $(5 \times 6) \times 3 = 5 \times (6 \times \blacksquare)$ **36.** $9 \times (5 \times 2) = (\blacksquare \times 5) \times 2$

37. $(10 \times 5) \times 4 = 10 \times (\blacksquare \times 4)$ **38.** $10 \times (7 \times 2) = (\blacksquare \times 7) \times 2$

39. $(15 \times 2) \times 3 = 15 \times (\blacksquare \times 3)$ **40.** $8 \times (4 \times 6) = (8 \times 4) \times \blacksquare$

Write which property of multiplication is shown.

41. $94 \times 36 = 36 \times 94$ **42.** $18 \times (6 \times 3) = (18 \times 6) \times 3$

43. $(9 \times 6) \times 9 = 9 \times (6 \times 9)$ **44.** $(4 \times 83) \times 9 = 4 \times (83 \times 9)$

45. $426 \times 893 = 893 \times 426$ **46.** $10 \times 100 = 100 \times 10$

Use properties of ALGEBRA to multiply.

DIVISION OF WHOLE NUMBERS
By 1- or 2-Digit Numbers

Divide: 95 ÷ 4.

```
         ┌──────── Quotient
      23 R3 ◄──── Remainder
Divisor ──► 4)95  ◄──── Dividend
```

Estimate the tens digit.	**Multiply and subtract.**	**Bring down the ones. Estimate the ones digit.**	**Multiply and subtract. Write the remainder.**	**Check.**

Estimate the tens digit.

4)95

4)9 is about 2.
Try 2 as the tens digit.

Multiply and subtract.

```
    Tens | Ones
      2  |
4)    9  |  5
      8  |
      1  |
```

Bring down the ones. Estimate the ones digit.

```
    Tens | Ones
      2  |
4)    9  |  5
      8  |
      1  |  5
```

4)15 is about 3.
Try 3 as the ones digit.

Multiply and subtract. Write the remainder.

```
    Tens | Ones
      2  |  3  R 3
4)    9  |  5
      8  |
      1  |  5
      1  |  2
         |  3
```

Check.

```
   23   Quotient
 ×  4   Divisor
   92
 +  3   Remainder
   95   Dividend
```

Divide: 496 ÷ 12.

12)496   Estimate the quotient.   100 × 12 = 1,200 ──► quotient too big
           The quotient is   ? × 12 = 496
           between 10 and 100.   10 × 12 = 120 ──► quotient too small

Estimate the tens digit.	**Multiply and subtract.**	**Estimate the ones digit.**	**Multiply and subtract.**	**Check.**

Estimate the tens digit.

10
12)496

Round 12 to 10.
1)4 is 4.
Try 4 as the tens digit.

Multiply and subtract.

```
     H | T | O
       | 4 |
12)  4 | 9 | 6
     4 | 8 |
       | 1 |
```

Estimate the ones digit.

```
     H | T | O
       | 4 | 1
12)  4 | 9 | 6
     4 | 8 |
       | 1 | 6
```

Multiply and subtract.

```
     H | T | O
       | 4 | 1 R 4
12)  4 | 9 | 6
     4 | 8 |
       | 1 | 6
       | 1 | 2
           | 4
```

Check.

```
   41
 × 12
  492
 +  4
  496
```

GUIDED PRACTICE

Divide.
Estimate the quotient first.

1. 7)849   **2.** 9)2,804   **3.** 10)3,540   **4.** 19)236   **5.** 48)2,986

FOCUS | Use NUMBER skills to divide whole numbers.

PRACTICE

Divide.

6. $5\overline{)6,750}$ **7.** $6\overline{)3,252}$ **8.** $3\overline{)7,984}$ **9.** $4\overline{)2,060}$ **10.** $8\overline{)4,267}$

11. $7\overline{)3,485}$ **12.** $1\overline{)7,924}$ **13.** $9\overline{)1,962}$ **14.** $2\overline{)1,436}$ **15.** $20\overline{)8,536}$

16. $19\overline{)3,069}$ **17.** $35\overline{)30,870}$ **18.** $43\overline{)7,846}$ **19.** $27\overline{)9,207}$ **20.** $59\overline{)3,467}$

21. $91\overline{)24,348}$ **22.** $61\overline{)25,750}$ **23.** $87\overline{)55,975}$ **24.** $90\overline{)33,191}$ **25.** $73\overline{)41,698}$

26. A family is planning to travel 2,472 miles during their 24-day vacation. What is the average number of miles they must travel each day?

27. An airline shuttle carried 2,482 passengers to Los Angeles on 17 flights. What was the average number of passengers on each flight?

MIXED PRACTICE
Maintaining and Reviewing Skills

Solve.

28. $(36 \div 6) \times 8 = t$ **29.** $(18 - 8) \times (7 + 4) = k$ **30.** $(15 \div 3) \times 1 = b$

31. $(96 \div 96) \times (49 \div 7) = n$ **32.** $(9 \times 10) \div (10 \times 9) = l$ **33.** $16 \times (9 - 9) = m$

34. $27 \times s = 810$ **35.** $x + 546 = 825$ **36.** $52 \times t = 3,120$

CHALLENGE

Addition is commutative because changing the order of addends does not change the sum.

$$3 + 4 = 4 + 3$$

Multiplication is commutative because changing the order of factors does not change the product.

$$5 \times 6 = 6 \times 5$$

37. Is division commutative?

38. Is subtraction commutative?

*39. Write an explanation of why division is not commutative. Give an example.

*40. Write an explanation of why subtraction is not commutative. Give an example.

DIVISION OF WHOLE NUMBERS
By 1- or 2-Digit Numbers

Divide: $2,856 \div 42$.

Estimate the quotient. $100 \times 42 = 4,200 \longrightarrow$ quotient too big
The quotient is $? \times 42 = 2,856$
between 10 and 100. $10 \times 42 = 420 \longrightarrow$ quotient too small

Estimate the tens digit.

40

$42)\overline{2856}$

Round 42 to 40.
$4)\overline{28}$ is 7. Try
7 as the tens
digit.

Multiply and subtract.

	Th	H	T	O
			7	
$42)$	2	8	5	6
	2	9	4	

$294 > 285$, so
7 is too big
for the tens
digit. Try 6.

Multiply and subtract.

	Th	H	T	O
			6	
$42)$	2	8	5	6
	2	5	2	
			3	3

Divide the ones.

	Th	H	T	O
			6	8
$42)$	2	8	5	6
	2	5	2	
		3	3	6
		3	3	6
				0

PRACTICE

Divide.

1. $4)\overline{2,468}$ 2. $5)\overline{1,530}$ 3. $8)\overline{3,360}$ 4. $9)\overline{4,398}$ 5. $7)\overline{2,168}$

6. $83)\overline{1,771}$ 7. $48)\overline{2,688}$ 8. $21)\overline{1,155}$ 9. $29)\overline{2,630}$ 10. $67)\overline{2,909}$

11. $31)\overline{2,418}$ 12. $24)\overline{5,016}$ 13. $38)\overline{38,769}$ 14. $40)\overline{10,160}$ 15. $86)\overline{34,483}$

16. $56)\overline{24,864}$ *17. $27)\overline{81,189}$ *18. $68)\overline{174,148}$ *19. $99)\overline{870,553}$ *20. $63)\overline{441,012}$

MIXED PRACTICE
Maintaining and Reviewing Skills

Multiply.

21.	22.	23.	24.	25.
428	$3,269$	$4,507$	$8,321$	$9,006$
$\times 5$	$\times 9$	$\times 76$	$\times 468$	$\times 705$

26. 7×349 27. $9 \times 8,607$ 28. $5 \times 3,874$ 29. $18 \times 2,361$ 30. $14 \times 6,564$

FOCUS   Use NUMBER skills to divide whole numbers.

Using Logic and Number Skills

Look at the magic square below. The sum of every row, column, and diagonal is equal. The magic square sum is 30.

16	2	12
6	10	14
8	18	4

←—— 6 + 10 + 14 = 30

16 + 6 + 8 = 30   16 + 10 + 4 = 30

This is the same magic square but each number in the square has been divided by 2. The new magic square sum is 15.

8	1	6
3	5	7
4	9	2

←——3 + 5 + 7 = 15

8 + 3 + 4 = 15   8 + 5 + 2 = 15

Copy each magic square below. Multiply or divide each number in the square by the number above the square. Then find the new magic square sum.

31. Divide by 7.

161	63	133
91	119	147
105	175	77

32. Multiply by 6.

40	5	30
15	25	35
20	45	10

33. Divide by 3.

24	3	18
9	15	21
12	27	6

34. Divide by 12.

132	48	108
72	96	120
84	144	60

35. Divide by 14.

266	168	238
196	224	252
210	280	182

36. Divide by 21.

420	273	378
315	357	399
336	441	294

37. Multiply by 15.

18	4	14
8	12	16
10	20	6

38. Divide by 19.

152	19	114
57	95	133
76	171	38

39. Multiply by 17.

11	4	9
6	8	10
7	12	5

Use LOGIC and NUMBER skills to complete magic squares.

Point of View

The solar system (the sun, the nine planets, and the other bodies that travel around the sun), the stars, and the galaxies exist in space. There are many galaxies in space. They are separated by vast distances. The galaxy that the solar system and the stars that we can see are in is called the Milky Way galaxy.

In mapping space, scientsits use the Earth as a starting point. Space begins where the Earth's atmosphere ends. There are five regions of space.

The first region of space begins just 100 miles above the Earth and extends to the Moon. It is called **cislunar** space, which means "on this side of the moon."

The second region is **translunar** space, which includes cislunar space and extends about 1,000,000 miles above the Earth. It includes all of space in which the combined gravitational force of the Earth and the moon have an effect.

Beyond translunar space is the third region of space, called **interplanetary** space. This is the region in which we find the other 8 planets and the sun. It includes all of the area affected by the sun's gravity and extends to about 50,000,000,000 miles above the Earth.

The fourth region of space is called **interstellar** space. This region extends to nearly 1,000,000,000,000,000,000 miles from Earth. It is often thought of as the space between the stars.

Beyond the stars of our galaxy lies **intergalactic** space—the space beyond our galaxy—containing all the other galaxies. This region of space has no end that we know about.

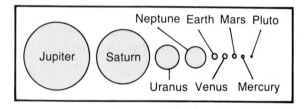

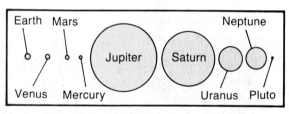

CRITICAL THINKING

1. Compare the two charts above. Describe the organization of each.

2. Why do you think scientists map space starting at the Earth?

3. If you know that Jupiter and Saturn are within 1,000,000,000 miles of the Earth, what do you know about Neptune's distance from the Earth?

4. Which chart above did you use to answer Question 3?

| FOCUS | Use NUMBER skills to learn about mapping in space.

The moon as seen from the Earth's orbit.

A relationship between the Earth, sun, and moon is shown from orbit.

Reviewing and Testing Chapter 7

In Chapter 7 you formulated problems about diving for silver ingots. To review, refer to pages 90 and 91.

1. How much time would it take the divers to raise the remaining ingots?

To review what you learned about multiplying by 1-, 2-, or 3-digit numbers, refer to pages 92 and 94.

Multiply.

2.   78
   × 3
	3. 243
	   × 4
		4. 503
		   × 9
			5. 784
			   × 8
				6. 213
				   × 42

7.   508
   × 36
	8. 524
	   × 135
		9. 704
		   × 205
			10. 7,296
			   × 87
				11. 3,254
				   × 80

12.   617
   × 88
	13. 342
	   × 98
		14. 384
		   × 648
			15. 185
			   × 248
				16. 853
				   × 392

You learned about dividing by 1-, or 2-digit numbers. To review, refer to page 98.

Divide.

17. $7\overline{)1,736}$	18. $14\overline{)3,402}$	19. $5\overline{)16,080}$	20. $26\overline{)18,446}$
21. $17\overline{)30,689}$	22. $9\overline{)6,498}$	23. $38\overline{)2,546}$	24. $8\overline{)46,312}$
25. $27\overline{)15,903}$	26. $36\overline{)1,512}$	27. $49\overline{)12,713}$	28. $32\overline{)24,832}$
29. $65\overline{)2,512}$	30. $40\overline{)3,440}$	31. $35\overline{)2,846}$	32. $58\overline{)38,222}$

You learned about using maps to plot planets and stars. Refer to page 100 to review how the five regions of space are plotted.

33. List the planets in order of their distance from the sun.

FOCUS   Review and test skills learned and practiced.

LOOKING AHEAD
Preparing for New Skills for Chapter 8

In the next chapter you will focus on

- formulating problems about animals.
- multiplying whole numbers.
- finding patterns in multiplication.
- using multiplication properties to solve equations.

- dividing whole numbers.
- dividing whole numbers with remainders.
- finding patterns in division.
- how math is used in games.

Multiplying and dividing with larger whole numbers will be easier if you review multiplication using multiples of 10 and division with multiples of 10 used as divisors.

To multiply a number by a multiple of 10, multiply the nonzero digits and then add as many zeros as there are in the multiple.

Example 1:

$$600 \times 7 = 4,200$$

Example 2:

$$5,000 \times 9 = 45,000$$

To divide a whole number by a multiple of 10, follow the steps in Example 3.

Example 3:

Estimate the tens digit.	Multiply and subtract.	Estimate the ones digit.	Multiply and subtract.
$20\overline{)820}$ $2\overline{)8}$ is 4. Try 4 as the tens digit.	$\begin{array}{r} 4 \\ 20\overline{)820} \\ -80 \\ \hline 2 \end{array}$	$\begin{array}{r} 4 \\ 20\overline{)820} \\ -80\downarrow \\ \hline 20 \end{array}$ $2\overline{)2}$ is 1. Try 1 as the ones digit.	$\begin{array}{r} 41 \\ 20\overline{)820} \\ -80\downarrow \\ \hline 20 \\ -20 \\ \hline 0 \end{array}$

PRACTICE

Find each answer.

1. 400×2 **2.** 9×700 **3.** $6,000 \times 9$ **4.** $3 \times 3,000$

5. $30\overline{)2,340}$ **6.** $80\overline{)3,440}$ **7.** $40\overline{)1,160}$ **8.** $90\overline{)7,560}$

Review NUMBER skills in preparation for learning new skills.

FOCUS   Formulate problems using photo, data, and text.

8

Multiplication and Division With Larger Whole Numbers

DATA

Crocodile Breeding in Kenya

Number of crocodiles on ranch	5,000
Crocodiles returned to wild each year	1 out of 20
Eggs taken from the wild each year	2,500
Survival rate of eggs in captivity	7 out of 10
Survival rate of eggs in the wild	1 out of 20
Maturing time in captivity	2–5 years
Maturing time in the wild	5–10 years

People have long feared the crocodile as a menace to life and limb. But, in recent years, people have proven to be a greater threat to the crocodile than the crocodile might ever be to them. The demand for reptile hides has nearly swept clean the crocodile population from many parts of the globe.

Look at the picture of the crocodile ranchers in Kenya transferring baby crocodiles to a shallow pond. The babies have been raised in captivity. As you can see from the data, five thousand crocodiles have survived to maturity on this crocodile ranch.

Why is it so difficult for crocodiles to survive in the wild? What reasons can you suggest for these 5,000 crocodiles surviving on this ranch? Predict some possible results of this breeding and evaluate them.

By 1-, 2-, 3-, or 4-Digit Numbers

In one journey a pilot logged 1,747 miles. How many miles would he log for 125 journeys of the same length?

Multiply: $125 \times 1{,}747$.

Multiply 1,747 by 5.

Th	H	T	O
1	7	4	7
× 1	2	5	
8	7	3	5

Multiply 1,747 by 20.

TTh	Th	H	T	O
	1	7	4	7
×		1	2	5
	8	7	3	5
3	4	9	4	0

Multiply 1,747 by 100.

HTh	TTh	Th	H	T	O
		1	7	4	7
	×		1	2	5
		8	7	3	5
	3	4	9	4	0
1	7	4	7	0	0

Add the products.

HTh	TTh	Th	H	T	O
		1	7	4	7
	×		1	2	5
		8	7	3	5
	3	4	9	4	0
1	7	4	7	0	0
2	1	8	3	7	5

The pilot would log 218,375 miles.

When multiplying by a number that has a zero in it use a shortcut.

Multiply: $205 \times 1{,}389$.

Write in zeros.

```
    1,389
 ×    205
    6 945
   00 000  ←—— Write in zeros.
  277 800
  284,745
```

Shortcut

```
    1,389
 ×    205
    6 945
  277 800  ←——
  284,745
```
Omit extra line of zeros. Write a zero in the ones and in the tens places. Continue multiplying.

GUIDED PRACTICE

Multiply. Use the shortcut if there is a zero in the multiplier.

1.
```
   213
 ×  32
   426
  ▮▮90
```

2.
```
   675
 ×  49
  ▮▮75
 ▮▮▮▮0
```

3.
```
   831
 ×  52
  ▮▮▮2
 ▮▮▮▮0
```

4.
```
 5,487
× 405
```

5.
```
 5,236
×  204
```

FOCUS Use NUMBER skills to multiply whole numbers.

PRACTICE

Multiply.

6. $\begin{array}{r} 312 \\ \times\ \ \ 4 \\ \hline \end{array}$	**7.** $\begin{array}{r} 543 \\ \times\ \ 21 \\ \hline \end{array}$	**8.** $\begin{array}{r} 746 \\ \times\ \ 38 \\ \hline \end{array}$	**9.** $\begin{array}{r} 3,241 \\ \times\ \ \ \ 20 \\ \hline \end{array}$	**10.** $\begin{array}{r} 4,212 \\ \times\ \ \ 321 \\ \hline \end{array}$
11. $\begin{array}{r} 5,624 \\ \times\ \ \ 213 \\ \hline \end{array}$	**12.** $\begin{array}{r} 8,962 \\ \times\ \ \ 204 \\ \hline \end{array}$	**13.** $\begin{array}{r} 7,638 \\ \times\ \ \ 320 \\ \hline \end{array}$	**14.** $\begin{array}{r} 5,061 \\ \times\ \ \ 308 \\ \hline \end{array}$	**15.** $\begin{array}{r} 6,870 \\ \times\ \ \ 300 \\ \hline \end{array}$
16. $\begin{array}{r} 4,209 \\ \times\ \ \ 509 \\ \hline \end{array}$	**17.** $\begin{array}{r} 3,845 \\ \times\ \ \ 639 \\ \hline \end{array}$	**18.** $\begin{array}{r} 7,521 \\ \times\ \ \ 444 \\ \hline \end{array}$	**19** $\begin{array}{r} 5,302 \\ \times\ \ \ 986 \\ \hline \end{array}$	**20.** $\begin{array}{r} 7,080 \\ \times\ \ \ 506 \\ \hline \end{array}$
21. $\begin{array}{r} 9,872 \\ \times\ \ \ 708 \\ \hline \end{array}$	**22.** $\begin{array}{r} 3,860 \\ \times\ \ \ 953 \\ \hline \end{array}$	**23.** $\begin{array}{r} 5,721 \\ \times\ \ \ 686 \\ \hline \end{array}$	**24.** $\begin{array}{r} 4,334 \\ \times\ \ \ 817 \\ \hline \end{array}$	**25.** $\begin{array}{r} 5,000 \\ \times\ \ \ 333 \\ \hline \end{array}$
26. $\begin{array}{r} 6,002 \\ \times\ \ \ 708 \\ \hline \end{array}$	***27.** $\begin{array}{r} 42,121 \\ \times\ \ 2,342 \\ \hline \end{array}$	***28.** $\begin{array}{r} 50,607 \\ \times\ \ 3,025 \\ \hline \end{array}$	***29.** $\begin{array}{r} 24,153 \\ \times\ \ 3,217 \\ \hline \end{array}$	***30.** $\begin{array}{r} 235,460 \\ \times\ \ \ 3,006 \\ \hline \end{array}$

31. 756×39 **32.** $6,318 \times 502$ **33.** $49,601 \times 717$

*34. $58,793 \times 7,052$ ***35.** $35,468 \times 3,269$ ***36.** $40,630 \times 1,005$

MIXED PRACTICE
Maintaining and Reviewing Skills

Add or subtract.

37. $\begin{array}{r} 567,314 \\ +\ 372,685 \\ \hline \end{array}$	**38.** $\begin{array}{r} 762,057 \\ -\ 349,613 \\ \hline \end{array}$	**39.** $\begin{array}{r} 763,408 \\ +\ \ 15,761 \\ \hline \end{array}$	**40.** $\begin{array}{r} 853,219 \\ -\ 853,019 \\ \hline \end{array}$	**41.** $\begin{array}{r} 189,236 \\ -\ \ \ \ \ \ 703 \\ \hline \end{array}$

Solve.

42. A printing press can print 8,500 sheets of paper in one hour. How many sheets can be printed in 15 hours?

43. A folding machine can fold 12,000 sheets of paper in one hour. How many sheets can be folded in 18 hours?

CHALLENGE

Why do exercises 44–47 have the same solution?

*44. $9 \times 84 \times 362 \times 205 \times 15 \times 0 = y$ ***45.** $17 \times 86 \times 4 \times 0 \times 8 = t$

*46. $439 \times 25 \times 6 \times 57 \times 0 \times 17 = x$ ***47.** $35 \times 16 \times 942 \times 0 \times 683 \times 5 = n$

MULTIPLICATION OF WHOLE NUMBERS
Patterns in Multiplication

Study these patterns.

$8 \times 1 = 8$	$38 \times 1 = 38$
$8 \times 10 = 80$	$38 \times 10 = 380$
$8 \times 100 = 800$	$38 \times 100 = 3,800$
$8 \times 1,000 = 8,000$	$38 \times 1,000 = 38,000$
$8 \times 10,000 = 80,000$	$38 \times 10,000 = 380,000$
$8 \times 100,000 = 800,000$	$38 \times 100,000 = 3,800,000$

Notice the zeros in each product.

5	50	500	5,000	50,000
$\times 6$	$\times 6$	$\times 6$	$\times 6$	$\times 6$
30	300	3,000	30,000	300,000
1 zero	2 zeros	3 zeros	4 zeros	5 zeros

PRACTICE

Multiply.

1. $\begin{array}{r}10\\ \times\ 7\\\hline\end{array}$	**2.** $\begin{array}{r}20\\ \times\ 4\\\hline\end{array}$	**3.** $\begin{array}{r}300\\ \times 2\\\hline\end{array}$	**4.** $\begin{array}{r}700\\ \times\ 8\\\hline\end{array}$	**5.** $\begin{array}{r}900\\ \times\ 6\\\hline\end{array}$
6. $\begin{array}{r}5,000\\ \times\ 3\\\hline\end{array}$	**7.** $\begin{array}{r}8,000\\ \times\ 4\\\hline\end{array}$	**8.** $\begin{array}{r}3,000\\ \times\ 9\\\hline\end{array}$	**9.** $\begin{array}{r}40,000\\ \times\ 6\\\hline\end{array}$	**10.** $\begin{array}{r}80,000\\ \times\ 9\\\hline\end{array}$
11. $\begin{array}{r}400,000\\ \times\ 2\\\hline\end{array}$	**12.** $\begin{array}{r}100,000\\ \times\ 3\\\hline\end{array}$	**13.** $\begin{array}{r}6,000,000\\ \times\ 3\\\hline\end{array}$	**14.** $\begin{array}{r}8,000,000\\ \times\ 5\\\hline\end{array}$	**15.** $\begin{array}{r}9,000,000\\ \times\ 9\\\hline\end{array}$

16. $900,000 \times 6$ **17.** $30,000 \times 4$ **18.** $200,000 \times 9$

19. $600,000,000 \times 1$ **20.** $500,000,000 \times 3$ **21.** $700,000,000 \times 8$

MIXED PRACTICE
Maintaining and Reviewing Skills

Solve.

22. $6^3 = a$ **23.** $7^2 = b$ **24.** $21^3 = d$ **25.** $15^4 = k$ **26.** $20^3 = t$

27. $25^4 = t$ **28.** $4^7 = x$ **29.** $8^8 = w$ **30.** $5^9 = m$ **31.** $10^6 = k$

32. $5 \times 10^3 = g$ **33.** $4 \times 10^2 = w$ **34.** $17 \times 10^3 = n$ **35.** $215 \times 10^3 = s$ **36.** $368 \times 10^5 = r$

FOCUS	Use PATTERNS to multiply whole numbers by 10, 100, and 1,000.

APPLICATION
Using Multiplication Properties

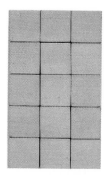

5 rows of cubes
3 cubes in each row
5 × 3 = 15

Factors   Product

3 rows of cubes
5 cubes in each row
3 × 5 = 15

Factors   Product

Commutative Property of Multiplication
Changing the order of factors does not change the product.

3 × 5 = 5 × 3 $a \times b = b \times a$ 25 × 15 = 15 × 25

Associative Property of Multiplication
Changing the grouping of factors does not change the product.

2 × (3 × 4) = (2 × 3) × 4 $a \times (b \times c) = (a \times b) \times c$
(15 × 10) × 2 = 15 × (10 × 2)

Distributive Property
3 × (2 + 4) = (3 × 2) + (3 × 4) $a \times (b + c) = (a \times b) + (a \times c)$
3 ×   6   =   6   +   12
       18   =   18

Property of One
$n \times 1 = n$ 278 × 1 = 278

Property of Zero
$z \times 0 = 0$ 3,064 × 0 = 0

Solve. Write which property you used to get each answer.

37. 5 × 1 = n

38. 6 × (7 + 2) = (6 × b) + (6 × c)

39. 2 × (3 × 8) = (2 × x) × 8

40. 36 × 0 = w

41. 8 × 9 = s × 8

42. 796 × t = 796

Use properties of ALGEBRA to solve equations.

DIVISION OF WHOLE NUMBERS
By 1-, 2-, or 3-Digit Numbers

A cargo plane flew 312 trips. It flew a total of 95 166 km. What was the average distance of each trip?

Divide: 95 166 ÷ 312.

$312\overline{)95\,166}$

Estimate the quotient. The quotient is between 100 and 1,000.

$$1,000 \times 312 = 312,000 \rightarrow \text{Quotient too big}$$
$$? \times 312 = 95,166$$
$$100 \times 312 = 31,200 \rightarrow \text{Quotient too small}$$

Estimate the hundreds digit. Multiply and subtract.

TTh	Th	H	T	O
		3		
312) 9	5	1	6	6
9	3	6		
	1	5		

Estimate the tens digit. Multiply and subtract.

TTh	Th	H	T	O
		3	0	
312) 9	5	1	6	6
9	3	6	↓	
	1	5	6	

Estimate the ones digit. Multiply and subtract.

TTh	Th	H	T	O	
		3	0	5	R6
312) 9	5	1	6	6	
9	3	6		↓	
	1	5	6	6	
	1	5	6	0	
				6	

Round 312 to 300.
$3\overline{)9}$ is 3, so try 3 as the hundreds digit.

$3\overline{)1}$ No 3 in 1, so write 0 as the tens digit.

$3\overline{)15}$ is 5, so try 5 as the ones digit.

Each trip was about 305 km.

Check to see if the answer is correct.

```
quotient    305
divisor   × 312
            610
          3 050
         91 500
         95 160
```

```
   95 160
 +      6  ← Remainder
   95 166  ← Dividend
```

GUIDED PRACTICE

Divide and check. Remember to estimate the quotient first.

1. $215\overline{)23,220}$ 2. $322\overline{)80,888}$ 3. $431\overline{)89,660}$ 4. $516\overline{)53,148}$ 5. $299\overline{)30,199}$

6. $300\overline{)64,200}$ 7. $208\overline{)50,960}$ 8. $458\overline{)76,486}$ 9. $276\overline{)28,528}$ 10. $327\overline{)666,426}$

FOCUS | Use NUMBER skills and ESTIMATION to divide whole numbers.

PRACTICE

Divide.

11. $6\overline{)4,506}$ 12. $8\overline{)6,747}$ 13. $7\overline{)16,338}$ 14. $9\overline{)54,189}$ 15. $4\overline{)39,683}$

16. $21\overline{)897}$ 17. $31\overline{)999}$ 18. $53\overline{)3,604}$ 19. $61\overline{)19,825}$ 20. $79\overline{)16,116}$

21. $85\overline{)26,265}$ 22. $62\overline{)145,142}$ 23. $43\overline{)259,806}$ 24. $68\overline{)245,418}$ 25. $81\overline{)243,324}$

26. $413\overline{)96,229}$ 27. $288\overline{)67,400}$ 28. $624\overline{)40,569}$ 29. $397\overline{)11,910}$ 30. $431\overline{)89,660}$

31. $323\overline{)69,135}$ 32. $204\overline{)63,698}$ *33. $534\overline{)663,762}$ *34. $432\overline{)995,328}$ *35. $172\overline{)516,189}$

Solve.

36. Mr. Diego averages 250 km a day on driving trips. How many days will it take him to travel 1 500 km?

37. Ms. Firenza assembled one bicycle in 3 hours. How many bicycles can she assemble in 48 hours?

38. Mr. Montana packages his pencils 144 to a box. How many boxes will he need to package 36,000 pencils?

39. Zahari used 3,240 screws to assemble 30 gym sets. How many screws did he use for each set?

40. Write a paragraph to explain how you estimate a quotient.

MIXED PRACTICE
Maintaining and Reviewing Skills

Add, subtract, or multiply.

41. 562,398
    $+ 245,167$

42. 876,500
    $- 235,495$

43. 4,682
    $\times \quad 37$

44. 5,241
    $\times \quad 356$

45. 85,214
    $+ 3,025$

46. 497,362
    $+ 9,831$

47. 3,901
    $\times \quad 72$

48. 470,209
    $- 26,872$

49. 267,335
    $- 8,989$

50. 62,934
    $+ 7,508$

51. 37,021
    $- \quad 38$

52. 704,511
    $+ 4,906$

53. 301,422
    $- 7,668$

54. 83,507
    $- 929$

55. 74,086
    $+37,398$

CHALLENGE

Write the next three numbers in each sequence.

*56. 1, 5, 9, 14, 19, 25, ■, ■, ■

*57. 87, 76, 86, 75, 85, ■, ■, ■

DIVISION OF WHOLE NUMBERS
Remainders in Division

Divide: 49,894 ÷ 215.

215)‾49,894   Estimate the quotient.   1,000 × 215 = 215,000 ⟶ Quotient too big
              The quotient is between   ? × 215 = 49,894
              100 and 1,000.   100 × 215 = 21,500 ⟶ Quotient too small

Estimate the hundreds digit. Multiply and subtract.

	TTh	Th	H	T	O
		2			
215)	4	9	8	9	4
	4	3	0		
		6	8		

Round 215 to 200.
2)‾4 is 2, so
try 2 as the
hundreds digit.

Estimate the tens digit. Multiply and subtract.

	TTh	Th	H	T	O
			2	3	
215)	4	9	8	9	4
	4	3	0		
		6	8	9	
		6	4	5	
			4	4	

2)‾6 is 3, so try 3
as the tens digit.

Estimate the ones digit. Multiply and subtract.

	TTh	Th	H	T	O
			2	3	2 R14
215)	4	9	8	9	4
	4	3	0		
		6	8	9	
		6	4	5	
			4	4	4
			4	3	0
				1	4

2)‾4 is 2, so try 2
as the ones digit.

Check: 232   49,880
          × 215   +   14 ⟵ Remainder
          1 160   49,894 ⟵ Dividend
          2 320
         46 400
         49,880

PRACTICE

Divide.

1. 6)‾49   2. 8)‾94   3. 7)‾73   4. 9)‾238   5. 5)‾1,623

6. 8)‾4,860   7. 13)‾12,490   8. 65)‾13,297   9. 50)‾34,590   10. 83)‾49,846

11. 236)‾14,053 12. 307)‾8,909 13. 541)‾19,882 14. 930)‾200,480 15. 426)‾146,867

*16. 7,586,873 ÷ 3,682   *17. 749,736 ÷ 2,314   *18. 802,112 ÷ 1,328

*19. 48,265,207 ÷ 9,653   *20. 1,335,015 ÷ 3,069   *21. 14,342,220 ÷ 4,687

22. There are 3,023 cans of fruit juice packaged 24 cans per carton. How many full cartons are there?

23. There are 468 lockers in a gym. There are 156 lockers in each row. How many rows are there?

FOCUS | Use NUMBER skills to find remainders in division.

MIXED PRACTICE
Maintaining and Reviewing Skills

Solve.

24. $15 + y = 68$ **25.** $n - 16 = 30$ **26.** $5 \times 9 = a$ **27.** $m \times 3 = 24$ **28.** $18 \times t = 18$

29. $c \div 5 = 7$ **30.** $d + 9 = 50$ **31.** $54 \div f = 6$ **32.** $8 \times k = 72$ **33.** $29 \times n = 0$

APPLICATION
Using Patterns

One number is **divisible** by another if, after dividing, there is a zero remainder.

■ A number is divisible by 2 if its ones digit is 0, 2, 4, 6, or 8.
The number 26 is divisible by 2 because the ones digit is 6.

■ A number is divisible by 5 if its ones digit is 0 or 5.
The number 45 is divisible by 5 because the ones digit is 5.

■ A number is divisible by 10 if its ones digit is 0.
The number 60 is divisible by 10 because the ones digit is 0.

■ A number is divisible by 3 if the sum of its digits is divisible by 3.
The number 12 is divisible by 3 because $1 + 2 = 3$, and 3 is divisible by 3.

■ A number is divisible by 9 if the sum of its digits is divisible by 9.
The number 72 is divisible by 9 because $7 + 2 = 9$, and 9 is divisible by 9.

Which of these numbers are divisible by 2, 3, 5, 9, or 10?
Some numbers are divisible by more than one number.

34. 20	**35.** 12	**36.** 25	**37.** 36	**38.** 42
39. 45	**40.** 39	**41.** 50	**42.** 115	**43.** 90
44. 48	**45.** 30	**46.** 270	**47.** 460	**48.** 234

Use PATTERNS to determine divisibility.

The Game of Nim

Nim is the name of a game. The term *nim* can be traced back in the English language to between the seventh and sixteenth centuries. Originally it meant "to take or steal." We no longer use the word in that context, but the game of nim is a game of taking and logic.

Nim is played by two people. No game board or special playing pieces are needed. It is played with stones or other small objects (more than 5 and less than 20 is best).

The object of the game is to pick up the last stone or stones. At the start of the game the players decide who will go first and how many stones can be picked up at each turn. For example, players can decide that no more than 3 stones can be picked up at a time. It is then up to each player to pick one, two, or three stones at each turn.

Nim requires logic. The strategy of "counting" the remaining stones in order to develop a way to pick up the last stone can be very complex. You need to use a strategy that plans your next move and following moves.

Say you started with 4 stones and planned that the maximum number of stones a player could pick up at a turn is 3. Whoever went first would lose. No matter how many stones the first player took, the second player would be able to take the last stone or stones.

This also works for larger numbers that are multiples of 4. The first player would lose if his or her opponent always left a multiple of 4.

Here is a sample game of nim. The players have decided to pick up between one and three stones for each turn from the pile of 12 stones. They have also decided that Player B will start the game.

1. Player B picks up 3 stones from the pile, leaving 9 stones.
2. Player A picks up 1 stone from the pile, leaving 8 stones.
3. Player B picks up 3 stones from the pile, leaving 5 stones.
4. Player A picks up 1 stone from the pile, leaving 4 stones.
5. Player B picks up 3 stones from the pile, leaving 1.
6. Player A takes 1 stone and wins.

For an alternative game, the player who takes the last stone is the loser.

CRITICAL THINKING

1. How can making the first move be the beginning of losing the game?

2. How could Player A have lost?

3. Is it possible to come up with a strategy so that the game can always be won?

FOCUS | Use NUMBER skills and LOGIC to learn the strategy of the game of nim.

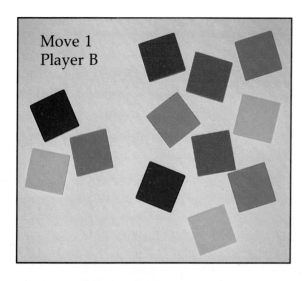

Move 1
Player B

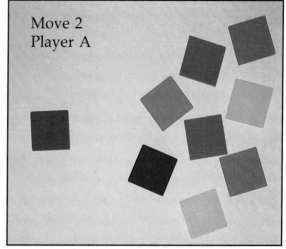

Move 2
Player A

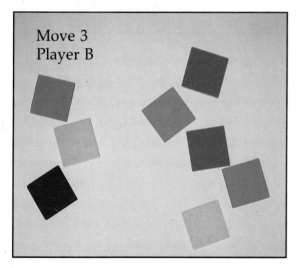

Move 3
Player B

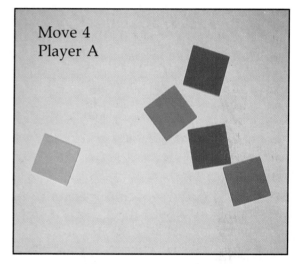

Move 4
Player A

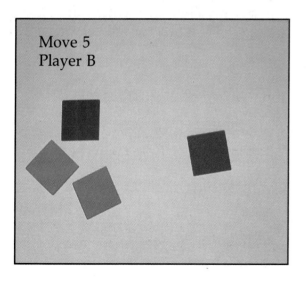

Move 5
Player B

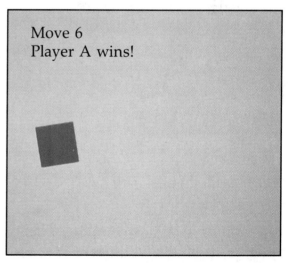

Move 6
Player A wins!

LOOKING BACK
Reviewing and Testing Chapter 8

In Chapter 8 you formulated problems about breeding crocodiles. Refer to pages 104 and 105.

1. What are some ways in which we can protect crocodiles in the wild?

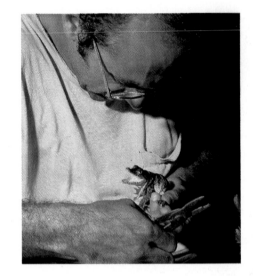

To review what you learned about multiplying by 1-, 2-, 3-, or 4-digit numbers, refer to page 106.

Multiply.

2. 6,539 × 257	3. 527 × 26	4. 4,678 × 9	5. 3,468 × 2,091	6. 684 × 43
7. 7,843 × 6	8. 34,682 × 2,643	9. 1,783 × 926	10. 5,382 × 1,853	11. 786 × 95

To review patterns in multiplication, refer to page 108.

12. 6,000 × 7	13. 70,000 × 4	14. 36,000 × 9	15. 30,000 × 5	16. 800,000 × 8

You learned about dividing by 1-, 2-, or 3-digit numbers. To review, refer to page 110.

Divide.

17. 22)924   18. 68)1,564   19. 184)35,512   20. 7)441   21. 43)11,099

22. 214)50,290   23. 438)266,301   24. 370)148,370   25. 195)44,070   26. 9)1,009

27. 37)3,515   28. 288)67,400   29. 34)8,289   30. 64)5,568   31. 304)24,444

You learned about using logic and strategy when playing the game of NIM. Refer to page 114.

32. What determines the number of stones player 1 should pick up on the first move?

FOCUS | Review and test skills learned and practiced.

116

LOOKING AHEAD
Preparing for New Skills for Chapter 9

In the next chapter you will focus on

- formulating problems about hot air balloons.
- finding the GCF.
- using the GCF to simplify fractions.
- using patterns to check divisibility.
- using a problem-solving strategy.
- finding the LCM.
- using prime factorization to find LCM.
- solving multi-step problems.
- how math is used in Islamic art.

Finding the greatest common factor and least common multiple will be easier if you review how to find factors, prime factors, and multiples of a number.

Example 1:

The multiples of 6 are
6, 12, 18, 24, 30, . . .

Example 2:

The multiples of 19 are
19, 38, 57, 76, 95, . . .

A **prime number** is a number with exactly two factors, 1 and itself. Since 1 and 3 are the only factors of 3, it is a prime number. A whole number greater than 1 with more than two factors is a **composite number**. The numbers 0 and 1 are neither prime nor composite.

Example 3:

List the factors of 18.

$$18 = 1 \times 18$$
$$2 \times 9$$
$$3 \times 6$$

Factors of 18: 1, 2, 3, 6, 9, 18

Example 4:

Use a factor tree to find the **prime factorization** of 18.

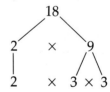

$$18 = 2 \times 3 \times 3$$

PRACTICE

List the first five multiples for each number.

1. 4   **2.** 10   **3.** 7   **4.** 5   **5.** 11

List the factors for each. Then write the prime factorization.

6. 12   **7.** 10   **8.** 20   **9.** 8   **10.** 14

Review NUMBER skills in preparation for learning new skills.

Write the letter of the correct answer.

Identify the place value of each underlined digit.

1. 658,362
   - A. hundreds
   - B. millions
   - C. thousands
   - D. billions

2. 1,202,464
   - E. hundred thousands
   - F. thousands
   - G. millions
   - H. ten millions

3. 16,050,175
   - A. thousands
   - B. ten thousands
   - C. millions
   - D. ten millions

4. 6,530,100,720
   - E. millions
   - F. billions
   - G. hundreds
   - H. ten thousands

Round to the nearest million.

5. 3,851,000
   - A. 3,000,000
   - B. 3,500,000
   - C. 4,000,000
   - D. 4,800,000

6. 8,498,600
   - E. 8,500,000
   - F. 8,000,000
   - G. 9,000,000
   - H. 8,400,000

7. 750,000
   - A. 1,000,000
   - B. 0
   - C. 500,000
   - D. 800,000

8. 5,500,331
   - E. 5,000,000
   - F. 5,600,000
   - G. 5,500,000
   - H. 6,000,000

Identify the standard form for each.

9. 5^2
   - A. 10
   - B. 25
   - C. 50
   - D. 15

10. 4^4
    - E. 16
    - F. 24
    - G. 256
    - H. 40

11. 4×3^2
    - A. 36
    - B. 13
    - C. 144
    - D. 49

12. 9×2^2
    - E. 18
    - F. 83
    - G. 85
    - H. 36

13. 3×4^3
    - A. 73
    - B. 129
    - C. 192
    - D. 81

Solve.

14. $4 \times 3 - 2 + 2 = x$
    - E. 6
    - F. 4
    - G. 8
    - H. 12

15. $(64 \div 4 \times 2)^2 = a$
    - A. 1,024
    - B. 128
    - C. 64
    - D. 16

16. $10 - 5 + 6 \div 2 \times 3 = m$
    - E. 14
    - F. 17
    - G. 6
    - H. 12

17. $7^2 - (15 \div 3 + 2)^2$
    - A. 40
    - B. 0
    - C. 49
    - D. 98

FOCUS Review concepts and skills taught in Chapters 2–8.

Find the solution for each pair of inverse sentences.

18. $9 + 6 = n$ $n - 6 = 9$

   E. 12   **F.** 20   **G.** 15   **H.** 24

19. $c \div 5 = 9$ $5 \times 9 = c$

   A. 45   **B.** 54   **C.** 14   **D.** 4

Add or subtract.

20. $\begin{array}{r} 68 \\ + 23 \\ \hline \end{array}$ **E.** 85   **F.** 91   **G.** 95   **H.** 45

21. $\begin{array}{r} 115 \\ - \ 26 \\ \hline \end{array}$ **A.** 141   **B.** 191   **C.** 90   **D.** 89

22. $\begin{array}{r} 237 \\ + 385 \\ \hline \end{array}$ **E.** 666   **F.** 562   **G.** 622   **H.** 632

23. $\begin{array}{r} 2,036 \\ - \ 156 \\ \hline \end{array}$ **A.** 1,880   **B.** 1,920   **C.** 2,192   **D.** 1,980

24. $\begin{array}{r} 463 \\ 72 \\ + 1,309 \\ \hline \end{array}$ **E.** 1,754   **F.** 1,854   **G.** 1,844   **H.** 1,694

Identify the prime numbers.

25. A. 25   **B.** 26   **C.** 28   **D.** 29

26. E. 15   **F.** 16   **G.** 17   **H.** 18

27. A. 80   **B.** 81   **C.** 82   **D.** 83

28. E. 53   **F.** 54   **G.** 55   **H.** 56

Identify the prime factorization.

29. 70 **A.** $2 \times 4 \times 5$ **B.** $2 \times 5 \times 7$
     C. $7 \times 10 \times 1$ **D.** 2×35

30. 120 **E.** $2 \times 2 \times 3 \times 5$ **F.** $2^3 \times 3 \times 5$
     G. $3^2 \times 5 \times 2$ **H.** $3 \times 4 \times 10$

Multiply or divide.

31. $\begin{array}{r} 42 \\ \times \ 3 \\ \hline \end{array}$ **A.** 126   **B.** 45   **C.** 84   **D.** 125

32. $\begin{array}{r} 215 \\ \times \ 4 \\ \hline \end{array}$ **E.** 219   **F.** 860   **G.** 872   **H.** 760

33. $\begin{array}{r} 348 \\ \times \ 16 \\ \hline \end{array}$ **A.** 5,866   **B.** 6,028   **C.** 7,200   **D.** 5,568

34. $\begin{array}{r} 487 \\ \times \ 211 \\ \hline \end{array}$ **E.** 105,750   **F.** 95,857   **G.** 102,757   **H.** 10,757

35. $\begin{array}{r} 4,419 \\ \times \ 203 \\ \hline \end{array}$ **A.** 897,057   **B.** 879,075   **C.** 892,638   **D.** 901,476

36. $\begin{array}{r} 2,307 \\ \times \ 366 \\ \hline \end{array}$ **E.** 684,180   **F.** 484,662   **G.** 844,362   **H.** 874,162

37. $6\overline{)444}$ **A.** 64   **B.** 54   **C.** 74   **D.** 24

38. $9\overline{)1,782}$ **E.** 296   **F.** 202   **G.** 196   **H.** 198

39. $12\overline{)1,596}$ **A.** 93   **B.** 133   **C.** 136   **D.** 163

40. $24\overline{)6,744}$ **E.** 281   **F.** 218   **G.** 216   **H.** 272

41. $93\overline{)21,633}$ **A.** 323 R19   **B.** 230 R17   **C.** 232 R57   **D.** 320 R71

42. $70\overline{)38,019}$ **E.** 542 R85   **F.** 534 R19   **G.** 535 R47   **H.** 543 R9

FOCUS   Formulate problems using photo, data, and text.

CHAPTER 9

Greatest Common Factor and Least Common Multiple

DATA

How to Fly a Hot-air Balloon

To rise 1 meter in altitude, burn $\frac{1}{2}$ liter of fuel.

To lower the balloon 1 meter, release $\frac{1}{2}$ liter of hot air from the balloon.

The wind at 1 000 meters is blowing due west at 5 km/h.

The wind at 500 meters is blowing due east at 3 km/h.

The eastern landing field is 33 km away.

The western landing field is 50 km away.

It was a perfect day for a hot-air balloon exhibition. The beautiful balloons, caught by the gentle wind, soared up, up, and away. George said to his little brother, Nickie, "They look so wonderful from the ground but I'm not sure I'd want to go up in one."

As the exhibition ended, George turned to leave and realized that Nickie had not heard a word he had said. His brother had climbed into the basket of a balloon. As George quickly jumped aboard to get him, the ropes holding the balloon to the ground snapped. The balloon drifted up into the air!

Now George must fly the balloon. He knows that a balloon travels in whatever direction the wind blows. The pilot controls the way a balloon flies by rising or descending to find a wind blowing in the direction wanted.

All George wants is a safe landing. Does the data indicate how he can best steer the balloon and land it safely? What are some questions George might want answers for as soon as possible?

Greatest Common Factor

The Greatest Common Factor (GCF) of 2 or more numbers is the largest number that is a factor of all the numbers.

Find the greatest common factor of 12 and 40:
List factors of 12: **1**, **2**, 3, **4**, 6, 12
List factors of 40: **1**, **2**, **4**, 5, 8, 10, 20, 40
List the common factors: **1**, **2**, **4**

Choose the largest number.
The GCF of 12 and 40 is 4.

To find the greatest common factor another way:
List the factors of the smaller number, 12.
Factors of 12: 1, 2, 3, 4, 6, 12
Divide 40 by the largest factor, 12.
Is 40 divisible by 12? **NO**

Divide 40 by the next largest factor, 6.
Is 40 divisible by 6? **NO**

Divide 40 by the next factor, 4.
Is 40 divisible by 4? **YES**
The GCF of 12 and 40 is 4.

Two numbers are **relatively prime** if 1 is their greatest common factor.

Find the greatest common factor of 8 and 35.
List the factors of 8: 1, 2, 4, 8
List the factors of 35: 1, 5, 7, 35

The GCF of 8 and 35 is 1. Therefore the numbers are relatively prime.

GUIDED PRACTICE

Find the greatest common factor for each pair.

1. 15 and 45
Factors of 15: 1, 3, ■, ■
Factors of 45: 1, 3, ■, ■, ■, ■

2. 6 and 27
Factors of 6: 1, 2, ■, ■
Factors of 27: 1, 3, ■, ■

3. 24 and 30

4. 9 and 24

FOCUS | Use NUMBER skills and PATTERNS to find the GCF.

PRACTICE

Find the greatest common factor for each exercise.

5. 6 and 15   **6.** 10 and 30   **7.** 18 and 54

8. 3 and 9   **9.** 14 and 35   **10.** 12 and 20

11. 16 and 52   **12.** 18 and 36   **13.** 15 and 28

14. 7 and 13   **15.** 27 and 12   **16.** 8 and 11

17. 30 and 66   **18.** 42 and 78   **19.** 21 and 28

20. 8, 12, and 20   **21.** 16, 24, and 20   **22.** 9, 12, and 18

23. 9, 24, and 42   **24.** 8, 11, and 19   **25.** 17, 34, and 51

26. 6, 20, and 22   **27.** 15, 25, and 95   **28.** 8, 60, and 78

MIXED PRACTICE
Maintaining and Reviewing Skills

Choose the answer that best completes each sentence.

29. When one number is a multiple of another, the greatest common factor of the two numbers is always the (smaller, larger) number.

30. The greatest common factor of two prime numbers is always (zero, one).

31. Consecutive numbers, such as 9 and 10, or 26 and 27, are always (prime, relatively prime).

Which property of multiplication is shown?

32. $25 \times 64 = 64 \times 25$ **33.** $(17 \times 6) \times 4 = 17 \times (6 \times 4)$

CHALLENGE

Find the GCF for each group of 4 numbers.

*34. 10, 8, 4, and 6   ***35.** 6, 24, 30, and 18

*36. 8, 30, 27, and 24   ***37.** 9, 30, 27, and 24

GREATEST COMMON FACTOR
Simplifying Fractions

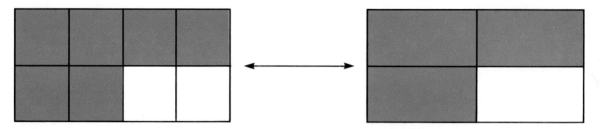

6 out of 8 parts shaded ↔ 3 out of 4 parts shaded

Fractions describe these pictures. The same part of the whole is shaded, so the fractions have equal values.

$$\frac{\text{part}}{\text{whole}} \leftrightarrow \frac{\text{numerator}}{\text{denominator}} \leftrightarrow \frac{6}{8} = \frac{3}{4} \text{ simplest terms}$$

A fraction is in **simplest terms** when the greatest common factor of the numerator and denominator is 1.

Use the Greatest Common Factor (GCF) of the numerator and denominator to simplify $\frac{6}{8}$.

The GCF of 6 and 8 is 2.

$$\frac{6 \div 2}{8 \div 2} = \frac{3}{4} \quad \begin{array}{l} \text{Divide the numerator by 2.} \\ \text{Divide the denominator by 2.} \end{array}$$

PRACTICE

Divide the numerator and denominator by the GCF to simplify each fraction.

1. $\frac{3}{9}$ 2. $\frac{4}{20}$ 3. $\frac{7}{35}$ 4. $\frac{8}{12}$ 5. $\frac{10}{25}$

6. $\frac{27}{36}$ 7. $\frac{7}{63}$ 8. $\frac{11}{44}$ 9. $\frac{32}{64}$ 10. $\frac{36}{48}$

11. $\frac{54}{72}$ 12. $\frac{14}{56}$ 13. $\frac{27}{81}$ 14. $\frac{34}{85}$ 15. $\frac{26}{39}$

16. $\frac{16}{32}$ 17. $\frac{18}{45}$ 18. $\frac{25}{40}$ 19. $\frac{16}{96}$ 20. $\frac{24}{72}$

21. $\frac{18}{100}$ 22. $\frac{12}{16}$ 23. $\frac{18}{81}$ *24. $\frac{13}{28}$ *25. $\frac{105}{135}$

FOCUS   Use NUMBER skills and PATTERNS to simplify fractions.

MIXED PRACTICE
Maintaining and Reviewing Skills

Which of the following are already in simplest terms? Why?
Simplify if possible.

26. $\frac{21}{28}$ **27.** $\frac{22}{35}$ **28.** $\frac{48}{50}$ **29.** $\frac{19}{36}$ **30.** $\frac{15}{19}$

Write the meaning of each exponential expression. Then
write the value. The first one has been done for you.

31. $5^3 = 5 \times 5 \times 5 = 125$ **32.** 7^4 **33.** 2^9 **34.** 38^3

Multiply.

35. 326×14 **36.** 493×12 **37.** 876×20 **38.** 954×42

APPLICATION
Using Patterns

A number is **divisible by 4** if the number formed by the tens and ones digits is divisible by 4. 132 is divisible by 4.

$$132$$
$$\downarrow\downarrow$$
$$32 \div 4 = 8 \quad \text{yes}$$

A number is **divisible by 6** if the number is divisible by 2 and by 3. 84 is divisible by 6.

$$84 \div 2 = 42$$
$$84 \div 3 = 28$$
$$84 \div 6 = 14 \quad \text{yes}$$

A number is **divisible by 8** if the number formed by the hundreds, tens, and ones digits is divisible by 8. 19,872 is divisible by 8.

$$19,872$$
$$\downarrow\downarrow\downarrow$$
$$872 \div 8 = 109 \quad \text{yes}$$

Is each number divisible by 4? Write *yes* or *no*.

39. 1,424   **40.** 7,639   **41.** 25,816   **42.** 78,042   **43.** 97,948

Is each number divisible by 6? Write *yes* or *no*.

44. 534   **45.** 5,359   **46.** 2,094   **47.** 58,986   **48.** 79,633

Is each number divisible by 8? Write *yes* or *no*.

49. 7,249   **50.** 12,731   **51.** 23,687   **52.** 26,072   **53.** 54,648

Use PATTERNS to determine divisibility.

Solving Multi-Step Problems

The five important steps to solving problems are READ, KNOW, PLAN, SOLVE, and CHECK. One or more of these steps may have to be performed several times in order to SOLVE a problem. More than one operation may be needed to answer the question.

1. READ Every day, 243,000 pairs of women's jeans and 590,000 pairs of men's jeans are manufactured in the United States. At this rate, how many pairs of jeans are produced in a year?

2. KNOW Ask yourself: What do I need to find out?

Key facts: women's jeans per day   243,000
             men's jeans per day   590,000
             days in a year   365

3. PLAN Use two steps in this order:
  a. Add to find the total number of men's and women's jeans manufactured in a day.
  b. Use the answer obtained above as a factor. Then multiply to find the total number of jeans manufactured in a year.

4. SOLVE

a.
$$\begin{array}{r} 590,000 \\ + 243,000 \\ \hline 833,000 \end{array}$$

b.
$$\begin{array}{r} 833,000 \\ \times 365 \\ \hline 4\ 165\ 000 \\ 49\ 980\ 00 \\ 249\ 900\ 0 \\ \hline 304,045,000 \end{array}$$

Each year 304,045,000 pairs of jeans are manufactured in the United States.

5. CHECK Reread the question and check your steps. Ask yourself: Why is the answer reasonable?

Check by rounding:

$$\begin{array}{r} 590,000 \longrightarrow 600,000 \\ + 243,000 \longrightarrow + 200,000 \\ \hline 800,000 \end{array}$$

$$365 \longrightarrow 400$$

$$\begin{array}{r} 800,000 \\ \times 400 \\ \hline 320,000,000 \end{array}$$

The answer 304,045,000 is reasonable because it is about 320,000,000.

| FOCUS | Solve multi-step problems as part of the Five–Step PROBLEM–SOLVING Plan. |

PRACTICE

List the operations needed to solve each problem. Then
SOLVE and CHECK.

1. Every day, Americans eat 56,000 gallons of honey. This is enough to fill seven tractor trailer trucks. How many quarts can a tractor trailer hold?

2. Each year, pet owners in the United States buy about 400,000 sweaters for their dogs. About how many sweaters do they buy per day?

3. Every day, dentists use 80 pounds of gold to fill people's cavities. If gold sells for $329 an ounce, what is the value of the gold used this way each day?

4. Each day, people in the United States spend $300 million on clothes. About how much do they spend on clothes each minute?

5. Every day, 100,000 bushels of broccoli are taken to American markets. If half of the broccoli is eaten fresh, about how many bushels of fresh broccoli are eaten per year?

* 6. About 125 books a day are published in the United States. Of those, 15 are fiction books and 8 are books for children. At this rate, how many more fiction books are published each year than children's books?

7. Daily 550,000 pounds of toothpaste are used by Americans. At this rate, how much would they use during the month of October?

8. Every day, 20,000 people write a letter to the President of the United States. How many letters are written every 4 weeks?

9. In one year, America mines 1,038,098 metric tons of copper. If each ton is worth $1,687.20, what is the total value of the copper mined?

10. In one year, 317,905,000 passengers travel by air in the United States. How many passengers travel each week?

Class Project

Each day, Americans jog 28 million miles. Work with a few classmates and use a calculator to figure out three ways to describe this distance. For example, 28 million miles is enough to travel every road in the United States seven times. Try to think of examples that help you imagine how far this really is.

Least Common Multiple

The **Least Common Multiple** (LCM) of 2 or more numbers is the smallest nonzero number that is a multiple of all of them.

To find the least common multiple of 7 and 9, ask:

What are the multiples of 7?

7, 14, 21, 28, 35, 42, 49, 56, 63, . . .

What are the multiples of 9?

9, 18, 27, 36, 45, 54, 63, 72, . . .

What is the smallest number in both lists? 63
The LCM of 7 and 9 is 63.

Find the least common multiple of 4 and 6:

Multiples of 4: 4, 8, (12,) 16, 20, (24,) 28, 32, (36,) . . .

Multiples of 6: 6, (12,) 18, (24,) 30, (36,) . . .

Common multiples: 12, 24, and 36
The Least Common Multiple (LCM) of 4 and 6 is 12.

To find the least common multiple of 2, 4, and 6 ask:

What are the multiples of 2? 2, 4, 6, 8, 12, 14, . . .
What are the multiples of 4? 4, 8, 12, 16, 20, . . .
What are the multiples of 6? 6, 12, 18, 24, . . .
What is the smallest number in all three lists? 12

The LCM of 2, 4, and 6 is 12.

GUIDED PRACTICE

Find the LCM of each pair. Remember to include the number as the first multiple.

1. 6 and 15   Multiples of 6: 6, 12, ■, ■, ■, . . .
               Multiples of 15: 15, 30, ■, ■, ■, . . .

2. 4 and 20   Multiples of 4: 4, 8, ■, ■, ■, . . .
               Multiples of 20: 20, 40, ■, ■, ■, . . .

3. 7 and 12   4. 10 and 25   5. 12 and 16

| FOCUS | Use NUMBER skills and PATTERNS to determine the LCM. |

PRACTICE

Find the least common multiple for each exercise.

6. 6 and 10   **7.** 8 and 12   **8.** 15 and 20   **9.** 8 and 20

10. 3 and 8   **11.** 5 and 9   **12.** 6 and 10   **13.** 9 and 12

14. 13 and 4   **15.** 5 and 8   **16.** 3 and 7   **17.** 6 and 12

18. 6 and 7   **19.** 6 and 8   **20.** 9 and 15   **21.** 11 and 9

22. 4 and 15   **23.** 10 and 80   **24.** 13 and 14   **25.** 6 and 11

26. 25, 10, 4   **27.** 7, 5, 10   **28.** 10, 2, 25   **29.** 25, 6, 30, 5

Solve.

30. On opening day at a new food market, every 10th customer wins a free pound of flour. Every 16th customer wins a free pound of fruit mix. What number customer will be the first to win both the flour and the fruit mix?

31. Beginning at the first parking space, every 4th car in a row is blue. Every 15th car is a van. How many cars will you have to count before you come to a blue van?

MIXED PRACTICE
Maintaining and Reviewing Skills

Write the first five multiples of each number.

32. 3   **33.** 11   **34.** 14   **35.** 30   **36.** 126

Write the factors of each number.

37. 3   **38.** 11   **39.** 14   **40.** 30   ***41.** 126

Write the prime factorization of each number.

42. 3   **43.** 11   **44.** 14   **45.** 30   **46.** 126

47. 72   **48.** 86   **49.** 57   **50.** 75   **51.** 48

CHALLENGE

*52. Write the next five numbers in the sequence.

$$\frac{1}{3}, \frac{1}{5}, \frac{1}{7}, \frac{1}{10}, \frac{1}{13}, \frac{1}{17}, \frac{1}{\blacksquare}, \frac{1}{\blacksquare}, \frac{1}{\blacksquare}, \frac{1}{\blacksquare}, \frac{1}{\blacksquare}$$

LEAST COMMON MULTIPLE
Using Prime Factorization

To find the Least Common Multiple (LCM) of 6 and 9 using prime factorization:

- Write the prime factorization of 6: 2×3.
- Write the prime factorization of 9: 3^2.
- Multiply the highest powers of each factor: $2 \times 3^2 = 2 \times 3 \times 3 = 18$.

The LCM of 6 and 9 is 18.

This method works well for large numbers. Find the LCM of 18 and 30.

- Write the prime factorization of 18: 2×3^2
- Write the prime factorization of 30: $2 \times 3 \times 5$
- Multiply the highest powers of each factor: $2 \times 3^2 \times 5 = 2 \times 3 \times 3 \times 5 = 90$

The LCM of 18 and 30 is 90.

PRACTICE

Find the LCM using prime factorization.

1. 12 and 6   **2.** 12 and 5   **3.** 12 and 8   **4.** 8 and 9

5. 6 and 16   **6.** 10 and 8   **7.** 5 and 7   **8.** 12 and 15

9. 50 and 12   **10.** 24 and 18   **11.** 32 and 20   **12.** 50 and 12

13. 2, 6, and 12   **14.** 3, 6, and 7   **15.** 2, 5, and 12   **16.** 3, 4, and 16

17. 5, 8, and 10   ***18.** 7, 8, and 9   ***19.** 2, 6, 5, and 10   ***20.** 2, 3, 5, and 6

MIXED PRACTICE
Maintaining and Reviewing Skills

Compare. Use the symbols >, <, or = .

21. 17 ● 87   **22.** 62 ● 162   **23.** 325 ● 315

24. 579 ● 579   **25.** 907 ● 970   **26.** 2,684 ● 2,684

27. 3,421 ● 3,321   **28.** 8,007 ● 8,070   **29.** 9,643 ● 9,364

*30. LCM of 32 and 25 ● LCM of 40 and 15

FOCUS | Use NUMBER skills and PATTERNS to determine the LCM by prime factorization.

Solving Problems

31. On a class trip to a botanical park, Glenn visited the rock garden. Every fifteenth rock was yellow and every eighteenth rock was a crystal. Which rock will be a yellow crystal?

32. Ann has two broken clocks. One chimes every 3 hours. The other chimes every 4 hours. At 2 A.M. they both chimed. When is the next time they will both chime together?

Problem Solving: Solving Multi-Step Problems

In order to solve certain problems, you must use more than one step and more than one operation.

Choose the correct operation. Then solve.

33. Mr. Foster is preparing to paint his apartment. He bought 5 cans of paint at $9 a can. How much change did he get from $50?
Which operation is used to find the cost of the paint?
Which operation is used to find Mr. Foster's change?

34. Andrew bought a bike that costs $165. As a down payment, he paid $75. He will pay the balance in 3 equal payments. What is the amount of each payment?
Which operation is used to find the balance?
Which operation is used to find each payment?

35. Rose drove 1,210 miles in 3 days. She drove 470 miles in the first day and 455 miles the second day. How many miles did she drive on the third day of her trip?
Which operation is used to find the miles driven in 2 days?
Which operation is used to find the miles driven on the third day?

36. Folders are on sale at the bookstore at 3 for $3.29. Each folder usually costs $1.35. How much would you save in all by buying 3 folders at the sale price?
Which operation is used to find the cost of 3 folders not on sale?
Which operation is used to find the savings?

*37. A weather reporter noticed that every ninth day beginning on October 1 was below 40°F. Every twelfth day was rainy. What was the date of the first rainy day that was below 40°F? Which operation is used to find the date?

*38. Cups come in sets of 6, plates in sets of 8, and napkins in sets of 12. How many packages are needed to get the same number of cups, plates, and napkins without leftovers? Which operation is used to find the number of packages?

Solve multi-step problems and apply the Five-step PROBLEM-SOLVING Plan.

Tessellations

Geometric patterns are very important in the art of Islam. From Spain to India for over 1,000 years Islamic artists created and repeated these patterns. They appear on the walls and tile floors of buildings. They are carved on wooden doors. They decorate the surfaces of glazed bowls and platters, and are woven into rugs and tapestries.

These geometric patterns are reproduced with great detail in the illustrations in Persian books, like this page from the Shah-Nameh (the Book of Kings).

It seems hard to believe that all the geometric patterns of the Islamic artists were created with only the compass and the straight edge. The main figure is the circle. Then a straight edge is used to draw equilateral triangles, squares, and regular hexagons. These are the shapes from which all the artists' designs were developed.

The design is repeated across the entire surface, starting from the center.

Patterns of this type are called tessellations. A **tessellation** is a pattern repeated in a design which covers the whole surface.

Most Islamic patterns are based on two kinds of grids—squares and equilateral triangles. Regular hexagons are formed by combinations of equilateral triangles.

Besides geometric patterns, Islamic artists used plant life and calligraphy in their designs. Calligraphy means **beautiful writing**. It decorates Islamic shrines, metalwork, dishes, and textiles, as well as books.

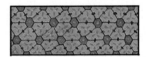 

CRITICAL THINKING

1. The floor pattern in the illustration is made up of stars and regular polygons.
   a. Name the regular polygon. How many sides does it have?
   b. Describe the star.
   c. This pattern can be drawn on a grid of equilateral triangles. What is the smallest number of triangles that will join to form a regular hexagon? A six-pointed star?
   d. How many degrees are in an angle made by the point of the star?

2. Which regular polygons tessellate? Why? Do regular pentagons tessellate?

3. Look at the illustration. Can you find other repeated patterns? Can you find floral designs? Can you find calligraphy?

| FOCUS | Use GEOMETRY to learn about tessellation in Islamic art. |

At least seven tessellated patterns add to the beautiful design of this detail of
the *Shah-Nameh*.

LOOKING BACK

Reviewing and Testing Chapter 9

In Chapter 9 you formulated problems about flying hot-air balloons. To review, refer to page 121.

1. A balloon's altitude is 900 meters. How much air must be released in order for the balloon to drop to 850 meters?

To review what you learned about the greatest common factor (GCF), refer to the example on page 122.

Find the GCF of each pair.

2. 12 and 18   **3.** 15 and 36   **4.** 10 and 45   **5.** 9 and 30

6. 27 and 72   **7.** 24 and 25   **8.** 16 and 24   **9.** 21 and 35

You learned about using the GCF to simplify fractions. To review, refer to page 124.

Rewrite each fraction in simplest terms.

10. $\frac{2}{4}$ **11.** $\frac{6}{8}$ **12.** $\frac{5}{15}$ **13.** $\frac{14}{21}$ **14.** $\frac{15}{25}$ **15.** $\frac{9}{27}$

Use the Five-Step Problem Solving Plan to solve this problem. Refer to page 126.

16. The Nile River is 3,206 miles longer than the Ohio River. The Ohio River is 3,019 miles shorter than the Amazon River. The Amazon River is 4,000 miles long. How long is the Nile River?

To review what you learned about least common multiple (LCM), refer to page 128.

Find the LCM of each pair.

17. 3 and 5   **18.** 2 and 14   **19.** 7 and 6   **20.** 6 and 8

You learned about how Islamic artists used patterns. Refer to page 132 to review how tessellations are used.

21. On a separate sheet of paper, design your own tessellation. (Be sure to fill the whole page.)

| FOCUS | Review and test skills learned and practiced. |

LOOKING AHEAD
Preparing for New Skills for Chapter 10

In the next chapter you will focus on

- formulating problems about a soap-box derby.
- finding equivalent fractions.
- using cross products to find equivalent fractions.
- solving multi-step problems.
- comparing fractions.
- ordering fractions.
- simplifying fractions.
- how math was used in ancient number systems.

Learning about equivalent fractions will be easier if you review finding the least common multiple (LCM) and comparing whole numbers using > and <. Study the examples.

On a number line, the greater number is always to the right.

Example 1:

$5 > 3$

Example 2:

$4 < 8$

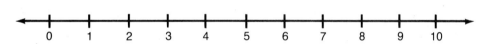

To find the LCM (least common multiple) of two numbers, find the smallest number that is a multiple of both numbers.

Example 3:

Find the LCM of 8 and 12.

Multiples of 8: 8, 16, ⟨24⟩ 32, . . .
Multiples of 12: 12, ⟨24⟩ 36, 48, . . .
LCM: 24

Example 4:

Find the LCM of 6 and 9.

Multiples of 6: 6, 12, ⟨18⟩ 24, 30, ⟨36⟩ . . .
Multiples of 9: 9, ⟨18⟩ 27, ⟨36⟩ 45, . . .
LCM: 18

PRACTICE

Compare. Use > or <.

1. 5 ● 12

2. 45 ● 54

3. 1,110 ● 1,101

4. 34,243 ● 34,098

Find the LCM of each pair of numbers.

5. 3, 5

6. 4, 12

7. 12, 15

8. 10, 11

Review NUMBER skills in preparation for learning new skills.

FOCUS Formulate problems using photo, data, and text.

CHAPTER 10

Equivalent Fractions and Ordering Fractions

DATA

The All-American Soap Box Derby Junior Division

Length of the racetrack
at Derby Downs   953.75 ft

Track sections and number of ft the track drops every 100 ft

Length	Drop Rate
First 53.75 ft	16 ft
Next 530 ft	6 ft
Last 370 ft	2 ft

Age of driver   9–12

Weight of driver
plus car   220 lb maximum

The All-American Soap Box Derby at Derby Downs in Akron, Ohio is the final race, the "Indy 500" of those motorless wonders, the soap box cars. Soap box cars may not have motors, but the rules for entry in this event are as exacting as they are for any "real" automobile race.

These cars must be constructed by the racers themselves—with carefully limited adult help—to strict specifications of size, building materials, and parts. The result of these specifications is that the Junior division cars all look the same except for the paint color.

The cars are not the same, though, because some win and others do not. Clearly, good workmanship can make the difference. Just as motor-driven cars must make the best use of gasoline, a soap box car must make the best use of its "fuel," gravity.

Suggest some problems that may arise both before and during the race. Justify your answers. What may a driver ask himself or herself about his or her chance of winning the race?

Using Cross Products

A fraction can describe part of a whole when a figure is separated into parts of the same size.

A fraction can describe part of a set of objects.

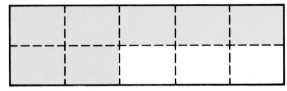

$\frac{7}{10}$ of the rectangle is yellow.

$\frac{2}{5}$ of the triangles are green.

The name of a fraction can be changed without changing its value. Fractions having the same value are called **equivalent fractions**. Multiply the numerator and the denominator by the same nonzero number to find an equivalent fraction.

List 4 equivalent fractions for $\frac{2}{3}$.

$$\frac{2 \times 2}{3 \times 2} = \frac{4}{6} \qquad \frac{2 \times 3}{3 \times 3} = \frac{6}{9} \qquad \frac{2 \times 4}{3 \times 4} = \frac{8}{12} \qquad \frac{2 \times 5}{3 \times 5} = \frac{10}{15} \qquad \frac{2 \times 6}{3 \times 6} = \frac{12}{18}$$

$\frac{2}{3}, \frac{4}{6}, \frac{6}{9}, \frac{8}{12}, \frac{10}{15}$, and $\frac{12}{18}$ are equivalent fractions.

Are $\frac{2}{3}$ and $\frac{14}{21}$ equivalent fractions? Use cross products to check.

$\frac{2}{3} \ \blacksquare \ \frac{14}{21}$?

If the cross products are equal, the fractions are equivalent.

$\frac{2}{3} \diagdown\!\!\!\!\!\diagup \frac{14}{21}$

Yes, $\frac{2}{3} = \frac{14}{21}$.

$2 \times 21 = 42$
$3 \times 14 = 42$

GUIDED PRACTICE

List the next 5 equivalent fractions for each fraction.

1. $\frac{1 \times 2}{2 \times 2} = \frac{\blacksquare}{\blacksquare}, \frac{1 \times 3}{2 \times 3} = \frac{\blacksquare}{\blacksquare}, \frac{1 \times 4}{2 \times 4} = \frac{\blacksquare}{\blacksquare}, \frac{\blacksquare}{\blacksquare}, \frac{\blacksquare}{\blacksquare}, \frac{\blacksquare}{\blacksquare}, \frac{\blacksquare}{\blacksquare}$

2. $\frac{3}{5}$ 3. $\frac{2}{7}$ 4. $\frac{4}{9}$ 5. $\frac{5}{11}$ 6. $\frac{2}{4}$

| FOCUS | Use NUMBER skills to find equivalent fractions. |

PRACTICE

List the next 4 equivalent fractions.

7. $\frac{3}{4}$ **8.** $\frac{7}{10}$ **9.** $\frac{3}{6}$ **10.** $\frac{4}{5}$ **11.** $\frac{3}{8}$

Find the missing numerator or denominator.

12. $\frac{1}{2} = \frac{\blacksquare}{10}$ **13.** $\frac{2}{3} = \frac{\blacksquare}{36}$ **14.** $\frac{3}{4} = \frac{\blacksquare}{12}$ **15.** $\frac{2}{5} = \frac{\blacksquare}{35}$ **16.** $\frac{7}{10} = \frac{42}{\blacksquare}$

17. $\frac{7}{8} = \frac{35}{\blacksquare}$ **18.** $\frac{3}{10} = \frac{\blacksquare}{80}$ **19.** $\frac{9}{10} = \frac{90}{\blacksquare}$ **20.** $\frac{3}{3} = \frac{\blacksquare}{9}$ **21.** $\frac{27}{45} = \frac{3}{\blacksquare}$

22. $\frac{4}{5} = \frac{16}{\blacksquare}$ **23.** $\frac{9}{12} = \frac{\blacksquare}{4}$ **24.** $\frac{21}{24} = \frac{\blacksquare}{8}$ **25.** $\frac{6}{15} = \frac{2}{\blacksquare}$ **26.** $\frac{21}{30} = \frac{\blacksquare}{10}$

Use cross products to tell whether each pair is equivalent.

27. $\frac{1}{3}$ and $\frac{4}{12}$ **28.** $\frac{1}{5}$ and $\frac{3}{15}$ **29.** $\frac{1}{8}$ and $\frac{4}{30}$ **30.** $\frac{5}{6}$ and $\frac{25}{30}$ **31.** $\frac{4}{5}$ and $\frac{7}{8}$

32. $\frac{3}{15}$ and $\frac{9}{45}$ **33.** $\frac{7}{20}$ and $\frac{21}{80}$ **34.** $\frac{8}{13}$ and $\frac{48}{78}$ **35.** $\frac{18}{50}$ and $\frac{10}{25}$ **36.** $\frac{3}{16}$ and $\frac{18}{96}$

MIXED PRACTICE
Maintaining and Reviewing Skills

Multiply.

37. $\begin{array}{r} 543 \\ \times\ 78 \\ \hline \end{array}$ **38.** $\begin{array}{r} 365 \\ \times\ 49 \\ \hline \end{array}$ **39.** $\begin{array}{r} 726 \\ \times\ 63 \\ \hline \end{array}$ **40.** $\begin{array}{r} 692 \\ \times\ 56 \\ \hline \end{array}$ **41.** $\begin{array}{r} 657 \\ \times\ 46 \\ \hline \end{array}$

42. $\begin{array}{r} 7{,}054 \\ \times\ \ 78 \\ \hline \end{array}$ **43.** $\begin{array}{r} 5{,}006 \\ \times\ \ 49 \\ \hline \end{array}$ **44.** $\begin{array}{r} 8{,}002 \\ \times\ \ 43 \\ \hline \end{array}$ **45.** $\begin{array}{r} 9{,}106 \\ \times\ \ 72 \\ \hline \end{array}$ **46.** $\begin{array}{r} 6{,}310 \\ \times\ \ 56 \\ \hline \end{array}$

Divide.

47. $9\overline{)828}$ **48.** $5\overline{)6{,}365}$ **49.** $46\overline{)966}$ **50.** $5\overline{)845}$ **51.** $54\overline{)810}$

52. $33\overline{)5{,}346}$ **53.** $159\overline{)3{,}498}$ **54.** $40\overline{)640}$ **55.** $23\overline{)5{,}382}$ **56.** $17\overline{)6{,}341}$

CHALLENGE

*57. Complete. Draw the final figure.

 is to 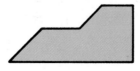 as is to

EQUIVALENT FRACTIONS

Using Cross Products

Equivalent fractions are different names for the same value. To find equivalent fractions, multiply or divide the numerator or denominator by the same nonzero number.

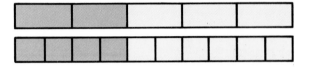 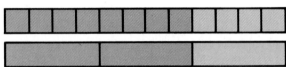

5 times what number equals 10?

$$\frac{2}{5} = \frac{\blacksquare}{10}$$

12 divided by what number equals 3?

$$\frac{8}{12} = \frac{\blacksquare}{3}$$

Multiply the numerator and the denominator by 2. ($5 \times 2 = 10$)

$$\frac{2}{5} = \frac{2 \times 2}{5 \times 2} = \frac{4}{10}$$

Divide the numerator and the denominator by 4. ($12 \div 4 = 3$)

$$\frac{8}{12} = \frac{8 \div 4}{12 \div 4} = \frac{2}{3}$$

Use cross products to check.

$$\frac{2}{5} \diagup\!\!\!\!\!\diagdown \frac{4}{10} \qquad \begin{array}{l} 2 \times 10 = 20 \\ 5 \times 4 = 20 \end{array}$$

Use cross products to check.

$$\frac{8}{12} \diagup\!\!\!\!\!\diagdown \frac{2}{3} \qquad \begin{array}{l} 8 \times 3 = 24 \\ 12 \times 2 = 24 \end{array}$$

PRACTICE

Find the missing numerator or denominator.

1. $\dfrac{4}{15} = \dfrac{\blacksquare}{75}$

2. $\dfrac{1}{4} = \dfrac{6}{\blacksquare}$

3. $\dfrac{5}{8} = \dfrac{\blacksquare}{72}$

4. $\dfrac{4}{9} = \dfrac{\blacksquare}{27}$

5. $\dfrac{2}{5} = \dfrac{20}{\blacksquare}$

6. $\dfrac{4}{11} = \dfrac{24}{\blacksquare}$

7. $\dfrac{9}{10} = \dfrac{\blacksquare}{50}$

8. $\dfrac{8}{22} = \dfrac{\blacksquare}{44}$

9. $\dfrac{6}{10} = \dfrac{\blacksquare}{5}$

10. $\dfrac{21}{30} = \dfrac{7}{\blacksquare}$

11. $\dfrac{2}{7} = \dfrac{\blacksquare}{42}$

12. $\dfrac{1}{9} = \dfrac{3}{\blacksquare}$

13. $\dfrac{8}{10} = \dfrac{4}{\blacksquare}$

14. $\dfrac{3}{5} = \dfrac{\blacksquare}{35}$

15. $\dfrac{1}{4} = \dfrac{\blacksquare}{16}$

16. $\dfrac{2}{9} = \dfrac{10}{\blacksquare}$

17. $\dfrac{4}{7} = \dfrac{\blacksquare}{42}$

18. $\dfrac{5}{12} = \dfrac{\blacksquare}{60}$

19. $\dfrac{3}{8} = \dfrac{18}{\blacksquare}$

20. $\dfrac{3}{4} = \dfrac{24}{\blacksquare}$

Complete the sequence. Write the missing numbers.

21. $\dfrac{2}{3} = \dfrac{\blacksquare}{6} = \dfrac{8}{\blacksquare} = \dfrac{\blacksquare}{24} = \dfrac{\blacksquare}{\blacksquare}$

22. $\dfrac{\blacksquare}{5} = \dfrac{\blacksquare}{15} = \dfrac{18}{30} = \dfrac{36}{\blacksquare} = \dfrac{\blacksquare}{\blacksquare}$

| FOCUS | Use NUMBER skills to determine equivalent fractions. |

MIXED PRACTICE
Maintaining and Reviewing Skills

Multiply.

23. $9 \times 8,888 = $ ■   **24.** $5 \times 8,300 = $ ■   **25.** $25 \times 1,623 = $ ■   **26.** $16 \times 2,597 = $ ■

27. $36 \times 516 = $ ■   **28.** $87 \times 136 = $ ■   **29.** $205 \times 2,490 = $ ■   **30.** $195 \times 3,008 = $ ■

APPLICATION
Problem Solving: Solving Multi-Step Problems

Sometimes you must do more than one operation to solve word problems. Plan the steps before solving these problems. Remember to READ, KNOW, PLAN, SOLVE, and CHECK.

31. Last week Rose Bud Florist ran a $\frac{1}{2}$-page ad at the combo rate. This week they doubled their ad size. How much more will they pay for the larger combo ad? How much will they pay for both ads?

32. What is the savings in ordering a $\frac{1}{8}$-page ad at the weekly rate rather than the daily rate? How many days are you actually paying for by using the weekly rate? What is the difference per day in the weekly rate from the daily rate?

Ad Size	Weekly Rate Wednesday–Tuesday	Combo Rate Sunday–Monday	Daily Rate
$\frac{1}{8}$ page	$110	$38	$22
$\frac{1}{6}$ page	$149	$52	$28
$\frac{1}{4}$ page	$216	$70	$37
$\frac{1}{3}$ page	$299	$94	$49
$\frac{1}{2}$ page	$373	$116	$60
Full page	$572	$172	$88

33. An order was placed for a full page ad to run for 3 consecutive weeks. How much will the total order cost if the third week's ad runs at a 50% discount?

34. Mrs. Wilson is having a one-day garage sale. She wants to spend $60 and run an ad in the newspaper as many times as possible. Which order should she place?

35. Jim has a budget of $44. What is the largest size ad he can order at the daily rate? Would he save any money running two smaller ads?

*36. Three stores will run $\frac{1}{2}$ page ads for 3 weeks. If they pay the weekly rate for 2 weeks and get a 25% discount for the third week, how much will they pay?

Solve multi-step problems and apply the Five-Step PROBLEM-SOLVING Plan.

Compare and Order

Lou and Lori are classmates. Lou read $\frac{3}{7}$ of the assignment. Lori read $\frac{5}{7}$ of the assignment. Who read more?

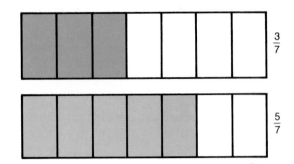

To compare fractions with like denominators, compare numerators.

Compare $\frac{3}{7}$ and $\frac{5}{7}$. Since $3 < 5$, $\frac{3}{7} < \frac{5}{7}$.

Lori read more of the assignment.

To compare fractions with unlike denominators, find equivalent fractions with like denominators, then compare. Use the Least Common Multiple (LCM) of the denominators.

Compare $\frac{3}{4}$ and $\frac{2}{5}$. The LCM of 4 and 5 is 20.

$$\frac{3}{4} = \frac{\blacksquare}{20} \qquad \frac{3 \times 5}{4 \times 5} = \frac{15}{20} \qquad \frac{3}{4} = \frac{15}{20}$$

$$\frac{2}{5} = \frac{\blacksquare}{20} \qquad \frac{2 \times 4}{5 \times 4} = \frac{8}{20} \qquad \frac{2}{5} = \frac{8}{20}$$

Now compare $\frac{15}{20}$ and $\frac{8}{20}$. Since $15 > 8$, $\frac{15}{20} > \frac{8}{20}$, $\frac{3}{4} > \frac{2}{5}$.

The Least Common Multiple of the denominators is called the **Least Common Denominator (LCD)**.

GUIDED PRACTICE

Write equivalent fractions with like denominators. Use cross products to check.

1. $\frac{1}{3}$ and $\frac{2}{5}$

$$\frac{1}{3} = \frac{\blacksquare}{15} \qquad \frac{2}{5} = \frac{\blacksquare}{15}$$

2. $\frac{2}{3}$ and $\frac{4}{7}$

$$\frac{2}{3} = \frac{\blacksquare}{21} \qquad \frac{4}{7} = \frac{\blacksquare}{21}$$

Compare. Use the symbols $>$, $<$, or $=$.

3. $\frac{5}{8} \,\bullet\, \frac{3}{8}$ 　　　**4.** $\frac{9}{12} \,\bullet\, \frac{10}{12}$ 　　　**5.** $\frac{2}{3} \,\bullet\, \frac{4}{7}$ 　　　**6.** $\frac{5}{8} \,\bullet\, \frac{11}{12}$

PRACTICE

Find the equivalent fractions with like denominators.
Use the Least Common Denominator (LCD).

7. $\frac{1}{2}$ and $\frac{2}{3}$

8. $\frac{2}{3}$ and $\frac{4}{5}$

9. $\frac{1}{4}$ and $\frac{3}{5}$

10. $\frac{2}{7}$ and $\frac{1}{8}$

11. $\frac{5}{9}$ and $\frac{6}{11}$

12. $\frac{3}{4}$ and $\frac{5}{6}$

13. $\frac{7}{10}$ and $\frac{6}{8}$

14. $\frac{2}{4}$ and $\frac{7}{8}$

15. $\frac{5}{12}$ and $\frac{7}{15}$

16. $\frac{7}{16}$ and $\frac{12}{16}$

17. $\frac{4}{9}$ and $\frac{7}{12}$

18. $\frac{2}{3}$ and $\frac{3}{8}$

19. $\frac{1}{2}, \frac{2}{3}, \frac{3}{4}$

20. $\frac{1}{4}, \frac{2}{5}, \frac{7}{10}$

21. $\frac{3}{4}, \frac{5}{8}, \frac{4}{6}$

22. $\frac{3}{5}, \frac{7}{8}, \frac{1}{4}$

Compare. Use the symbols >, <, or =.

23. $\frac{3}{5} \bullet \frac{2}{3}$

24. $\frac{2}{7} \bullet \frac{1}{8}$

25. $\frac{1}{2} \bullet \frac{6}{9}$

26. $\frac{12}{20} \bullet \frac{7}{8}$

27. $\frac{4}{5} \bullet \frac{3}{4}$

28. $\frac{5}{6} \bullet \frac{8}{9}$

29. $\frac{3}{4} \bullet \frac{9}{12}$

30. $\frac{9}{16} \bullet \frac{1}{2}$

Order the fractions from least to greatest.

31. $\frac{6}{7}, \frac{2}{7}, \frac{15}{7}$

32. $\frac{3}{4}, \frac{4}{5}, \frac{1}{6}$

33. $\frac{7}{9}, \frac{4}{5}, \frac{2}{15}$

34. $\frac{1}{2}, \frac{5}{6}, \frac{3}{12}$

35. $\frac{5}{8}, \frac{3}{4}, \frac{1}{2}$

36. $\frac{5}{6}, \frac{1}{2}, \frac{2}{3}$

37. $\frac{2}{3}, \frac{5}{8}, \frac{3}{4}$

38. $\frac{2}{3}, \frac{5}{6}, \frac{4}{9}$

MIXED PRACTICE
Maintaining and Reviewing Skills

Divide.

39. $63\overline{)488}$

40. $86\overline{)358}$

41. $23\overline{)260}$

42. $58\overline{)862}$

43. $2\overline{)7,910}$

44. $3\overline{)8,198}$

45. $63\overline{)8,653}$

46. $25\overline{)1,775}$

47. $46\overline{)3,689}$

48. $77\overline{)4,399}$

49. $18\overline{)6,250}$

50. $62\overline{)8,866}$

CHALLENGE

Write the rule for each. The first one is done for you.

*51.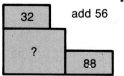

*52.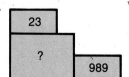

*53.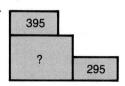

*54.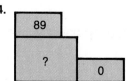

FRACTIONS

Compare and Order

Compare: $\frac{4}{5}$ and $\frac{2}{5}$.

To compare two or more fractions with like denominators, compare their numerators.

$$\frac{4}{5}, \frac{2}{5} \qquad \text{Since } 4 > 2, \frac{4}{5} > \frac{2}{5}.$$

Compare $\frac{3}{4}$ and $\frac{5}{6}$.

If two or more fractions have unlike denominators, find equivalent fractions with like denominators.

First find the Least Common Multiple (LCM) of 4 and 6. The LCM of 4 and 6 is 12.

$$\begin{array}{cc} \frac{3}{4} & \text{and } \frac{5}{6} \\ \downarrow & \downarrow \\ \frac{9}{12} & \frac{10}{12} \end{array}$$

Write equivalent fractions. Use 12 as a denominator.

To compare these fractions, compare the numerators.

Since $9 < 10$, $\frac{9}{12} < \frac{10}{12}$. Therefore $\frac{3}{4} < \frac{5}{6}$.

PRACTICE

Compare. Use the symbols $>$, $<$, or $=$.

1. $\frac{7}{10} \bullet \frac{4}{5}$ 　 2. $\frac{2}{3} \bullet \frac{8}{12}$ 　 3. $\frac{4}{10} \bullet \frac{6}{15}$ 　 4. $\frac{5}{7} \bullet \frac{1}{2}$ 　 5. $\frac{7}{8} \bullet \frac{5}{6}$

6. $\frac{3}{4} \bullet \frac{7}{12}$ 　 7. $\frac{5}{8} \bullet \frac{11}{12}$ 　 8. $\frac{5}{12} \bullet \frac{1}{2}$ 　 9. $\frac{5}{8} \bullet \frac{2}{3}$ 　 10. $\frac{2}{15} \bullet \frac{1}{5}$

List the fractions in order from least to greatest.

11. $\frac{7}{8}, \frac{7}{10}, \frac{7}{12}$ 　 12. $\frac{1}{2}, \frac{3}{4}, \frac{2}{5}$ 　 13. $\frac{1}{2}, \frac{8}{9}, \frac{3}{4}$ 　 14. $\frac{5}{8}, \frac{1}{2}, \frac{2}{3}$

MIXED PRACTICE
Maintaining and Reviewing Skills

Multiply.

15. $\begin{array}{r} 409 \\ \times \quad 9 \\ \hline \end{array}$ 　 16. $\begin{array}{r} 78 \\ \times \quad 38 \\ \hline \end{array}$ 　 17. $\begin{array}{r} 257 \\ \times \quad 44 \\ \hline \end{array}$ 　 18. $\begin{array}{r} 706 \\ \times \quad 21 \\ \hline \end{array}$ 　 19. $\begin{array}{r} 425 \\ \times \quad 27 \\ \hline \end{array}$

20. $\begin{array}{r} 1,986 \\ \times \quad 64 \\ \hline \end{array}$ 　 21. $\begin{array}{r} 353 \\ \times \quad 182 \\ \hline \end{array}$ 　 22. $\begin{array}{r} 6,124 \\ \times \quad 19 \\ \hline \end{array}$ 　 23. $\begin{array}{r} 1,624 \\ \times \quad 372 \\ \hline \end{array}$ 　 24. $\begin{array}{r} 767 \\ \times \quad 321 \\ \hline \end{array}$

FOCUS 　 Use NUMBER skills to compare and order fractions.

APPLICATION
Using Number Skills

A fraction is in simplest terms if the Greatest Common Factor (GCF) of the numerator and the denominator is 1.

Simplify $\frac{8}{12}$.

To change a fraction to simplest terms, divide the numerator and the denominator by their greatest common factor.

Divide by the GCF, 4.

$$\frac{8}{12} = \frac{8 \div 4}{12 \div 4} = \frac{2}{3}$$

Since the GCF of 2 and 3 is 1, $\frac{2}{3}$ is in simplest terms.

Simplify $\frac{32}{48}$.

If the factor you use is not the greatest common factor, you can keep dividing by a common factor until the fraction is in simplest terms.

Suppose you divide both 36 and 48 by 6.

$$\frac{36}{48} = \frac{36 \div 6}{48 \div 6} = \frac{6}{8}$$

Since $\frac{6}{8}$ is not in simplest terms, you can divide again.

Suppose you divide by 2.

$$\frac{6}{8} = \frac{6 \div 2}{8 \div 2} = \frac{3}{4}$$

Since the GCF of 3 and 4 is 1, $\frac{3}{4}$ is in simplest terms.

Simplify.

25. $\frac{35}{140}$ **26.** $\frac{24}{92}$ **27.** $\frac{6}{58}$ **28.** $\frac{15}{90}$ **29.** $\frac{20}{20}$

30. $\frac{108}{100}$ **31.** $\frac{93}{36}$ **32.** $\frac{144}{60}$ **33.** $\frac{17}{19}$ **34.** $\frac{53}{39}$

35. $\frac{18}{12}$ **36.** $\frac{60}{15}$ **37.** $\frac{95}{25}$ **38.** $\frac{87}{13}$ **39.** $\frac{135}{2}$

Use NUMBER skills and LOGIC to simplify fractions.

Ancient Numbers

The first numbers were tally marks scratched in the sand by primitive people. As the need grew for a more permanent record of counting, the tally marks were carved onto pieces of bone or wooden sticks.

It is not surprising that the first numbers were an outgrowth of these tally marks. We see in Egyptian hieroglyphics that the number 3 is III . In the early Roman numbers 1, 2, and 3 were represented by I, II, and III . The Babylonians had a writing tool called a **stylus** that made a wedge-shaped stroke ▼ . The idea was the same as in the Egyptian and Roman systems—one stroke stood for 1 ▼ , two strokes stood for 2 ▼ ▼ and so on.

To make tally marks easier to read, ancient people began grouping the strokes in bundles of 3, 5, or in visual patterns. See these examples below.

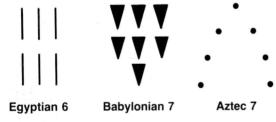

Egyptian 6   **Babylonian 7**   **Aztec 7**

Although grouping made the numbers easier to read, it was still awkward to write so many strokes. Thus the need for using symbols for numbers became clear.

The process of using symbols to represent numbers is called **cipherization**. The first example of cipherization on ancient tally sticks was the number 10 represented by V or X . The earliest ancient symbols were usually 5, 10, and higher powers of 10. The Egyptians had picture-symbols for the powers of 10 through one million:

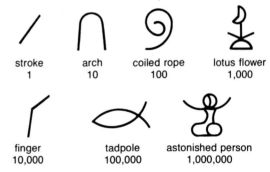

| stroke 1 | arch 10 | coiled rope 100 | lotus flower 1,000 |

| finger 10,000 | tadpole 100,000 | astonished person 1,000,000 |

Numbers were written by combining these symbols, as in adding.

 = 311

CRITICAL THINKING

1. Describe some advantages of having cipherized symbols to represent numbers.

2. What number system sometimes used today most resembles the tally mark system?

3. Why do you think the number 10 was the first cipherization to appear on ancient tally sticks?

These scenes from a 3400-year-old mural painting at Abd-el-Qurna show two different processes which call for the use of numbers. One shows the tallying of separate items. The other shows the recording of the results of measurements. This differentiation of uses marked an important step in the development of mathematics.

LOOKING BACK
Reviewing and Testing Chapter 10

In Chapter 10 you formulated problems about soap box cars. Refer to pages 136 and 137.

1. What are some factors that can affect the speed of a soap box car?

To review what you learned about equivalent fractions, look at the example on page 138.

List the next four equivalent fractions.

2. $\frac{1}{8}$ 3. $\frac{2}{5}$ 4. $\frac{4}{7}$ 5. $\frac{3}{10}$ 6. $\frac{2}{7}$

Find the equivalent fractions with like denominators.

7. $\frac{1}{2}$ and $\frac{1}{3}$ 8. $\frac{2}{4}$ and $\frac{4}{6}$ 9. $\frac{2}{3}$ and $\frac{5}{7}$ 10. $\frac{2}{5}$ and $\frac{3}{4}$

You learned about comparing and ordering fractions. To review, refer to pages 142 and 144.

Compare. Use the symbols >, <, or = .

11. $\frac{5}{8}$ ● $\frac{6}{10}$ 12. $\frac{7}{3}$ ● $\frac{5}{4}$ 13. $\frac{8}{12}$ ● $\frac{2}{3}$ 14. $\frac{3}{4}$ ● $\frac{6}{10}$

15. $\frac{11}{20}$ ● $\frac{3}{5}$ 16. $\frac{1}{11}$ ● $\frac{3}{33}$ 17. $\frac{2}{5}$ ● $\frac{7}{15}$ 18. $\frac{1}{5}$ ● $\frac{11}{15}$

19. $\frac{1}{5}$ ● $\frac{3}{10}$ 20. $\frac{5}{8}$ ● $\frac{11}{16}$ 21. $\frac{1}{2}$ ● $\frac{4}{8}$ 22. $\frac{3}{8}$ ● $\frac{1}{4}$

Order the fractions from least to greatest.

23. $\frac{3}{8}, \frac{5}{16}, \frac{1}{2}$ 24. $\frac{11}{15}, \frac{2}{3}, \frac{7}{10}$ 25. $\frac{3}{16}, \frac{3}{4}, \frac{1}{2}$

You learned about using marks and symbols for numbers. Refer to page 146 to review how the Egyptians used picture symbols for numbers.

26. Write 132,123 in Egyptian picture symbols.

FOCUS   Review and test skills learned and practiced.

148

LOOKING AHEAD
Preparing for New Skills for Chapter 11

In the next chapter you will focus on

- formulating problems about painting an apartment.
- adding fractions.
- adding mixed numbers.
- using a problem solving strategy.
- subtracting fractions.
- subtracting mixed numbers.
- graphing equivalent fractions.
- how math is used in science.

Sometimes when adding and subtracting mixed numbers, you will have to write equivalent fractions using the least common denominator (LCD). The LCD of two or more fractions is the LCM of their denominators. To rename fractions in simplest terms, find the greatest common factor (GCF).

Example 1:

Find fractions equivalent to $\frac{2}{3}$ and $\frac{4}{5}$ with like demominators.

The LCD is 15.

$\frac{2}{3} = \frac{2 \times 5}{3 \times 5} = \frac{10}{15}$ $\frac{4}{5} = \frac{4 \times 3}{5 \times 3} = \frac{12}{15}$

Example 2:

Rename $\frac{8}{10}$ in simplest terms.

The GCF of 8 and 10 is 2.

$\frac{8}{10} = \frac{8 \div 2}{10 \div 2} = \frac{4}{5}$

Example 3:

Rename 1 as four different fractions.

$1 = \frac{2}{2} = \frac{3}{3} = \frac{4}{4} = \frac{5}{5}$

Example 4:

Rename $2\frac{1}{5}$ as a mixed number with an improper fraction.

$2\frac{1}{5} = 1 + \frac{5}{5} + \frac{1}{5} = 1\frac{6}{5}$

PRACTICE

Find equivalent fractions with like denominators.

1. $\frac{2}{3}$ and $\frac{3}{4}$ **2.** $\frac{1}{5}$ and $\frac{3}{8}$ **3.** $\frac{1}{3}$ and $\frac{3}{7}$ **4.** $\frac{1}{8}$ and $\frac{2}{9}$

Rename in simplest terms.

5. $\frac{10}{15}$ **6.** $\frac{27}{36}$ **7.** $\frac{9}{18}$ **8.** $\frac{21}{49}$

Regroup.

9. $3\frac{4}{5} = 2\frac{\blacksquare}{5}$ **10.** $8\frac{5}{9} = 7\frac{\blacksquare}{9}$ **11.** $2\frac{1}{8} = 1\frac{\blacksquare}{8}$ **12.** $6\frac{2}{7} = 5\frac{\blacksquare}{7}$

Review NUMBER skills in preparation for learning new skills.

Addition and Subtraction of Fractions and Mixed Numbers

DATA

Number of people	5
Cost of paint per	
gallon	$10.99
square feet covered	
per gallon	500
Cost of brushes	
1-inch	$2.45
2-inch	$3.75
Cost of roller and pan set	$5.90
Size of living room	
Floor	14 ft × 10 ft
Ceiling height	9 ft
Size of kitchen	
Floor	10 ft × 7 ft
Ceiling height	8 ft
Size of bedroom	
Floor	12 ft × 12 ft
Ceiling height	10 ft
Size of bathroom	
Floor	8 ft × 4 ft
Ceiling height	8 ft

Moving into a new house or apartment can be a lot of fun—but it also involves a lot of hard work. The people in the picture have gotten together to help Todd paint his new apartment. For several days Todd has been planning the work that needs to be done. First he measured each room to determine how much paint he would need. Then he made a list of necessary equipment—brushes, rollers, pans, and at least one stepladder. Finally Todd decided on the color he wanted to paint each room.

Imagine that you are going to paint a room in your home or school. What color would you choose? Measure the room to find out its dimensions, then use the data to determine how much paint you would need. Do you have the necessary equipment? Make a list of the things you would have to buy.

ADDITION OF FRACTIONS AND MIXED NUMBERS
With Regrouping

Mr. Roberto walked $\frac{8}{10}$ mile before lunch and $\frac{6}{10}$ mile after lunch. How far did he walk in all?

To add fractions with like denominators, add the numerators and the denominators stay the same.

Like denominators: $\frac{8}{10}$ ← Add the numerators.

$+\frac{6}{10}$ ← Change to a mixed number.

The denominator stays the same. → $\frac{14}{10} = 1\frac{4}{10} = 1\frac{2}{5}$ in simplest terms.

Mr. Roberto walked $1\frac{2}{5}$ miles.

Ms. Clark walked $1\frac{5}{8}$ miles in the morning and $1\frac{1}{2}$ miles in the evening. How far did she walk in all?

To add fractions with different denominators, find equivalent fractions with a common denominator. Then add.

Find common denominators. The LCD of 8 and 2 is 8.

$1\frac{5}{8} = 1\frac{5}{8}$

$+1\frac{1}{2} = 1\frac{4}{8}$

Write equivalent fractions. Add the fractions.

$1\frac{5}{8} = 1\frac{5}{8}$

$+1\frac{1}{2} = 1\frac{4}{8}$

$\frac{9}{8}$

Add whole numbers. Simplify.

$1\frac{5}{8} = 1\frac{5}{8}$

$+1\frac{1}{2} = 1\frac{4}{8}$

$2\frac{9}{8} = 2 + 1\frac{1}{8} = 3\frac{1}{8}$

Ms. Clark walked $3\frac{1}{8}$ miles.

GUIDED PRACTICE

Add. Remember to simplify answers.

1. $\frac{1}{2} = \frac{\blacksquare}{6}$

$+\frac{1}{3} = \frac{\blacksquare}{6}$

2. $2\frac{2}{6} = 2\frac{\blacksquare}{24}$

$+1\frac{4}{8} = 1\frac{\blacksquare}{24}$

3. $\frac{5}{6} = \frac{\blacksquare}{12}$

$+\frac{4}{12} = \frac{\blacksquare}{12}$

4. $4\frac{3}{4} = 4\frac{\blacksquare}{20}$

$+3\frac{1}{5} = 3\frac{\blacksquare}{20}$

FOCUS | Use NUMBER skills to add fractions and mixed numbers.

152

PRACTICE

Add. Remember to simplify answers.

5. $\dfrac{3}{8}$
$+\dfrac{2}{8}$

6. $7\dfrac{5}{10}$
$+8\dfrac{3}{10}$

7. $\dfrac{2}{15}$
$+\dfrac{11}{15}$

8. $3\dfrac{5}{7}$
$+2\dfrac{4}{7}$

9. $\dfrac{5}{9}$
$+\dfrac{1}{3}$

10. $\dfrac{4}{6}$
$+\dfrac{2}{5}$

11. $\dfrac{5}{7}$
$+\dfrac{4}{5}$

12. $\dfrac{2}{6}$
$+\dfrac{3}{4}$

13. $4\dfrac{2}{3}$
$+4\dfrac{4}{5}$

14. $\dfrac{9}{11}$
$+\dfrac{5}{8}$

15. $\dfrac{13}{20}$
$+\dfrac{7}{8}$

16. $3\dfrac{2}{3}$
$+2\dfrac{11}{12}$

17. $\dfrac{5}{6}$
$+\dfrac{7}{9}$

18. $11\dfrac{3}{4}$
$+6\dfrac{11}{14}$

19. $\dfrac{2}{3}$
$+\dfrac{23}{25}$

20. $11\dfrac{7}{12}$
$+5\dfrac{3}{4}$

21. $9\dfrac{2}{3}$
$+8\dfrac{4}{7}$

22. $3\dfrac{3}{4}$
$+4\dfrac{5}{16}$

23. $1\dfrac{3}{8}$
$+1\dfrac{2}{3}$

24. $4\dfrac{3}{10}$
$+6\dfrac{5}{10}$

25. $2\dfrac{3}{5} + 4\dfrac{5}{8}$

26. $1\dfrac{1}{2} + 2\dfrac{3}{5}$

27. $4\dfrac{7}{12} + 5\dfrac{5}{12}$

28. $3\dfrac{2}{3} + 4\dfrac{1}{2}$

*29. $\dfrac{2}{3} + \dfrac{3}{4} + \dfrac{5}{6}$

*30. $\dfrac{1}{2} + \dfrac{7}{9} + \dfrac{3}{4}$

*31. $\dfrac{3}{5} + \dfrac{4}{6} + \dfrac{2}{3}$

*32. $\dfrac{13}{15} + \dfrac{9}{12} + \dfrac{1}{4}$

MIXED PRACTICE
Maintaining and Reviewing Skills

Solve.

33. $25 = n - 25$

34. $z - 15 = 9$

35. $139 = x - 47$

36. $x - 136 = 142$

37. $54 = 60 - n$

38. $45 = b - 18$

39. $35 - t = 9$

40. $73 = h - 46$

41. $39 = x - 53$

42. $s = 102 - 87$

43. $73 - k = 16$

44. $v - 26 = 35$

45. $n - 28 = 34$

46. $35 = x - 97$

47. $z - 16 = 38$

48. $r - 28 = 156$

CHALLENGE

In each example the missing numerators are the same.

*49. $\dfrac{7}{20} + \dfrac{\blacksquare}{20} + \dfrac{\blacksquare}{20} + \dfrac{\blacksquare}{20} = \dfrac{4}{5}$

*50. $\dfrac{17}{60} + \dfrac{\blacksquare}{60} + \dfrac{\blacksquare}{60} + \dfrac{\blacksquare}{60} + \dfrac{\blacksquare}{60} = \dfrac{3}{4}$

ADDITION OF FRACTIONS AND MIXED NUMBERS
With Regrouping

Dominic picked $3\frac{1}{3}$ baskets of strawberries. Gloria picked $2\frac{1}{6}$ baskets. How many baskets did they pick in all?

Write equivalent fractions. The LCD of 3 and 6 is 6.

$$3\frac{1}{3} = 3\frac{2}{6}$$
$$+\ 2\frac{1}{6} = 2\frac{1}{6}$$

Add the fractions.

$$3\frac{1}{3} = 3\frac{2}{6}$$
$$+\ 2\frac{1}{6} = 2\frac{1}{6}$$
$$\frac{3}{6}$$

Add the whole numbers. Simplify.

$$3\frac{1}{3} = 3\frac{2}{6}$$
$$+\ 2\frac{1}{6} = 2\frac{1}{6}$$
$$5\frac{3}{6} = 5\frac{1}{2}$$

Dominic and Gloria picked $5\frac{1}{2}$ baskets.

Add $4\frac{2}{3} + 3\frac{4}{5}$.

Write equivalent fractions. The LCD of 3 and 5 is 15.

$$4\frac{2}{3} = 4\frac{10}{15}$$
$$+\ 3\frac{4}{5} = 3\frac{12}{15}$$

Add the fractions. Add the whole numbers.

$$4\frac{2}{3} = 4\frac{10}{15}$$
$$+\ 3\frac{4}{5} = 3\frac{12}{15}$$
$$7\frac{22}{15}$$

Regroup fractions greater than one, then simplify.

$$\frac{22}{15} = 1\frac{7}{15}$$

$$7 + 1\frac{7}{15} = 8\frac{7}{15}$$

PRACTICE

Add. Remember to simplify.

1. $\quad 3\frac{1}{2}$
  $+\ 2\frac{1}{4}$

2. $\quad 5\frac{2}{3}$
  $+\ 3\frac{1}{6}$

3. $\quad 7\frac{5}{8}$
  $+\ 4\frac{4}{6}$

4. $\quad 5\frac{1}{3}$
  $+\ 4\frac{3}{8}$

5. $\quad 7\frac{3}{10}$
  $+\ 7\frac{2}{5}$

6. $\quad 4\frac{5}{8}$
  $+\ 2\frac{1}{4}$

7. $\quad 3\frac{1}{2}$
  $+\ 2\frac{1}{3}$

8. $\quad 1\frac{1}{3}$
  $+\ 1\frac{1}{8}$

9. $\quad 2\frac{4}{9}$
  $+\ 3\frac{1}{2}$

10. $\quad 3\frac{1}{4}$
  $+\ 2\frac{1}{3}$

11. $\quad 4\frac{3}{5}$
  $+\ 2\frac{5}{6}$

12. $\quad 8\frac{3}{4}$
  $+\ 4\frac{3}{16}$

13. $\quad 4\frac{3}{8}$
  $+\ 2\frac{5}{8}$

14. $\quad 3\frac{7}{8}$
  $+\ 4\frac{1}{4}$

15. $\quad 9\frac{1}{2}$
  $+\ 3\frac{11}{12}$

FOCUS   Use NUMBER skills to add fractions and mixed numbers.

MIXED PRACTICE
Maintaining and Reviewing Skills

Solve each equation.

16. $48 = 15 + y$ **17.** $16 + p = 25$ **18.** $87 = x + 21$ **19.** $59 + a = 85$

20. $124 = z + 15$ **21.** $n + 97 = 143$ **22.** $41 + a = 78$ **23.** $64 = 35 + y$

APPLICATION
Solving Problems

24. Tim used $4\frac{1}{2}$ bags of plaster to make concrete flower pot molds. He also used $\frac{3}{4}$ of another bag of plaster to make more concrete molds. How many bags of plaster did he use in all to make the flower pot molds?

25. In one day, Kathleen spent $2\frac{7}{8}$ hours varnishing an antique table. On the next day she spent $3\frac{1}{2}$ hours varnishing a rocking chair. How much time in all did she spend varnishing furniture?

26. Gavin made a race car for his scout project. It took him $2\frac{1}{5}$ hours to carve out a model from a block of wood. Then he spent $2\frac{1}{4}$ hours sanding the car. How many hours in all did he spend on the project?

27. Mr. Peters is recovering some furniture. He used $26\frac{7}{8}$ yards of solid fabric, 59 yards of striped fabric, and $6\frac{1}{2}$ yards of checked fabric. How much fabric did he use in all?

28. Sara spent $2\frac{11}{12}$ hours tracing shapes for puppets. Eric spent $3\frac{4}{5}$ hours cutting fabric, and Jenny spent $4\frac{9}{10}$ hours sewing the puppets together. How much time in all did they spend making puppets?

29. Ed spent $3\frac{1}{2}$ hours putting together a wooden rocking horse. He also spent $2\frac{1}{4}$ hours sanding it and $1\frac{1}{6}$ hours painting the horse. How much time in all did he spend on the rocking horse?

30. Bill used $4\frac{1}{2}$ yards of solid blue fabric to make a banner. He used $2\frac{3}{4}$ yards of yellow fabric to make a trim and $1\frac{7}{8}$ yards of white fabric to cut out letters. How much fabric in all did he use on the banner?

31. During the recycling drive, Mrs. Ross's class collected $164\frac{1}{2}$ pounds of newspapers, $120\frac{3}{4}$ pounds of glass bottles and 27 pounds of aluminum cans. How much material in all did they bring in?

Use NUMBER skills to solve problems with fractions and mixed numbers.

PROBLEM SOLVING
Selecting a Strategy: Using a Diagram

The five important steps for solving problems are READ, KNOW, PLAN, SOLVE, and CHECK. Using a diagram is a strategy that can help you KNOW, PLAN, SOLVE, and CHECK some kinds of problems. Sometimes a diagram is included in a problem, and sometimes you need to draw your own.

1. READ There are 5 people in a room. If everyone shakes hands with everyone else once, how many handshakes will there be in all?

2. KNOW Ask yourself: What do I need to find out? What is the number of handshakes in all?

Key facts: a. There are 5 people in all.
b. Everyone shakes hands with everyone else once.

3. PLAN Select a strategy: Try using a diagram. Draw a diagram to show what is happening. Then count to find the answer.

4. SOLVE Each number represents one of the people. Each arrow represents one handshake.

Use the diagrams to solve this problem.

The first person shakes hands with each of the others.

Since person 2 already shook hands with person 1, ...

Since person 3 already shook hands with 1 and 2, ...

Since person 4 already shook hands with 1, 2, and 3, ...

Go back and count all the arrows to find how many handshakes there were. $4 + 3 + 2 + 1 = 10$

There will be 10 handshakes in all.

5. CHECK Look at the diagrams to see that the answer is reasonable because each person has shaken hands only once with every other person. Why is there no diagram for person 5?

FOCUS | Use a diagram as part of the Five–Step PROBLEM–SOLVING Plan.

PRACTICE

Draw a diagram to help SOLVE or CHECK each of the following problems.

1. There are 7 people in a room. Everyone shakes hands with everyone else in the room once. How many handshakes are there altogether?

2. There are 5 children standing in a circle. Each child throws a ball to every other child once. How many times is the ball thrown?

3. Joanne had 20 miles to walk. She walked half the distance the first day. She walked half of the remaining distance the second day. How far did she have to walk the third day to finish the trip?

4. Three turtles were in a race. Turtle A was 2 feet behind turtle B. Turtle C was 4 feet ahead of turtle A. Turtle B was 6 feet from the starting line. Which turtle was ahead?

Use the diagram at the right to answer each of the questions.

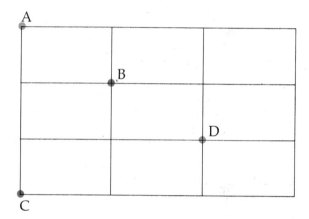

5. If you can move only right and down, in any order, how many paths are there from A to B?

6. If you can move only right and up, in any order, how many paths are there from C to B?

7. If you can move only left and up, in any order, how many paths are there from D to A?

Class Project

Form a group with several classmates. Have one student in each group draw a picture using geometric shapes. Have a second student look at the picture and describe it for the remaining students to draw. Do not let students look at the original picture while they are drawing. When everyone has finished, compare the drawings with the original. Are they close?

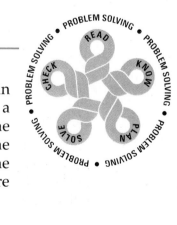

SUBTRACTION OF FRACTIONS AND MIXED NUMBERS
With Regrouping

Jessica rode her bicycle 4 miles and Mario rode his bike $2\frac{2}{4}$ miles. How much farther did Jessica ride her bike?

Regroup 4 as $3\frac{4}{4}$.

Regroup.

$$4 = 3\frac{4}{4}$$
$$-2\frac{2}{4} = 2\frac{2}{4}$$

Subtract.

$$4 = 3\frac{4}{4}$$
$$-2\frac{2}{4} = 2\frac{2}{4}$$
$$1\frac{2}{4} = 1\frac{1}{2}$$

Jessica rode her bike $1\frac{1}{2}$ miles farther.

Sometimes it is necessary to regroup a mixed number.

Subtract $38\frac{1}{3} - 14\frac{2}{3}$.

Since $\frac{2}{3}$ is larger than $\frac{1}{3}$ regroup $38\frac{1}{3}$ as $37\frac{4}{3}$.

Regroup.

$$38\frac{1}{3} = 37\frac{4}{3}$$
$$-14\frac{2}{3} = 14\frac{2}{3}$$

Subtract.

$$38\frac{1}{3} = 37\frac{4}{3}$$
$$-14\frac{2}{3} = 14\frac{2}{3}$$
$$23\frac{2}{3}$$

Sometimes it is necessary to find equivalent fractions and regroup before you can subtract.

Subtract: $13\frac{1}{6} - 11\frac{3}{4}$.

Write equivalent fractions.

Since $\frac{9}{12}$ is larger than $\frac{2}{12}$ regroup $13\frac{2}{12}$ as $12\frac{14}{12}$.

Regroup.

$$13\frac{1}{6} = 13\frac{2}{12} = 12\frac{14}{12}$$
$$-11\frac{3}{4} = 11\frac{9}{12} = 11\frac{9}{12}$$

Subtract.

$$12\frac{14}{12}$$
$$-11\frac{9}{12}$$
$$1\frac{5}{12}$$

GUIDED PRACTICE

Complete.

1. $14\frac{4}{5} = 13\frac{\blacksquare}{5}$

2. $6\frac{3}{8} = 5\frac{\blacksquare}{8}$

3. $11\frac{4}{5} = 10\frac{\blacksquare}{15}$

4.
$$8\frac{7}{8}$$
$$-5\frac{4}{8}$$

5. $12\frac{2}{3} = 12\frac{10}{15}$
$$-7\frac{3}{5} = 7\frac{9}{15}$$

6. $26\frac{2}{5} = 26\frac{12}{30} = 25\frac{\blacksquare}{30}$
$$-18\frac{5}{6} = 18\frac{25}{30} = 18\frac{25}{30}$$

FOCUS | Use NUMBER skills to subtract fractions and mixed numbers.

158

PRACTICE

Subtract.

7. 5
$- 3\frac{2}{3}$

8. 23
$- 12\frac{7}{8}$

9. 19
$- 17\frac{3}{5}$

10. $4\frac{3}{5}$
$- 2\frac{4}{5}$

11. $9\frac{1}{8}$
$- 4\frac{7}{8}$

12. $8\frac{1}{4}$
$- 2\frac{1}{2}$

13. $9\frac{1}{3}$
$- 5\frac{1}{4}$

14. $23\frac{2}{5}$
$- 10\frac{1}{2}$

15. $14\frac{2}{3}$
$- 12\frac{1}{6}$

16. $12\frac{8}{9}$
$- 6\frac{1}{3}$

17. 43
$- 24\frac{1}{2}$

18. $25\frac{1}{4}$
$- 14\frac{3}{4}$

19. $37\frac{1}{3}$
$- 34\frac{1}{2}$

20. $17\frac{5}{7}$
$- 11\frac{1}{3}$

21. $41\frac{3}{5}$
$- 35\frac{4}{5}$

22. $25\frac{1}{6}$
$- 12\frac{6}{7}$

23. $56\frac{2}{3}$
$- 42\frac{7}{8}$

24. $25\frac{1}{5}$
$- 16\frac{7}{9}$

25. $36\frac{1}{10}$
$- \frac{2}{5}$

26. $40\frac{2}{5}$
$- 39\frac{5}{6}$

27. $19 - 6\frac{4}{15}$

28. $41\frac{1}{12} - 15\frac{1}{3}$

29. $27\frac{1}{8} - 14\frac{1}{3}$

30. $67\frac{1}{4} - 42\frac{5}{6}$

31. Pearl rowed $7\frac{5}{8}$ miles. Tyrone rowed $11\frac{1}{4}$ miles. How much farther did Tyrone row?

MIXED PRACTICE
Maintaining and Reviewing Skills

Estimate the fraction and mixed number sums.
Use < or >.

32. $\frac{7}{8} + \frac{5}{8} \; \bullet \; \frac{1}{2}$

33. $\frac{7}{8} + \frac{7}{8} \; \bullet \; 2$

34. $1\frac{1}{4} + \frac{7}{8} \; \bullet \; 2$

35. $\frac{3}{4} + \frac{7}{9} \; \bullet \; 2$

36. $\frac{1}{12} + \frac{1}{4} \; \bullet \; \frac{1}{2}$

37. $\frac{3}{16} + \frac{1}{16} \; \bullet \; \frac{1}{2}$

38. $\frac{1}{2} + \frac{11}{12} \; \bullet \; 1$

39. $\frac{4}{5} + \frac{7}{8} + \frac{1}{2} \; \bullet \; 3$

40. $\frac{8}{9} + \frac{3}{4} + \frac{4}{5} \; \bullet \; 4$

CHALLENGE

Place a + or − symbol between each number to make the statement true.

*41. $2\frac{3}{4} \; \blacksquare \; \frac{1}{8} \; \blacksquare \; 1\frac{3}{8} \; \blacksquare \; \frac{2}{3} = \frac{5}{6}$

*42. $1\frac{1}{5} \; \blacksquare \; 2\frac{3}{10} \; \blacksquare \; 3\frac{1}{2} \; \blacksquare \; 4\frac{3}{10} = 2\frac{7}{10}$

SUBTRACTION OF FRACTIONS AND MIXED NUMBERS
With Regrouping

Chris had $5\frac{1}{7}$ empty pages in his photo album. He filled $3\frac{3}{7}$ pages with pictures. How many pages did he have left to fill?

Since $\frac{3}{7}$ is larger than $\frac{1}{7}$ regroup $5\frac{1}{7}$ as $4\frac{8}{7}$.

Regroup.

$$5\frac{1}{7} = 4\frac{8}{7}$$
$$-3\frac{3}{7} = 3\frac{3}{7}$$

Subtract.

$$5\frac{1}{7} = 4\frac{8}{7}$$
$$-3\frac{3}{7} = 3\frac{3}{7}$$
$$1\frac{5}{7}$$

Chris had $1\frac{5}{7}$ pages left to fill.

Subtract: $9\frac{1}{2} - 4\frac{2}{3}$.

Write equivalent fractions.

Since $\frac{4}{6}$ is larger than $\frac{3}{6}$ regroup $9\frac{3}{6}$ as $8\frac{9}{6}$.

Regroup.

$$9\frac{1}{2} = 9\frac{3}{6} = 8\frac{9}{6}$$
$$-4\frac{2}{3} = 4\frac{4}{6} = 4\frac{4}{6}$$

Subtract.

$$8\frac{9}{6}$$
$$-4\frac{4}{6}$$
$$4\frac{5}{6}$$

PRACTICE

Subtract. Simplify the answers.

1. $7\frac{6}{8}$
   $-4\frac{1}{8}$

2. $3\frac{1}{7}$
   $-1\frac{3}{7}$

3. $9\frac{1}{2}$
   $-6\frac{3}{4}$

4. $3\frac{7}{8}$
   $-\frac{11}{12}$

5. 8
   $-4\frac{7}{9}$

6. $2\frac{1}{2}$
   $-1\frac{7}{8}$

7. 10
   $-7\frac{5}{6}$

8. $14\frac{3}{5}$
   $-9\frac{1}{10}$

9. 20
   $-8\frac{3}{10}$

10. $12\frac{1}{6}$
    $-6\frac{7}{8}$

MIXED PRACTICE
Maintaining and Reviewing Skills

Copy the number line below. Label the points given.

11. $B = \frac{3}{4}$
12. $C = 1\frac{1}{2}$
13. $D = 2\frac{1}{4}$
14. $E = 3$
15. $F = \frac{7}{2}$

FOCUS — Use NUMBER skills to subtract fractions and mixed numbers from whole numbers.

APPLICATION
Using Geometry

Here is a graph of the following numerators and denominators

$$\frac{1}{2}, \frac{2}{4}, \frac{3}{6}, \frac{4}{8}, \frac{5}{10}$$

Look at the equivalent fractions plotted on the grid.

The numerator tells you the first point to plot. The denominator tells you the second point to plot.

To graph $\frac{1}{2}$, plot the point (1,2). Start at zero. Move 1 space to the right and 2 spaces up.

To graph $\frac{2}{4}$, plot the point (2,4). Start at zero. Move 2 spaces to the right and 4 spaces up.

This has been done for the fractions $\frac{3}{6}$, $\frac{4}{8}$, and $\frac{5}{10}$.

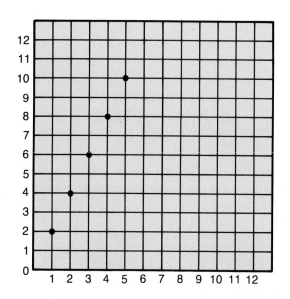

Notice the pattern formed on the grid. From point to point, each point is 1 more space to the right and 2 more spaces up.

Numerator	Denominator
1	2
2	4
3	6
4	8
5	10

Use the grid to answer the following questions.

16. Name the points for the fractions $\frac{3}{6}$, $\frac{4}{8}$, and $\frac{5}{10}$.

17. If you connected the points for the equivalent fractions of $\frac{1}{2}$, you would get a ■.

Use graph paper. Label three separate graphs like the ones above. Graph each set of equivalent fractions given below.

18. $\frac{1}{4} = \frac{2}{8} = \frac{3}{12} = \frac{4}{16} = \frac{5}{20}$

19. $\frac{2}{5} = \frac{4}{10} = \frac{6}{15} = \frac{8}{20}$

20. $\frac{2}{3} = \frac{4}{6} = \frac{6}{9} = \frac{8}{12} = \frac{10}{15} = \frac{12}{18}$

Use GEOMETRY to graph equivalent fractions.

Gravity

How high can you jump? Can you touch the ceiling? If you were standing on the Moon you could. You can jump very high on the moon because of gravity. **Gravity** is the force that pulls objects toward the surface of a planet. The larger the planet, the stronger the pull of gravity. Since the moon is smaller than the Earth, it has less gravity. The chart below shows how high you could jump on some of the different planets.

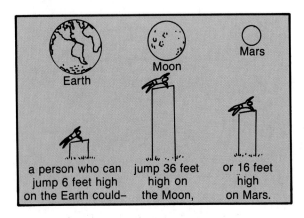

a person who can jump 6 feet high on the Earth could– jump 36 feet high on the Moon, or 16 feet high on Mars.

Which of these planets is the biggest? Which is the smallest?

A rocket taking off for space, uses much more power to take off than an airplane. This is because of the mass of the rocket. The **mass** is determined by the weight of an object, and the materials it is made of. A rocket ship is much bigger and heavier than an airplane. Bigger and heavier things have more trouble fighting the pull of gravity, so they need more power. For the same reason, a person weighing 100 pounds should be able to jump quicker than a person weighing 200 pounds. The heavier person needs to push harder to beat the pull of gravity. This doesn't mean that the lighter person will be able to jump higher. Much of that depends on athletic ability. But the lighter person should get off the ground faster.

A rocket taking off for space moves very slowly while it fights the pull of gravity. Once free from the Earth's gravity, it moves quickly and easily.

Great scientists like Newton and Einstein helped prove a lot about the Earth's gravity. However, there is no single mathematical formula to explain it. Many formulas are used, involving complicated physics. There is still work to be done in this field. It is easier to determine the mass of an object, and this helps explain how different objects are affected by gravity.

CRITICAL THINKING

1. Why is it possible to throw a baseball farther on the moon than on the Earth?

2. If a rock is the same size as a tennis ball, which do you think has a greater mass? Why?

3. Can a person jump higher on the Earth or on Mars?

FOCUS | Use LOGIC to understand gravity.

The Spacelab D-1 astronauts experience the effects of weightlessness.

LOOKING BACK
Reviewing and Testing Chapter 11

In Chapter 11 you formulated problems about painting a room. Refer to page 151 for data.

1. If 2,500 ft² of surface is going to be painted, what will the cost of the paint be?

To review addition of fractions and mixed numbers with regrouping, refer to page 152.

Add. Rename in simplest terms.

2.	3.	4.	5.	6.
$3\frac{2}{3}$	$1\frac{1}{3}$	$2\frac{1}{8}$	$2\frac{3}{5}$	$4\frac{5}{6}$
$+2\frac{1}{2}$	$+\frac{4}{12}$	$+3\frac{3}{8}$	$+3\frac{4}{7}$	$+3\frac{4}{5}$

7. $\frac{3}{4} + \frac{1}{5}$
8. $3\frac{1}{3} + 6\frac{2}{9}$
9. $4\frac{3}{5} + 3\frac{4}{15}$
10. $7\frac{4}{9} + 4\frac{2}{9}$
11. $6\frac{1}{6} + 6\frac{4}{15}$

Use a diagram to solve this problem. Refer to page 157.

12. Eight children have entered a checkers tournament. Each child will play one game with every other child. How many games will be played?

To review subtraction of fractions and mixed numbers with regrouping, refer to page 158.

Subtract. Rename in simplest terms.

13.	14.	15.	16.	17.
$7\frac{4}{8}$	16	$42\frac{2}{6}$	$19\frac{1}{8}$	$7\frac{7}{12}$
$-3\frac{5}{8}$	$-6\frac{4}{8}$	$-27\frac{3}{5}$	$-14\frac{4}{6}$	$-4\frac{8}{24}$

18. $9 - 6\frac{2}{3}$
19. $5\frac{3}{8} - 2\frac{6}{8}$
20. $9\frac{4}{5} - 1\frac{3}{10}$
21. $5\frac{1}{6} - 2\frac{3}{4}$
22. $11\frac{7}{8} - 4\frac{1}{2}$

You learned about gravity. Refer to the chart on page 162 to answer the following.

23. How many times higher can a person jump on the moon than on the earth?

FOCUS | Review and test skills learned and practiced.

LOOKING AHEAD
Preparing for New Skills for Chapter 12

In the next chapter you will focus on

- formulating problems about a meal.
- finding area of a rectangle.
- finding area of a triangle.
- finding area of a parallelogram.
- finding area of an irregular figure.
- how math is used in technology.

Finding area will be easier if you review geometric figures and how to multiply a whole number by $\frac{1}{2}$. Study the examples.

Example 1:

Triangle

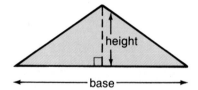

Example 2:

Rectangle

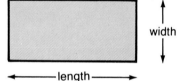

Example 3:

Parallelogram

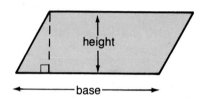

To find the product of a whole number and $\frac{1}{2}$, divide the whole number by 2.

Example 4:

$24 \times \frac{1}{2} \rightarrow 24 \div 2 = 12$

Example 5:

$\frac{1}{2} \times 18 \rightarrow 18 \div 2 = 9$

Example 6:

$100 \times \frac{1}{2} \rightarrow 100 \div 2 = 50$

PRACTICE

Name each figure.

1.

2.

3.

4.

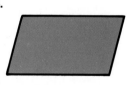

Multiply.

5. $\frac{1}{2} \times 16$

6. $\frac{1}{2} \times 48$

7. $\frac{1}{2} \times 38$

8. $28 \times \frac{1}{2}$

9. $200 \times \frac{1}{2}$

10. $\frac{1}{2} \times 88$

11. $456 \times \frac{1}{2}$

12. $1,000 \times \frac{1}{2}$

Review NUMBER skills and GEOMETRY in preparation for learning new skills.

FOCUS Formulate problems using photo, data, and text.

12

Area of Figures

DATA

Activity	Filling a pizza order
Large pie	8 slices, $7.50
Small pie	8 slices, $5.50

Toppings

Peppers	Onions
Anchovies	Meatballs
Mushrooms	Extra Cheese
Sausage	Ham

Topping Policy
   Any combination of
   toppings on a whole
   pie or half pie.

No individual slices sold.

"A large pie, please," said the three customers at the table. "But we'd like it sliced so we each get equal portions."

"I'll have to check," said Marysa. "The chef cuts pies only into eight slices. Would you like any toppings?"

"Onions," said Antonio. "Anchovies and mushrooms," said Thea. "Extra cheese, please," said Barnaby. "And peppers," Antonio added. "Meatballs, too," said Barnaby, "but I hate anchovies." "I can skip onions and extra cheese," said Thea. "No onions or anchovies on mine," Barnaby stated firmly.

Marysa wrote all this down, then gave the order to the chef.

"Do you want to drive me crazy?" he shouted. "Give them our topping policy and tell them that a pie has eight slices, and that's that."

"But we're not busy now, and I have an idea that will keep the customers happy and won't make us crazy. Will you let me try it?"

What do you think Marysa plans to do? What problems must she solve? Do you think she will succeed?

AREA
Finding the Area of a Rectangle

The area of a figure is the number of square units that cover the surface of the figure. Here are some common units used to measure area.

METRIC		CUSTOMARY	
square millimeters	mm^2	square inches	in^2
square centimeters	cm^2	square feet	ft^2
square meters	m^2	square yards	yd^2
square kilometers	km^2	square miles	mi^2

Gary has arranged some tiles into a rectangle. Count the squares to find the area.

You can also find the area (A) of a rectangle by multiplying the length (l) by the width (w).

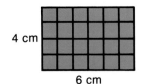

$$A = l \times w$$
$$A = 6 \times 4$$
$$A = 24$$

The area is 24 cm^2.

Find the area of a rectangle with a length of 20 feet and a width of 9 feet.

$$A = l \times w$$
$$A = 20 \times 9$$
$$A = 180$$

The area is 180 ft^2.

GUIDED PRACTICE

Find the area of each rectangle.

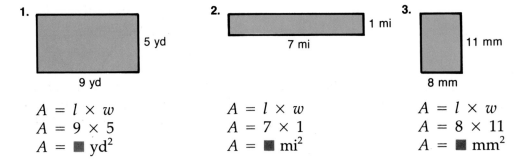

1.
$$A = l \times w$$
$$A = 9 \times 5$$
$$A = \blacksquare \ yd^2$$

2.
$$A = l \times w$$
$$A = 7 \times 1$$
$$A = \blacksquare \ mi^2$$

3.
$$A = l \times w$$
$$A = 8 \times 11$$
$$A = \blacksquare \ mm^2$$

FOCUS | Use MEASUREMENT and NUMBER skills to find the area of a rectangle.

PRACTICE

Find the area of each rectangle.

4. 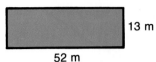 13 m

52 m

5. 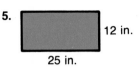 12 in.

25 in.

6. 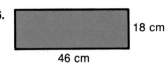 18 cm

46 cm

7. 37 ft

15 ft

8. 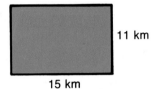 11 km

15 km

9. 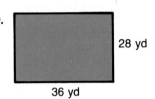 28 yd

36 yd

10. $l = 62$ in.
$w = 45$ in.

11. $l = 22$ cm
$w = 12$ cm

12. $l = 42$ mi
$w = 2$ mi

13. $l = 7$ mm
$w = 5$ mm

14. $l = 71$ ft
$w = 2$ ft

15. $l = 44$ m
$w = 17$m

16. $l = 21$ cm
$w = 14$ cm

17. $l = 32$ in.
$w = 31$ in.

18. $l = 14$ km
$w = 3$ km

19. $l = 8$ m
$w = 6$m

20. $l = 19$ m
$w = 18$ m

21. $l = 25$ yd
$w = 7$ yd

22. $l = 27$ m
$w = 13$ m

23. $l = 29$ km
$w = 20$ km

24. $l = 25$ ft
$w = 14$ ft

25. $l = 31$ mm
$w = 16$ mm

MIXED PRACTICE
Maintaining and Reviewing Skills

Solve.

26. $42 + m = 84$

27. $27 + n = 39$

28. $62 + z = 89$

29. $94 + q = 186$

30. $23 + p = 97$

31. $83 + b = 105$

32. $236 + c = 321$

33. $586 + n = 923$

34. $13 \times n = 39$

35. $4 \times q = 48$

36. $6 \times m = 360$

37. $12 \times b = 144$

38. $81 \div m = 9$

39. $625 \div z = 25$

40. $90 \div n = 18$

41. $224 \div c = 4$

CHALLENGE

Solve.

*42. A solar collector has 100 solar panels. Each panel measures 4 meters by 2 meters. What is the total area of the panels?

*43. A rectangular picnic area is 26 m long. If the area of the rectangle is 390 m^2, what is the width of the picnic area?

AREA

Finding the Area of a Triangle

This rectangle is formed by two triangles of the same size and shape. You can see by counting the squares that the area of the unshaded triangle is one half $\left(\frac{1}{2}\right)$ the area of the rectangle. The formula for finding the area of a triangle is $A = \frac{1}{2} \times b \times h$.

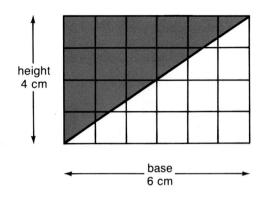

height
4 cm

base
6 cm

$$A = \frac{1}{2} \times b \times h$$
$$A = \frac{1}{2} \times 6 \times 4$$
$$A = 12 \text{ cm}^2$$

This rectangle is formed by two shaded triangles and one unshaded triangle. The shaded triangles can be put together to match exactly the unshaded triangle. So the area of the unshaded triangle is one half the area of the rectangle.

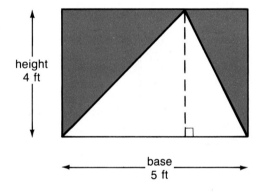

height
4 ft

base
5 ft

$$A = \frac{1}{2} \times b \times h$$
$$A = \frac{1}{2} \times 5 \times 4$$
$$A = 10 \text{ ft}^2$$

Note the symbol for right angle.

PRACTICE

Find the area of each triangle.

1.

12 cm

36 cm

2.

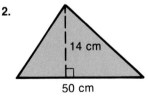

14 cm

50 cm

3.

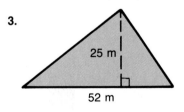

25 m

52 m

4. $b = 4$ in
  $h = 26$ in

5. $b = 7$ ft
  $h = 8$ ft

6. $b = 26$ cm
  $h = 41$ cm

7. $b = 30$ m
  $h = 60$ m

8. $b = 14$ yd
  $h = 14$ yd

9. $b = 21$ ft
  $h = 26$ ft

10. $b = 4$ in.
  $h = 14$ in.

11. $b = 38$ mm
  $h = 9$ mm

| FOCUS | Use MEASUREMENT and NUMBER skills to find the area of a triangle. |

Maintaining and Reviewing Skills

Solve. Parentheses show which operation to do first.

12. $8 \times (3 + 6) = n$

13. $14 \times (6 - 4) = q$

14. $21 \div (7 - 4) = m$

15. $64 \div (32 - 24) = b$

16. $(81 - 7) \times 3 = z$

17. $(26 + 4) \times 156 = f$

18. $(2 \times 3) \times (9 + 6) = r$

19. $(9 - 7) \times (126 - 31) = s$ **20.** $(21 \div 7) \times (3 \times 4) = t$

APPLICATION
Using Measurement

To find the area of the figure at the right, divide it into a rectangle and a triangle. Then find the area of each and add them to find the area of the figure.

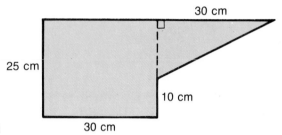

30 cm

25 cm

10 cm

30 cm

Area of a rectangle $= l \times w$

$$A = 30 \times 25, \text{ or } 750 \text{ cm}^2$$

Area of a triangle $= \frac{1}{2} \times b \times h$

$$A = \frac{1}{2} \times 15 \times 30, \text{ or } 225 \text{ cm}^2$$

Area of figure $= 750 \text{ cm}^2 + 225 \text{ cm}^2, \text{ or } 975 \text{ cm}^2$

Find the area for each figure.

21.

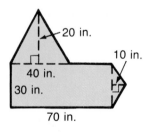

20 in.

10 in.

40 in.

30 in.

70 in.

22.

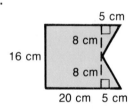

5 cm

8 cm

16 cm

8 cm

20 cm   5 cm

23.

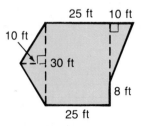

25 ft   10 ft

10 ft

30 ft

8 ft

25 ft

24.

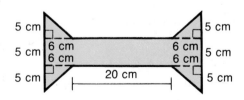

5 cm

5 cm

6 cm

6 cm

5 cm

20 cm

5 cm

5 cm

6 cm

6 cm

5 cm

Find Areas of Parallelograms

The figure to the right is a parallelogram. A **parallelogram** is a quadrilateral with opposite sides that are parallel.

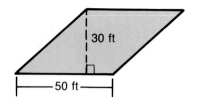

To find the area of a parallelogram, form a rectangle by sliding one of the two triangles across to the other end.

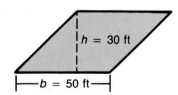
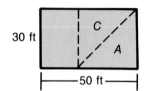

Now find the area of the rectangle. The formula for the area of a rectangle is length × width.

$$A = l \times w$$
$$A = 50 \times 30$$
$$A = 1,500$$

The area is 1,500 ft^2.

Another way to find the area of a parallelogram is to multiply the length of the base by the height.

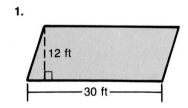

$$A = b \times h$$
$$A = 50 \times 30$$
$$A = 1,500 \text{ ft}^2$$

GUIDED PRACTICE

Find the area of each parallelogram.

1.

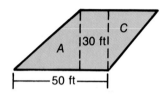

2.

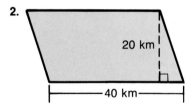

3.

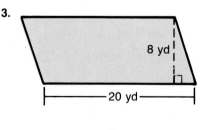

$30 \times 12 = \blacksquare$ ft^2 $40 \times \blacksquare = \blacksquare$ km^2 $\blacksquare \times 8 = \blacksquare$ yd^2

FOCUS   Use MEASUREMENT and NUMBER skills to find areas of parallelograms.

PRACTICE

Find the area of each parallelogram.

4.

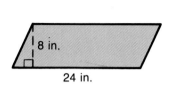

8 in.

24 in.

5.

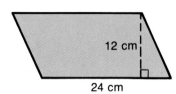

12 cm

24 cm

6.

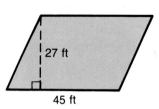

27 ft

45 ft

Find the area of each parallelogram using the given base (*b*) and height (*h*).

7. $b = 10$ cm
$h = 3$ cm

8. $b = 12$ m
$h = 14$ m

9. $b = 13$ mm
$h = 6$ mm

10. $b = 15$ yd
$h = 8$ yd

11. $b = 16$ in.
$h = 9$ in.

12. $b = 8$ mi
$h = 22$ mi

13. $b = 25$ ft
$h = 8$ ft

14. $b = 13$ km
$h = 6$ km

15. $b = 24$ yd
$h = 6$ yd

16. $b = 19$ m
$h = 26$ m

17. $b = 35$ cm
$h = 10$ cm

18. $b = 36$ mi
$h = 11$ mi

19. $b = 7$ in.
$h = 21$ in.

20. $b = 10$ mm
$h = 9$ mm

21. $b = 30$ km
$h = 12$ km

22. $b = 27$ ft
$h = 4$ ft

MIXED PRACTICE
Maintaining and Reviewing Skills

Add or subtract. Write answers in simplest terms.

23. $27\frac{1}{4} + 33\frac{1}{7}$

24. $96\frac{2}{3} - 12\frac{1}{4}$

25. $11\frac{1}{2} + 26\frac{6}{11}$

26. $41\frac{1}{5} + 56\frac{3}{8}$

27. $31\frac{1}{3} - 14\frac{7}{8}$

28. $14\frac{3}{4} + 12\frac{7}{8}$

29. $23\frac{4}{5} - 17\frac{1}{3}$

30. $37\frac{2}{7} - 26\frac{1}{3}$

31. $44\frac{1}{4} + 44\frac{1}{7}$

32. $138\frac{1}{2} - 41\frac{7}{9}$

33. $46\frac{1}{6} - 19\frac{3}{4}$

34. $22\frac{7}{9} + 14\frac{1}{6}$

CHALLENGE

Parallelograms with areas of 50 in² can have different dimensions, for example: $b = 5$ in., $h = 10$ in.; $b = 4$ in., $h = 12.5$ in.

Give several possible dimensions for the following parallelograms.

*35. $A = 100$ m²

*36. $A = 144$ ft²

*37. $A = 65$ cm²

*38. $A = 42$ mi²

AREA

Rectangles, Triangles, and Parallelograms

Use the following formulas to find the areas of rectangles, triangles, and parallelograms.

Area of a rectangle = length × width

$$A = l \times w$$
$$A = 10 \times 5$$
$$A = 50$$

The area is 50 mi^2.

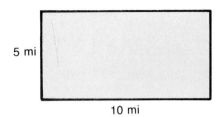

5 mi

10 mi

Area of a triangle $= \frac{1}{2} \times$ base × height

$$A = \frac{1}{2} \times b \times h$$
$$A = \frac{1}{2} \times 30 \times 8$$
$$A = 120$$

The area is 120 cm^2.

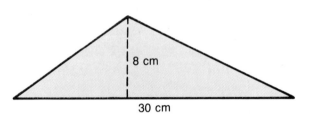

8 cm

30 cm

Area of a parallelogram = base × height

$$A = b \times h$$
$$A = 10 \times 5$$
$$A = 50$$

The area is 50 km^2.

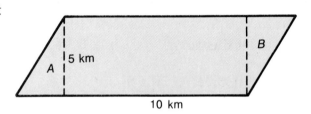

B

5 km

A

10 km

PRACTICE

Find the area of each figure.

1.

18 cm

20 cm

2.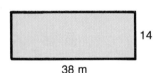

14 m

38 m

3.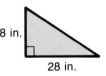

18 in.

28 in.

4. parallelogram
$b = 13$ ft, $h = 8$ ft

5. triangle
$b = 19$ mm, $h = 22$ mm

6. rectangle
$l = 18$ m, $w = 11$ m

7. triangle
$b = 6$ in., $h = 8$ in.

8. rectangle
$l = 27$ cm, $w = 15$ cm

9. parallelogram
$b = 24$ km, $h = 26$ km

10. rectangle
$l = 17$ mi, $w = 12$ mi

11. parallelogram
$b = 22$ m, $h = 6$ m

12. triangle
$b = 38$ ft, $h = 12$ ft

FOCUS | Use MEASUREMENT and NUMBER skills to find the areas of rectangles, triangles, and parallelograms.

Maintaining and Reviewing Skills

Find the Greatest Common Factor (GCF) for each pair of numbers.

13. 16 and 20   **14.** 6 and 15   **15.** 10 and 25   **16.** 9 and 36

17. 20 and 28   **18.** 14 and 21   **19.** 7 and 56   **20.** 35 and 45

21. 30 and 5   **22.** 8 and 16   **23.** 48 and 72   **24.** 72 and 90

APPLICATION
Using Measurement

Look at the figure to the right. It is made up of several regular figures. To find the area of this figure divide it into familiar shapes such as rectangles, triangles, and parallelograms.

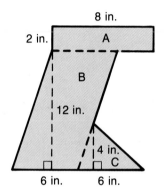

The area of Rectangle A = 16 in^2
The area of Parallelogram B = 72 in^2
The area of Triangle C = 12 in^2

Area of the figure = 16 in^2 + 72 in^2 + 12 in^2 = 100 in^2

Find the area of each figure.

25.

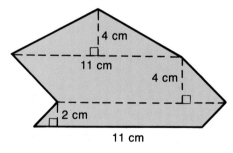

26.

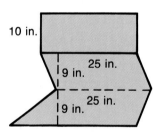

27.

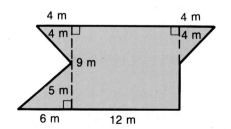

28.

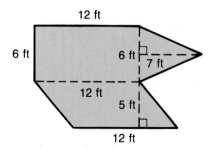

Use MEASUREMENT to find the areas of irregular figures.

Writing an Algorithm

See how a computer can be programmed to solve a problem:

Find the area of a rectangle whose length is 8 inches and whose width is 3 inches.

Before getting the computer to find the area of the rectangle, we must know how to do it ourselves.

Step 1: The area of a figure is the number of square units that cover the surface.

3 in.

8 in.

Step 2: To find the area of a rectangle, multiply the length by the width. Thus, the area of this rectangle is $8 \times 3 = 24$ square inches, or 24 in.^{2}

For the computer to solve this problem, it must be given a step-by-step procedure called an **algorithm**. It is like a formula.

To write the algorithm, first describe the solution in words, then with symbols.

$$Area = length \times width$$
$$A = l \times w$$
$$A = L * W$$

The algorithm for this problem consists of just one equation. For some problems, the algorithm consists of several equations and computations. In computer work an asterisk (*) is used to show multiplication, and a slash (/) is used to show division. For addition and subtraction, the usual plus and minus signs are used.

Now that an algorithm has been written, write the plan for a computer solution. To write a plan, ask "What should the computer do in order to solve the problem using the algorithm?"

Plan for Telling the Computer How to Find the Area of a Rectangle

1. Tell the computer the length (L).
2. Tell the computer the width (W). (Do not tell the computer anything else—it will tell us the area!)
3. The computer will calculate area $A = L * W$.
4. The computer will print the area, A.

Later, this plan will be used to write a program.

CRITICAL THINKING

1. What is the difference between the use of an algorithm and a plan in solving a problem on the computer?

2. Why must we be able to perform an operation ourselves before writing a plan for the computer to perform it?

FOCUS   Use LOGIC, GEOMETRY, and MEASUREMENT to write an algorithm for a computer program to find the area of a rectangle.

A recipe is like a formula. It is a step-by-step procedure so it is an example of an algorithm.

CHEESE SOUFFLE

1. Stir $\frac{1}{4}$ cup flour into $\frac{1}{4}$ cup butter (which has been melted in a pan).

2. Add 1 cup milk and stir, until thickened, for 5 minutes.

3. Add 1 cup grated cheese, 1 teaspoon salt, $\frac{1}{8}$ teaspoon paprika, and $\frac{1}{2}$ teaspoon mustard. Mix, then remove from the stove.

4. Gradually mix in 4 well-beaten *egg yolks*.

5. Then, slowly fold in 4 stiffly beaten *egg whites*.

6. Pour into a greased casserole dish and bake at 350°F for 50–60 minutes.

LOOKING BACK
Reviewing and Testing Chapter 12

In Chapter 12 you formulated problems about ordering in a restaurant. To review, refer to page 167 for data.

1. There are 6 people at a pizzeria. They have $14 to spend. What order(s) can they place?

You learned how to find the area of a rectangle. To review, refer to page 168.

Find the area of each rectangle.

2. $l = 36$ ft
   $w = 18$ ft

3. $l = 47$ in.
   $w = 53$ in.

4. $l = 19$ cm
   $w = 16$ cm

5. $l = 25$ km
   $w = 11$ km

6. $l = 4$ in.
   $w = 12$ in.

7. $l = 19$ m
   $w = 37$ m

8. $l = 34$ yd
   $w = 29$ yd

9. $l = 100$ ft
   $w = 29$ ft

You learned about finding the area of a triangle. To review, refer to page 170.

Find the area of each triangle.

10. $b = 6$ in.
    $h = 13$ in.

11. $b = 34$ cm
    $h = 14$ cm

12. $b = 16$ yd
    $h = 14$ yd

13. $b = 5$ ft
    $h = 12$ ft

To review how to find the area of a parallelogram, refer to page 172.

Find the area of each parallelogram.

14. $b = 8$ cm
    $h = 6$ cm

15. $b = 23$ m
    $h = 16$ m

16. $b = 12$ in.
    $h = 19$ in.

17. $b = 18$ m
    $h = 22$ m

18. $b = 17$ mm
    $h = 30$ mm

19. $b = 21$ km
    $h = 26$ km

20. $b = 9$ yd
    $h = 11$ yd

21. $b = 13$ km
    $h = 14$ km

You learned about writing an algorithm for a computer program. To review, refer to page 176.

22. Write an algorithm for a computer program for the area of a triangle.

FOCUS | Review and test skills learned and practiced.

LOOKING AHEAD
Preparing for New Skills for Chapter 13

In the next chapter you will focus on

- formulating problems about commuting on a train.
- classifying angles.
- classifying triangles by angles.
- classifying triangles by sides.

- finding the measures of angles in a triangle.
- classifying quadrilaterals.
- working with polygons.
- how math is used in consumer education.

Learning about angles and triangles and other polygons will be easier if you review measuring angles using a protractor. Study the examples.

Example 1: Read the top scale.
m ∠ A = 55°

read the bottom scale

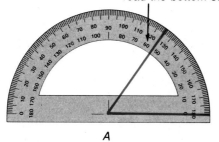

A

Example 2: Read the bottom scale.
m ∠ B = 132°

read the top scale

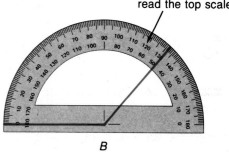

B

PRACTICE

Use a protractor to measure each angle.

1.

A

2.

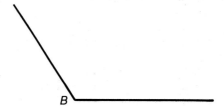

B

3.

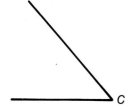

C

4.

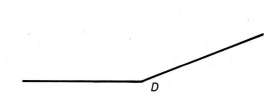

D

Review GEOMETRY in preparation for learning new skills.

FOCUS   Formulate problems using photo, data, and text.

Triangles and Quadrilaterals

DATA

Museum opening time	11:00 AM
Planned meeting time	10:30 AM
Distance from Bert's house to museum	3 mi
Distance from Andre's house to museum	30 mi
Bert's travel time	
Walking	45 min
or	
Bicycling	15 min
Andre's expected travel time	
Train	$1\frac{1}{2}$ hours
and	
City bus	$\frac{1}{2}$ hour
Train departure time	7:00 AM
Announced train delay	45 min

Bert and Andre plan to go to the museum on Saturday to see the exhibit, "Guitars of the Stars." They arranged to meet a half-hour before the doors open so that they can be at the head of the ticket-holders' line. It is a very popular exhibit, and this is its final week.

Bert lives in the city and can get to the museum easily. Andre, however, has to travel thirty miles. Andre has heard his parents' complaints about the commuter train. He knows they are often late for work or late getting home from work because of train delays. Andre has taken an early train, which should arrive in the city with more than an hour to spare.

As he stares out the train window, daydreaming about guitars, the conductor announces, "Because of mechanical problems, there will be a forty-five minute delay." The train stops between stations.

If nothing else goes wrong, what are Andre's chances of meeting Bert on time? Under the circumstances, what other problems might arise? Using the data, suggest other unexpected events for Andre and how he might deal with them.

Angles and Triangles

An **angle** is formed by two rays with a common endpoint. The endpoint is called the **vertex** of the angle.

In naming an angle, the middle letter names the vertex such as ∠*EAI*.

An angle can also be named by using the vertex such as ∠*A*.

m∠*A* means "the measure of angle *A*."

Since m∠*A* = 90°, ∠*A* is a right angle.

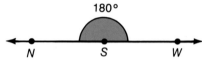

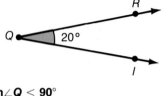

m∠*Q* < 90°
∠*Q* is an acute angle.

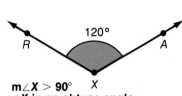

m∠*X* > 90°
∠*X* is an obtuse angle.

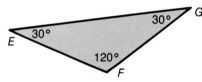

m∠*S* = 180°
∠*S* is a straight angle.

Triangles can be classified according to their angles. △ means triangle.

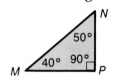

△**MNP** has *one* right angle.
△**MNP** is a right triangle.

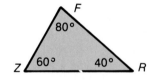

△**EFG** has *one* obtuse angle.
△**EFG** is an obtuse triangle.

△**ZFR** has *all* acute angles.
△**ZFR** is an acute triangle.

GUIDED PRACTICE

Use your protractor to find the measure of each angle.

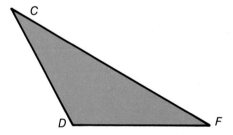

1. m∠*C* = 30°

2. m∠*D* = ■°

3. m∠*F* = ■°

4. Does △*CDF* contain a right angle?

5. Does △*CDF* contain an obtuse angle?

6. Does △*CDF* contain all acute angles?

7. Is △*CDF* a right triangle, an obtuse triangle, or an acute triangle?

FOCUS | Use GEOMETRY to study angles and triangles.

PRACTICE

Measure each angle. Then tell whether it is acute, obtuse, or right.

8.

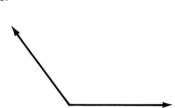

9.

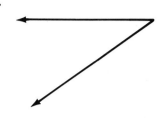

10.

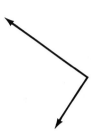

Use your protractor to find the measure of each angle in each triangle.

11. m∠A

12. m∠B

13. m∠C

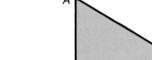

14. Is △ABC a right triangle, an obtuse triangle, or an acute triangle?

15. m∠J

16. m∠K

17. m∠L

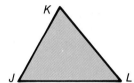

18. Is △JKL a right triangle, an obtuse triangle, or an acute triangle?

MIXED PRACTICE
Maintaining and Reviewing Skills

Add, subtract, multiply, or divide.

19. 6,246 + 597   **20.** 8,432 − 689   **21.** 384 × 9   **22.** 336 ÷ 8

23. 9,016 − 785   **24.** 782 × 13   **25.** 4,613 + 948   **26.** 1,122 ÷ 17

27. 8,421 + 639   **28.** 482 ÷ 23   **29.** 5,283 − 438   **30.** 649 × 32

CHALLENGE

∠MNQ is called an **exterior angle**.

To find m∠MNQ complete these steps.

*31. Find m∠RNQ. (The interior angle.)

*32. Subtract m∠RNQ from 180°.

*33. m∠MNQ = ▦

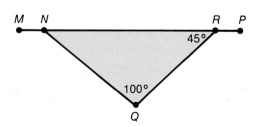

GEOMETRY
Sides of Triangles

Triangles also can be classified according to their sides.

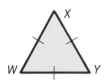

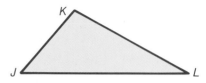

All 3 sides have the same length. △*WYX* is an equilateral triangle.

Two sides have the same length. △*MNP* is an isosceles triangle.

No sides have the same length. △*JKL* is a scalene triangle.

To show sides that are exactly the same length, use small lines on the sides of equal length.

same length

PRACTICE

Write whether each triangle is equilateral, isosceles, or scalene.

1.    **2.**   **3.**   **4.**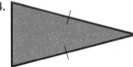

Write the letter of the triangle that is a (an)

5. isosceles, right triangle.

6. equilateral, acute triangle.

7. scalene, acute triangle.

8. isosceles, obtuse triangle.

9. scalene, right triangle.

10. scalene, obtuse triangle.

a.    **b.**

c.    **d.**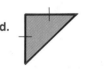

e.   **f.**

MIXED PRACTICE
Maintaining and Reviewing Skills

Add. Write answers in simplest terms.

11. $5\frac{1}{2} + 2\frac{1}{5} + \frac{3}{5}$ **12.** $1\frac{1}{8} + \frac{8}{9} + 3\frac{1}{3}$ **13.** $3\frac{2}{3} + 2\frac{1}{3} + 5\frac{1}{3}$ **14.** $3\frac{1}{2} + 4\frac{1}{5} + 1\frac{3}{8}$

FOCUS | Use GEOMETRY to study triangles.

APPLICATION
Using Geometry

Jim leans a ladder against his house. He knows that the ladder makes a 50° angle with the ground. He wants to know the measure of the angle that the ladder makes with the side of the house.

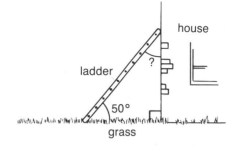

To find the measure of an unknown angle in a triangle, when two angles are known, follow these steps:

■ Add the measures of the two known angles.
$90° + 50° = 140°$

■ Then subtract the sum of the two known angles from 180° to find the measure of the unknown angle. (Remember the sum of the measures of the angles of a triangle is 180°.)
$180° - 140° = 40°$

The measure of the angle that the ladder makes with the side of the house is 40°.

Find the measure of ∠A in each triangle.

15.

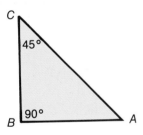

16.

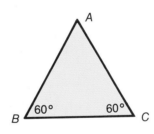

17.

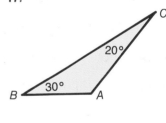

18.

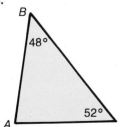

19. **20.**

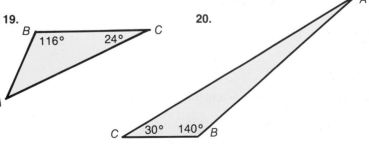

Use GEOMETRY to study angles of a triangle.

Angles of Quadrilaterals

A **quadrilateral** is a polygon with four sides. These figures are examples of quadrilaterals.

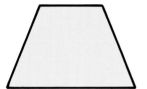

Trapezoid

A trapezoid is a quadrilateral with one pair of parallel sides.

Parallelogram

A parallelogram is a quadrilateral whose opposite sides are parallel and the same length.

Rectangle

A rectangle is a parallelogram with four right angles and two pairs of opposite sides the same length.

Square

A square is a rectangle with four right angles and four sides the same length.

The sum of the angle measures of a rectangle is 360°. A square is also a rectangle. A right angle measures 90°. Add the measures of the four angles. 90° + 90° + 90° + 90° = 360°.

The sum of the angle measures *in a square* is 360°.

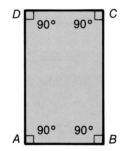

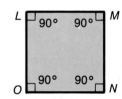

The sum of the angle measures of quadrilateral *ABCD* equals the sum of the angle measures of △*ABD* and △*BCD*. The sum of the angle measures in a triangle is 180°. 180° + 180° = 360°

Divide quadrilateral *ABCD* into two triangles.

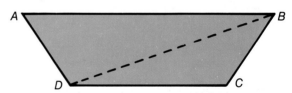

The sum of the angle measures in any quadrilateral is 360°.

GUIDED PRACTICE

Use rectangle *HIJK* to answer the following.

1. Find the sum of the angle measures of △*HJI*.

2. Find the sum of the angle measures of △*HJI* and △*HJK*.

3. Find the sum of the angle measures of rectangle *HIJK*.

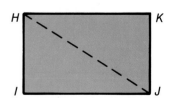

FOCUS | Use GEOMETRY to study quadrilaterals.

PRACTICE

In a parallelogram, adjacent angles are supplementary angles. The sum of the measures of the adjacent angles is 180°.

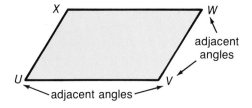

Find the missing measures of the angles for each parallelogram.

4.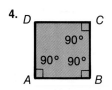

5.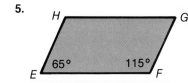

6.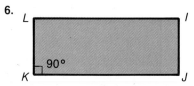

7.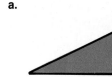

8.

*9.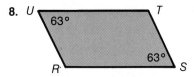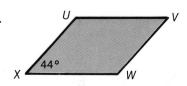

MIXED PRACTICE
Maintaining and Reviewing Skills

10. Three crews repaved a road. Crew A did $67\frac{1}{10}$ miles, Crew B did $77\frac{4}{5}$ miles, and Crew C did 80 miles. To the nearest half mile, how many miles were repaved altogether?

11. On another road, a crew has repaved $92\frac{3}{5}$ miles of a 215-mile highway. If 20 more miles are repaved, how many miles of highway will remain to be repaved?

CHALLENGE

Angles whose measures have a sum of 90° are **complementary angles.**

*12. In which figures are $\angle A$ and $\angle B$ complementary?

a.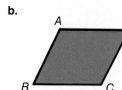

b.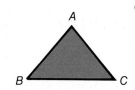

c.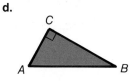

d.

GEOMETRY
Angles of Polygons

Regular Pentagon
5 sides

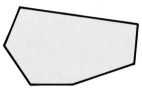
Irregular Hexagon
6 sides

Regular Octagon
8 sides

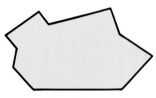
Irregular Decagon
10 sides

If the angles of a polygon all have the same measure, then the polygon is a **regular polygon**.

If the angles of a polygon have different measures, then the polygon is an **irregular polygon**.

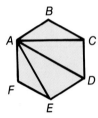

The hexagon at the right has had all the **diagonals** from vertex *A* drawn. Notice that 4 triangles are made. Since the sum of the measures of each triangle is 180°, then the sum of the measures of the interior angles of the hexagon is 4 × 180°, or 720°.

PRACTICE

Draw a pentagon like the one to the right. Use your drawing to complete the following.

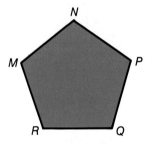

1. Label the vertices of the pentagon *M, N, P, Q* and *R*.

2. Draw all the diagonals from vertex *M*.

3. How many triangles are formed?

4. Write a multiplication sentence to show the sum of the measures of the angles of a pentagon.

Draw a regular octagon like the one to the right. Use your drawing to complete the following.

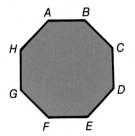

5. Draw all the diagonals from vertex *A*.

6. How many triangles are formed?

7. Write a multiplication sentence to show the sum of the measures of the angles of an octagon.

*8. What is the measure of each angle?

| FOCUS | Use GEOMETRY to study polygons. |

188

MIXED PRACTICE
Maintaining and Reviewing Skills

Find the area of each rectangle. Use $A = l \times w$.

9. $l = 14$ cm
$w = 9$ cm

10. $l = 25$ mi
$w = 4$ mi

11. $l = 30$ km
$w = 6$ km

12. $l = 14$ m
$w = 12$ m

13. $l = 13$ in.
$w = 9$ in.

Find the area of each triangle. Use $A = \frac{1}{2} \times b \times h$.

14. $b = 42$ ft
$h = 6$ ft

15. $b = 12$ in.
$h = 38$ in.

16. $b = 13$ km
$h = 30$ km

17. $b = 54$ cm
$h = 7$ cm

18. $b = 12$ mm
$h = 14$ mm

APPLICATION
Using Geometry

The sum of the angle measures of a triangle is 180°. The sum of the angle measures of a rectangle or a square is 360°.

Draw a triangle like the one to the right. Shade the interior angles as shown. Cut the angles on the dotted lines. Place the shaded angles side by side. Notice that they form a straight angle.

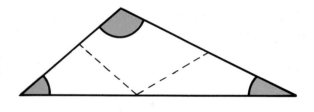

19. Draw an isosceles, a right, and an equilateral triangle. Repeat the experiment with each triangle. What do you notice about the sum of the angle measures for each triangle?

20. Draw a rectangle like the one on the right. Shade the interior of each angle as shown. Cut the angles on the dotted lines. Arrange the shaded angles side by side. What is the total measure of the angles?

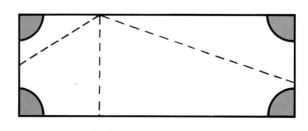

21. Try this activity using a square. Then try a quadrilateral other than a rectangle or a square. What is the sum of the measures of the angles of each quadrilateral?

Use GEOMETRY to find the sum of the angle measures of polygons.

Buying in Quantity

Imagine you are on a walk and spot a sign that reads

Do you buy one apple or 5 apples? To decide, compare the cost of one apple at $0.25 and the cost of one apple at 5 for $1.00.

To find the cost of one apple at 5 for $1.00, you must find the **unit price** of one apple. The **unit price** is the cost for one item. To calculate, divide the total cost by the quantity.

Unit price = $1.00 ÷ 5 or $0.20

If you want to save money per apple, then you would buy 5 for $1.00.

The advantage of buying single items or items in quantity varies with each situation.

Imagine you see a large box of your favorite laundry soap next to a giant box of a brand you have never tried. The soap in the giant box might cost less per wash, but it may not be worth it if it does not get your clothes as clean as you would like.

When deciding whether to purchase items in quantity, it is best to consider your needs carefully.

CRITICAL THINKING

1. What is the cost per pound of the economy-sized Sudso? Giant-sized Sudso?

2. Compare the large-sized Sudso with the stupendous size. What is the price of each per pound?

3. Why might the stupendous size *not* be the best buy?

Large Size	Giant Size	Economy Size	Stupendous Size
4 oz for $0.80	8 oz for $1.50	2 lb for $4.50	5 lb for $8.00

FOCUS | Use NUMBER skills to consider factors that enter into buying in quantity.

The wide variety of products available, many with different brands, sizes, and prices, make it more important than ever to be a wise consumer.

LOOKING BACK
Reviewing and Testing Chapter 13

In Chapter 13 you formulated problems about schedules. To review, refer to page 181 for data.

1. If Andre must be home at 7:00 P.M., what time should he leave the city?

To review angles and triangles, refer to pages 182 and 184.

Use your protractor to find the measures of the angles in each triangle.

2. m∠A

3. m∠B

4. m∠C

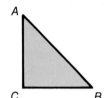

5. m∠A

6. m∠B

7. m∠C

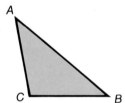

Tell whether each triangle is equilateral, isosceles, or scalene.

8.

9.

10.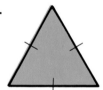

11.

To review angles of quadrilaterals, refer to page 186.

Find the measures of the angles for each parallelogram.

12.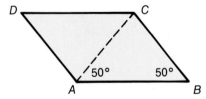

13.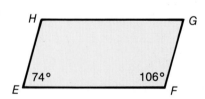

To review consumer education, refer to page 190.

14. Find the per unit cost of each product and decide the best value: Potatoes 10 lb for $1.85; 20 lb for $2.84; 50 lb for $5.25.

LOOKING AHEAD
Preparing for New Skills for Chapter 14

In the next chapter you will focus on
- **formulating problems about fighting forest fires.**
- **finding mean, median, mode, and range of a group of numbers.**
- **using a problem solving strategy.**
- **making a frequency table.**
- **interpreting graphs.**
- **how math is used in social studies.**

Arranging lists of numbers in order will help you work with median and mode. Study the examples.

Example 1:

Write the numbers in order. Be sure to repeat numbers that appear more than once.

80, 68, 85, 79, 83, 71, 80, 83, 70, 76, 80, 81

85 83 83 81 80 80 80 79 76 71 70 68 ⟵ greatest to least

68 70 71 76 79 80 80 80 81 83 83 85 ⟵ least to greatest

Tally marks can be used to show how many times a number occurs in a list.

Example 2:

6, 8, 9, 7, 8, 8, 8, 6, 6, 9, 7, 7,
8, 6, 9, 6, 8, 6, 8, 6, 6, 9, 6, 8

Number	Tally
6	ⅲ |||
7				
8	ⅲ |||
9					

PRACTICE

Write each list in order from least to greatest and then from greatest to least.

1. 7, 12, 15, 10, 8, 9, 11, 15, 10, 15, 9, 9

2. 88, 96, 82, 100, 98, 80, 85, 93, 89, 94, 81

Copy and complete the chart.

3. 1, 2, 2, 2, 1, 1, 1, 1, 2, 2, 2, 2, 1
2, 2, 2, 1, 1, 2, 1, 2, 1, 2, 1, 2, 1

Number	Tally
1	
2	

Review NUMBER and STATISTICS skills in preparation for learning new skills.

FOCUS | Formulate problems using photo, data, and text.

14

Mean, Median, Range, and Mode

DATA

Location	Montana
Major forest fires	3
Minor blazes	9
Acres of timberland destroyed	86,000
Communities threatened	2
Today's weather conditions	
Wind direction	north/northeast
Wind speed	22 mph
Forecast	hot and dry
Number of smokejumpers	120
Ground crew	500
Backfires	0
Number of planes	16
Number of helicopters	10

Everyone agrees it is the worst fire season in memory. Major fires burn out of control, while winds whip the smaller blazes. Most of the 120 smokejumpers from the Forest Service Aerial Fire Depot in Missoula, Montana are already assigned, when a dangerous new fire is spotted.

Five smokejumpers parachute to the scene to try to contain the fire until a ground crew of firefighters arrives on foot. If the smokejumpers can clear an area at least 18 inches wide of all burnable materials, and the wind dies down, the fire will not be able to continue beyond this point. However, if the wind keeps up, or gets stronger, the fire may be able to jump this line.

If the wind changes direction, the firefighters may try to "fight fire with fire" by setting a backfire. A backfire is a carefully controlled fire that leaves only burned material behind. When the original forest fire reaches the backfire area, there is nothing there to burn, and the fire cannot continue.

What problems do the smokejumpers face?

DATA
Finding Mean, Median, Range, and Mode

Sara kept a record of her test scores. She arranged this data, in order from greatest to least, so that she could analyze her scores.

100	**Range**	Difference between greatest and least numbers: $100 - 70 = 30$
95		
95		
90		
90 ⟵	**Median**	Middle number: 90
75		
75	**Mode**	Number that occurs most often: 75
75		
70		
765	**Mean**	Average: $765 \div 9 = 85$

The **range** is the difference between the greatest number and the least number.

The **median** is the middle number in a list arranged from least to greatest or from greatest to least. When there are two middle numbers, the median is the average of the two middle numbers.

The **mode** is the item or items that occur most frequently. If all of the items occur with the same frequency, there is no mode.

The **mean** is an average found by adding the numbers and dividing by how many numbers there are.

GUIDED PRACTICE

Use the list of numbers below to answer the following.

75   80   65   72   80   68   70   68   74   68

1. Divide the sum of the numbers by the number of items in the list. What is the mean?

2. Arrange the numbers in order. Subtract the least number from the greatest number. What is the range?

3. Which number occurs more often than the others? What is the mode?

4. Which two numbers are the middle numbers of the list? Find the mean of those two numbers to find the median. What is the median?

FOCUS	Use STATISTICS to determine mean, median, range, and mode.

PRACTICE

Find the mean and median for each list.

5. 3, 2, 5, 10

6. 15, 8, 17, 5, 0

7. 16, 13, 9, 8, 29

8. 50, 80, 90, 40, 60, 70

9. 199, 197, 207

10. 61, 7, 23, 12, 22, 1

11. 73, 18, 3, 32, 0, 48

12. 12, 32, 4, 12, 19, 75, 42

13. 5,231, 7,000, 1,293, 304

14. 3,375, 6,000, 4,377, 526, 2,597

15. 317, 624, 218, 401

16. 100, 100, 0, 80, 90

17. 75, 60, 60, 90, 90

18. 140, 140, 210, 190, 250, 330

19. 9, 6, 52, 12, 19, 31, 4

20. 410, 580, 640, 620, 530, 490, 755

Find the range, mode, mean, and median for each list.

21. 15, 18, 19, 16, 15, 19, 15, 16, 20

22. 36, 38, 39, 36, 35, 38, 35, 36, 31

23. 89, 63, 48, 69, 100, 83, 71, 0, 40, 57

24. 63, 69, 66, 58, 59, 61, 66, 70, 64

MIXED PRACTICE
Maintaining and Reviewing Skills

Solve for n.

25. $n + 126 = 243$

26. $139 = n - 47$

27. $n \times 4 = 868$

28. $160 - n = 103$

29. $n \times 63 = 882$

30. $n + 138 = 500$

31. $477 = 53 \times n$

32. $126 = 18 \times n$

33. $1,226 - n = 941$

34. $385 = n \times 77$

35. $n \times 15 = 1,110$

36. $n + 287 = 479$

37. $196 = n \times 7$

38. $26 \times n = 3,874$

39. $n + 371 = 565$

40. $437 = 921 - n$

CHALLENGE

*41. List the next 5 numbers in the sequence.
1, 1, 2, 3, 5, 8, 13, ■, ■, ■, ■, ■

DATA

Finding Mean, Median, Range, and Mode

Ms. Taber is examining the scores that her students received on their mathematics final exam.

| 80 | 100 | 76 | 65 | 76 | 96 | 60 | 83 | 87 | 76 | 91 | 70 |

She calculated the **mean** (average) by finding the sum of the scores and then dividing by the number of scores.

$$960 \div 12 = 80 \longleftarrow \text{Mean}$$

Total — Number of scores

To find the **median** (middle number), she found the average of the two middle numbers. First she had to arrange the scores in order.

$$80 + 76 = 156 \qquad 156 \div 2 = 78 \qquad \text{Median}$$

The **mode** or the test score that most students received was 76.

Ms. Taber calculated the **range** by finding the difference between the highest and lowest scores.

$$100 - 60 = 40 \qquad \text{Range}$$

PRACTICE

Find the range, mode, mean, and median for each list. Sometimes there may be no mode.

1. 80, 87, 100, 80, 91, 96

2. 55, 96, 100, 0, 99

3. 90, 89, 92, 75, 88, 8, 62

4. 97, 97, 79, 79, 84, 97, 90

5. 200, 800, 700, 500, 200, 600

6. 8,220; 6,990; 7,590; 50,000

MIXED PRACTICE

Maintaining and Reviewing Skills

Find the least common multiple for each pair.

7. 9 and 12

8. 15 and 30

9. 12 and 15

10. 3 and 7

11. 8 and 5

12. 2 and 9

13. 8 and 10

14. 5 and 7

| FOCUS | Use STATISTICS to determine mean, median, range, and mode. |

APPLICATION
Using Statistics

Data can be organized into a chart, table, or graph. Here is a chart Mr. Dijoun made of the number of students in each of his 5 French classes.

MR. DIJOUN'S STUDENTS	
1st period	18 students
2nd period	16 students
3rd period	22 students
4th period	21 students
5th period	18 students

Graphs are often used to visually show comparisons in numbers. The bar graph below represents the data from the chart.

Here is how the data was analyzed.

The range of the data for student enrollment is 4.

The mode is 3rd period since more students are in that class than are in any other class.

The mean of the data for student enrollment is 19.

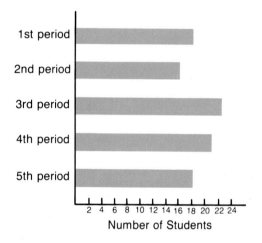

Number of Students

The scouts sold magazine subscriptions for charity. The chart shows the types of magazines and the number of each type sold. This data was used to make a bar graph.

TYPES OF MAGAZINES			
Movie	8	Computer	15
Business	18	Puzzles	6
Sports	21	Science	12
	Hobbies	18	

15. What does the graph show?

16. Which two types of magazines sold a total of 23 subscriptions?

17. For what type of magazine were 12 subscriptions sold?

18. What was the mean for total subscriptions sold?

19. What was the range of the data for all subscriptions?

20. Which type of magazine is the mode?

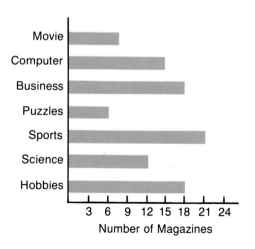

Number of Magazines

Use STATISTICS to interpret graphs.

Selecting a Strategy: Finding a Pattern

The five important steps for solving problems are READ, KNOW, PLAN, SOLVE, and CHECK.

Finding a pattern is a strategy that can help you PLAN and SOLVE some kinds of problems. Finding a pattern means discovering the rule that explains the relationship between numbers or items in a group.

1. READ   What are the next two numbers in this number pattern?   20, 24, 12, 16, 8, ■, ■

2. KNOW   Ask yourself: What do I need to find out? What is the rule for the number pattern?

Key fact: From left to right, the size of the next number alternates from greater than to less than that number.

3. PLAN   Select a strategy: try finding a pattern. Identify the pattern that shows how the numbers are related to each other. Addition and multiplication make numbers larger. Subtraction and division make numbers smaller.

4. SOLVE   The second number is 4 more than the first number. The third number is half the second number. The same pattern works for the next two numbers.

$$20 + 4 = 24 \quad 24 \div 2 = 12 \quad 12 + 4 = 16 \quad 16 \div 2 = 8$$

The rule is: Add 4 to get one number, divide by 2 to get the next number.

The next two numbers are 12 and 6.

5. CHECK   Look at the numbers once again. Apply the rule. It seems reasonable that if adding 4 and dividing by 2 gives the next 2 numbers, then that same pattern will give 12 and 6, the next 2 numbers, to continue the pattern. Ask yourself: Does it work every time? What are the next two numbers in the number pattern?

| FOCUS | Find a pattern as part of the Five-Step PROBLEM–SOLVING Plan. |

PRACTICE

Write the letter of the rule that describes each pattern. Then copy and complete the pattern.

1. 12, 18, 24, 30, ▨ ▨

   A. Add 6.   **B.** Multiply by 2.   **C.** Subtract 6.   **D.** Divide by 3.

2. 4.03, 4.10, 4.17, 4.24, ▨, ▨

   A. Multiply by 0.07. **B.** Divide by 0.7   **C.** Add 0.07.   **D.** Multiply by 1.07.

3. 36, 44, 39, 47, 42, ▨, ▨

   A. Add 8.   **B.** Subtract 5.

   C. Subtract 6 to get one number, add 5 to get the next number.   **D.** Add 8 to get one number, subtract 5 to get the next number.

4. 0.12, 0.27, 0.57, 1.17, ▨, ▨

   A. Add 0.15.   **B.** Subtract 0.15.

   C. Multiply each number by 2, then add 0.03 to the product.   **D.** Divide each number by 2, then add 0.03 to the quotient.

Write the rule. Then copy and complete the pattern.

5. 3, 9, 27, 81, ▨, ▨

6. $\frac{1}{2}$, $\frac{3}{4}$, 1, $1\frac{1}{4}$, ▨, ▨

7. 2.22, 2.10, 1.98, 1.86, ▨, ▨

8. 4, 12, 6, 18, 12, ▨, ▨

9. 86, 43, 54, 27, 38, ▨, ▨

10. 2, 8, 4, 16, 8, ▨, ▨

Class Project

Form a group with several classmates. Make a list of five number patterns that require two operations to figure out each number. Make up symbols to represent the rules for each pattern. For example, # might mean: "Multiply by 3, then add 2." Place the symbol between each number in the pattern so it looks like this: 3 # 11 # 35 # 107. Use a different symbol for each number pattern. Trade lists with another group and determine what the symbols mean in the list you receive.

FREQUENCY TABLES
Using Range and Mode

Mr. Martin reviewed the scores his students received on their exam.

He organized the information or data into a frequency table using tally marks to record each test score.

Here is how to make a frequency table.

Step 1: Make a chart with 3 columns and label them *Data, Tally,* and *Frequency*.

Step 2: List the items in the data column in order from least to greatest.

Step 3: Make a tally mark to show how often each item occurs.

Step 4: Count the tally marks and record the number in the frequency column.

FINAL EXAM SCORES					
75	90	60	80	75	80
65	75	80	65	90	70
100	80	95	65	90	85
80	85	70	80	80	90
85	70	80	100	75	85

FREQUENCY TABLE		
Data/Scores	Tally	Frequency
60	|	1
65	|||	3
70	|||	3
75	||||	4
80	ⅢⅢ |||	8
85	||||	4
90	||||	4
95	|	1
100	||	2

Here are the conclusions Mr. Martin reached.

The **range** was 40. It is the difference between the greatest and least test score.

The **mode** was 80. It is the score that most students received on the test.

GUIDED PRACTICE

Use the frequency table to the right to answer the following questions.

1. What was the difference between the highest and lowest scores (the range)?

2. What number was scored the most (the mode)?

3. How many 70s were scored?

4. Which score occurred 3 times?

Scores	Tally	Frequency
60	||	2
70	ⅢⅢ	5
80	ⅢⅢ |	6
90	||	2
100	|||	3

FOCUS	Use STATISTICS to find the range and mode using a frequency table.

MIXED PRACTICE

Solve.

6. $\dfrac{2}{5} = \dfrac{\blacksquare}{15}$ **7.** $\dfrac{4}{7} = \dfrac{\blacksquare}{14}$ **8.** $\dfrac{3}{8} = \dfrac{\blacksquare}{24}$ **9.** $\dfrac{2}{3} = \dfrac{\blacksquare}{15}$

10. $\dfrac{4}{5} = \dfrac{\blacksquare}{25}$ **11.** $\dfrac{1}{2} = \dfrac{\blacksquare}{12}$ **12.** $\dfrac{9}{10} = \dfrac{\blacksquare}{20}$ **13.** $\dfrac{5}{6} = \dfrac{\blacksquare}{12}$

14. $\dfrac{2}{3} = \dfrac{\blacksquare}{6}$ **15.** $\dfrac{5}{8} = \dfrac{\blacksquare}{24}$ **16.** $\dfrac{2}{3} = \dfrac{\blacksquare}{12}$ **17.** $\dfrac{1}{6} = \dfrac{\blacksquare}{24}$

APPLICATION
Using Statistics

The area of mathematics that deals with presenting data so that it can be analyzed is called **statistics**.

Graphs are diagrams which are used to show comparisons and differences in data.

The line graph below shows the number of badges awarded in a scout troop during the first half of the year.

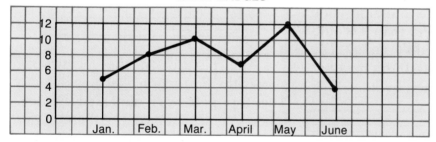

MERIT BADGES

Use the line graph above to answer the following questions.

18. What was the range of badges for the entire 6 months? the first 3 months?

19. Which month was the mode?

20. Choose one of the following topics or think of one yourself. Then arrange your statistics from a frequency table onto a graph.

Presidents' Ages   Olympic Medals Won

Classmates Heights

Use STATISTICS to interpret graphs.

205

The Parthenon

On the top of a hill called the Acropolis in Athens, Greece, there is a famous temple. It is to the goddess Athena, the goddess of wisdom. The name of the temple is the Parthenon. It was built in honor of a victory by the Athenians over the Persians and was finished in 438 B.C.

The architectural style of the Parthenon is Doric. Doric buildings have rounded columns. Each column is topped by a square capital. As you can see in the drawing below, the columns are not perfect cylinders. They are narrower at the top than at the bottom. This shape makes the building look lighter and more graceful than it would with columns that didn't taper. The Doric column "lifts" its burden rather than being pressed down by it.

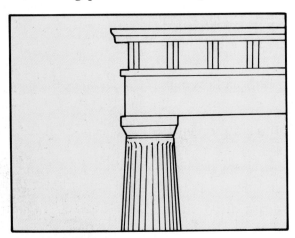

The Parthenon is of special interest to mathematicians. Its dimensions form a Golden Rectangle. The ratio of its length to its width forms a golden ratio which has a decimal value of 1.6. The Golden Rectangle is said to be one of the most beautiful and pleasing of geometric shapes.

The scale drawing below shows how the Parthenon fits this ratio. If you measure the rectangle with a ruler and divide the length by the width, you will indeed get just about 1.6.

The picture on the facing page shows the Parthenon as its looks today. The top part was damaged in 1687, when Venice attacked Athens. More damage took place the following year during an attack by Turks.

CRITICAL THINKING

1. Give reasons why the Greeks may have named a city Athens.

2. Many buildings in Washington, D.C. are designed in Greek style. Suggest a reason for this.

3. Design a small picture frame based on the Golden Rectangle. Draw it actual size.

FOCUS   Use GEOMETRY to learn about the Golden Rectangle of the Parthenon.

The composition and harmony of the Parthenon was further enhanced by color, carvings, and bronze and gold accessories.

Reviewing and Testing Chapter 14

In Chapter 14 you formulated problems about forest fires. Refer to page 195 for data.

1. If 2,000 acres were destroyed in the minor blazes, what was the average number of acres destroyed in each major forest fire?

You learned about finding mean, median, range and mode. To review, refer to page 196.

Find the mean and median for each list.

2. 19, 20, 23, 27, 36, 40, 45

3. 9, 38, 16, 18, 29, 15, 36, 3

4. 63, 38, 14, 30, 29, 83, 30

5. 117, 235, 79, 127, 38, 400

Find the range, mode, mean, and median for each list.

6. 26 27 25 29 26 29 27 25 29

7. 82 90 80 81 93 84 91 84 89

8. 57 22 71 15 26 79 53 51 33 73

Use the Five–Step Problem Solving Plan to write the rule and complete each pattern. Refer to page 200.

9. 12, 6, 24, 12, 48, 24, 96, , ■

10. 19, 10, 20, 11, 22, 13, 26, ■, ■

To review what you learned about a frequency table refer to page 202.

Use the frequency table to find the following.

11. range

12. mode

Data	Tally	Frequency
10	||	2
12	|||	3
14	|||	3
16	||||	4

You learned about the Parthenon and the golden rectangle. To review, refer to page 206.

13. Draw three rectangles that have a length to width ratio of 1.6.

FOCUS Review and test skills learned and practiced.

LOOKING AHEAD
Preparing for New Skills for Chapter 15

In the next chapter you will focus on

- formulating problems about arranging furniture.
- multiplying fractions.
- using reciprocals.
- using fractions to estimate answers.
- dividing fractions.
- solving word problems involving fractions.
- how math is used in technology.

Multiplying and dividing fractions will be easier if you know how to simplify fractions. Study the examples.

Example 1:

$$\frac{5}{1} = 5$$

Example 2:

$$\frac{16}{20} = \frac{16 \div 4}{20 \div 4} = \frac{4}{5}$$

Example 3:

$$1\frac{15}{30} = 1\frac{1}{2} \qquad \frac{15 \div 15}{30 \div 15} = \frac{1}{2}$$

Improper fractions can be written as mixed numbers and whole numbers can be written in fractional form.

Example 4:

$$8 = \frac{8}{1} = \frac{16}{2} = \ldots$$

Example 5:

$$\frac{9}{7} = 1\frac{2}{7} \qquad \begin{array}{r} 1 \\ 7\overline{)9} \\ -7 \\ \hline 2 \end{array}$$

Example 6:

$$\frac{22}{8} = 2\frac{6}{8} = 2\frac{3}{4} \qquad \begin{array}{r} 2 \\ 8\overline{)22} \\ -16 \\ \hline 6 \end{array}$$

PRACTICE

Rename each fraction in simplest terms.

1. $\frac{7}{1}$
2. $\frac{6}{8}$
3. $\frac{12}{20}$
4. $1\frac{8}{24}$

Write each whole number in fractional form with 1 as a denominator.

5. 6
6. 3
7. 12
8. 15

Write each fraction as a mixed number in simplest terms.

9. $\frac{13}{7}$
10. $\frac{11}{6}$
11. $\frac{12}{5}$
12. $\frac{38}{7}$
13. $\frac{15}{9}$
14. $\frac{24}{10}$
15. $\frac{44}{8}$
16. $\frac{56}{10}$

Review NUMBER skills in preparation for learning new skills.

radiator

door to room

closet

15

Multiplication and Division With Fractions

DATA

Floor plan for Arvin and Ray's room:

1 square = 1 square foot

Doorway and door

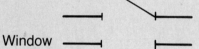

Window ⊢——⊣   ⊢——⊣

Room height   10' (floor to ceiling)

Furniture

2 beds, each 6' × 3' × 2'

2 desk units with shelves,
each 3' × 1$\frac{1}{2}$' × 6'

2 night tables,
each 1$\frac{1}{2}$' × 1$\frac{1}{2}$' × 2'

1 bookcase, 4' × 1' × 6'

Arvin and Ray were really excited when their father told them the good news—he had been promoted by his company and the family would be moving to the city. The brothers were happy until they got the bad news—they would have to share a bedroom.

With memories of their spacious separate rooms in the country, they set about rearranging their room.

As the floor plan shows, the windows and radiator are all in one part of the room. They cannot block the windows, radiator, or doorways with furniture.

Both Arvin and Ray will have a bed with built-in drawers that pull out, as well as other furniture listed in the data section. The beds are low enough to fit below the windows.

The floor plan shows the room without furniture. The size of each piece of furniture is listed with the data. The first number is the length, the second is the width, and the last number is the height.

The boys want to arrange the furniture so that the room is divided as equally as possible. Will this be easy? Can any problems be foreseen?

Multiplying a Fraction by a Fraction

Carmen uses $\frac{2}{3}$ of her garden for vegetables. She plants beans in $\frac{1}{4}$ of the vegetable patch. How much of her garden is used for beans?

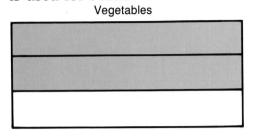

Vegetables

Beans

$\frac{2}{3}$ of the garden for vegetables

$\frac{1}{4}$ of $\frac{2}{3}$ for beans

$\frac{1}{4}$ of $\frac{2}{3}$ is the same as $\frac{1}{4} \times \frac{2}{3}$.

To multiply fractions:

■ Multiply the numerators.

■ Multiply the denominators.

■ Simplify.

$$\frac{1}{4} \times \frac{2}{3} = \frac{1 \times 2}{4 \times 3} = \frac{2}{12} = \frac{1}{6}$$

Try a short cut. Divide the numerator and denominator by common factors to simplify before multiplying.

The numbers 2 and 4 have 2 as a common factor. Carmen uses $\frac{1}{6}$ of the garden for beans.

$$\frac{1}{4} \times \frac{2}{3} = \frac{1 \times \overset{1}{\cancel{2}}}{\underset{2}{\cancel{4}} \times 3} = \frac{1}{6}$$

Multiply: $\frac{5}{8} \times \frac{4}{15} \times \frac{1}{2}$.

Simplify. Divide the numerator and denominator by common factors.

$$\frac{5}{8} \times \frac{4}{15} \times \frac{1}{2} = \frac{\overset{1}{\cancel{5}} \times \overset{1}{\cancel{4}} \times 1}{\underset{2}{\cancel{8}} \times \underset{3}{\cancel{15}} \times 2} = \frac{1}{12}$$

GUIDED PRACTICE

Multiply.

1. $\frac{2}{3} \times \frac{1}{5} = \frac{2 \times 1}{3 \times 5} = $ ■

2. $\frac{4}{10} \times \frac{5}{7} = \frac{4 \times 5}{10 \times 7} = $ ■

3. $\frac{2}{6} \times \frac{3}{4} = \frac{2 \times 3}{6 \times 4} = $ ■

4. $\frac{3}{5} \times \frac{1}{6} = \frac{3 \times 1}{5 \times 6} = $ ■

5. $\frac{1}{4} \times \frac{12}{11} = \frac{1 \times 12}{4 \times 11} = $ ■

6. $\frac{32}{45} \times \frac{5}{8} = \frac{32 \times 5}{45 \times 8} = $ ■

| FOCUS | Use NUMBER skills to multiply fractions. |

PRACTICE

Multiply. Simplify the answers.

7. $\frac{1}{2} \times \frac{1}{3}$ **8.** $\frac{1}{5} \times \frac{2}{3}$ **9.** $\frac{7}{9} \times \frac{3}{5}$ **10.** $\frac{3}{4} \times \frac{2}{8}$

11. $\frac{4}{5} \times \frac{10}{12}$ **12.** $\frac{6}{7} \times \frac{2}{10}$ **13.** $\frac{4}{5} \times \frac{3}{7}$ **14.** $\frac{1}{11} \times \frac{3}{5}$

15. $\frac{3}{9} \times \frac{3}{12}$ **16.** $\frac{5}{25} \times \frac{3}{4}$ **17.** $\frac{10}{15} \times \frac{4}{30}$ **18.** $\frac{9}{16} \times \frac{4}{27}$

19. $\frac{1}{2} \times \frac{3}{5} \times \frac{1}{4}$ **20.** $\frac{2}{5} \times \frac{3}{4} \times \frac{1}{3}$ **21.** $\frac{5}{8} \times \frac{4}{7} \times \frac{3}{10}$ **22.** $\frac{6}{7} \times \frac{14}{18} \times \frac{5}{20}$

*23. $\frac{7}{9} \times \frac{3}{10} \times \frac{4}{21}$ ***24.** $\frac{8}{9} \times \frac{2}{5} \times \frac{1}{7}$ ***25.** $\frac{8}{9} \times \frac{2}{72} \times \frac{1}{20}$ ***26.** $\frac{5}{6} \times \frac{7}{6} \times \frac{1}{6}$

27. Carmen canned $\frac{3}{5}$ of the beans she grew. She gave away $\frac{2}{3}$ of the canned beans. What part of the beans grown were given away?

28. One day $\frac{1}{6}$ of the class wore blue, and $\frac{2}{3}$ of those wearing blue also wore red. What part of the class wore blue and red?

MIXED PRACTICE
Maintaining and Reviewing Skills

Change each fraction to a mixed number in simplest terms.

29. $\frac{22}{7}$ **30.** $\frac{15}{4}$ **31.** $\frac{39}{8}$ **32.** $\frac{67}{9}$ **33.** $\frac{45}{8}$

34. $\frac{87}{9}$ **35.** $\frac{90}{7}$ **36.** $\frac{56}{10}$ **37.** $\frac{38}{12}$ **38.** $\frac{95}{10}$

39. $\frac{47}{2}$ **40.** $\frac{86}{3}$ **41.** $\frac{125}{7}$ **42.** $\frac{400}{15}$ **43.** $\frac{290}{8}$

CHALLENGE

Solve.

*44. Complete the magic square. The sums of the rows, horizontally, vertically, and diagonally, equal $1\frac{2}{3}$.

$\frac{8}{9}$	$\frac{1}{9}$	a
$\frac{1}{3}$	b	$\frac{7}{9}$
$\frac{4}{9}$	c	$\frac{2}{9}$

MULTIPLICATION OF FRACTIONS
Reciprocals

If the product of 2 numbers is 1, those numbers are **reciprocals** of each other.

$$\frac{1}{3} \times \frac{3}{1} = \frac{3}{3} = 1 \qquad \frac{2}{5} \times \frac{5}{2} = \frac{10}{10} = 1 \qquad \frac{9}{1} \times \frac{1}{9} = \frac{9}{9} = 1$$

To find the reciprocal of $\frac{3}{4}$, reverse the numerator and denominator. Multiply to check that the product is 1.

$$\frac{3}{4} \times \frac{4}{3} = \frac{12}{12} = 1 \qquad \text{The reciprocal of } \frac{3}{4} \text{ is } \frac{4}{3}.$$

What is the reciprocal of 8?

Write the whole number in fraction form by dividing the number by 1. Then reverse the numerator and denominator. Multiply to check that the product is 1.

$$\frac{8}{1} \times \frac{1}{8} = \frac{8}{8} = 1 \qquad \text{The reciprocal of 8 is } \frac{1}{8}.$$

PRACTICE

Give the reciprocal.

1. $\frac{5}{6}$ 2. $\frac{7}{9}$ 3. $\frac{3}{2}$ 4. 9   5. $\frac{1}{7}$ 6. $\frac{4}{5}$

7. $\frac{1}{10}$ 8. 12   9. $\frac{11}{12}$ 10. $\frac{6}{7}$ 11. 14   12. $\frac{1}{12}$

Multiply. Simplify your answers.

13. $\frac{5}{6} \times \frac{3}{8}$ 14. $\frac{2}{5} \times \frac{15}{24}$ 15. $\frac{6}{9} \times \frac{12}{15}$ 16. $\frac{3}{7} \times \frac{7}{3}$

MIXED PRACTICE
Maintaining and Reviewing Skills

Compare using $>$, $<$, or $=$.

17. $\frac{2}{3} \bullet \frac{4}{5}$ 18. $\frac{1}{2} \bullet \frac{25}{50}$ 19. $\frac{3}{11} \bullet \frac{5}{22}$ 20. $\frac{5}{6} \bullet \frac{11}{12}$

21. $\frac{3}{5} \bullet \frac{5}{8}$ 22. $\frac{7}{8} \bullet \frac{7}{12}$ 23. $\frac{2}{5} \bullet \frac{1}{2}$ 24. $\frac{5}{6} \bullet \frac{7}{10}$

FOCUS   Use NUMBER skills to find the reciprocal of a fraction.

PRACTICE

Complete the division. Simplify.

7. $4 \div \frac{3}{4} = \blacksquare$ **8.** $6 \div \frac{1}{3} = \blacksquare$ **9.** $5 \div \frac{2}{5} = \blacksquare$ **10.** $\frac{3}{4} \div \frac{1}{4} = \blacksquare$

11. $\frac{7}{8} \div \frac{1}{8} = \blacksquare$ **12.** $14 \div \frac{2}{7} = \blacksquare$ **13.** $12 \div \frac{6}{10} = \blacksquare$ **14.** $\frac{5}{8} \div \frac{1}{4} = \blacksquare$

15. $\frac{1}{2} \div \frac{1}{4} = \blacksquare$ **16.** $\frac{8}{9} \div \frac{1}{9} = \blacksquare$ **17.** $25 \div \frac{5}{7} = \blacksquare$ **18.** $33 \div \frac{3}{8} = \blacksquare$

19. $16 \div \frac{4}{10} = \blacksquare$ **20.** $\frac{11}{12} \div \frac{11}{15} = \blacksquare$ **21.** $24 \div \frac{12}{13} = \blacksquare$ **22.** $\frac{3}{4} \div \frac{1}{12} = \blacksquare$

23. Three meat pies are divided into fifths. Are there enough portions to feed 16 people?

24. Five quarts of tomato juice is divided into sixths. Is there enough for 25 drinks?

25. Six pizzas are divided into eighths. Is there enough pizza for 45 people to have one slice each?

*26. Four melons are cut into twelfths. Are there enough wedges for 25 people to have 2 wedges each?

MIXED PRACTICE
Maintaining and Reviewing Skills

Change to whole numbers or fractions.

27. $\frac{15}{3} = \frac{\blacksquare}{1} = \blacksquare$ **28.** $\frac{24}{2} = \frac{\blacksquare}{1} = \blacksquare$ **29.** $\frac{35}{5} = \frac{\blacksquare}{1} = \blacksquare$ **30.** $\frac{14}{7} = \frac{\blacksquare}{1} = \blacksquare$ **31.** $\frac{64}{8} = \frac{\blacksquare}{1} = \blacksquare$

32. $5 = \frac{\blacksquare}{5}$ **33.** $14 = \frac{\blacksquare}{2}$ **34.** $81 = \frac{\blacksquare}{10}$ **35.** $7 = \frac{\blacksquare}{11}$ **36.** $16 = \frac{\blacksquare}{2}$

Simplify.

37. $\frac{18}{12} = \blacksquare$ **38.** $\frac{42}{6} = \blacksquare$ **39.** $\frac{7}{3} = \blacksquare$ **40.** $\frac{21}{17} = \blacksquare$ **41.** $\frac{80}{7} = \blacksquare$

CHALLENGE

Give the next five numbers in the sequence.

*42. $3\frac{2}{8}$, $4\frac{3}{9}$, $5\frac{4}{10}$, $\blacksquare$, $\blacksquare$, $\blacksquare$, $\blacksquare$, $\blacksquare$

DIVISION OF FRACTIONS
Dividing a Fraction by a Fraction

To divide a fraction by a fraction, multiply the dividend by the reciprocal of the divisor.

Divide: $\dfrac{9}{10} \div \dfrac{2}{5}$.

Multiply by the reciprocal of the divisor.

Find common factors and simplify.

Multiply and rename in simplest terms.

$\dfrac{9}{10} \times \dfrac{5}{2}$ $\dfrac{5}{2}$ and $\dfrac{2}{5}$ are reciprocals

$\dfrac{9}{\underset{2}{10}} \times \dfrac{\overset{1}{5}}{2}$

$\dfrac{9}{2} \times \dfrac{1}{2} = \dfrac{9}{4} = 2\dfrac{1}{4}$

To divide a fraction by a whole number, or a whole number by a fraction, write the whole number as a fraction. Then multiply the dividend by the reciprocal of the divisor.

Divide: $\dfrac{4}{5} \div 8$.

Write as a fraction. Multiply by the reciprocal of the divisor.

Multiply and rename in simplest terms.

$\dfrac{4}{5} \div \dfrac{8}{1} = \dfrac{4}{5} \times \dfrac{1}{8}$

$\dfrac{\overset{1}{4}}{5} \times \dfrac{1}{\underset{2}{8}} = \dfrac{1}{10}$

$\dfrac{1}{8}$ and $\dfrac{8}{1}$ are reciprocals

Divide: $6 \div \dfrac{3}{8}$.

Write as a fraction. Multiply by the reciprocal of the divisor.

Multiply and rename in simplest terms.

$\dfrac{6}{1} \div \dfrac{3}{8} = \dfrac{6}{1} \times \dfrac{8}{3}$

$\dfrac{\overset{2}{6}}{1} \times \dfrac{8}{\underset{1}{3}} = \dfrac{16}{1} = 16$

$\dfrac{8}{3}$ and $\dfrac{3}{8}$ are reciprocals

PRACTICE

Divide.

1. $7 \div \dfrac{1}{3} = \blacksquare$

2. $\dfrac{3}{4} \div 5 = \blacksquare$

3. $\dfrac{9}{10} \div \dfrac{1}{4} = \blacksquare$

4. $\dfrac{6}{7} \div 3 = \blacksquare$

5. $\dfrac{2}{3} \div \dfrac{1}{4} = \blacksquare$

6. $\dfrac{4}{9} \div \dfrac{2}{3} = \blacksquare$

7. $6 \div \dfrac{2}{7} = \blacksquare$

8. $3 \div \dfrac{2}{11} = \blacksquare$

9. $\dfrac{8}{13} \div \dfrac{6}{7} = \blacksquare$

10. $\dfrac{1}{2} \div 26 = \blacksquare$

11. $\dfrac{1}{21} \div 2 = \blacksquare$

12. $\dfrac{3}{7} \div \dfrac{2}{5} = \blacksquare$

13. $\dfrac{3}{4} \div 2 = \blacksquare$

14. $\dfrac{5}{2} \div \dfrac{1}{4} = \blacksquare$

15. $\dfrac{3}{8} \div \dfrac{2}{3} = \blacksquare$

16. $5 \div \dfrac{5}{8} = \blacksquare$

17. $\dfrac{1}{4} \div \dfrac{3}{5} = \blacksquare$

18. $\dfrac{1}{5} \div 3 = \blacksquare$

19. $\dfrac{1}{2} \div \dfrac{4}{5} = \blacksquare$

20. $\dfrac{5}{6} \div \dfrac{7}{12} = \blacksquare$

FOCUS Use NUMBER skills to divide fractions and whole numbers.

MIXED PRACTICE
Maintaining and Reviewing Skills

Add or subtract. Write in simplest terms.

21. $\frac{1}{5} + \frac{1}{3}$ **22.** $\frac{5}{6} - \frac{3}{4}$ **23.** $\frac{2}{3} + \frac{5}{9}$ **24.** $\frac{7}{12} - \frac{3}{12}$

25. $\frac{7}{8} - \frac{5}{8}$ **26.** $\frac{2}{9} + \frac{5}{6}$ **27.** $3\frac{1}{2} + 3\frac{3}{10}$ **28.** $3\frac{5}{6} - 1\frac{1}{4}$

29. $4\frac{1}{2} + 6\frac{3}{5}$ **30.** $12\frac{4}{5} - 6\frac{1}{2}$ **31.** $\frac{4}{5} - \frac{1}{2}$ **32.** $\frac{2}{9} + \frac{5}{7}$

33. $5\frac{2}{3} + 3\frac{1}{12}$ **34.** $2\frac{2}{3} + 6\frac{1}{6}$ **35.** $9\frac{3}{4} - 7\frac{7}{12}$ **36.** $11\frac{5}{6} - 4\frac{1}{2}$

APPLICATION
Problem Solving

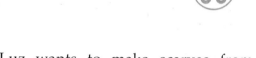

Solve.

37. Luis had $3\frac{1}{2}$ gal of paint. He used $2\frac{4}{5}$ gal to paint a room. How much paint did he have left?

38. Luz wants to make scarves from $\frac{3}{4}$ yd of silk. If she needs $\frac{1}{8}$ yd for each, how many scarves can she make?

39. The scouts marked $3\frac{1}{2}$ miles of a hiking trail. One troop marked $\frac{1}{3}$. Another marked $\frac{1}{2}$. The third troop marked the rest. How many miles of the trail did the third troop mark?

40. The perimeter of Lake Attitash is twelve miles. There are cabins lining the lake along the perimeter. There is a cabin every $\frac{1}{3}$ mile. How many cabins are on the lake?

41. David had 150 stickers. He gave $\frac{1}{5}$ of them to Fritz for his birthday. He traded $\frac{1}{3}$ of what was left to Pat for a kite. What fraction of the original number of stickers did David have left? How many stickers were left?

42. Larry bought 12 watermelons for a picnic. The adults ate half of the melons. The children ate one sixth. The teenagers ate another sixth. What fraction was left over? How many melons were left?

43. Mrs. Peal jogged $1\frac{1}{2}$ miles every day for a week. The second week she increased the distance she ran by $\frac{1}{5}$. How many miles did she run daily?

44. A candidate sent 750 questionnaires to people in her district. Only $\frac{2}{5}$ of the questionnaires were returned. How many were returned?

Use PROBLEM SOLVING to solve problems with fractions.

Using an Algorithm to Write a Computer Program

Now we can write a computer program. The language that we will be using is called BASIC. This stands for *Beginner's All-purpose Symbolic Instruction Code.*

In order to write the program, we must have a plan. We want to calculate the area of a rectangle.

Plan	Computer Instructions
1. Tell the computer the length L	10 INPUT L
2. Tell the computer the width W	20 INPUT W
3. Calculate A = L × W	30 A = L*W
4. Print the answer, A	40 PRINT A
5. Nothing else is to be done	50 END

Look carefully at the computer program. Notice that:
- Every computer instruction in BASIC must have a line number in front of it. The computer will follow the instructions in numerical order, even if they were typed out of order.
- The lines are usually numbered in multiples of ten, so that if something is mistakenly left out, it can later be inserted using a line number that falls in between the multiples of ten.
- When the computer reaches an INPUT statement, it stops and waits for data to be entered.

- Every computer program must have the instruction "END" for its last statement. This tells the computer that no other instructions will be coming.

Running Your Program

To run your program, first enter it by typing in each line. At the end of each line, press the button marked "RETURN" or "ENTER". When you have entered the entire program, then type in the word RUN and press RETURN. A question mark will appear every time the computer reaches an INPUT statement. At this point, enter the number and press RETURN.

This is how the output will look if data is input for a rectangle whose length is 7 units and whose width is 5 units. (The area is 35 square units.)

```
RUN
?5
?7
35
```

CRITICAL THINKING

1. What types of statements will cause the computer to stop?

2. When does the computer display the contents of a memory cell?

FOCUS   Use LOGIC to write a computer program using an algorithm.

At computer camps, computer instruction is a daily activity along with swimming, hiking, and horseback riding.

LOOKING BACK
Reviewing and Testing Chapter 15

In Chapter 15 you formulated problems about a floor plan. Refer to pages 210 and 211.

1. Draw a floor plan of a room in your home. Then show where each piece of furniture belongs.

You learned about multiplying a fraction by a fraction. To review, refer to pages 212 and 214.

Multiply. Write your answers in simplest terms.

2. $\frac{1}{8} \times \frac{3}{5}$

3. $\frac{3}{4} \times \frac{1}{3}$

4. $\frac{2}{7} \times \frac{3}{4}$

5. $\frac{1}{6} \times \frac{5}{7}$

6. $\frac{5}{12} \times \frac{3}{5}$

7. $\frac{4}{16} \times \frac{1}{4}$

8. $\frac{2}{11} \times \frac{3}{8}$

9. $\frac{1}{2} \times \frac{4}{8}$

10. $\frac{7}{16} \times \frac{2}{4}$

11. $\frac{8}{15} \times \frac{3}{16}$

12. $\frac{3}{8} \times \frac{4}{9}$

13. $\frac{6}{7} \times \frac{1}{2}$

14. $\frac{7}{10} \times \frac{3}{4}$

15. $\frac{2}{6} \times \frac{4}{7}$

16. $\frac{5}{8} \times \frac{9}{11}$

Give the reciprocal.

17. $\frac{3}{5}$

18. 12

19. $\frac{3}{8}$

20. $\frac{7}{9}$

21. $\frac{1}{8}$

To review what you learned about dividing a fraction by a fraction, refer to page 216.

Divide. Write your answers in simplest terms.

22. $\frac{3}{4} \div \frac{1}{3}$

23. $5 \div \frac{1}{3}$

24. $\frac{3}{5} \div \frac{2}{6}$

25. $3 \div \frac{1}{4}$

26. $4 \div \frac{5}{8}$

27. $\frac{8}{10} \div \frac{2}{3}$

28. $7 \div \frac{1}{7}$

29. $\frac{8}{9} \div \frac{1}{5}$

30. $\frac{7}{11} \div \frac{1}{2}$

31. $\frac{3}{4} \div \frac{9}{16}$

32. $8 \div \frac{3}{4}$

33. $\frac{5}{8} \div \frac{1}{4}$

34. $\frac{3}{10} \div \frac{4}{5}$

35. $\frac{5}{9} \div \frac{2}{3}$

36. $9 \div \frac{3}{5}$

You learned about using an algorithm to write a computer program. To review, refer to pages 220 and 221.

37. Why are the lines numbered in numerical order?

FOCUS   Review and test skills learned and practiced

LOOKING AHEAD

Preparing for New Skills for Chapter 16

In the next chapter you will focus on

- formulating problems about comparing ages.
- multiplying fractions and mixed numbers.
- dividing fractions and mixed numbers.
- using logic.
- how math is used in games.

Learning to multiply and divide using mixed numbers will be easier if you review multiplying and dividing fractions and renaming mixed numbers. Study the examples.

Example 1:

$$\frac{5}{6} \times \frac{5}{7} = \frac{5 \times 5}{6 \times 7} = \frac{25}{42}$$

Example 2:

$$\frac{2}{3} \times \frac{9}{14} = \frac{\cancel{2}^1}{\cancel{3}_1} \times \frac{\cancel{9}^3}{\cancel{14}_7} = \frac{3}{7}$$

Example 3:

$$\frac{2}{3} \div \frac{9}{14} = \frac{2}{3} \times \frac{14}{9} = \frac{28}{27} = 1\frac{1}{27}$$

Example 4:

$$\frac{5}{6} \div \frac{10}{11} = \frac{\cancel{5}^1}{6} \times \frac{11}{\cancel{10}_2} = \frac{11}{12}$$

Mixed numbers and whole numbers can be written as fractions.

Example 5:

$$7 = \frac{7}{1}$$

Example 6:

$$3\frac{1}{4} = \frac{(3 \times 4) + 1}{4} = \frac{13}{4}$$

PRACTICE

Multiply or divide.

1. $\frac{1}{4} \times \frac{3}{4}$
2. $\frac{3}{7} \times \frac{2}{5}$
3. $\frac{7}{8} \times \frac{4}{21}$
4. $\frac{5}{6} \times \frac{2}{15}$
5. $\frac{3}{5} \div \frac{1}{2}$
6. $\frac{7}{8} \div \frac{2}{3}$
7. $\frac{9}{20} \div \frac{7}{10}$
8. $\frac{11}{12} \div \frac{3}{4}$

Rename as fractions.

9. 17
10. 6
11. $4\frac{9}{10}$
12. $3\frac{4}{5}$

Review NUMBER skills in preparation for learning new skills.

CHAPTER 16

Multiplication and Division With Whole Numbers, Fractions, and Mixed Numbers

DATA

Ken's Age (x)	Mr. Stein's Age (y)
11	34 (this year)
12	35 (next year)
13	36
14	37
15	38
16	39
17	40
18	41
19	42
20	43

The age equation for this year:
x = Ken's age
y = Mr. Stein's age
$3x + 1 = y$

The age equation for next year:
$2x + 11 = y$

Ken noticed gray hairs in Mr. Stein's beard. "You're getting old."

"It happens," said Mr. Stein.

"How old are you?" Ken asked.

"If you can solve a simple equation, you can calculate my age."

Ken groaned. "Don't teachers ever just give easy answers?"

Mr. Stein laughed. "Not if we can help it. Now, how old are you?"

"Eleven," said Ken. "But I want to know your age."

"You will if you use this equation." Mr. Stein wrote on the blackboard:

$$3x + 1 = y$$

Ken calculated. "You're three times my age, plus one year. You're thirty-four."

"Some day, I won't even be twice your age. I'm catching up," said Mr. Stein.

Ken made a table like the one in the data column, only longer. "You are catching up, in a way. But in twelve years the age equation will stop changing." Is Ken's prediction correct?

Fractions and Mixed Numbers

There are $2\frac{2}{3}$ panels of fence left to paint. Aretha's job is to paint $\frac{1}{2}$ of it. How many panels will Aretha paint?

Multiply: $\frac{1}{2} \times 2\frac{2}{3}$.

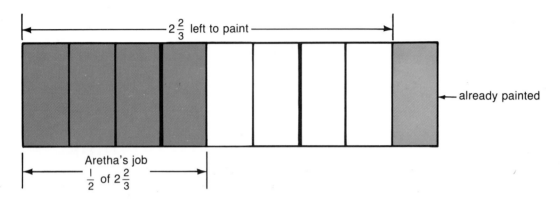

Change a mixed number to a fraction.

$$\frac{1}{2} \times 2\frac{2}{3} = \frac{1}{2} \times \frac{8}{3}$$

Find common factors. Simplify if possible.

$$\frac{1}{\underset{1}{\cancel{2}}} \times \frac{\overset{4}{\cancel{8}}}{3}$$

Multiply and rename in simplest terms.

$$\frac{1}{1} \times \frac{4}{3} = \frac{4}{3} = 1\frac{1}{3}$$

Aretha will paint $1\frac{1}{3}$ panels of the fence.

Multiply: $3\frac{1}{5} \times 4\frac{3}{8}$.

Change mixed numbers to fractions.

$$3\frac{1}{5} \times 4\frac{3}{8} = \frac{16}{5} \times \frac{35}{8}$$

Find common factors. Simplify if possible.

$$\frac{\overset{2}{\cancel{16}}}{\underset{1}{\cancel{5}}} \times \frac{\overset{7}{\cancel{35}}}{\underset{1}{\cancel{8}}}$$

Multiply and rename in simplest terms.

$$\frac{2}{1} \times \frac{7}{1} = \frac{14}{1} = 14$$

GUIDED PRACTICE

Multiply. Remember to find common factors and simplify before multiplying. Rename in simplest terms.

1. $2\frac{1}{2} \times \frac{2}{7} = \frac{\blacksquare}{2} \times \frac{2}{7} = \blacksquare$

2. $1\frac{1}{4} \times 1\frac{1}{4} = \frac{\blacksquare}{4} \times \frac{\blacksquare}{4} = \blacksquare$

3. $2\frac{1}{3} \times 9\frac{2}{5} = \frac{7}{3} \times \frac{\blacksquare}{\blacksquare} = \blacksquare$

4. $6\frac{1}{3} \times \frac{2}{3} = \frac{\blacksquare}{3} \times \frac{2}{3} = \blacksquare$

5. $\frac{3}{8} \times 12\frac{1}{4} = \frac{3}{8} \times \frac{\blacksquare}{4} = \blacksquare$

6. $\frac{1}{2} \times 6\frac{1}{10} = \frac{1}{2} \times \frac{\blacksquare}{10} = \blacksquare$

FOCUS | Use NUMBER skills to multiply fractions and mixed numbers.

PRACTICE

Multiply. Rename in simplest terms.

7. $\dfrac{2}{3} \times \dfrac{3}{4}$ **8.** $\dfrac{3}{5} \times \dfrac{15}{12}$ **9.** $3\dfrac{1}{4} \times \dfrac{3}{5}$ **10.** $\dfrac{3}{7} \times 2\dfrac{1}{3}$

11. $2\dfrac{1}{4} \times \dfrac{2}{3}$ **12.** $\dfrac{3}{8} \times 2\dfrac{1}{2}$ **13.** $5\dfrac{1}{7} \times \dfrac{3}{10}$ **14.** $\dfrac{8}{9} \times \dfrac{1}{2}$

15. $8\dfrac{1}{3} \times \dfrac{3}{5}$ **16.** $\dfrac{2}{3} \times 6\dfrac{1}{4}$ **17.** $\dfrac{9}{10} \times \dfrac{5}{7}$ **18.** $2\dfrac{4}{5} \times \dfrac{5}{8}$

19. $10\dfrac{1}{6} \times \dfrac{1}{3}$ **20.** $\dfrac{7}{11} \times 1\dfrac{12}{21}$ **21.** $\dfrac{1}{8} \times 9\dfrac{4}{5}$ **22.** $\dfrac{4}{7} \times \dfrac{21}{50}$

23. $\dfrac{3}{17} \times \dfrac{51}{60}$ **24.** $\dfrac{1}{5} \times 5\dfrac{5}{7}$ **25.** $\dfrac{2}{7} \times \dfrac{4}{11}$ **26.** $2\dfrac{3}{4} \times \dfrac{9}{10}$

27. $3\dfrac{1}{2} \times 4\dfrac{1}{5}$ **28.** $4\dfrac{2}{5} \times \dfrac{5}{6}$ ***29.** $2\dfrac{1}{3} \times \dfrac{3}{4} \times \dfrac{2}{7}$ ***30.** $4\dfrac{3}{8} \times \dfrac{4}{5} \times \dfrac{1}{2}$

31. The Davis family had $345\dfrac{1}{2}$ mi to drive on a trip. They drove $\dfrac{2}{3}$ of the way on the first day. How far did they drive?

32. On a slow day, the bakery made $\dfrac{3}{4}$ of their daily amount of bread. They only sold $\dfrac{2}{3}$ of that. What fraction of the daily amount was sold?

MIXED PRACTICE
Maintaining and Reviewing Skills

Write the reciprocals.

33. $\dfrac{3}{5}$ **34.** $\dfrac{9}{7}$ **35.** $\dfrac{1}{23}$ **36.** $\dfrac{1}{54}$

Divide.

37. $\dfrac{3}{8} \div \dfrac{1}{4}$ **38.** $\dfrac{7}{10} \div \dfrac{1}{2}$ **39.** $\dfrac{5}{9} \div \dfrac{2}{3}$ **40.** $\dfrac{9}{12} \div \dfrac{3}{4}$

41. $\dfrac{3}{4} \div \dfrac{1}{12}$ **42.** $\dfrac{5}{6} \div \dfrac{2}{3}$ **43.** $\dfrac{5}{7} \div \dfrac{10}{21}$ **44.** $\dfrac{2}{3} \div \dfrac{5}{9}$

CHALLENGE

*45. Two identical books are side by side on a shelf. Each cover is $\dfrac{1}{16}$ in. thick. Each book without its covers is $1\dfrac{3}{4}$ in. thick. How far is it from the first page of the first book to the last page of the second book?

MULTIPLICATION
Fractions and Mixed Numbers

Mr. Kostas has $10\frac{1}{2}$ yards of drapery material in stock. He cut $\frac{4}{5}$ of that to fill an order. How much material did Mr. Kostas cut?

Multiply: $\frac{4}{5} \times 10\frac{1}{2}$.

Change mixed numbers to fractions.

$$\frac{4}{5} \times 10\frac{1}{2} = \frac{4}{5} \times \frac{21}{2}$$

Find common factors and simplify.

$$\frac{\overset{2}{\cancel{4}}}{5} \times \frac{21}{\underset{1}{\cancel{2}}}$$

Multiply and rename in simplest terms.

$$\frac{42}{5} = 8\frac{2}{5}$$

Mr. Kostas needs $8\frac{2}{5}$ yards of material.

Multiply: $4\frac{7}{8} \times 1\frac{1}{3}$.

Change mixed numbers to fractions.

$$4\frac{7}{8} \times 1\frac{1}{3} = \frac{39}{8} \times \frac{4}{3}$$

Find common factors. Simplify if possible.

$$\frac{\overset{13}{\cancel{39}}}{\underset{2}{\cancel{8}}} \times \frac{\overset{1}{\cancel{4}}}{\underset{1}{\cancel{3}}}$$

Multiply and rename in simplest terms.

$$\frac{13}{2} = 6\frac{1}{2}$$

PRACTICE

Multiply. Rename in simplest terms.

1. $1\frac{2}{5} \times 1\frac{3}{8}$ 2. $2\frac{3}{4} \times 2\frac{8}{9}$ 3. $8\frac{1}{4} \times 1\frac{1}{3}$ 4. $\frac{6}{7} \times 2\frac{1}{3}$ 5. $5\frac{2}{3} \times \frac{3}{4}$

6. $2\frac{1}{2} \times 1\frac{5}{6}$ 7. $7\frac{3}{8} \times \frac{1}{4}$ 8. $25\frac{1}{3} \times \frac{1}{2}$ 9. $\frac{5}{8} \times 4\frac{4}{7}$ 10. $3\frac{1}{2} \times \frac{2}{3}$

11. $7\frac{3}{7} \times 1\frac{1}{2}$ 12. $\frac{1}{4} \times 12\frac{1}{2}$ 13. $\frac{2}{3} \times 6\frac{2}{3}$ *14. $\frac{1}{2} \times \frac{2}{3} \times 2\frac{1}{3}$ *15. $3\frac{1}{4} \times \frac{1}{4} \times \frac{1}{2}$

MIXED PRACTICE
Maintaining and Reviewing Skills

Write the mean for each set of numbers.

16. 49, 57, 61, 59, 58, 52

17. 38, 66, 54, 42, 62, 38

18. 136, 144, 215, 172, 225, 164

19. 140, 138, 159, 157, 150, 138

FOCUS   Use NUMBER skills to multiply fractions and mixed numbers.

APPLICATION
Using Patterns

In 1617, the great Scottish mathematician John Napier described a shortcut for doing multiplication. His multiplication table was put onto ivory rods. People nicknamed the rods Napier's Bones. This is how the chart works.

Each "bone" on the chart is the product of the row number × the column number. Look at the "bone" for Row 3, Column 5. It looks like [1/5]

The product of 3 × 5 = 15.

Napier's Bones	Column								
Row	1	2	3	4	5	6	7	8	9
0	0/0	0/0	0/0	0/0	0/0	0/0	0/0	0/0	0/0
1	0/1	0/2	0/3	0/4	0/5	0/6	0/7	0/8	0/9
2	0/2	0/4	0/6	0/8	1/0	1/2	1/4	1/6	1/8
3	0/3	0/6	0/9	1/2	1/5	1/8	2/1	2/4	2/7
4	0/4	0/8	1/2	1/6	2/0	2/4	2/8	3/2	3/6
5	0/5	1/0	1/5	2/0	2/5	3/0	3/5	4/0	4/5
6	0/6	1/2	1/8	2/4	3/0	3/6	4/2	4/8	5/4
7	0/7	1/4	2/1	2/8	3/5	4/2	4/9	5/6	6/3
8	0/8	1/6	2/4	3/2	4/0	4/8	5/6	6/4	7/2
9	0/9	1/8	2/7	3/6	4/5	5/4	6/3	7/2	8/1

Here is the way to use Napier's Bones to find 27 × 59.

Look at Row 2. Find the bone under Column 5 and the bone under Column 9.

Look at Row 7. Find the bone under Column 5 and the bone under Column 9.

Stack the bones as shown.

Add the numbers diagonally, from right to left.

Check the answer, 1,593, by solving the problem.

Use Napier's Bones to find the product for each.

20. 23 × 14   **21.** 56 × 73   **22.** 80 × 67   **23.** 9 × 87

24. 125 × 32   **25.** 37 × 42   **26.** 92 × 35   ***27.** 2,138 × 409

Use PATTERNS to multiply with Napier's Bones method.

Fractions and Mixed Numbers

It takes Bill $\frac{3}{4}$ of an hour to assemble a sailboat. How many sailboats can he assemble in $4\frac{1}{2}$ hours?

Divide: $4\frac{1}{2} \div \frac{3}{4}$.

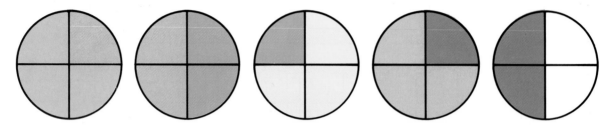

Write the mixed number as a fraction.

$4\frac{1}{2} \div \frac{3}{4} = \frac{9}{2} \div \frac{3}{4}$

Write the reciprocal of the divisor.

$\frac{9}{2} \times \frac{4}{3}$

$\frac{4}{3}$ is the reciprocal of $\frac{3}{4}$

Find common factors. Simplify if possible.

$\frac{\overset{3}{\cancel{9}}}{\underset{1}{\cancel{2}}} \times \frac{\overset{2}{\cancel{4}}}{\underset{1}{\cancel{3}}}$

Multiply and rename in simplest terms.

$\frac{3}{1} \times \frac{2}{1} = \frac{6}{1} = 6$

There are 6 "$\frac{3}{4}$" in $4\frac{1}{2}$ hours.

So, Bill can make 6 sailboats in $4\frac{1}{2}$ hours.

Divide: $4\frac{3}{5} \div 1\frac{4}{5}$.

Write the mixed numbers as fractions.

$4\frac{3}{5} \div 1\frac{4}{5} = \frac{23}{5} \div \frac{9}{5}$

Write the reciprocal of the divisor.

$\frac{23}{5} \times \frac{5}{9}$

$\frac{5}{9}$ is the reciprocal of $\frac{9}{5}$

Find common factors. Simplify if possible.

$\frac{23}{\underset{1}{\cancel{5}}} \times \frac{\overset{1}{\cancel{5}}}{9}$

Multiply and rename in simplest terms.

$\frac{23}{1} \times \frac{1}{9} = \frac{23}{9} = 2\frac{5}{9}$

GUIDED PRACTICE

Divide. Remember to find the reciprocal and common factors. Then simplify and rename in simplest terms.

1. $8\frac{1}{2} \div \frac{2}{3} = \frac{17}{2} \div \frac{2}{3} = \frac{17}{2} \times \frac{\blacksquare}{\blacksquare} = \blacksquare$

2. $2\frac{2}{5} \div \frac{2}{5} = \frac{12}{5} \div \frac{2}{5} = \frac{12}{5} \times \frac{\blacksquare}{\blacksquare} = \blacksquare$

3. $3\frac{3}{4} \div \frac{5}{7} = \frac{\blacksquare}{\blacksquare} \div \frac{5}{7} = \frac{\blacksquare}{\blacksquare} \times \frac{\blacksquare}{\blacksquare} = \blacksquare$

4. $2\frac{2}{3} \div \frac{1}{4} = \frac{\blacksquare}{\blacksquare} \div \frac{1}{4} = \frac{\blacksquare}{\blacksquare} \times \frac{\blacksquare}{\blacksquare} = \blacksquare$

FOCUS | Use NUMBER skills to divide fractions and mixed numbers.

PRACTICE

Divide.

5. $3\frac{1}{2} \div \frac{1}{2}$ **6.** $\frac{2}{3} \div 1\frac{2}{3}$ **7.** $\frac{15}{16} \div 2\frac{1}{8}$ **8.** $7\frac{1}{2} \div 4\frac{1}{2}$

9. $\frac{3}{4} \div 5\frac{1}{2}$ **10.** $3\frac{1}{7} \div 4\frac{1}{7}$ **11.** $4\frac{1}{8} \div 2\frac{1}{4}$ **12.** $10\frac{1}{4} \div 2\frac{3}{4}$

13. $2\frac{1}{2} \div \frac{1}{3}$ **14.** $3\frac{2}{3} \div \frac{3}{8}$ **15.** $5\frac{6}{7} \div \frac{4}{7}$ **16.** $7\frac{3}{9} \div \frac{1}{3}$

17. $\frac{3}{4} \div 1\frac{1}{2}$ **18.** $\frac{5}{6} \div 2\frac{1}{6}$ **19.** $\frac{4}{5} \div 3\frac{1}{3}$ **20.** $\frac{5}{6} \div 2\frac{5}{6}$

21. $3\frac{2}{3} \div 2\frac{1}{6}$ **22.** $5\frac{4}{7} \div 4\frac{1}{3}$ **23.** $8\frac{3}{5} \div 2\frac{1}{3}$ **24.** $9\frac{5}{8} \div 2\frac{3}{6}$

25. $6\frac{2}{3} \div \frac{2}{3}$ **26.** $8\frac{1}{8} \div \frac{7}{8}$ **27.** $5\frac{1}{2} \div \frac{6}{7}$ **28.** $8\frac{3}{10} \div \frac{83}{84}$

29. $2\frac{5}{8} \div 2\frac{1}{3}$ **30.** $1\frac{3}{8} \div 5\frac{1}{2}$ **31.** $2\frac{2}{3} \div 1\frac{1}{6}$ **32.** $3\frac{3}{4} \div 1\frac{1}{9}$

33. $5\frac{5}{7} \div 2\frac{1}{2}$ **34.** $2\frac{1}{4} \div \frac{2}{3}$ **35.** $3\frac{1}{2} \div 2\frac{3}{4}$ **36.** $1\frac{1}{3} \div \frac{1}{4}$

MIXED PRACTICE
Maintaining and Reviewing Skills

Add or subtract. Simplify answers.

37. $\begin{array}{r} 25\frac{1}{3} \\ + 42\frac{5}{7} \\ \hline \end{array}$ **38.** $\begin{array}{r} 38\frac{7}{8} \\ + 26\frac{15}{16} \\ \hline \end{array}$ **39.** $\begin{array}{r} 46\frac{7}{9} \\ - 22\frac{1}{3} \\ \hline \end{array}$ **40.** $\begin{array}{r} 25\frac{1}{4} \\ - 15\frac{2}{3} \\ \hline \end{array}$

Solve.
Which operations did you use?

41. Mrs. Long bought $4\frac{1}{2}$ yards of blue ribbon, and $5\frac{1}{3}$ yards of red ribbon. She also bought white ribbon which was 2 times as long as the sum of the length of the blue and red ribbons. How much white ribbon did she buy?

CHALLENGE

Find the next three numbers in the sequence.

*42. $\frac{1}{3}, \frac{2}{3}, 1\frac{1}{3}, 2\frac{2}{3}, 5\frac{1}{3}, 10\frac{2}{3}$, ▪, ▪, ▪   ***43.** $1, \frac{1}{2}, \frac{1}{4}, \frac{1}{8}$, ▪, ▪, ▪

DIVISION
Fractions and Mixed Numbers

Divide: $6\frac{3}{4} \div \frac{3}{5}$.

Write the mixed number as a fraction.	**Write the reciprocal of the divisor.**	**Find common factors. Simplify if possible.**	**Multiply and rename in simplest terms.**
$6\frac{3}{4} \div \frac{3}{5} = \frac{27}{4} \div \frac{3}{5}$	$\frac{27}{4} \times \frac{5}{3}$	$\frac{\overset{9}{\cancel{27}}}{4} \times \frac{5}{\underset{1}{\cancel{3}}}$	$\frac{45}{4} = 11\frac{1}{4}$

Divide: $5\frac{1}{3} \div 2\frac{2}{3}$.

Write mixed numbers as fractions.	**Write the reciprocal of the divisor.**	**Find common factors. Simplify if possible.**	**Multiply and rename in simplest terms.**
$5\frac{1}{3} \div 2\frac{2}{3} = \frac{16}{3} \div \frac{8}{3}$	$\frac{16}{3} \times \frac{3}{8}$	$\frac{\overset{2}{\cancel{16}}}{\underset{1}{\cancel{3}}} \times \frac{\overset{1}{\cancel{3}}}{\underset{1}{\cancel{8}}}$	$\frac{2}{1} = 2$

PRACTICE

Divide. Rename in simplest terms.

1. $2\frac{1}{3} \div \frac{1}{3}$ **2.** $3\frac{4}{5} \div 2\frac{1}{5}$ **3.** $1\frac{3}{8} \div \frac{1}{4}$ **4.** $5\frac{5}{7} \div \frac{3}{7}$

5. $8\frac{1}{2} \div \frac{3}{4}$ **6.** $\frac{7}{8} \div 1\frac{2}{3}$ **7.** $5\frac{1}{5} \div 2\frac{1}{2}$ **8.** $4\frac{1}{5} \div 2\frac{5}{8}$

9. $\frac{9}{10} \div 2\frac{1}{6}$ **10.** $\frac{10}{15} \div 5\frac{1}{5}$ **11.** $23\frac{1}{3} \div 1\frac{3}{7}$ **12.** $1\frac{6}{7} \div \frac{1}{7}$

MIXED PRACTICE
Maintaining and Reviewing Skills

Find the measure of each missing angle.

13.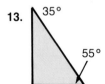
14.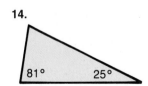
15.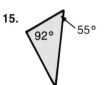
16.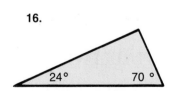

17. Angle A has a measure of $\frac{2}{3}$ the total angle measure of a triangle. What does $\angle A$ measure?

FOCUS | Use NUMBER skills to divide fractions and mixed numbers.

Using Logic

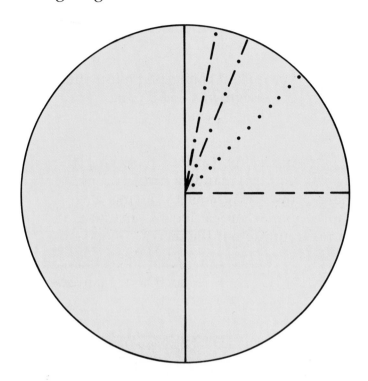

Study the circle above.

18. If one diameter is drawn across the circle, how many parts will there be?

19. What is each part called in fractional terms?

20. If one part is cut into two equal parts, what is the new fractional name for each new part?

21. If one of these parts is cut into two equal parts, what is the fractional name for each of the new parts?

22. What pattern do you notice when studying the denominators of the parts?

23. Imagine you continue cutting each part in two. Write the next 5 fractional names for each of the new parts.

*24. If you had instruments precise enough to cut forever, what is the smallest part you would eventually have?

*25. What is the largest number of equal parts into which you can cut the circle?

Use LOGIC to explore the density of fractions.

The Tangram Puzzle

Tangrams have been amusing people for almost 4,000 years. Napoleon is said to have spent many hours working with a set of tangram pieces during his years of exile.

A tangram is made by cutting a square into seven sections. These sections can be arranged and rearranged in many ways to form different pictures.

Here is a square with the tangram pieces numbered. You can see how the pieces have been rearranged to form the picture of a boat.

square and connecting midpoints of the line segments, you can construct a tangram of your own.

Tangrams are best made out of oaktag or cardboard so that they are easy to handle. You can make your own tangrams by taking a square of paper or cardboard, marking it, and cutting out the pieces.

This square has been marked A, B, C, D, E, F so that we can identify the lines to be drawn.

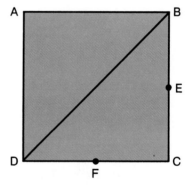

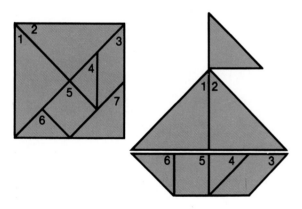

A, B, C, and D are the corners of the square. The line segment from B to D is a **diagonal**. It connects the two opposite corners of the square. Point E is halfway between B and C. Point E is called the middle point or midpoint of line segment BC.

Point F is the midpoint of line segment CD. By carefully dividing the

CRITICAL THINKING

1. What is the geometric shape of each piece of the tangram?

2. Why can we say that a midpoint bisects a line segment?

3. How do the two triangles formed by diagonal BD compare in size?

4. Why might we say that a diagonal bisects a square?

FOCUS Use GEOMETRY to understand the tangram puzzle.

LOOKING BACK
Reviewing and Testing Chapter 16

In Chapter 16 you formulated problems about age differences. Refer to pages 224 and 225.

1. Write an equation showing the difference between your age and your mother's age.

To review what you learned about multiplication of fractions and mixed numbers, refer to page 226.

Multiply. Write your answers in simplest terms.

2. $\frac{1}{3} \times \frac{9}{16}$ 3. $3\frac{1}{3} \times \frac{9}{10}$ 4. $2\frac{1}{7} \times 3\frac{1}{3}$ 5. $\frac{4}{9} \times \frac{3}{8}$ 6. $\frac{1}{6} \times \frac{2}{3}$

7. $\frac{1}{5} \times 5\frac{1}{10}$ 8. $\frac{5}{10} \times \frac{3}{4}$ 9. $4\frac{1}{4} \times 1\frac{1}{9}$ 10. $2\frac{11}{12} \times \frac{7}{10}$ 11. $3\frac{2}{5} \times \frac{5}{17}$

12. $\frac{3}{7} \times 4\frac{1}{9}$ 13. $1\frac{19}{20} \times 3\frac{4}{5}$ 14. $3\frac{11}{14} \times 7\frac{1}{8}$ 15. $3\frac{1}{2} \times 4\frac{1}{7}$ 16. $6\frac{2}{4} \times 4\frac{2}{5}$

17. Diane has $11\frac{1}{3}$ yards of material. She uses $\frac{3}{4}$ of that for a dress. How much material does she use?

18. There are $3\frac{1}{6}$ fences to paint. If $\frac{2}{5}$ of the fences get painted, how many fences are left to paint?

You learned about division of fractions and mixed numbers. To review, refer to page 230.

Divide. Write your answers in simplest terms.

19. $4\frac{1}{3} \div \frac{1}{4}$ 20. $2\frac{1}{8} \div \frac{6}{7}$ 21. $3\frac{1}{4} \div \frac{2}{5}$ 22. $\frac{1}{3} \div \frac{2}{3}$ 23. $\frac{4}{5} \div \frac{1}{10}$

24. $2\frac{2}{3} \div 1\frac{1}{6}$ 25. $4\frac{4}{7} \div 3\frac{1}{3}$ 26. $7\frac{3}{5} \div 2\frac{1}{4}$ 27. $5\frac{6}{7} \div 4\frac{1}{8}$ 28. $2\frac{3}{4} \div 1\frac{5}{6}$

You learned about the tangram puzzle. To review, refer to pages 234 and 235.

29. How many different geometric shapes make up the pieces of the tangram puzzle? What are they?

> **In the next chapter you will focus on**
>
> - formulating problems about a school orientation.
> - changing fractions to decimals.
> - changing mixed numbers to decimals.
>
> - using a problem solving strategy.
> - changing decimals to fractions or mixed numbers.
> - finding decimal-fraction equivalents.
> - how math is used in science.

Finding decimal-fraction equivalents will be easier if you review dividing whole numbers and simplifying fractions. Study the examples.

To divide a whole number by a greater whole number:

- Write a decimal point and one or more zeros in the dividend. Remember, $2 = 2.0 = 2.00 = 2.000$, and so on.
- Place the decimal point in the quotient directly above the one in the dividend.
- Divide as if you were dividing with whole numbers.

Example 1:

$$2 \div 5 \rightarrow 5\overline{)2.0}$$

$$\begin{array}{r} 0.4 \\ 5\overline{)2.0} \\ -2\,0 \end{array}$$

Write a decimal point and one zero.

Example 2:

$$3 \div 8 \rightarrow 8\overline{)3.000}$$

$$\begin{array}{r} 0.375 \\ 8\overline{)3.000} \\ -2\,4 \\ \hline 60 \\ -56 \\ \hline 40 \\ -40 \\ \hline \end{array}$$

To simplify a fraction, divide both the numerator and denominator by the GCF of the two numbers.

Example 3:

$$\frac{5}{10} = \frac{5 \div 5}{10 \div 5} = \frac{1}{2}$$

The GCF of 5 and 10 is 5.

Example 4:

$$\frac{24}{40} = \frac{24 \div 8}{40 \div 8} = \frac{3}{5}$$

The GCF of 24 and 40 is 8.

PRACTICE

Divide.

1. $5\overline{)1}$ **2.** $10\overline{)8}$ **3.** $4\overline{)3}$

Simplify each fraction.

4. $\frac{10}{18}$ **5.** $\frac{27}{60}$ **6.** $\frac{35}{100}$

Review NUMBER skills in preparation for learning new skills.

Write the letter of the correct answer.

Find the GCF (Greatest Common Factor) for each pair.

1. 12 and 16   **A.** 4   **B.** 8
                   C. 12   **D.** 16

2. 75 and 3   **E.** 15   **F.** 25
                   G. 3   **H.** 5

Find the LCM (Least Common Multiple) for each pair.

3. 3 and 8   **A.** 15   **B.** 24
                 C. 11   **D.** 12

4. 10 and 13   **E.** 23   **F.** 26
                   G. 130   **H.** 113

Find the missing numerator or denominator.

5. $\frac{2}{6} = \frac{\blacksquare}{15}$ **A.** 7   **B.** 5
                                                 C. 13   **D.** 3

6. $\frac{3}{8} = \frac{9}{\blacksquare}$ **E.** 27   **F.** 4
                                               G. 3   **H.** 24

Use the LCD to find the greatest fraction.

7. **A.** $\frac{1}{2}$ **B.** $\frac{2}{5}$ **C.** $\frac{5}{10}$ **D.** $\frac{5}{8}$

8. **E.** $\frac{3}{10}$ **F.** $\frac{3}{4}$ **G.** $\frac{19}{24}$ **H.** $\frac{30}{40}$

9. **A.** $\frac{9}{12}$ **B.** $\frac{9}{15}$ **C.** $\frac{10}{20}$ **D.** $\frac{1}{3}$

Add or subtract. Then simplify.

10. $\frac{1}{3} + \frac{1}{2}$ **E.** $\frac{2}{5}$ **F.** $\frac{5}{6}$ **G.** $\frac{1}{6}$ **H.** $\frac{3}{2}$

11. $1\frac{3}{5} + 2\frac{3}{5}$ **A.** $3\frac{6}{10}$ **B.** $\frac{20}{5}$ **C.** $4\frac{1}{5}$ **D.** $10\frac{2}{5}$

12. $3\frac{1}{3} + 4\frac{1}{4}$ **E.** $7\frac{2}{7}$ **F.** $8\frac{1}{7}$ **G.** $7\frac{2}{12}$ **H.** $7\frac{7}{12}$

13. $\frac{8}{12} - \frac{1}{2}$ **A.** $\frac{1}{6}$ **B.** $\frac{7}{10}$ **C.** $\frac{9}{14}$ **D.** $\frac{1}{3}$

14. $6 - 2\frac{1}{7}$ **E.** $3\frac{2}{7}$ **F.** $4\frac{1}{7}$ **G.** $3\frac{6}{7}$ **H.** $\frac{30}{7}$

15. $5\frac{2}{3} - 2\frac{1}{2}$ **A.** $3\frac{1}{5}$ **B.** $3\frac{1}{2}$ **C.** $2\frac{5}{6}$ **D.** $3\frac{1}{6}$

16. $9\frac{2}{5} - 6\frac{3}{4}$ **E.** $2\frac{13}{20}$ **F.** $3\frac{1}{5}$ **G.** $2\frac{1}{2}$ **H.** $2\frac{3}{4}$

Find the area of each figure.

17.

16 cm
10 cm

A. 160 cm²   **B.** 300 cm²
C. 52 cm²   **D.** 170 cm²

18. $l = 16$ cm, $w = 12$ cm

E. 172 cm²   **F.** 180 cm²
G. 38 cm²   **H.** 192 cm²

19. $l = 9$ m, $w = 8$ m

A. 17 m²   **B.** 72 m²
C. 170 m²   **D.** 80 m²

20.

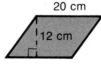

20 cm
12 cm

E. 120 cm²   **F.** 320 cm²
G. 240 cm²   **H.** 60 cm²

| FOCUS | Review concepts and skills taught in Chapters 9–16. |

Use your protractor to find the measure of each angle in triangle *EFG*.

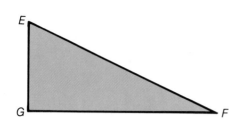

21. m∠*E*   **A.** 75°   **B.** 65°
         C. 90°   **D.** 100°

22. m∠*F*   **E.** 30°   **F.** 15°
         G. 25°   **H.** 10°

23. m∠*G*   **A.** 90°   **B.** 180°
         C. 100°   **D.** 45°

Without using a protractor, find the measure of the angles for each parallelogram.

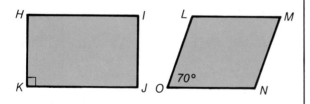

24. m∠*I*   **E.** 180°   **F.** 360°
         G. 45°   **H.** 90°

25. m∠*J*   **A.** 90°   **B.** 105°
         C. 72°   **D.** 80°

26. m∠*L*   **E.** 70°   **F.** 90°
         G. 160°   **H.** 110°

27. m∠*M*   **A.** 80°   **B.** 70°
         C. 45°   **D.** 60°

Find the mean, mode, range, and median for (23, 25, 25, 28, 34, 37, 38).

28. mode   **E.** 25   **F.** 30   **G.** 34   **H.** 28

29. mean   **A.** 28   **B.** 30   **C.** 31   **D.** 25

30. median   **E.** 30   **F.** 28   **G.** 31   **H.** 38

31. range   **A.** 38   **B.** 28   **C.** 30   **D.** 15

Use the frequency table to find the range and mode.

Score	Tally	Frequency
18		1
21				2
23						5
26					3

32. mode   **E.** 23   **F.** 8   **G.** 22   **H.** 21

33. range   **A.** 26   **B.** 18   **C.** 8   **D.** 4

Multiply or divide. Simplify.

34. $\frac{5}{6} \times \frac{6}{12}$ **E.** $\frac{5}{12}$ **F.** $\frac{11}{72}$ **G.** $\frac{11}{12}$ **H.** $\frac{5}{18}$

35. $\frac{3}{4} \div \frac{2}{8}$ **A.** $\frac{6}{24}$ **B.** $\frac{5}{12}$ **C.** $\frac{3}{16}$ **D.** 3

36. $6 \div \frac{2}{3}$ **E.** $\frac{12}{3}$ **F.** $\frac{1}{2}$ **G.** 9   **H.** 6

37. $2\frac{1}{3} \times \frac{3}{4}$ **A.** $1\frac{1}{2}$ **B.** $\frac{2}{4}$ **C.** $\frac{2}{3}$ **D.** $1\frac{3}{4}$

38. $\frac{1}{6} \times 6\frac{4}{5}$ **E.** $1\frac{1}{6}$ **F.** $1\frac{2}{15}$ **G.** $2\frac{6}{15}$ **H.** $1\frac{1}{8}$

39. $8\frac{1}{2} \div 3\frac{3}{4}$ **A.** $2\frac{4}{15}$ **B.** $2\frac{1}{2}$ **C.** $2\frac{2}{5}$ **D.** $3\frac{2}{15}$

40. $5\frac{5}{10} \div \frac{25}{30}$ **E.** $6\frac{1}{5}$ **F.** $5\frac{3}{4}$ **G.** $6\frac{3}{5}$ **H.** $6\frac{3}{4}$

Write the letter of the correct answer.

Identify the place value of each underlined digit.

1. 581,322
   A. hundreds   B. thousands
   C. millions   D. ten thousands

2. 69,387,403
   E. billions   F. ten thousands
   G. millions   H. ten millions

Round to the nearest hundred thousand.

3. 449,800   A. 400,000   B. 500,000
              C. 450,000   D. 449,000

4. 862,111   E. 800,000   F. 860,000
              G. 900,000   H. 870,000

Multiply or divide.

5.   23   A. 276   B. 45
   × 12   C. 236   D. 190

6.   326   E. 3,521   F. 35,210
   × 108   G. 35,208 H. 4,340

7. 6) 246   A. 141   B. 14
             C. 36   D. 41

8. 13) 351   E. 28   F. 27
             G. 270   H. 17

9. 107) 1,926   A. 28   B. 180
                C. 18   D. 81

Find the GCF (Greatest Common Factor) for each pair.

10. 15 and 24   E. 2   F. 3
                G. 8   H. 5

11. 17 and 51   A. 17   B. 1
                C. 34   D. 51

12. 23 and 67   E. 18   F. 67
                G. 23   H. 1

Find the LCM (Least Common Multiple) for each pair.

13. 2 and 9   A. 11   B. 36
               C. 18   D. 4

14. 8 and 6   E. 48   F. 14
               G. 24   H. 16

Add or subtract. Then simplify.

15. $\frac{3}{8} + \frac{1}{8}$ A. $\frac{1}{2}$ B. $\frac{2}{8}$ C. $\frac{5}{8}$ D. $\frac{1}{4}$

16. $\frac{2}{4} + \frac{1}{3}$ E. $\frac{2}{3}$ F. $\frac{5}{6}$ G. $\frac{11}{12}$ H. $\frac{3}{7}$

17. $1\frac{6}{9} + 1\frac{8}{9}$ A. $3\frac{1}{9}$ B. $2\frac{2}{9}$ C. $3\frac{5}{9}$ D. $3\frac{7}{9}$

18. $3\frac{9}{10} + 4\frac{2}{5}$ E. $8\frac{3}{10}$ F. $7\frac{7}{15}$ G. $8\frac{1}{15}$ H. $7\frac{9}{25}$

19. $\frac{5}{8} - \frac{1}{4}$ A. $\frac{1}{2}$ B. $\frac{2}{8}$ C. $\frac{4}{4}$ D. $\frac{3}{8}$

20. $5 - 3\frac{6}{10}$ E. $2\frac{4}{10}$ F. $\frac{4}{5}$ G. $1\frac{2}{5}$ H. $1\frac{6}{10}$

21. $8\frac{4}{5} - 2\frac{2}{3}$ A. $6\frac{10}{15}$ B. $6\frac{2}{15}$ C. $5\frac{9}{15}$ D. $6\frac{1}{5}$

22. $9\frac{1}{3} - \frac{5}{6}$ E. $8\frac{1}{2}$ F. $9\frac{1}{6}$ G. $8\frac{5}{6}$ H. $9\frac{1}{12}$

FOCUS   Review concepts and skills taught in Chapters 2–16.

Multiply or divide. Then simplify.

23. $\frac{3}{4} \times \frac{1}{2}$ **A.** $\frac{1}{4}$ **B.** $\frac{4}{6}$ **C.** $\frac{3}{8}$ **D.** $\frac{4}{8}$

24. $\frac{2}{5} \times \frac{6}{10}$ **E.** $\frac{6}{25}$ **F.** $\frac{8}{15}$ **G.** $\frac{12}{15}$ **H.** $\frac{3}{4}$

25. $2\frac{3}{8} \times \frac{2}{3}$ **A.** $4\frac{1}{4}$ **B.** $1\frac{7}{12}$ **C.** $1\frac{9}{12}$ **D.** $1\frac{6}{24}$

26. $\frac{3}{7} \times 4\frac{7}{14}$ **E.** $2\frac{3}{10}$ **F.** 7 **G.** $2\frac{1}{2}$ **H.** $1\frac{13}{14}$

27. $\frac{4}{5} \div \frac{2}{10}$ **A.** $\frac{4}{25}$ **B.** 3 **C.** $\frac{2}{5}$ **D.** 4

28. $\frac{8}{9} \div \frac{8}{6}$ **E.** $\frac{64}{54}$ **F.** $\frac{2}{3}$ **G.** $\frac{16}{15}$ **H.** $\frac{24}{35}$

29. $9 \div \frac{2}{3}$ **A.** $13\frac{1}{3}$ **B.** $\frac{6}{9}$ **C.** $13\frac{1}{2}$ **D.** 6

30. $7\frac{1}{2} \div 1\frac{5}{7}$ **E.** $4\frac{3}{8}$ **F.** $7\frac{3}{7}$ **G.** $4\frac{7}{8}$ **H.** $7\frac{1}{3}$

Find the area of each rectangle or parallelogram.

31.

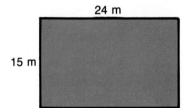

24 m

15 m

A. 78 m²   **B.** 39 m²   **C.** 360 m²   **D.** 120 m²

32. $l = 7$ ft, $w = 4$ ft

E. 32 ft²   **F.** 28 ft²   **G.** 22 ft²   **H.** 11 ft²

33.

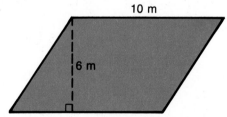

10 m

6 m

A. 60 m²   **B.** 30 m²   **C.** 16 m²   **D.** 32 m²

34. $b = 15$ in., $h = 6$ in.

E. 90 in.   **F.** 21 in.²   **G.** 90 in.²   **H.** 42 in.²

Find the area of each triangle.

35.

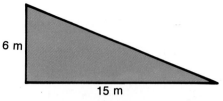

6 m

15 m

A. 90 m²   **B.** 45 m²   **C.** 21 m²   **D.** 42 m²

36.

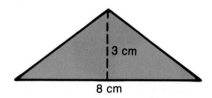

3 cm

8 cm

E. 12 cm²   **F.** 24 cm²   **G.** 11 cm²   **H.** 16 cm²

37. $b = 13$ in., $h = 4$ in.

A. 52 in²   **B.** 17 in²   **C.** 26 in²   **D.** 34 in²

38. $b = 1$ yd, $h = 2$ yd

E. 3 yd²   **F.** 1 yd²   **G.** 4 yd²   **H.** 6 yd²

Find the mean, mode, range, and median for each set of numbers.

{8, 9, 9, 11, 13}

39. mean   **A.** 8   **B.** 13   **C.** 9   **D.** 10

40. mode   **E.** 9   **F.** 11   **G.** 10   **H.** 8

41. range   **A.** 13   **B.** 5   **C.** 18   **D.** 11

42. median   **E.** 9   **F.** 11   **G.** 5   **H.** 13

{75, 76, 81, 82, 85, 85, 90}

43. mean   **A.** 80   **B.** 83   **C.** 82   **D.** 85

44. mode   **E.** 82   **F.** 90   **G.** 15   **H.** 85

45. range   **A.** 15   **B.** 82   **C.** 20   **D.** 85

46. median   **E.** 81   **F.** 80   **G.** 82   **H.** 90

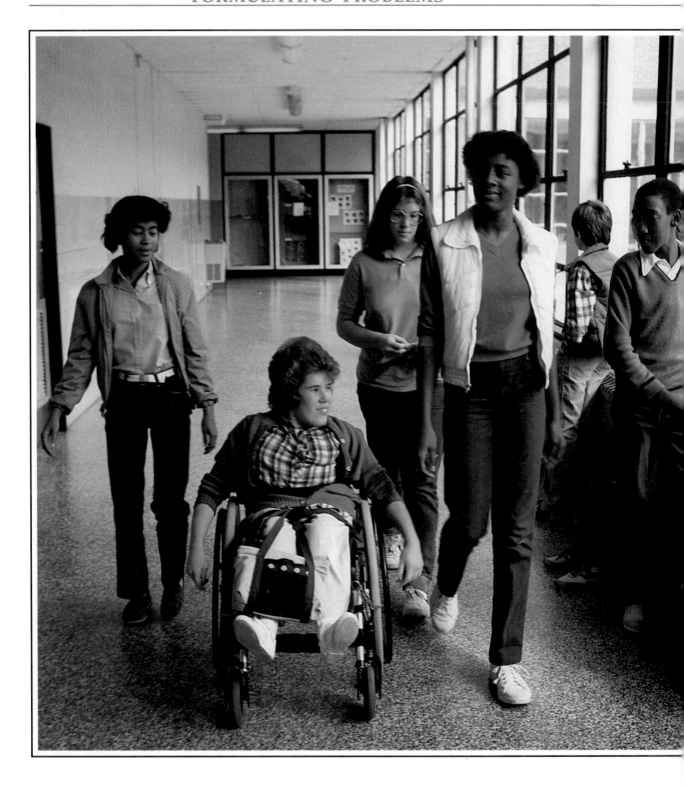

Formulate problems using photo, data, and text.

CHAPTER 17

Fractions, Mixed Numbers, and Decimals

DATA

Event	Orientation
Place	Wilson Middle School
Date	June 10
Time	9:30 AM–2:30 PM
Number of students in incoming class	120
Number of student guides	15
Length of class period	40 min
Wilson school enrollment	490

Each student receives
    Name tag
    Information packet
    Lunch ticket

Activities planned so far
    Introduction
    Tour of building
    Lunch
    Visiting classes
    Speeches and discussions

Starting out at a new school is always a little confusing, especially when it means changing from elementary to middle school. The Student Council at Wilson Middle School wants to make the transition for new students as smooth as possible. They are planning a day-long orientation for students who will be sixth graders next September. They have talked a lot about what they want to include in the day, but there are still many decisions to be made. Planning a day for 120 people is a challenge.

What would be the best way to plan an orientation for students coming into your school? Make a list of the things that are most important for a new student to know. Then use these ideas to plan a program that is both informative and enjoyable.

Changing Fractions to Decimals

Every fraction can be written as an equivalent decimal.

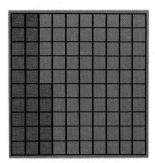

$\frac{1}{4}$ or $\frac{25}{100}$ of the square is shaded.
0.25 of the square is shaded.

To write a fraction as a decimal, divide the numerator by the denominator.

$$\frac{1}{4} \rightarrow 4\overline{)1.00} \quad \begin{array}{r} 0.25 \\ \underline{8} \\ 20 \\ \underline{20} \\ 0 \end{array}$$ ← zero remainder

0.25 is a **terminating decimal**. The digits in the quotient do not repeat.

$$\frac{5}{11} \rightarrow 11\overline{)5.0000} \quad \begin{array}{r} 0.4545... \\ \underline{44} \\ 60 \\ \underline{55} \\ 50 \\ \underline{44} \\ 60 \\ \underline{55} \\ 5 \end{array}$$ ← remainder

0.4545 . . . is a **repeating decimal**. The digits in the quotient keep repeating. Place a bar over the digits that repeat.

0.4545 . . . = $0.\overline{45}$

GUIDED PRACTICE

Write each fraction as a decimal. Label *repeating* or *terminating*.

1. $\frac{2}{5} \rightarrow \quad 5\overline{)2.0} \quad 0.\blacksquare$

2. $\frac{5}{8} \rightarrow \quad 8\overline{)5.000} \quad 0.\blacksquare\blacksquare\blacksquare$

3. $\frac{2}{9} \rightarrow \quad 9\overline{)2.00} \quad 0.\blacksquare\blacksquare$

4. $\frac{1}{3}$

5. $\frac{5}{6}$

6. $\frac{3}{8}$

7. $\frac{4}{5}$

8. $\frac{7}{9}$

FOCUS — Use NUMBER skills to change fractions to decimals.

PRACTICE

Tell which are repeating decimals and which are terminating decimals. Write repeating decimals using a bar.

9. 0.15   **10.** 0.8   **11.** 0.005   **12.** 0.6666 . . .   **13.** 0.232323 . . .

14. 0.253   **15.** 0.7999 . . .   **16.** 0.4268   **17.** 0.0922   **18.** 0.012012012 . . .

Change each fraction to a decimal. Use a bar to show repeating decimals.

19. $\frac{3}{4}$ **20.** $\frac{3}{5}$ **21.** $\frac{2}{3}$ **22.** $\frac{7}{10}$ **23.** $\frac{5}{9}$

24. $\frac{9}{20}$ **25.** $\frac{1}{11}$ **26.** $\frac{7}{8}$ **27.** $\frac{11}{16}$ **28.** $\frac{23}{25}$

29. $\frac{1}{6}$ **30.** $\frac{5}{22}$ **31.** $\frac{3}{11}$ **32.** $\frac{7}{12}$ **33.** $\frac{1}{5}$

34. $\frac{9}{11}$ **35.** $\frac{2}{30}$ **36.** $\frac{5}{3}$ **37.** $\frac{6}{11}$ **38.** $\frac{5}{6}$

39. $\frac{4}{9}$ **40.** $\frac{1}{2}$ **41.** $\frac{7}{20}$ **42.** $\frac{3}{8}$ **43.** $\frac{7}{9}$

MIXED PRACTICE
Maintaining and Reviewing Skills

Write the standard decimal.

44. Four hundred two thousandths   **45.** Three tenths

46. Eight and seventy-six thousandths   **47.** Twenty-two hundredths

48. Three thousand five hundred fifty-nine ten-thousandths

CHALLENGE

*****49.** Which figure is different?

A.
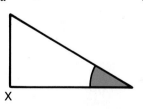

B.
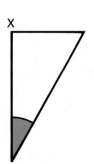

C.
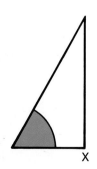

D.
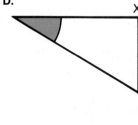

MIXED NUMBERS AND DECIMALS
Changing Mixed Numbers to Decimals

Write $2\frac{3}{4}$ as a decimal.

Rename $\frac{3}{4}$ as a decimal.

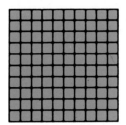 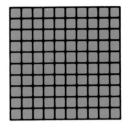 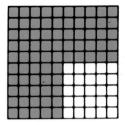

$$\frac{3}{4} \longrightarrow 4\overline{)3.00}^{\,0.75}$$

$$2\frac{3}{4} = 2\frac{75}{100} = 2.75$$

Then write the whole number, 2, to the left of the decimal point.   2.

Write the decimal equivalent of the fraction.   2.75

The fraction $2\frac{3}{4}$ as a decimal is 2.75.

PRACTICE

Write as decimals. Remember to use the bar for repeating digits.

1. $1\frac{1}{2}$ **2.** $2\frac{3}{5}$ **3.** $4\frac{1}{4}$ **4.** $3\frac{5}{8}$ **5.** $6\frac{3}{10}$

6. $10\frac{1}{5}$ **7.** $2\frac{5}{6}$ **8.** $3\frac{1}{3}$ **9.** $7\frac{1}{8}$ **10.** $8\frac{35}{100}$

11. $4\frac{1}{20}$ **12.** $3\frac{3}{22}$ **13.** $4\frac{3}{4}$ **14.** $2\frac{9}{11}$ **15.** $11\frac{11}{12}$

*16. $10\frac{5}{400}$ ***17.** $20\frac{7}{300}$ ***18.** $300\frac{3}{500}$ ***19.** $40\frac{5}{200}$ ***20.** $27\frac{365}{600}$

MIXED PRACTICE
Maintaining and Reviewing Skills

Add, subtract, multiply, or divide.

21. $3\frac{2}{3} + 4\frac{5}{6}$ **22.** $15\frac{7}{8} + 10\frac{2}{3}$ **23.** $14\frac{3}{10} - 8\frac{7}{10}$ **24.** $27\frac{1}{3} - 13\frac{4}{5}$ **25.** $19 - 12\frac{6}{7}$

26. $\frac{4}{5} \times \frac{2}{3}$ **27.** $3\frac{3}{5} \times 4\frac{3}{8}$ **28.** $\frac{9}{10} \div \frac{3}{5}$ **29.** $3\frac{1}{3} \div \frac{5}{6}$ **30.** $4\frac{7}{8} \times 9\frac{3}{10}$

31. $31\frac{2}{3} \div 3\frac{6}{8}$ **32.** $18\frac{1}{5} \div 9\frac{1}{10}$ **33.** $42\frac{1}{3} \times 3\frac{4}{7}$ **34.** $93\frac{2}{3} \times 27\frac{3}{4}$ **35.** $42\frac{7}{8} \div 3\frac{1}{4}$

FOCUS   Use NUMBER skills to change mixed numbers to decimals.

APPLICATION

Using Measurement

Here is how to find what decimal part one number is of another.

What decimal part of a decade is 2 years?

Write what is given as a fraction.

$\dfrac{2}{10}$ —years
—years in a decade

Simplify. $\dfrac{\overset{1}{\cancel{2}}}{\underset{5}{\cancel{10}}} = \dfrac{1}{5}$

Change the fraction into an equivalent decimal by dividing the numerator by the denominator.

$\dfrac{1}{5} = 1 \div 5 = 5\overline{)1.0}^{\,0.2}$

Two years is $\dfrac{1}{5}$ or 0.2 of a decade.

Write a fraction and a decimal for each.

36. One year is ■ of a decade.

37. Five years is ■ of a decade.

38. Seven years is ■ of a decade.

39. Eight years is ■ of a decade.

What part of a century (100 years) is each? Write your answers as a decimal and a fraction in simplest terms.

40. 30 years	**41.** 44 years	**42.** 25 years	**43.** 10 years
44. 5 years	**45.** 26 years	**46.** 50 years	**47.** 60 years
48. 85 years	**49.** 75 years	**50.** 78 years	**51.** 47 years

What part of a millennium (1,000 years) is each? Write your answers as a decimal and a fraction in simplest terms.

52. 250 years	**53.** 330 years	**54.** 75 years	**55.** 200 years
56. 500 years	**57.** 225 years	**58.** 600 years	**59.** 50 years
60. 450 years	**61.** 750 years	**62.** 475 years	**63.** 980 years

Use MEASUREMENT to write time periods as fractions and decimals.

Selecting a Strategy: Making a List

The five important steps to solving problems are READ, KNOW, PLAN, SOLVE, and CHECK. Making a list can help you PLAN and SOLVE a problem. A list can be used to find all the possible answers and to eliminate impossible ones.

1. READ   How many different 4-digit even numbers can you write using all of the digits 4, 5, 7, and 0 in each number?

2. KNOW   Ask yourself: What do I need to find out? How many even 4-digit numbers can be made using all of the digits 4, 5, 7, and 0 in each number?
Key facts: a. The digits are 4, 5, 7, 0.

b. Each number will be a 4-digit number.

c. Each 4-digit number will be an even number.

3. PLAN   Select a strategy: Try making a list.

a. Make a list of all the possible 4-digit numbers that can be made by using the digits 4, 5, 7, and 0 in each number.

b. Count the even numbers in the list.

4. SOLVE

4570	5470	7540
4507	5407	7504
4750	5704	7450
4705	5740	7405
4075	5074	7045
4057	5047	7054

There are 10 4-digit even numbers that can be written from the digits 4, 5, 7, and 0.

5. CHECK   Reread the question and check your steps. Ask yourself: Does the list contain all the possible 4-digit numbers? Recount the even numbers in the list. Are there 10? Count the odd numbers. How many are there?

FOCUS   Make a list as part of the Five-Step PROBLEM-SOLVING Plan.

PRACTICE

Make a list to find all the possible answers for each problem.

1. List as many different 3-digit odd numbers as you can make using the digits 4, 5, 7, and 0. No number should contain the same digit more than once.

2. A cash register drawer has a tray of $20 bills, a tray of $10 bills, a tray of $5 bills, and a tray of $1 bills. How many ways can you make change for a $20 bill using fewer than 6 bills?

3. Find two single-digit numbers whose difference is 3 and whose quotient is 2.

4. Find two single-digit numbers whose sum is 9 and whose product is 14.

5. Find a 1-digit number and a 2-digit number whose sum is 49 and whose product is 258.

6. How many ways can you give change from a $50 bill for a $28 purchase using only two $1 bills?

7. How many ways can you give change from three $100 bills for a $252 purchase if the customer requests at least one $20 bill and at least one $10 bill?

8. How many different ways can 4 letters be arranged with the letters A, B, C, and D? No arrangement should contain the same letter more than once.

9. How many different ways can you have 50¢ using quarters, dimes, and nickels?

*10. How many ways can 3 letters be arranged with the letters A, B, and C? The letters may be used more than once in each arrangement.

Class Project

Work with several classmates to estimate the cost of a yearly supply of toothpaste for all the students in your class. Start by carefully making a list of all the items you need to think about in order to make an estimate. Share your estimate with the other groups and explain how you arrived at it. Then make a list of all the estimates. How close were they? Which group had the highest estimate? Which group had the lowest estimate? What was the difference between the highest and the lowest estimate?

Changing Decimals to Fractions and Mixed Numbers

Every decimal has an equivalent fraction.

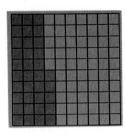

Change 0.35 to a fraction.

Write the decimal as a fraction.   **Simplify.**

$$0.35 = \frac{35}{100}$$

$$\overset{7}{\underset{20}{\frac{\cancel{35}}{\cancel{100}}}} = \frac{7}{20}$$

Change 3.025 to a mixed number.

   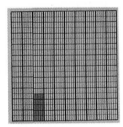

**Write the whole number part.
Then write the decimal part as
a fraction.**

$$3.025 = 3\frac{25}{1{,}000}$$

Simplify.

$$3\,\overset{1}{\underset{40}{\frac{\cancel{25}}{\cancel{1{,}000}}}} = 3\frac{1}{40}$$

GUIDED PRACTICE

Write each as a fraction. Simplify if possible.

1. $0.2 = \frac{\blacksquare}{10} = \frac{\blacksquare}{5}$ **2.** $0.35 = \frac{\blacksquare}{100} = \frac{\blacksquare}{20}$ **3.** $0.075 = \frac{\blacksquare}{1{,}000} = \frac{\blacksquare}{40}$

4. 0.4 **5.** 0.16 **6.** 0.142

Write each as a mixed number. Simplify if possible.

7. $2.5 = 2\frac{\blacksquare}{10} = 2\frac{\blacksquare}{2}$ **8.** $5.05 = \blacksquare\frac{\blacksquare}{100} = \blacksquare\frac{\blacksquare}{20}$ **9.** $4.375 = \blacksquare\frac{\blacksquare}{1{,}000} = \blacksquare\frac{\blacksquare}{8}$

10. 25.8 **11.** 3.75 **12.** 12.125

| FOCUS | Use NUMBER skills to change decimals to fractions and mixed numbers. |

PRACTICE

Write each as a fraction. Simplify if possible.

13. 0.48   **14.** 0.18   **15.** 0.06   **16.** 0.125   **17.** 0.625

18. 0.25   **19.** 0.50   **20.** 0.32   **21.** 0.67   **22.** 0.375

23. 0.95   **24.** 0.56   **25.** 0.07   **26.** 0.029   **27.** 0.639

28. 0.875   **29.** 0.05   **30.** 0.025   **31.** 0.005   **32.** 0.244

33. 0.35   **34.** 0.123   **35.** 0.075   **36.** 0.843   **37.** 0.0075

Write each as a mixed number. Simplify if possible.

38. 2.5   **39.** 3.25   **40.** 5.10   **41.** 7.45   **42.** 8.97

43. 5.375   **44.** 6.125   **45.** 9.33   **46.** 12.80   **47.** 15.6

48. 43.375   **49.** 56.625   **50.** 17.328   **51.** 25.075   **52.** 30.003

53. 14.782   **54.** 26.324   **55.** 19.655   **56.** 83.745   **57.** 96.368

MIXED PRACTICE
Maintaining and Reviewing Skills

Compare. Use $<$, $>$, or $=$. Change to a decimal if necessary.

58. 0.5 ● 0.$\overline{5}$ **59.** 0.06 ● 0.60 **60.** 1.35 ● 1.$\overline{3}$ **61.** 0.36 ● $\frac{36}{50}$ **62.** 2.9 ● 2.$\overline{6}$

63. $\frac{1}{3}$ ● 0.$\overline{4}$ **64.** 0.0$\overline{4}$ ● 0.4 **65.** $\frac{7}{8}$ ● 0.$\overline{7}$ **66.** 0.25 ● $\frac{2}{5}$ **67.** 2.8 ● 2$\frac{8}{100}$

68. $\frac{1}{8}$ ● 0.1$\overline{2}$ **69.** 0.3 ● $\frac{3}{8}$ **70.** $\frac{5}{9}$ ● 0.$\overline{5}$ **71.** 62.$\overline{3}$ ● 62.4 **72.** 0.018 ● 0.017$\overline{9}$

73. $\frac{7}{20}$ ● 0.35 **74.** 8.$\overline{8}$ ● 8.889 **75.** 6.6 ● 6.06 **76.** $\frac{4}{5}$ ● 0.9 **77.** 0.8 ● $\frac{8}{9}$

CHALLENGE

Solve.

*78. There are eight tins. Five tins contain paper clips. Three tins contain rubber bands. Two tins contain both paper clips and rubber bands. How many of the tins contain neither paper clips nor rubber bands?

FRACTIONS AND DECIMALS
Common Equivalents

Study these commonly used equivalents. Look for patterns.

COMMON FRACTION-DECIMAL EQUIVALENTS	
$\frac{1}{2} = 0.50$, or 0.5	$\frac{3}{4} = 0.75$
$\frac{1}{3} = 0.333 \ldots$, or $0.\overline{3}$	$\frac{2}{5} = 0.40$, or 0.4
$\frac{1}{4} = 0.25$	$\frac{3}{5} = 0.60$, or 0.6
$\frac{1}{5} = 0.20$, or 0.2	$\frac{4}{5} = 0.80$, or 0.8
$\frac{1}{6} = 0.166 \ldots$, or $0.1\overline{6}$	$\frac{5}{6} = 0.833 \ldots$, or $0.8\overline{3}$
$\frac{1}{8} = 0.125$	$\frac{3}{8} = 0.375$
$\frac{1}{10} = 0.10$, or 0.1	$\frac{5}{8} = 0.625$
$\frac{2}{3} = 0.666 \ldots$, or $0.\overline{6}$	$\frac{7}{8} = 0.875$

PRACTICE

Give the decimal equivalents. Use the chart to help.

1. $\frac{2}{5}$ 2. $\frac{3}{4}$ 3. $\frac{5}{6}$ 4. $\frac{1}{3}$ 5. $\frac{7}{8}$

6. $\frac{1}{9}$ 7. $\frac{2}{3}$ 8. $\frac{3}{8}$ 9. $\frac{4}{5}$ 10. $\frac{5}{8}$

*11. $\frac{3}{6}$ *12. $\frac{5}{9}$ *13. $\frac{4}{6}$ *14. $\frac{8}{9}$ *15. $\frac{8}{8}$

MIXED PRACTICE
Maintaining and Reviewing Skills

Solve.

16. $23 \times x = 92$ 17. $945 \div n = 63$ 18. $w - 368 = 793$ 19. $564 + a = 936$

20. $14 \times m = 378$ 21. $264 \div z = 12$ 22. $q - 583 = 321$ 23. $987 + y = 1,585$

FOCUS | Use PATTERNS with common decimal-fraction equivalents.

APPLICATION
Using a Calculator

$\frac{23}{27}$ $\begin{array}{c}23\\ \text{divided by}\\ 27\end{array}$ $23 \div 27$ $27\overline{)23.000}$

Changing fractions to decimals is very easy to do using a calculator.

$\frac{23}{27}$ Key: $\boxed{2}\ \boxed{3}\ \boxed{\div}\ \boxed{2}\ \boxed{7}\ \boxed{=}$.   See: 0.8518518. Write: $0.\overline{851}$.

Most calculators show 8 or 9 decimal places. Write the decimal you see on the display. Check to see if it is a terminating or a repeating decimal. If it is a repeating decimal, place a bar over the digits that repeat.

$\frac{6}{125}$ Key: $\boxed{6}\ \boxed{\div}\ \boxed{1}\ \boxed{2}\ \boxed{5}\ \boxed{=}$. See: 0.048. Write: 0.048.

Change to decimals using a calculator. Copy the calculator display. Then write the answer.

	See:	Write:			See:	Write:
24. $\frac{5}{8}$	▨	▨	**25.** $\frac{7}{9}$	▨	▨
26. $\frac{33}{40}$	▨	▨	**27.** $\frac{51}{75}$	▨	▨
28. $\frac{11}{27}$	▨	▨	**29.** $\frac{13}{25}$	▨	▨
30. $\frac{21}{55}$	▨	▨	**31.** $\frac{5}{12}$	▨	▨
32. $\frac{19}{40}$	▨	▨	**33.** $\frac{15}{44}$	▨	▨
34. $\frac{111}{148}$	▨	▨	**35.** $\frac{125}{333}$	▨	▨
36. $\frac{205}{328}$	▨	▨	**37.** $\frac{33}{500}$	▨	▨
38. $\frac{5}{74}$	▨	▨	**39.** $\frac{3,003}{4,000}$	▨	▨

Use a CALCULATOR to change fractions to decimals.

Energy Conservation

Can you imagine what life would be like without energy? There would be no electricity, no oil to heat homes, and no gasoline for cars. This is a scary thought, because we have become accustomed to having all the energy we want. However, energy is not always replaceable. Some day, we may use up all our energy resources. That is why energy conservation has become such an important issue in the 1980s.

The United States uses more energy than any other country in the world. We get our energy from all of the sources pictured below.

Coal   Oil   Gas   Sun   Water

Most of these sources are not permanent like the sun. Can you see why solar energy may be important for our future? Oil, gas, water, and coal are all natural resources that may be used up some day.

One of the areas of energy in which conservation is important is electricity. Electricity is not a natural resource. It is a form of energy produced by natural resources, like oil, coal, and water.

A watt is a unit of power in electricity. Every month, your home receives an electric bill for the total number of watts used. Since a watt is a very small unit, electric companies use a unit called a kilowatt-hour (kwh). A kilowatt is equal to 1,000 watts, and a kilowatt-hour is equivalent to the energy expended in 1 hour by 1 kilowatt of power. If you look at an electric bill, you will see a number that represents kilowatt-hours. If this number is 756, for example, it means that your home used 756,000 watts during that month.

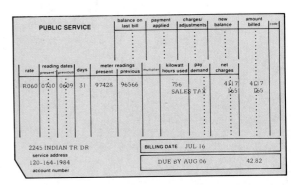

By comparing each monthly electric bill, we can tell whether we are increasing or reducing our use of electricity.

CRITICAL THINKING

1. Identify some of the sources for energy.

2. Define watt and kilowatt.

3. Explain two ways that we can reduce our use of electricity.

FOCUS | Use NUMBER skills to learn about energy conservation.

The Diablo Dam, on the Skagit River in Northwestern Washington, is part of the Seattle Power System.

LOOKING BACK
Reviewing and Testing Chapter 17

In Chapter 17 you formulated problems about a school orientation. Refer to page 243 for data.

1. If each information packet costs $2.00 to print, how much will be spent for the orientation?

You learned about changing fractions and mixed numbers to decimals. To review, refer to page 244.

Which are terminating and which are repeating decimals?

2. $0.4333\ldots$ 3. 0.79 4. 0.36 5. $0.5555\ldots$

Change each fraction to a decimal. Write your answer to the ten-thousandth's place if necessary. Do not round.

6. $\dfrac{4}{5}$ 7. $\dfrac{2}{13}$ 8. $\dfrac{8}{14}$ 9. $\dfrac{6}{11}$ 10. $\dfrac{3}{7}$

11. $2\dfrac{1}{4}$ 12. $1\dfrac{5}{7}$ 13. $7\dfrac{7}{9}$ 14. $11\dfrac{12}{14}$ 15. $9\dfrac{1}{14}$

Use the Five–Step Problem–Solving Plan to solve these problems. Refer to page 248.

16. How many different four-digit even numbers can be made with the digits 4, 6, 2, and 7?

17. How many different four-digit odd numbers can be made with the digits 1, 3, 5, and 4?

To review what you learned about changing decimals to fractions and mixed numbers, refer to page 250.

Write as fractions. Rename in simplest terms.

18. 0.53 19. 0.09 20. 0.80 21. 0.010 22. 0.020

23. 0.075 24. 0.85 25. 0.36 26. 0.65 27. 0.12

You learned about energy conservation. To review, refer to page 254.

28. How many watts are there in 1,453 kilowatts?

FOCUS | Review and test skills learned and practiced.

LOOKING AHEAD
Preparing for New Skills for Chapter 18

In the next chapter you will focus on

- **formulating problems about a sports opinion poll.**
- **rounding decimals to the nearest thousandth.**
- **using a calculator.**
- **compare and order decimals to ten-thousandths.**
- **rounding, comparing, and ordering money.**
- **how math is used in technology.**

Rounding and comparing decimals will be easier if you review rounding and comparing whole numbers.

Example 1:

8,635 rounded to the nearest ten

8,635
└─5 or greater
8,640

Example 2:

63,834 rounded to the nearest ten thousand

63,834
└─less than 5
60,000

Example 3:

┌─same─┐
62,573 > 62,419
5 is greater
than 4

Example 4:

┌─same─┐
73,001 < 73,010
0 is less
than 1

To read a decimal, you read the number and then name the place value of the last digit.

Example 5:

0.43   forty-three hundredths

Example 6:

0.007   seven thousandths

PRACTICE

Round to the nearest thousand.

1. 8,623   **2.** 4,487   **3.** 56,210   **4.** 398,516

Compare. Use > or <.

5. 12,791 ● 12,971   **6.** 65,560 ● 65,506   **7.** 48,843 ● 48,834   **8.** 860,219 ● 806,219

Review NUMBER skills in preparation for learning new skills.

FOCUS   Formulate problems using photo, data, and text.

18

Round, Compare, and Order Decimals

DATA

Conducting an Opinion Poll
Students surveyed	500
Total number of students	550
Students involved in sports	20%

Questionnaire
Sports events attended per season
10 or more	8%
6 to 9	11%
1 to 5	46%
none	35%

Reasons for not attending
Too busy	6%
Not interested	12%
Home team losses	25%
Unaware of game schedule	48%
Not sure	9%

Would attend more if
Home teams won more	10%
Games scheduled at different times	25%
Added new sports	58%
Not sure	7%

"The problem is, we don't know what people are thinking," said Coach Lambert. "We don't know why they come to games and why they don't." Coach Lambert was talking to the Millbrook Athletic Council about the problem of dwindling attendance at school sports events.

"I suggest that we conduct an opinion poll," said Ms. Moritz, the school principal.

"Great idea!" exclaimed Lori and Darin, the council's two student representatives.

"Well," laughed Ms. Moritz, "I think I know who should be in charge of the poll. How about it, Lori and Darin?"

The results of Lori's and Darin's poll are shown in the data. Try to analyze the reasons for Millbrook's problem. What might the Athletic Council do, based on the responses? What other questions might have been asked on the questionnaire? What are the chances of changing the situation?

To the Nearest Hundredth or Thousandth

Place Names:

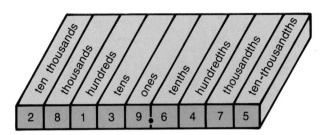

Place Values: $20,000 + 8,000 + 100 + 30 + 9 + 0.6 + 0.04 + 0.007 + 0.0005$

Read: twenty-eight thousand, one hundred thirty-nine
and six thousand, four hundred seventy-five
ten-thousandths

Round 0.7368 to the nearest hundredth.

The digit 3 is in the hundredths place.
Look at the digit just to the right of 3.
This digit is 6.

Digit in place to be rounded ⟶ 0.7368 ⟵ Digit one place to the right.

If the digit to the right of the place to be rounded is:

- less than 5, round down.
- 5 or greater, round up.

To round 0.7368 to the nearest hundredth, use the digit in
the thousandths place. This digit is 6. Since 6 is greater
than 5, the 3 in the hundredths place is increased to 4.

To the nearest hundredth, 0.7368 is 0.74.

GUIDED PRACTICE

Round to the nearest hundredth. Remember to look at the
digit to the right of the one being rounded.

1. 0.452   Look at the 2. It is less than 5.

2. 0.5678 Look at the 7. It is greater than 5.

Round to the nearest thousandth.

3. 3.6491   Look at the 1. It is less than 5.

4. 54.0566 Look at the 6. It is greater than 5.

FOCUS | Use NUMBER skills and ESTIMATION to round decimals.

PRACTICE

Round to the nearest tenth.

5. 4.37	**6.** 9.42	**7.** 14.66	**8.** 17.79	**9.** 38.89
10. 10.23	**11.** 5.84	**12.** 3.17	**13.** 25.02	**14.** 19.58
15. 20.483	**16.** 85.751	**17.** 4.8463	**18.** 12.2598	**19.** 72.5752

Round to the nearest hundredth.

20. 12.273	**21.** 11.581	**22.** 9.142	**23.** 7.0348	**24.** 81.326
25. 14.647	**26.** 3.342	**27.** 15.715	**28.** 42.004	**29.** 14.781

Round to the nearest thousandth.

30. 8.6721	**31.** 10.0536	**32.** 21.4755	**33.** 17.3208	**34.** 27.8947
35. 9.30265	**36.** 4.07059	**37.** 3.00091	**38.** 8.00050	**39.** 13.84696

40. Lori ran the 50-yard dash three times during gym period. Her times were: 10.93 seconds, 10.84 seconds, and 10.675 seconds. Round each time to the nearest tenth. Which is the fastest time?

MIXED PRACTICE
Maintaining and Reviewing Skills

Copy and complete the chart. Round to the given place.

		Whole Number	Tenth	Hundredth	Thousandth
41.	362.85				
42.	4.9796				
43.	72.0303				
44.	19.5641				
45.	421.3266				

CHALLENGE

*46. Give the next three fractions in the sequence. How many fractions are in the complete sequence?

$$1, \frac{1}{2}, \frac{1}{4}, \frac{1}{8}, \frac{1}{16}, \frac{1}{32}, \blacksquare \blacksquare \blacksquare$$

ROUND DECIMALS
To the Nearest Hundredth or Thousandth

A chest of gold coins was recovered from a shipwreck. One coin weighed 6.7346 grams. Round the weight of the coin to the nearest hundredth.

Ones	Tenths	Hundredths	Thousandths	Ten-thousandths
6	7	3	4	6

Look at the digit to the right of the hundredths place.

If the number to the right of the one being rounded is:

> 5, the digit increases by 1
= 5, the digit increases by 1
< 5, the digit remains the same

Rounded to the nearest hundredth, 6.7346 is 6.73.

PRACTICE

Copy and complete this table.

		Nearest Hundredth	Nearest Thousandth
1.	6.5764		
2.	6.3272		
3.	7.0143		
4.	7.1155		
5.	7.9284		
6.	6.6972		
7.	8.3121		
8.	9.1249		
9.	5.8917		

MIXED PRACTICE
Maintaining and Reviewing Skills

Round 67.70194 to the nearest place indicated.

10. whole number
11. hundredth
12. tenth
13. ten-thousandth
14. ten

Round 114.0092 to the nearest place indicated.

15. hundredth
16. ten
17. tenth
18. thousandth
19. one

FOCUS Use NUMBER skills and ESTIMATION to round decimals.

APPLICATION
Using a Calculator

The fraction $\frac{4}{9}$ means $4 \div 9$. Dividing 4 by 9 results in a repeating decimal, $0.444444\ldots$. To round this decimal to the nearest thousandth, carry it out to ten-thousandths. To the nearest thousandth, $0.4444\ldots$ is 0.444.

Use a calculator to convert these fractions to decimals. Write the first four digits to the right of the decimal point, then round to the nearest thousandth.

	Change to Decimals	Key	Display	Round to Nearest Thousandth
20.	$\frac{1}{3}$	1 ÷ 3 =	0.3333	
21.	$\frac{5}{7}$	5 ÷ 7 =	0.7142	
22.	$\frac{2}{3}$	2 ÷ 3 =		
23.	$\frac{7}{9}$	7 ÷ 9 =		
24.	$\frac{8}{11}$	8 ÷ 11 =		
25.	$\frac{2}{7}$	2 ÷ 7 =		

Use the steps shown in the chart above as a guide to convert the following fractions to decimals. Then round each decimal to the nearest thousandth.

26. $\frac{4}{11}$ **27.** $\frac{8}{15}$ **28.** $\frac{1}{21}$ **29.** $\frac{1}{23}$ **30.** $\frac{1}{87}$

31. $\frac{1}{267}$ **32.** $\frac{2}{3,695}$ **33.** $\frac{7}{11}$ **34.** $\frac{6}{53}$ **35.** $\frac{12}{663}$

36. $\frac{15}{47}$ **37.** $\frac{91}{1,001}$ **38.** $\frac{88}{554}$ **39.** $\frac{51}{97}$ **40.** $\frac{102}{407}$

41. $\frac{371}{425}$ **42.** $\frac{80}{96}$ **43.** $\frac{11}{13}$ **44.** $\frac{17}{31}$ **45.** $\frac{7}{19}$

46. $\frac{2}{111}$ **47.** $\frac{65}{79}$ **48.** $\frac{94}{95}$ **49.** $\frac{121}{321}$ **50.** $\frac{891}{999}$

51. $\frac{56}{85}$ **52.** $\frac{27}{39}$ **53.** $\frac{59}{64}$ **54.** $\frac{99}{111}$ **55.** $\frac{21}{33}$

Use a CALCULATOR to convert fractions to decimals.

To Ten-Thousandths

Barbara has a pumpkin with a mass of 16.81 kilograms. Tim has a pumpkin with a mass of 16.87 kilograms. Who grew the heavier pumpkin?

To find the answer, compare the decimals 16.81 and 16.87. The tens, ones, and tenths are the same. Look at the digits in the hundredths place.

Compare 1 and 7: $1 < 7$

16.81 $<$ 16.87   Tim grew the heavier pumpkin.

Compare 12.66 and 12.663. Make sure each number has the same number of digits.

12.66 $=$ 12.660

Now compare 12.660 and 12.663. The tens, ones, tenths, and hundredths are the same. Compare the digits in the thousandths place.

$0 < 3$ 12.660 $<$ 12.663

Now put these numbers in order from least to greatest.

6.73   6.735   6.653
6.73 $<$ 6.735   Therefore, 6.653 $<$ 6.73 $<$ 6.735.

GUIDED PRACTICE

Compare the decimals. Use $<$, $>$, or $=$.

1. 6.72 ● 6.54 The ones are the same. Compare the tenths.

2. 0.39 ● 0.396 Remember, 0.39 = 0.390.

Write in order from least to greatest.

3. 9.083   9.721   9.236   Compare the tenths.

4. 7.0378   7.0562   7.0136   Compare the hundredths.

Write in order from greatest to least.

5. 4.357   4.350   4.352   Compare the thousandths.

6. 8.3675   8.3677   8.3679   Compare the ten-thousandths.

| FOCUS | Use NUMBER skills to compare and order decimals. |

PRACTICE

Compare. Use $<$, $>$, or $=$.

7. 9.278 ● 9.321   **8.** 2.9 ● 2.8   **9.** 6.36 ● 6.63   **10.** 19.763 ● 19.765

11. 7.14 ● 7.04   **12.** 5.6 ● 5.60   **13.** 12.421 ● 12.368   **14.** 23.76 ● 24.76

15. 11.54 ● 11.540   **16.** 9.07 ● 9.007   **17.** 42.96 ● 42.9   **18.** 19.678 ● 19.578

19. 61.700 ● 61.7   **20.** 3.2100 ● 3.2140   **21.** 10.100 ● 10.001   **22.** 29.016 ● 29.011

23. 8.7610 ● 8.7160   **24.** $3.59 ● $3.95   **25.** 4.003 ● 4.300   **26.** 84.7892 ● 84.7891

Write each group in order from least to greatest.

27. 0.5439   0.4395   0.3594   **28.** 7.1095   7.1062   7.6105

Write each group in order from greatest to least.

29. 0.834   0.83   0.843   **30.** 6.9124   6.2194   6.2491

MIXED PRACTICE
Maintaining and Reviewing Skills

Compare the fractions. Write $<$, $>$, or $=$.

31. $\frac{5}{15}$ ● $\frac{15}{45}$ **32.** $\frac{4}{27}$ ● $\frac{9}{61}$ **33.** $\frac{6}{31}$ ● $\frac{8}{17}$ **34.** $\frac{25}{49}$ ● $\frac{1}{2}$ **35.** $\frac{2}{3}$ ● $\frac{32}{99}$

Order from least to greatest.

*36. $\frac{12}{12}$, $\frac{1}{12}$, $\frac{1}{6}$, $\frac{2}{3}$, $\frac{1}{2}$, $\frac{5}{12}$, $\frac{1}{4}$, $\frac{7}{12}$, $\frac{1}{3}$, $\frac{5}{6}$, $\frac{3}{4}$, $\frac{11}{12}$

37. Robin and Tammy are on the diving team. After two dives, Robin scored 9.039 points and Tammy scored 9.036 points. Who scored more points?

*38. Kara and Mary both ran in a 100 meter race. Kara ran the race in 14.19 seconds. Mary ran the race in 14.2 seconds. Who ran faster?

CHALLENGE

Round each decimal to thousandths. Then write in order from greatest to least.

*39. $6.65\overline{65}$ $6.6\overline{6}$ $6.60\overline{60}$

*40. $2.02\overline{02}$ $2.09\overline{9}$ $2.12\overline{3123}$

COMPARE AND ORDER DECIMALS
To Ten-Thousandths

The top four skiers finished the race with these times:

> Racer A: 29.013 seconds
> Racer B: 29.394 seconds
> Racer C: 29.996 seconds
> Racer D: 29.674 seconds

Order these times from the fastest to the slowest. Remember, the fastest time will be the smallest number.

To compare these decimals, start with the place value of the digits at the extreme left. The whole numbers are the same. Compare the tenths. Since 0 is the least number of tenths, that time is the least, or fastest. Compare the tenths in the other decimals:

$0 < 3 < 6 < 9$ So: $29.013 < 29.394 < 29.674 < 29.996$

PRACTICE

Compare. Use $<$, $>$, or $=$.

1. 6.0909 ● 6.9009

2. 4.3773 ● 4.3377

3. 19.7932 ● 19.8362

4. 0.0021 ● 0.0102

5. 2.8974 ● 2.4897

6. 43.6279 ● 43.5989

7. 1.1055 ● 1.1505

8. 3.6644 ● 3.6446

9. 7.36540 ● 7.3654

Order from least to greatest.

10. 0.0316   0.0631   0.0063 **11.** 5.412   5.4   5.024   **12.** 31.32   31.3194   31.3201

Order from greatest to least.

13. 8.4628   8.4627   8.4629 **14.** 2.689   2.6   2.986   **15.** 12.1234 12.4321 12.3124

MIXED PRACTICE
Maintaining and Reviewing Skills

Add, subtract, multiply, or divide.

16. 52,834 × 3,025

17. 6,648 × 332

18. 97,834 × 8,642

19. 1,422,864 ÷ 369

20. 1,544,127 ÷ 221

21. 894,637 − 26,843

22. 2,489,673 − 486,789

23. 84,376 + 98,484

24. 287,894 + 846,327

| FOCUS | Use NUMBER skills to compare and order decimals. |

266

APPLICATION
Round, Compare, and Order Money

Some people invest in the stock market to earn money. A **share** of stock is part ownership of a company. As a stockholder, you may earn money by investing in a company.

Ryan wants to invest $1,000 in stock. Before he buys stock, he must know the price for each share. The chart below shows the price per share of stock for several companies.

Company	Price per Share	Company	Price per Share
Rollins Inc.	$16.05	CartCo	$14.04
A & Z Co.	$21.01	BT Electric	$18.90
Water Works	$ 9.25	Wall Works	$13.84
RAZ Plumbing	$17.59	Zena	$ 9.76
Homes Plus	$16.42	EagleAir	$14.76
Data Inc.	$21.22	Quick Shops	$13.15

Use the information in the table above to answer the following.

25. Copy the table. Round each price per share to the nearest dollar.

26. Order the prices per share from least to greatest.

27. Which company's share is the most expensive?

28. Which company's share is the least expensive?

29. On Monday, the price for one share of Zena stock was $9.68. On Tuesday it was $9.78. On Wednesday it was $9.76. On which day was the price the highest?

30. The WBF company stock is selling for $21.56 per share. Is that stock >, <, or = to the prices of the stocks listed in the table?

Complete by using <, >, or =.

31. 21.001 ● 14.765

32. 16.420 ● 16.055

33. 9.251 ● 9.768

34. 13.151 ● 13.847

35. 14.765 ● 14.04

36. 17.598 ● 18.905

37. 12.947 ● 12.497

38. 15.026 ● 15.030

39. 13.49 ● 13.049

Use NUMBER skills to round, compare, and order money.

How Do Computers Print Messages?

The result of a program that has been input into the computer is the **output**. The output appears on a computer display or monitor when the program is run.

Look at the three programs below. How will their outputs differ?

Program 1
```
10   INPUT X
20   PRINT X
30   END
```

Program 2
```
10   INPUT X
20   PRINT "MY AGE IS X."
30   END
```

Program 3
```
10   INPUT X
20   PRINT "MY AGE IS"; X
30   END
```

For all three programs, we will input the value 12 for X.

Here is the output for Program 1:

```
RUN
?12
12
```

In Program 2, a PRINT statement with quotes is used. This means that whatever is between the quotes will be printed out as a message. Thus, the output will be:

```
RUN
?12
MY AGE IS X
```

In Program 3, the PRINT statement has a message within quotes. The quotes are followed by a semicolon and the name of a memory cell. This means that the message will be printed first, and the number stored in the memory cell (12) will be printed afterwards. Thus, the output will look like this:

```
RUN
?12
MY AGE IS 12
```

Before writing the instructions for a program, you must plan your output. The output for a program that finds the area of a rectangle looks like this:

```
WHAT ARE THE LENGTH AND
WIDTH?
?12
?5
THE AREA IS 60.
```

Study the programs listed on page 269. Each can be used to find the area of a rectangle. How will their outputs differ?

CRITICAL THINKING

Examine each statement and identify the output that will result. How will the outputs differ from one another?

1. 10   PRINT "A; B; C"

2. 20   PRINT A; B; C

3. 30   PRINT "A"; "B"; "C"

FOCUS   Use LOGIC to learn how computers print messages.

268

Study these four programs and their outputs. How are
they alike? How do they differ?

```
10   INPUT L
20   INPUT W
30   A = L * W
40   PRINT A
50   END
RUN
? 8
? 4
 32
_
```

Original Program for
Area of a Rectangle

```
5    PRINT "WHAT ARE THE LENGTH AND WIDTH?"
10   INPUT L
20   INPUT W
30   A = L * W
40   PRINT "THE AREA IS"; A
50   END
RUN
WHAT ARE THE LENGTH AND WIDTH?
? 8
? 4
THE AREA IS 32
_
```

Program to Produce the
Planned Output

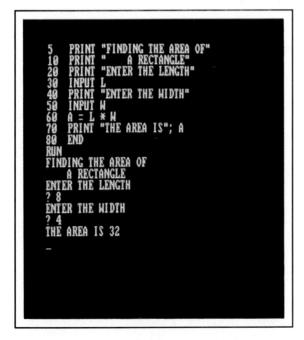

```
5    PRINT "FINDING THE AREA OF"
10   PRINT "    A RECTANGLE"
20   PRINT "ENTER THE LENGTH"
30   INPUT L
40   PRINT "ENTER THE WIDTH"
50   INPUT W
60   A = L * W
70   PRINT "THE AREA IS"; A
80   END
RUN
FINDING THE AREA OF
    A RECTANGLE
ENTER THE LENGTH
? 8
ENTER THE WIDTH
? 4
THE AREA IS 32

_
```

Another Improvement

```
10   PRINT "AREAS OF RECTANGLES"
20   PRINT "PROGRAM BY HELEN"
30   PRINT
40   PRINT "GIVE THE LENGTH AND WIDTH"
50   INPUT L, W
60   A = L * W
70   PRINT
80   PRINT A; "IS THE AREA"
90   END
RUN
AREAS OF RECTANGLES
PROGRAM BY HELEN

GIVE THE LENGTH AND WIDTH
? 8,4

32 IS THE AREA

_
```

Still Another Improvement

LOOKING BACK
Reviewing and Testing Chapter 18

In Chapter 18 you formulated problems about an opinion poll. To review, refer to page 259 for data.

1. How might the results of the poll change, if more students were surveyed?

You learned to round decimals to the nearest hundredth or thousandth. To review, refer to pages 260 and 262.

Round each decimal to the nearest tenth, hundredth and thousandth.

2. 9.87632   3. 14.6389   4. 12.3216   5. 47.83187

6. 71.12973   7. 87.6894   8. 1.12439   9. 32.98112

To review what you learned about comparing and ordering decimals, refer to pages 264 and 266.

Compare. Use <, >, or =.

10. 9.872 ● 9.862   11. 5.4 ● 5.40   12. 9.4320 ● 9.4230   13. 18.76 ● 18.761

14. 6.342 ● 6.344   15. 0.904 ● 0.909   16. 0.07 ● 0.77   17. 0.090 ● 0.009

18. 3.13 ● 3.130   19. 2.061 ● 2.016   20. 1.605 ● 1.645   21. 0.804 ● 0.814

Write in order from least to greatest.

22. 0.5678, 0.5768, 0.5876, 0.5867   23. 19.343, 19.342, 19.353, 19.354

Write in order from greatest to least.

24. 0.9876, 0.9983, 0.9974, 0.9764   25. 8.764, 8.676, 8.832, 8.842

To review what you learned about computer messages refer to page 268.

Examine each statement and identify the output.

26. 60 PRINT   "E; F"   27. 45 PRINT   5*6; "17"; "18"

| FOCUS | Review and test skills learned and practiced. |

LOOKING AHEAD
Preparing for New Skills for Chapter 19

In the next chapter you will focus on

- **formulating problems about packing for a trip.**
- **adding decimals.**
- **solving problems about a check register.**
- **subtracting decimals.**
- **solving problems about a bank statement.**
- **how math is used in games.**

Adding and subtracting decimals will be easier if you review place value and adding and subtracting whole numbers. Study the examples.

Tens	Ones	Tenths	Hundredths	Thousandths
3	2	6	5	1

Example 1:

The value of the digit in the tenths place is 6 tenths, or 0.6.

Example 2:

The value of the digit in the thousandths place is 1 thousandth, or 0.001.

Example 3:

$$\begin{array}{r} 1 \\ 4{,}756 \\ +\ 8{,}235 \\ \hline 12{,}991 \end{array}$$

When you add or subtract whole numbers, you begin by adding or subtracting with the ones place.

Example 4:

$$\begin{array}{r} 9\ 9 \\ 6\ 10\ 10\ 10 \\ 7{,}0\ 0\ 0 \\ -\ 5{,}1\ 3\ 2 \\ \hline 1{,}8\ 6\ 8 \end{array}$$

PRACTICE

Give the value of the 6 in each decimal.

1. 0.621

2. 0.836

3. 6.711

4. 0.061

Add or subtract.

5. 476
   + 321

6. 582
   + 408

7. 1,679
   + 3,527

8. 86,527
   + 35,187

9. 456
   − 213

10. 881
   − 756

11. 3,725
   − 1,468

12. 58,321
   − 48,715

Review NUMBER skills in preparation for learning new skills.

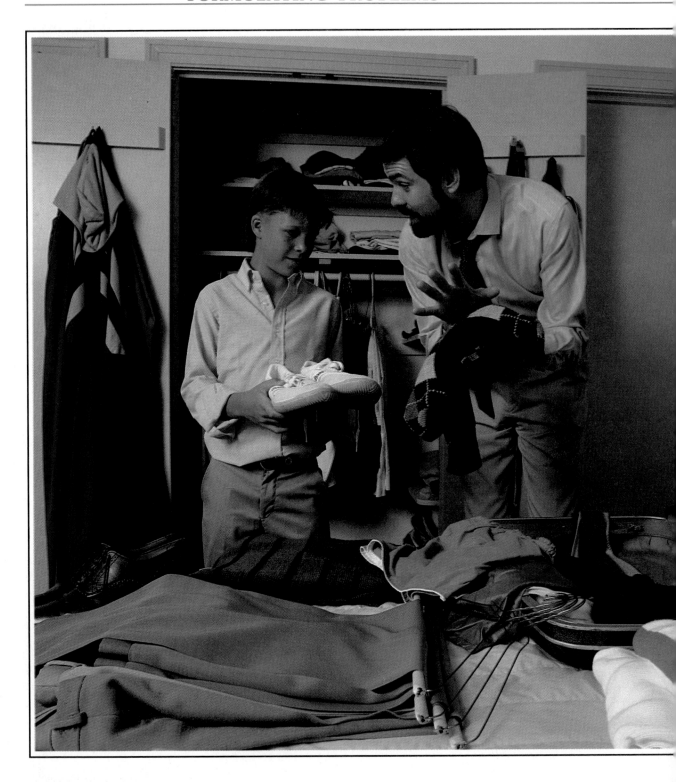

FOCUS   Formulate problems using photo, data, and text.

CHAPTER 19

Addition and Subtraction With Decimals

DATA

Mr. Marino's travel plans

Leave New York on Mon., Feb. 5

Stay in Buffalo, Mon.–Tues.,
Feb. 5–6

Stay in Washington, Wed.–Thurs.,
Feb. 7–8

Stay in Miami, Fri.–Sun.,
Feb. 9–11

Stay in Chicago, Mon., Feb. 12

Stay in Minneapolis, Tues.,
Feb. 13

Stay in Los Angeles, Wed.,
Feb. 14

Return to New York, Wed.,
Feb. 14

Predicted temperatures

New York (Feb. 5)	+ 35°F
Buffalo	− 5°F
Washington	+ 45°F
Miami	+ 85°F
Chicago	− 10°F
Minneapolis	− 25°F
Los Angeles	+ 90°F
New York (Feb. 14)	+ 30°F

"Tennis shorts, thermal shirts, wool suit . . ." Angelo Marino read his father's list. "Summer suit, bathing suit, insulated boots. I know you're going on a long business trip, but this is crazy!" Angelo held a heavy sweater in one hand, a bottle of suntan lotion in the other.

"If you check the places I'm going and the information I got from the National Weather Service, you will understand why I'm packing all these things."

Angelo looked over the itinerary and temperature data, then began adding and subtracting. "Wow!"

"What's so amazing, Angelo?"

"I just calculated that, with all the ups and downs, the temperature around you will change 415 degrees between the time you leave and the time you return."

Although Mr. Marino will not have to bear a single temperature change as great as Angelo's calculation, he may encounter other problems. Consider his schedule, his preparations, and the temperatures, and suggest why he might have made different plans.

To Thousandths

Ms. Hanami used 1.7 meters of blue fabric and 1.5 meters of yellow fabric to make a dress. How much fabric did she use in all?

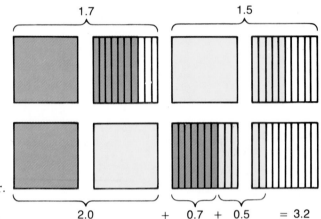

1.7   1.5

```
  1      Line up decimal points.
  1.7    Add in each place-value position.
+ 1.5    Regroup if necessary.
  3.2    Write the decimal point in the answer.
```

Ms. Hanami used 3.2 meters of fabric.

2.0   +   0.7 + 0.5   = 3.2

Add: 56.38 + 28.76

Add hundredths.

T	O	Ts	Hs
		1	
5	6	3	8
+ 2	8	7	6
			4

Line up decimal points.

Add tenths.

T	O	Ts	Hs
	1	1	
5	6	3	
+ 2	8	7	
		1	

Regroup if necessary.

Add whole numbers.

T	O	Ts	Hs
1	1	1	
5	6	3	8
+ 2	8	7	6
8	5	1	4

Write the decimal point in the answer.

Add: 45.678 + 36.09

T	O	Ts	Hs	Ths
4	5.6	7	8	
+ 3	6	0	9	
8	1	7	6	8

Write a zero to help ⟶

T	O	Ts	Hs	Ths
4	5.6	7	8	
+ 3	6	0	9	0
8	1	7	6	8

GUIDED PRACTICE

Add. Remember to line up the decimal points.

1.
```
  0.25
+ 0.34
  0.▇▇
```

2.
```
   1
  0.783
+ 0.659
 ▇.▇▇2
```

3.
```
  $0.37
+  0.95
```

4.
```
  27.09
+ 36.93
```

5.
```
  $89.59
+  76.98
```

FOCUS   Use NUMBER skills to add decimals to thousandths.

PRACTICE

Add.

6. 0.15
+ 0.23

7. 0.48
+ 0.21

8. 0.75
+ 0.03

9. 0.08
+ 0.94

10. 6.374
+ 2.04

11. $0.50
+ 0.95

12. $0.86
+ 0.25

13. 0.32
+ 0.407

14. 0.6
+ 0.009

15. 19.27
+ 6.32

16. 0.398
+ 0.245

17. 0.600
+ 0.32

18. 0.9
+ 0.724

19. 0.008
+ 0.4

20. 0.56
+ 3.097

21. $5.62
+ 7.84

22. $3.08
+ 4.79

23. 41.62
+ 2.136

24. 15.79
+ 24.4

25. 0.604
+ 7.406

26. 26.154
+ 9.37

27. 1.120
+ 0.476

28. 6.273
+ 13.844

29. 16.8
+ 64.072

30. 28.9
+ 57.613

31. 0.003
+ 124.3

32. 3.007
+ 0.322

33. 66.041
+ 9.28

34. 0.347
+ 1.004

35. 0.18
+ 2.947

MIXED PRACTICE
Maintaining and Reviewing Skills

Add or subtract. Write answers in simplest terms.

36. $3\frac{2}{5}$
$+ 9\frac{4}{7}$

37. $4\frac{3}{4}$
$+ 7\frac{5}{6}$

38. $15\frac{5}{8}$
$+ 7\frac{1}{6}$

39. $6\frac{4}{5}$
$+ 2\frac{7}{10}$

40. $8\frac{2}{3}$
$+ \frac{5}{6}$

41. $8\frac{2}{3}$
$- 3\frac{5}{12}$

42. $5\frac{1}{2}$
$- 2\frac{7}{8}$

43. $12\frac{2}{3}$
$- 7\frac{5}{6}$

44. $7\frac{8}{9}$
$- 1\frac{2}{9}$

45. $13\frac{9}{10}$
$- 4\frac{11}{15}$

CHALLENGE

*46. A snail is climbing out of a 30-foot well. Every hour it climbs up 3 feet, then slides back 2 feet in the mud. How many hours will it take the snail to climb out of the well?

ADDITION OF DECIMALS
To thousandths

Mathew's team ran in a relay race. Each runner's race time is shown in the chart at the right. What was the team's total relay time?

Relay Team	
Name	Time
Mattie	12.306 s
Elvin	10.17 s
Karen	11.009 s
Jeno	11.13 s

T	O	Ts	Hs	Ths			T	O	Ts	Hs	Ths	
		1	1						1	1		
1	2.	3	0	6			1	2.	3	0	6	
1	0.	1	7				1	0.	1	7	0	Write zeros to help.
1	1.	0	0	9			1	1.	0	0	9	
+ 1	1.	1	3		or		+ 1	1.	1	3	0	
4	4.	6	1	5			4	4.	6	1	5	Write decimal point.

Add thousandths.
Add hundredths.
Add tenths.
Add ones.
Add tens.

PRACTICE

Add.

1. 5.268
    4.31
  + 3.2

2. 25.42
    3.07
  + 42.8

3. 56.217
    25.009
  + 4.6

4. $56.39
    70.42
  + 9.50

5. $ 3.45
    17.32
  + 78.90

6. 52.489 + 3.76 + 25.7

7. 12.005 + 0.98 + 9.64 + 0.66

8. 325.2 + 4.89 + 0.006 + 45.793

9. 52.48 + 4.806 + 0.731

10. $3.37 + $245.65 + $17.93 + $0.42

11. 8.119 + 0.383 + 11.73 + 2.46

MIXED PRACTICE
Maintaining and Reviewing Skills

Subtract.

12. 3,487
   − 694

13. 5,748
   − 2,089

14. 26,773
   −   894

15. 70,425
   − 63,081

16. 42,633
   −   719

17. 18,853
   − 7,596

18. 420,661
   −   9,874

19. 368,092
   − 147,683

20. 500,603
   − 259,756

21. 921,006
   − 30,972

FOCUS	Use NUMBER skills to add three or more decimals.

APPLICATION
Using Consumer Skills

Below is part of a check register. A **check register** is a record of the activity in a checking account. It includes the **balance**, or amount of money in the account at a given time. It also includes the checks written and the **deposits** (money put into the account).

CK #	DATE	DESCRIPTION OF TRANSACTION	SUBTRACTIONS AMOUNT OF PAYMENT OR WITHDRAWAL (-)	✓	TAX OR OTHER	ADDITIONS AMOUNT OF DEPOSIT OR INTEREST (+)	BALANCE FORWARD 836 19
326	9/5	TO All-County Plumbing repair bathroom	167 15				BAL 669 04
327	9/6	TO Robes Department Store	46 39				BAL 622 65
328	9/8	TO Federal Savings Bank	550 00				BAL 72 65
	9/9	TO deposit				250 —	BAL
329	9/12	TO Townsville Water Supply	27 16				BAL
		TO					BAL

On September 5, Check 326 was written to All-County Plumbing for $167.15. After that check was written, the balance was $669.04.

Use the check register above to answer the questions.

22. How much money do Checks 326, 327, and 328 cover?

23. To whom is Check 328 written?

24. After Check 328 was written, the balance in the account was $72.65. What was the new balance after the deposit of $250 was made?

*25. After writing Check 329, the balance is $295.49. Will there be enough money in the account to write these checks: 330—$42.67, 331—$101.91, 332—$77.54?

Use number skills to read a check register.

To Thousandths

Marti paid $494.95 for a stereo. Ellen paid $379.49 for her stereo. How much more did Marti spend on his stereo than Ellen?

$$
\begin{array}{r}
{\scriptstyle 8\;14\;\;8\;15} \\
\$4\,9\,4\,.\,9\,5 \\
-\quad 3\,7\,9\,.\,4\,9 \\
\hline
\$1\,1\,5\,.\,4\,6
\end{array}
$$

Line up decimal points.
Subtract in each place-value position.
Regroup if necessary.
Write the decimal point in the answer.

Marti paid $115.46 more for his stereo than Ellen.

Sometimes you need to write one or more zeros to the right of the decimal point before you subtract.

Subtract: 566 − 87.359

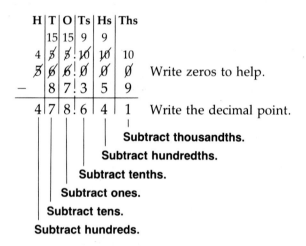

Write zeros to help.

Write the decimal point.

Subtract thousandths.
Subtract hundredths.
Subtract tenths.
Subtract ones.
Subtract tens.
Subtract hundreds.

GUIDED PRACTICE

Subtract. Remember to line up the decimal points.

1.
$$
\begin{array}{r}
{\scriptstyle 3\;10} \\
3\,.\,2\,4\,0 \\
-\,1\,.\,1\,3\,5 \\
\hline
\blacksquare\,.\,\blacksquare\blacksquare\,5
\end{array}
$$

2.
$$
\begin{array}{r}
{\scriptstyle 3\;\;11\;6\;17} \\
4\,.\,1\,7\,7 \\
-\,3\,.\,2\,6\,9 \\
\hline
\blacksquare\,.\,\blacksquare\blacksquare\,8
\end{array}
$$

3.
$$
\begin{array}{r}
4\,1\,2\,.\,\blacksquare\blacksquare\blacksquare \\
-\,2\,9\,6\,.\,4\,2\,2 \\
\hline
\blacksquare\blacksquare\blacksquare\,.\,\blacksquare\,7\,8
\end{array}
$$
←——Write 3 zeros.

4.
$$
\begin{array}{r}
5\,.\,1 \\
-\,3\,.\,3\,2\,6 \\
\end{array}
$$

5.
$$
\begin{array}{r}
6\,.\,1\,0\,3 \\
-\,3\,.\,4\,5 \\
\end{array}
$$

6.
$$
\begin{array}{r}
8\,3\,.\,3\,0 \\
-\,2\,3\,.\,2\,0\,7 \\
\end{array}
$$

7.
$$
\begin{array}{r}
2\,8\,.\,1\,2 \\
-\,6\,.\,0\,4 \\
\end{array}
$$

FOCUS | Use NUMBER skills to subtract decimals to thousandths.

PRACTICE

Subtract.

8. 9.27 − 5.96	**9.** 32.9 − 16.46	**10.** 0.218 − 0.174	**11.** 3.004 − 2.936	**12.** 16.48 − 8.5
13. 14.04 − 13.8	**14.** 16.84 − 9.9	**15.** 5.89 − 1.8	**16.** 96.11 − 7.01	**17.** 7.1 − 3.459
18. 29.196 − 17.4	**19.** 0.975 − 0.460	**20.** 58.164 − 2.09	**21.** 6.340 − 3.025	**22.** 0.828 − 0.237
23. 894.65 − 28.09	**24.** 3.596 − 1.632	**25.** 732.8 − 89.2	**26.** 3.047 − 1.829	**27.** 12.04 − 8.753
28. 5.071 − 3.256	**29.** 62.483 − 41.556	**30.** 21.2 − 17.397	**31.** 5.2 − 0.027	**32.** 0.429 − 0.377

33. $66.21 − $37.69

34. 42.3 − 10.23

35. 134.7 − 2.825

36. $16 − $2.75

37. 0.8 − 0.32

38. 0.1 − 0.01

MIXED PRACTICE
Maintaining and Reviewing Skills

Write the decimal.

39. seven tenths

40. nine tenths

41. two thousandths

42. twelve thousandths

43. six hundredths

44. forty-six thousandths

List each group of decimals in order from least to greatest.

45. 1.18, 1.81, 1.8

46. 0.9, 0.09, 0.909

47. 6.8, 8.66, 8.06

48. 4.0, 3.44, 4.044

49. 0.8, 0.88, 0.808

50. 97.6, 96.7, 97.06

CHALLENGE

***51.** List five numbers between 1.11 and 1.12.

***52.** List five numbers between 1.999 and 2.

SUBTRACTION OF DECIMALS
To Thousandths

When hit, a hockey puck had a speed of 45.55 meters per second. A golf ball had a speed of 28.371 meters per second. How much slower was the speed of the golf ball than the speed of the hockey puck?

Line up decimal points. Write zeros if necessary.

Regroup. Subtract the thousandths.	**Subtract the hundredths and tenths.**	**Subtract the tens and ones. Write the decimal point in the difference.**

T	O	Ts	Hs	Ths
		4	10	
4	5.5	5̸	0̸	
− 2	8 3	7	1	
			9	

T	O	Ts	Hs	Ths
			14	
		4	4̸	10
4	5.5̸	5̸	0̸	
− 2	8 3	7	1	
	1	7	9	

T	O	Ts	Hs	Ths
			14	
3	15 4	4̸	10	
4̸	5̸.5̸	5̸	0̸	
− 2	8 3	7	1	
1	7 1	7	9	

The speed of the golf ball was 17.179 meters per second slower than the hockey puck.

PRACTICE

Subtract.

1. $\begin{array}{r} 0.800 \\ -\ 0.762 \end{array}$ 2. $\begin{array}{r} 22.90 \\ -\ 18.2 \end{array}$ 3. $\begin{array}{r} 5.92 \\ -\ 0.499 \end{array}$ 4. $\begin{array}{r} 93 \\ -\ 5.8 \end{array}$ 5. $\begin{array}{r} 12.04 \\ -\ 8.753 \end{array}$

6. $\begin{array}{r} 35 \\ -\ 10.06 \end{array}$ 7. $\begin{array}{r} 9.27 \\ -\ 3.845 \end{array}$ 8. $\begin{array}{r} 4.75 \\ -\ 2.682 \end{array}$ 9. $\begin{array}{r} 0.063 \\ -\ 0.049 \end{array}$ 10. $\begin{array}{r} \$300 \\ -\ 125.49 \end{array}$

11. $710 - 709.95$ 12. $308 - 21.893$ 13. $250 - 9.999$

MIXED PRACTICE
Maintaining and Reviewing Skills

Solve.

14. $x - 341 = 270$ 15. $c \div 49 = 81$ 16. $14 \times b = 742$

17. $5,403 + d = 10,694$ 18. $12t = 24$ 19. $12 + q = 96$

20. $214 = a - 20$ 21. $b \div 53 = 24$ 22. $42t = 252$

FOCUS   Use NUMBER skills to subtract decimals to thousandths.

APPLICATION
Using Consumer Skills

Below is a bank statement that shows transactions in a checking account for a period of one month.

23. Are checks added or subtracted?

24. Are deposits added or subtracted?

25. Is the service charge added or subtracted?

Copy and complete the following bank statement.

	Date	Transaction	Amount	Balance	
	July 24			379.46	←—Previous Balance
26.	July 24	Deposit	326.49	705.95	
27.	Aug 06	Check	87.50	■	
28.	Aug 07	Check	53.07	■	
29.	Aug 08	Check	19.36	■	
30.	Aug 15	Deposit	326.49	■	
31.	Aug 16	Check	225.00	■	
32.	Aug 18	Check	8.65	■	
	Aug 21	Check	93.17	545.69	
	Aug 24	Service charge	5.00	540.69	
	Aug 24			540.69	←—Balance

33. What was the total amount deposited?

34. What was the total amount paid out in checks?

35. How much was the service charge?

Use the information below to find the end-of-month balance for a different bank statement.

36. previous balance: $1,907.68; checks written: $642.89; deposits: $850

37. previous balance: $504.03; checks written: $486.76; deposits: $747.62

Use NUMBER Skills to balance a checkbook.

The Soma Cube

The Soma Cube is a three-dimensional geometric puzzle. It is made up of 7 irregular shapes that, when fitted together, form a cube three units on a side. Each shape is made up of either three or four small cubes. The puzzle was invented about 40 years ago by a Danish engineer and writer, Piet Hein.

Hein first thought about combining cubes while listening to a lecture on space. In arranging two cubes, no matter which face of one cube is attached to any face of the second cube, the result is still the same.

Taking three cubes, Hein made one shape by lining them up in a row, and a different, irregular, shape by putting one cube on top of one of the other two, forming an angle.

Forms using three cubes

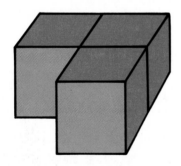

Next, Hein thought about four cubes. With four, he could form two regular shapes and 4 irregular shapes, each different from the others. These irregular shapes have "ins" and "outs." (They extend inward or outward.)

Regular shapes using four cubes

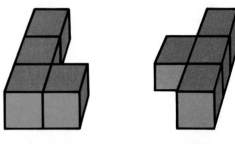

Irregular forms using four cubes

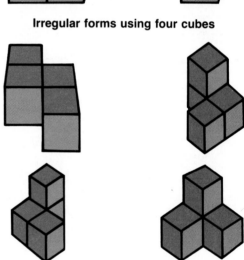

Hein found that using the six shapes made from four small cubes plus the one made from three cubes, he could form a cube that was three units on a side.

CRITICAL THINKING

1. If a 3 × 3 unit square is made up of 9 small squares, why does it take 27 cubes to make up a 3 × 3 × 3 cube?

2. Describe the difference between a regular and an irregular shape.

FOCUS | Use GEOMETRY to understand the Soma Cube.

The word *soma* comes from the ancient Greeks and means 'complete body'. The complete cube is considered the body. The individual shapes are considered inter-locking "cells."

Reviewing and Testing Chapter 19

In Chapter 19 you formulated problems about taking a trip. Refer to pages 272 and 273.

1. What things might you consider when packing for a trip?

To review what you learned about the addition of decimals, refer to page 274.

Add.

2.   0.157
   + 0.245
	3. 4.386
	   + 2.45
		4. 0.28
		   + 0.009
			5. 19.37
			   + 49.445
				6. 12.817
				   + 7.306

7.   4.35
   + 3.17
	8. 14.085
	   + 7.09
		9. 2.75
		   + 0.987
			10. 4.089
			   + 6.241
				11. 63.042
				   + 12.379

12. 1.58 + 8.14   13. 0.782 + 20.50   14. 85.5 + 2.638   15. 16.299 + 11.112

To review the subtraction of decimals, refer to page 278.

Subtract.

16.   8.45
   − 4.53
	17. 44.9
	   − 17.49
		18. 38.082
		   − 9.174
			19. 27.196
			   − 19.4
				20. 42.831
				   − 7.045

21.   23.41
   − 11.606
	22. 51.208
	   − 27.7
		23. 67.35
		   − 4.365
			24. 28.5
			   − 0.643
				25. 19.4
				   − 2.567

26. 83.7 − 43.82   27. 14.085 − 13.211   28. 76.982 − 43.794   29. 9.087 − 8.123

30. Mike runs 5 miles in 32.35 minutes. Hank runs the same distance in 26.9 minutes. How many minutes faster than Mike does Hank run 5 miles?

31. Martha walks 18.45 km to and from school each day. Ellen walks 19.87 km. How much farther does Ellen walk than Martha?

You learned about the Soma cube. To review, refer to pages 282 and 283.

32. If a 4-by 4-unit square is made up of 16 small squares, how many squares make up a 4-by 4-by 4-cube?

FOCUS   Review and test skills learned and practiced.

Preparing for New Skills for Chapter 20

In the next chapter you will focus on

- formulating problems about organizing activities for children.
- multiplying decimals by powers of 10.
- estimating products.
- using a problem-solving strategy.
- dividing decimals by powers of 10.
- estimating quotients.
- using mental arithmetic.
- how math is used in science.

Multiplying and dividing decimals by powers of 10 and estimating products and quotients will be easier if you review powers of 10 and rounding decimals.

Example 1:

10^2 means 10×10, or 100.

Example 2:

10^5 means $10 \times 10 \times 10 \times 10 \times 10$, or 100,000.

To round a decimal to a specified place, look at the digit in that place, then look at the digit to the right.

- If the digit to the right is 5 or more, add 1 to the place being rounded and drop all digits to the right.
- If the digit to the right is less than 5, drop all digits to the right of the place being rounded.

Example 3:

0.682 rounded to the nearest hundredth

$$0.682$$
— less than 5
$$0.68$$

Example 4:

0.5549 rounded to the nearest tenth

$$0.5549$$
— 5 or greater
$$0.6$$

PRACTICE

Write the standard number.

1. 10^3
2. 10^4
3. 10^6
4. 10^8

Round each decimal to the nearest tenth, then the nearest hundredth.

5. 0.642
6. 9.727
7. 43.482
8. 0.923
9. 3.855

Review NUMBER skills in preparation for learning new skills.

FOCUS Formulate problems using photo, data, and text.

20

Multiplication and Division With Decimal Powers of Ten

DATA

Time	8:45 AM–12:15 PM
Days	Mon. through Fri.
Place	Jefferson Park
Number of children enrolled	55
Daily attendance	30–45
Ages of children	5–7

Facilities
  Clubhouse (large room with small stage)
  Paved play area
  Open field
  Equipment area   swings
                        seesaws
                        jungle gym

Activities
  Organized sports
  Free play
  Arts and crafts
  Field trips

Average child's
  walking speed   3 mph

Planning activities for younger children can be a lot of fun—and at times quite a challenge! Marya and her two friends Danny and Malcolm are spending the summer assisting in the Children's Program at Jefferson Park. Each day they help Debbie, the program's leader, plan and supervise sports, crafts, and special trips. With at least 30 children present every morning, there's always plenty to do.

Try to plan a one-day—and then a one-week—schedule of park activities based on the data. Suggest what some of the "challenges" mentioned above might be.

What are some other opportunities to work with younger children? Which age group would be the most fun to plan activities for? Which age group would be the most difficult? Why?

By 10, 100, or 1,000

Multiply by 10:

$$
\begin{array}{r} 0.562 \\ \times \quad 10 \\ \hline 5.620 \end{array} = 5.62 \qquad
\begin{array}{r} 37.2 \\ \times \quad 10 \\ \hline 372.0 \end{array} = 372
$$

Shortcut: Move the decimal point 1 place to the right.

$$0.562 \times 10 = 5{.}62 = 5.62$$
$$37.2 \times 10 = 372{.} = 372$$

Multiply by 100:

$$
\begin{array}{r} 0.562 \\ \times \quad 100 \\ \hline 56.200 \end{array} = 56.2 \qquad
\begin{array}{r} 37.2 \\ \times \quad 100 \\ \hline 3{,}720.0 \end{array} = 3{,}720
$$

Shortcut: Move the decimal point 2 places to the right. Insert zeros as needed.

$$0.562 \times 100 = 56{.}2 = 56.2$$
$$37.2 \times 100 = 3720{.} = 3{,}720$$

Multiply by 1,000:

$$
\begin{array}{r} 0.562 \\ \times \quad 1{,}000 \\ \hline 562.000 \end{array} = 562 \qquad
\begin{array}{r} 37.2 \\ \times \quad 1{,}000 \\ \hline 37{,}200.0 \end{array} = 37{,}200
$$

Shortcut: Move the decimal point 3 places to the right. Insert zeros as needed.

$$0.562 \times 1{,}000 = 562{.} = 562$$
$$37.2 \times 1{,}000 = 37200{.} = 37{,}200$$

Notice the pattern. To multiply by a power of 10, move the decimal point to the right the same number of places as the number of zeros in the power of 10. Using exponents, the exponent tells how many places to move the decimal point.

$$0.562 \times 10^4 = 5620{.} = 5{,}620$$

GUIDED PRACTICE

Use the shortcut to place the decimal point.

1. $\begin{array}{r} 4.3 \\ \times \quad 10 \\ \hline 430 \end{array}$

2. $\begin{array}{r} 4.3 \\ \times 100 \\ \hline 4300 \end{array}$

3. $\begin{array}{r} 4.3 \\ \times 1{,}000 \\ \hline 43000 \end{array}$

4. $\begin{array}{r} 6.97 \\ \times \quad 10 \\ \hline 6970 \end{array}$

5. $\begin{array}{r} 6.97 \\ \times \quad 100 \\ \hline 69700 \end{array}$

6. $\begin{array}{r} 6.97 \\ \times \quad 1000 \\ \hline 697000 \end{array}$

| FOCUS | Use PATTERNS to multiply decimals by 10, 100, or 1,000. |

PRACTICE

Multiply.

7. 45.6
× 10

8. 3.51
× 10

9. 0.864
× 10

10. 0.07
× 10

11. 31.6
× 100

12. 0.052
× 100

13. 3.75
× 100

14. 0.006
× 100

15. 7.09
× 1,000

16. 82.67
× 1,000

17. 0.5603
× 1,000

18. 0.001
× 1,000

19. 0.835
× 100

20. 45.6
× 1,000

21. 0.072
× 1,000

22. 0.039
× 10,000

23. 0.318×100

24. 5.69×100

25. $0.56 \times 1,000$

26. $0.041 \times 10,000$

27. 5.2×10^3

28. 78.9×10^2

29. 0.62×10^4

30. 59.6×10^3

31. 0.04×10^5

32. 0.267×10^4

33. 0.089×10^5

34. 0.4×10^6

35. 0.003×10^3

MIXED PRACTICE
Maintaining and Reviewing Skills

Add or subtract.

36. $32\frac{7}{8}$
$+ 56\frac{3}{4}$

37. 63
$- 44\frac{5}{6}$

38. $39\frac{1}{4}$
$+ 14\frac{1}{20}$

39. $150\frac{1}{2}$
$- 74\frac{1}{3}$

40. $29\frac{2}{3}$
$+ 29\frac{2}{7}$

41. $49\frac{3}{8}$
$- 14\frac{4}{7}$

42. $81\frac{7}{8}$
$- 32\frac{1}{4}$

43. $732\frac{1}{5}$
$- 523\frac{1}{3}$

44. $326\frac{1}{4}$
$+ 112\frac{1}{12}$

45. $622\frac{5}{6}$
$- 333\frac{1}{3}$

MULTIPLICATION OF DECIMALS
Estimating Products

Estimate the product: 356.7×10^3

Round the decimal number to the nearest one and multiply.

$356.7 \rightarrow 357$
$357 \times 10^3 = 357,000$

Round the decimal number to the nearest ten and multiply.

$356.7 \rightarrow 360$
$360 \times 10^3 = 360,000$

Round the decimal number to the nearest hundred and multiply.

$356.7 \rightarrow 400$
$400 \times 10^3 = 400,000$

estimated product

Estimate the product: 0.358×10^4

Round the decimal number to the nearest tenth and multiply.

$0.358 \rightarrow 0.4$
$0.4 \times 10^4 = 4,000$

Round the decimal number to the nearest hundredth and multiply.

$0.358 \rightarrow 0.36$
$0.36 \times 10^4 = 3,600$

estimated product

PRACTICE

Estimate the products. Round as indicated.

1. 32.8×10^3 (nearest one)

2. 23.5×10^4 (nearest ten)

3. 5.55×10^2 (nearest one)

4. 251.79×10^5 (nearest ten)

5. 542.1×10^2 (nearest hundred)

6. 0.893×10^3 (nearest tenth)

7. 0.072×10^4 (nearest tenth)

8. 0.641×10^2 (nearest hundredth)

9. 0.72×10^4 (nearest tenth)

10. 0.235×10^3 (nearest hundredth)

MIXED PRACTICE
Maintaining and Reviewing Skills

Divide.

11. $10\overline{)3,420}$

12. $100\overline{)45,600}$

13. $1,000\overline{)45,000}$

14. $100\overline{)984,300}$

15. $7,800 \div 100$

16. $5,830 \div 10$

17. $97,000 \div 1,000$

18. $2,842,000 \div 1,000$

19. $84,200 \div 100$

20. $389,020 \div 10$

21. $102,000 \div 100$

22. $942,000 \div 1,000$

FOCUS | Use ESTIMATION to multiply decimals.

APPLICATION
Using Measurement

Use this chart to figure out how much U.S. dollars are worth in each country.

Example: How much is $100 worth in krone?

$100 = ■ krone
100 × 8.61 = 861
$100 = 861 krone

CURRENCY: RATES OF EXCHANGE		
Country	Currency	Rate
Denmark	krone	8.61 = $1
France	franc	6.86 = $1
Greece	drachma	83.58 = $1
Ireland	pound	0.73 = $1
Italy	lira	1,398.5 = $1
Portugal	escudo	92.53 = $1

23. $1,000 = ■ krone

24. $100 = ■ Irish pounds

25. $1,000 = ■ escudo

26. $100 = ■ lira

27. $10,000 = ■ drachma

28. $1,000 = ■ Irish pounds

29. $10,000 = ■ francs

30. $100,000 = ■ Irish pounds

31. $1,000 = ■ francs

32. $10,000 = ■ krone

33. $10 = ■ lira

34. $10,000 = ■ escudo

Using Mental Arithmetic

To change from larger to smaller units of measure, multiply by 10, 100, or 1 000.

1 gram	(g) =	1 g
1 dekagram	(dag) =	10 g
1 hectogram	(hg) =	100 g
1 kilogram	(kg) =	1 000 g

Complete. Multiply in your head. Use the shortcut.

35. 6.5 kg = ■ g
Think: 6.5 × 1 000 = ■ g

36. 0.72 hg = ■ g
Think: 0.72 × 100 = ■ g

37. 9.16 kg = ■ g

38. 4.9 dag = ■ g

39. 43.1 kg = ■ g

40. 8.7 hg = ■ g

41. 5.72 dag = ■ g

42. 0.95 kg = ■ g

43. 0.39 hg = ■ g

44. 125.2 dag = ■ g

45. 2.74 kg = ■ g

46. 33.1 hg = ■ g

Use MEASUREMENT to convert U.S. dollars into foreign currency and MENTAL ARITHMETIC to convert metric measures.

Selecting a Strategy: Using a Formula

The five important steps to solving problems are READ, KNOW, PLAN, SOLVE, and CHECK. Using a formula is a strategy that can help you PLAN and SOLVE a problem. A formula is an equation that uses letters to organize information. By substituting numbers for the letters in a formula, similar problems can be solved.

| 1. READ | Mrs. Ward's rectangular yard is 28 feet wide and 65 feet long. Mrs. Ward needs to find the area of her yard so she will know how much grass seed to buy. What is the area of Mrs. Ward's yard? |

1. READ Mrs. Ward's rectangular yard is 28 feet wide and 65 feet long. Mrs. Ward needs to find the area of her yard so she will know how much grass seed to buy. What is the area of Mrs. Ward's yard?

2. KNOW Ask yourself: What do I need to find out? What is the area of Mrs. Ward's yard?

Key facts: a. The yard is 28 feet wide and 65 feet long.
  b. The yard is shaped like a rectangle.

3. PLAN Select a strategy: Try using a formula. Use a formula to find the area of the yard. Since the yard is shaped like a rectangle, use the formula for finding the area of a rectangle:

$$\text{Area} = \text{length} \times \text{width}$$
$$A = l \times w$$

4. SOLVE length = 65 feet   width = 28 feet
Area = l (length) × w (width)
$A = 65 \times 28$ or 1,820
The area of Mrs. Ward's yard is 1,820 ft^2.

5. CHECK Reread the question and check your steps. Ask yourself: Did you choose the correct formula? Did you substitute the correct numbers for the letters in the formula? Draw a picture of Mrs. Ward's yard to help you picture the problem.

| FOCUS | Use a formula as part of the Five-Step PROBLEM-SOLVING Plan. |

PRACTICE

Choose the appropriate formula. Then solve each problem.

Area of a triangle	Area of a rectangle	Area of a circle	Area of a parallelogram
$A = \frac{1}{2} \times b \times h$	$A = l \times w$	$A = \pi \times r^2$	$A = b \times h$
b = base	l = length	π = 3.14	b = base
h = height	w = width	r = radius	h = height

1. A rectangular playground is 100 feet long and 56 feet wide. What is the area of the playground?

2. A round flower garden in a park has a radius of 14 feet. What is the area of the garden?

3. A football field is 48.8 meters wide and 109.7 meters long. What is the area of a football field?

4. A soccer field is 130 yards long and 100 yards wide. What is the area of the soccer field?

5. A triangular cape has a base of 6 feet and a height of 4 feet. How much material was used to make the cape?

6. A circular tablecloth has a radius of 35 inches. How much material was used to make the table cloth?

7. A parallelogram has a base of 64 cm and a height of 120 cm. What is the area of the parallelogram?

8. A triangle has a height of 47 meters and a base of 23 meters. What is the area of the triangle?

Class Project

Form a group with several of your classmates. Use the information below to compare the number of words in any three books. Use the following formula.

$$n = \frac{a + b + c + d + e}{5} \times p$$

n = number of words in a book
a, b, c, d, e = total number of words on any 5 pages you choose
p = total number of pages in the book

Which book has the most words? Which has the least words?

DIVISION OF DECIMALS
By 10, 100, or 1,000

Find the shortcut for dividing a decimal by 10, 100, or 1,000.

Divide: $985.2 \div 10$

$$\begin{array}{r} 98.52 \\ 10\overline{)985.20} \end{array}$$

Divide: $985.2 \div 100$

$$\begin{array}{r} 9.852 \\ 100\overline{)985.200} \end{array}$$

Divide: $985.2 \div 1,000$

$$\begin{array}{r} 0.9852 \\ 1,000\overline{)985.2000} \end{array}$$

In which direction does the decimal point move when a decimal is divided by 10, 100, or 1,000? How many places?

Shortcut to divide by 10:
Move the decimal point 1 place to the *left*. Insert zeros as needed.

$59.6 \div 10 = 5.96$

$0.32 \div 10 = 0.032$

Shortcut to divide by 100:
Move the decimal point 2 places to the *left*. Insert zeros as needed.

$398.25 \div 100 = 3.9825$

$7.56 \div 100 = 0.0756$

Shortcut to divide by 1,000:
Move the decimal point 3 places to the *left*. Insert zeros as needed.

$71,426 \div 1,000 = 71.426$

$819.5 \div 1,000 = 0.8195$

To divide by powers of 10, move the decimal point the proper number of places to the *left*. If the divisor is written in exponential form, the exponent shows the number of places to move the decimal point.

$98.3 \div 10^2 = 0.983$

↑

2 places

$98.3 \div 10^3 = 0.0983$

↑

3 places
zero inserted

GUIDED PRACTICE

Divide. Place the decimal point. Insert zeros as needed.

1. $671.2 \div 10 = 67 \blacksquare 12$

2. $671.2 \div 100 = 6712$

3. $671.2 \div 1,000 = 6712$

4. $0.689 \div 10 = 689$

5. $0.689 \div 100 = 689$

6. $0.689 \div 1,000 = 689$

7. $4,763.2 \div 10^3 = 47632$

8. $4,763.2 \div 10^4 = 47632$

9. $4,763.2 \div 10^5 = 47632$

| FOCUS | Use NUMBER skills and PATTERNS to divide decimals by 10, 100, or 1,000. |

PRACTICE

Divide.

10. $27.9 \div 10$

11. $5.2 \div 10$

12. $0.63 \div 10$

13. $0.071 \div 10$

14. $51.9 \div 100$

15. $0.064 \div 100$

16. $5.7 \div 100$

17. $0.583 \div 100$

18. $3,712 \div 1,000$

19. $526.8 \div 1,000$

20. $98.7 \div 1,000$

21. $0.43 \div 1,000$

22. $0.366 \div 100$

23. $49.94 \div 1,000$

24. $0.072 \div 100$

25. $32.7 \div 10$

26. $597.32 \div 100$

27. $6,792.4 \div 1,000$

28. $8,182.9 \div 10^3$

29. $75,462.5 \div 10^5$

30. $87,601.4 \div 10^3$

31. $66.01 \div 10^6$

32. $479.2 \div 10^2$

33. $93.24 \div 10^4$

34. $586 \div 10^3$

35. $13.5 \div 10^4$

36. $1,378.2 \div 10^2$

37. $7.92 \div 10^2$

38. $5,989.7 \div 10^5$

39. $3.1 \div 10^5$

40. $7,843.2 \div 10^3$

41. $4,763.2 \div 10^6$

42. $87,845 \div 10^3$

43. If 17.4 lb of gold nuggets are divided equally among 100 pirates, how much would each pirate get?

MIXED PRACTICE
Maintaining and Reviewing Skills

Solve.

44. $7^2 = w$

45. $3^4 = a$

46. $12^3 = n$

47. $5^6 = x$

48. $10^6 = b$

49. $10^{12} = s$

50. $100^2 = r$

51. $1,000^3 = n$

52. $5^4 = q$

53. $8^4 = z$

54. $11^3 = c$

55. $14^2 = m$

56. $6^5 = r$

57. $22^3 = b$

58. $16^4 = a$

59. $30^3 = x$

CHALLENGE

Complete the sequence.

*60. 12.3, 123, 0.123; 23.4, 234, 0.234; 34.5, ■, ■

DIVISION OF DECIMALS
Estimating Quotients

Estimate the quotient: $758.3 \div 10^3$

Round the decimal number to the nearest one and divide.

$758.3 \rightarrow 758$
$758 \div 10^3 = 0.758$

Round the decimal number to the nearest ten and divide.

$758.3 \rightarrow 760$
$760 \div 10^3 = 0.76$

Round the decimal number to the nearest hundred and divide.

$758.3 \rightarrow 800$
$800 \div 10^3 = 0.8$

estimated quotient

Estimate the quotient: $0.235 \div 10^4$

Round the decimal number to the nearest tenth and divide.

$0.235 \rightarrow 0.2$
$0.2 \div 10^4 = 0.00002$

Round the decimal number to the nearest hundredth and divide.

$0.235 \rightarrow 0.24$
$0.24 \div 10^4 = 0.000024$

estimated quotient

PRACTICE

Round numbers greater than 1 to the greatest place and numbers less than 1 to the nearest tenth. Then divide.

1. $73.3 \div 10$　　**2.** $89.7 \div 100$　　**3.** $294.8 \div 1{,}000$　　**4.** $3.5 \div 10$

5. $0.28 \div 10$　　**6.** $0.07 \div 10$　　**7.** $59.2 \div 100$　　**8.** $14.7 \div 100$

9. $3.67 \div 100$　　**10.** $79.3 \div 1{,}000$　　**11.** $32.1 \div 1{,}000$　　**12.** $0.714 \div 1{,}000$

13. $8.9 \div 10^3$　　**14.** $0.76 \div 10^2$　　**15.** $0.09 \div 10^4$　　**16.** $21.12 \div 10^2$

MIXED PRACTICE
Maintaining and Reviewing Skills

Multiply or divide.

17. $7\frac{3}{9} \times 4\frac{1}{2}$　　**18.** $8\frac{2}{3} \div 6$　　**19.** $12 \times \frac{3}{4}$　　**20.** $9 \div \frac{7}{8}$

21. $8\frac{3}{4} \times 2\frac{1}{3}$　　**22.** $9\frac{7}{8} \div 2\frac{1}{4}$　　**23.** $14\frac{3}{4} \times 2\frac{1}{2}$　　**24.** $17\frac{1}{2} \div 2\frac{1}{3}$

FOCUS　Use ESTIMATION to divide decimals.

APPLICATION
Using Mental Arithmetic

Use the shortcut to divide in your head. Move the decimal point to the *left*.

Example: $7{,}963 \div 1{,}000 = 7.963$

Think: 3 zeros   3 places left

25. $3{,}698 \div 10$

26. $746 \div 10$

27. $410 \div 10$

28. $2.7 \div 10$

29. $0.62 \div 10$

30. $0.08 \div 10$

31. $5{,}629 \div 100$

32. $273.4 \div 100$

33. $74.3 \div 100$

34. $7.12 \div 100$

35. $0.31 \div 100$

36. $0.02 \div 100$

37. $42{,}609 \div 1{,}000$

38. $5{,}291 \div 1{,}000$

39. $745 \div 1{,}000$

40. $27.9 \div 1{,}000$

41. $1.67 \div 1{,}000$

42. $0.321 \div 1{,}000$

43. $0.05 \div 1{,}000$

44. $0.007 \div 1{,}000$

45. $0.036 \div 1{,}000$

46. $3{,}814 \div 10^3$

47. $746 \div 10^4$

48. $0.32 \div 10^3$

Using Mental Arithmetic

To change from smaller to larger units of measure, divide by 10, 100 or 1 000.

meter	(m)	= 1 m
dekameter	(dam)	= 10 m
hectometer	(hm)	= 100 m
kilometer	(km)	= 1 000 m

Complete.

49. 7 254 m = ■ km
   Think: 7 254 ÷ 1 000 = ■ km

50. 9 842 m = ■ hm
   Think: 9 842 ÷ 100 = ■ hm

51. 416 m = ■ dam

52. 3 014 m = ■ km

53. 74 m = ■ hm

54. 641 m = ■ km

55. 0.5 m = ■ dam

56. 36.2 m = ■ hm

57. 3 811 m = ■ hm

58. 0.397 m = ■ dam

59. 893.2 m = ■ km

60. 44.61 m = ■ dam

Use MENTAL ARITHMETIC to divide decimals and to convert metric measures.

The Metric System

The metric system is different than the system that we are accustomed to using in the United States. Yet, almost every other country in the world uses metric units of measure.

The metric system has been in use for about two hundred years. It is simpler and easier to use than the old system, known as the British system.

This system is based on a limited number of units. These units are based on powers of ten. It is much easier to make calculations in the metric system because it is a base 10 system.

The metric system may be used to measure length, area, mass, capacity, and temperature. The base units of these measurements are as follows:

Length —meter
Area   —square meter
Mass   —gram
Capacity—liter
Temperature—degrees Celsius

The subdivisions of these base units are all powers of ten. The most important subdivisions are as follows:

$$\text{milli-} = \frac{1}{1\,000}$$
$$\text{centi-} = \frac{1}{100}$$
$$\text{kilo-} = 1\,000$$

Each subdivision can be used with any of the base units. For instance, one millimeter is equal to one-thousandth of one meter, and there are 1 000 millimeters in one meter. How many centimeters do you think are in one meter? A kilometer is equal to 1 000 meters. How many grams are in one kilogram?

The Celsius system of temperature is based on a scale of 100 degrees. In the Fahrenheit system that we still use in the United States, water freezes at 32° and boils at 212°. In the Celsius system, water freezes at 0° and boils at 100°. Isn't that easier to remember?

How many things can you think of that use the metric units of measure?

CRITICAL THINKING

1. Name the base units used in the metric units of measure.

2. Identify the three main subdivisions of the base units.

3. State how many degrees the Celsius system is based on.

FOCUS Use MEASUREMENT to learn the metric units of measure.

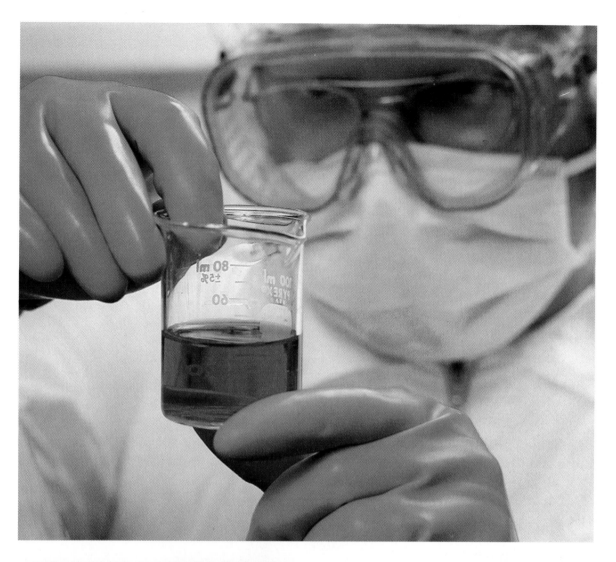

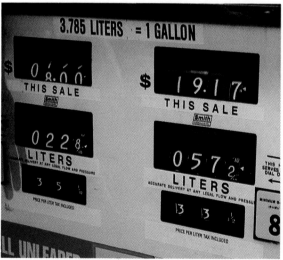

Chemists use beakers and other calibrated instruments to make precise metric measurements.

Use of the metric system in becoming increasingly common in this country. Note the measurements on the picture of the gas pump.

LOOKING BACK
Reviewing and Testing Chapter 20

In Chapter 20 you formulated problems about planning activities for young children. Refer to page 287 for data.

1. In planning the activities for children, what items were not included in the data? Make a list.

To review what you learned about multiplication of decimals by 10, 100, or 1,000, refer to page 288.

Multiply.

2.	48.3	3.	6.37	4.	0.7804	5.	758.7	6.	97.58
	× 10		× 100		× 1,000		× 10		× 1,000

7. 0.04×10^4 8. 0.9×10^5 9. 1.3×10^3 10. 0.14×10^5 11. 12.32×10^2

Estimating products was explained on page 290. Round as indicated. Then estimate the products.

12. 38.7×10^2 (nearest one)   13. 41.3×10^3 (nearest ten)   14. 0.68×10^4 (nearest tenth)

Use the Five–Step Problem–Solving Plan to solve this problem. Refer to page 292 for formulas.

15. A large clock at the top of a tower has a radius of 6 feet. What is the area of the clock face?

To review the division of decimals by 10, 100, or 1,000 refer to page 294.

Divide.

16. $57.8 \div 10$ 17. $7.085 \div 100$ 18. $48.36 \div 1,000$ 19. $583.4 \div 100$

20. $4.8 \div 10^3$ 21. $0.66 \div 10^4$ 22. $29.77 \div 10^2$ 23. $6.47 \div 10^3$

To review the metric system, refer to page 298.

24. Give one reason why the metric system of measures is easier to use than the British system.

FOCUS   Review and test skills learned and practiced.

LOOKING AHEAD
Preparing for New Skills for Chapter 21

In the next chapter you will focus on

- formulating problems about entering a walkathon.
- using metric units of length.
- using metric units of area.
- solving problems using metric measures.
- using metric units of capacity and mass.
- using measurement to find volume.
- how math is used in technology.

Working with metric units of measurement will be easier if you can multiply and divide by powers of 10. Study the examples.

To multiply by a power of 10, move the decimal point to the right as many places as there are zeros.

Example 1:

3 zeros   3 places

$8.32 \times 1,000 = 8\overline{320} = 8,320$

Example 2:

$0.52 \times 10 = 0.52 = 5.2$

To divide by a power of 10, move the decimal point to the left as many places as there are zeros.

Example 3:

2 zeros   2 places

$687 \div 100 = 6\overline{87} = 6.87$

Example 4:

$0.48 \div 10 = 0\,0.48 = 0.048$

PRACTICE

Multiply.

1. 45×10 **2.** 0.75×100 **3.** $3.901 \times 1,000$ **4.** 82.01×100

5. 0.03×10 **6.** 21.912×100 **7.** $8.6 \times 1,000$ **8.** 0.003×10

Divide.

9. $58 \div 10$ **10.** $0.3 \div 100$ **11.** $5.88 \div 10$ **12.** $435 \div 1,000$

13. $19.6 \div 100$ **14.** $34.2 \div 10$ **15.** $50.2 \div 100$ **16.** $3,461 \div 1,000$

Review NUMBER skills in preparation for learning new skills.

FOCUS   Formulate problems using photo, data, and text.

302

CHAPTER 21

Metric Measurements

DATA

Event	Walkathon
Place	town of Greenfield
Distance	10 miles
Check-in time	9 AM

Walkathon route
    corner West and Main
    Main St.
    Trinity Pl.
    Union Ave.
    First St.
    Maple Ave.
    Main St. to West St.

Checkpoint 1	
Public Library	3 mi
Checkpoint 2	
Memorial Field	5 mi
Checkpoint 3	
Madison Park	8 mi
Foot Repair Station	
Memorial Field	
Minimum pledge	10¢ per mile

Motorists driving through the center of Greenfield wondered what could possibly be going on. Thronging the sidewalks were hundreds of people dressed in shorts, T-shirts, and running shoes.

"What's happening?" called a man from his auto as he stopped for a red light.

"It's a walkathon to benefit local handicapped children," shouted Ruben, one of the walkers from Greenfield Junior High School. "We've all collected pledges from sponsors—so much per mile for each mile we walk. Our school hopes to raise $1,500."

"That sounds great," replied the motorist. "If you'll meet me on the other side of this light, I'll add my pledge to your list!"

Think of a worthwhile cause that could benefit from a walkathon. Make a list of the things that would need to be done to organize one. Consider whom it would be appropriate to ask to be sponsors. Try to predict any problems that might be involved in organizing the event. For example, what possible difficulty does Ruben's chat with the motorist suggest?

METRIC MEASURES
Of Length

millimeter mm	centimeter cm	decimeter dm	meter m	dekameter dam	hectometer hm	kilometer km
0.001 m	0.01 m	0.1 m	1 m	10 m	100 m	1 000 m

The **meter** is the basic unit of length in the metric system.

$$10 \text{ m} = 1 \text{ dam} \qquad 10 \text{ dm} = 1 \text{ m}$$
$$100 \text{ m} = 1 \text{ hm} \qquad 100 \text{ cm} = 1 \text{ m}$$
$$1\,000 \text{ m} = 1 \text{ km} \qquad 1\,000 \text{ mm} = 1 \text{ m}$$

Convert 6 409 m to km.
  Think: There are 1 000 meters in 1 kilometer.
         6 409 ÷ 1 000 = 6 409. = 6.409
         6 409 m = 6.409 km

Convert 543 m to cm.
  Think: There are 100 centimeters in 1 meter.
         543 × 100 = 54 300
         543 m = 54 300 cm

Convert 2.641 mm to cm.
  Think: There are 10 millimeters in 1 centimeter.
         2.641 ÷ 10 = 0.2641
         2.641 mm = 0.2641 cm

When measuring the length of objects choose the best unit of measure.

- length of a pencil   *centimeter*
- height of a door   *meter*
- thickness of a pencil line   *millimeter*
- distance from Dallas to Los Angles   *kilometer*

GUIDED PRACTICE

Choose the best unit of measure. Use mm, cm, m, or km.

1. height of a truck   **2.** thickness of a dime   **3.** width of a textbook

Convert.

4. 8 542 m to km
    8 542 ÷ 1 000 = ■
    8 542m = ■ km

5. 796 cm to m
    796 ÷ 100 = ■
    796 cm = ■ m

6. 6.31 km to m
    6.31 × 1 000 = ■
    6.31 km = ■ m

| FOCUS | Use MEASUREMENT to study metric units of measurement. |

PRACTICE

Choose the best unit of measure. Use millimeter (mm), centimeter (cm), meter (m), or kilometer (km).

7. height of a tree

8. length of an automobile

9. diameter of a tricycle wheel

10. distance from classroom to lunchroom

11. thickness of an eyeglass lens

12. length of a turtle

13. distance from Boston to Denver

14. height of a sparrow

15. height of a building

16. length of a school corridor

Convert.

17. 5 m = ■ cm

18. 9 cm = ■ mm

19. 8 km = ■ m

20. 6.8 m = ■ cm

21. 12.4 cm = ■ mm

22. 32.9 km = ■ m

23. 5 602 m = ■ km

24. 8 967 mm = ■ m

25. 752 mm = ■ cm

26. 419 m = ■ km

27. 9.3 m = ■ cm

28. 250 mm = ■ cm

29. 72 m = ■ km

30. 0.04 km = ■ m

31. 319 mm = ■ m

MIXED PRACTICE
Maintaining and Reviewing Skills

Multiply or divide.

32. $3\frac{2}{3} \times 5\frac{7}{8}$

33. $7\frac{3}{5} \div 2\frac{2}{3}$

34. $25 \times 6\frac{1}{9}$

35. $\frac{1}{4} \div 6$

36. 3.9×10^2

37. 0.84×10^3

38. 5.69×10^4

39. 0.12×10^5

40. $25.1 \div 10^2$

41. $4.3 \div 10^3$

42. $0.64 \div 10^3$

43. $0.02 \div 10^4$

CHALLENGE

***44.** Adam, Bill, Carla, Demetria, and Elia are friends. How many different teams of 3 members each can these 5 friends form?

METRIC MEASURES
Of Area

Mr. Chavez has to reseed a lawn that measures 208 meters in length and 125 meters in width. What is the area he must reseed?

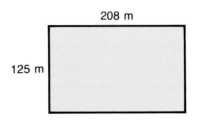

208 m

125 m

Area = length × width

$A = 208 \times 125$

$A = 26\ 000$

Mr. Chavez must reseed 26 000 m².

Remember that the measures for area are given in square units.

PRACTICE

Find the area.

1.
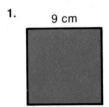
9 cm

2.
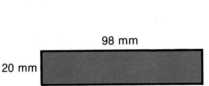
98 mm
20 mm

3.
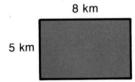
8 km
5 km

4. $l = 76$ cm; $w = 34$ cm

5. $l = 29$ dam; $w = 18$ dam

6. $l = 5$ cm; $w = 7$ cm

7. $l = 10$ dam; $w = 4$ dam

8. $l = 17$ km; $w = 5$ km

9. $l = 243$ m; $w = 115$ m

10. A book shelf has a length of 52 centimeters and a width of 28 centimeters. What is the area of the book shelf?

11. A canvas is used to cover a field. What is the area of the canvas if the length is 15 meters and the width is 11 meters?

MIXED PRACTICE
Maintaining and Reviewing Skills

Tell whether each statement is true, false, or open.

12. A century has 100 years.

13. She is a famous artist.

14. A decade has 1,000 years.

15. $x + 254 = 500$

16. $0.4063 = 0.4306$

17. $5.930 = 5.93$

18. $6,432 > b$

19. $54 \times a = 54$

20. $1,000 \div 50 = 20$

21. $928 \times 34 = 1,285$

FOCUS | Use MEASUREMENT to study metric units of measurement.

Solve.

22. A corn plant reaches a height of 2 meters in 60 days. How much does it grow per day?

23. A runner ran 3 kilometers in an hour. How many meters did he run per minute?

24. A paper clip is 3 centimeters long. There are 100 paper clips in a box. If the paper clips in 100 boxes were laid end to end, how far would they reach?

25. A stalagmite grows at the rate of 20 centimeters per year. How long will it take for the stalagmite to grow to a height of 3 meters?

26. A pressurized submarine dives at the rate of 5 meters per minute. How long will it take to reach the ocean floor, 1.2 kilometers below the surface?

27. A mountain is 3.5 kilometers high. A party of mountain climbers can only go 700 meters a day. How long will it take them to reach the summit?

28. A beach is eroding at an average rate of 50 centimeters per year. The beach is 100 meters wide. How many years will it take for the beach to erode completely?

29. Assuming the same rate of erosion, how wide was the beach a hundred years ago?
A thousand years ago?

Interpret the map.

30. In kilometers, about how high is the highest point in California?

31. What is the drop in elevation from the Sierra Nevada mountains to the Central Valley?

32. How many kilometers above sea level is the Mojave Desert?

33. The Sacramento River is 382 miles long. How many meters per mile does the river drop in elevation from its source to the Pacific Ocean?

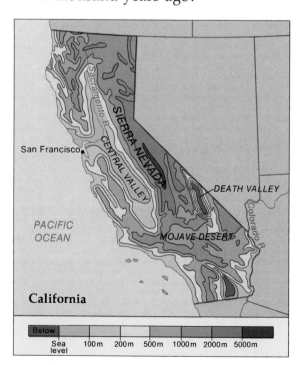

California

Below						
Sea level	100 m	200 m	500 m	1000 m	2000 m	5000 m

Use NUMBER skills to solve problems with metric units of measure.

Of Capacity and Mass

Capacity is the amount a container will hold.

The liter is the basic unit of capacity in the metric system. 1 000 milliliters (mL) = 1 liter (L)

A liter

Mass is the amount of matter in something.

The kilogram is the basic unit of mass in the metric system.

1 000 milligrams (mg) = 1 gram (g)
1 000 grams (g) = 1 kilogram (kg)
1 000 kilograms (kg) = 1 metric ton (t)

A kilogram

To convert metric measures follow these steps.

5 672 mL = ▇ L

Think: There are 1 000 mL in one L.

5 672 ÷ 1 000 = 5.672
5 672 mL = 5.672 L

8.4 kg = ▇ g

Think: There are 1 000 g in one kg.

8.4 × 1 000 = 8 400
8.4 kg = 8 400 g

When measuring capacity or mass of objects choose the best unit of measure.

What is the capacity of a container of yogurt?

200 mL or 200 L

The capacity is 200 mL.

What is the mass of a safety pin?

3 g or 3 kg

The mass is 3 g.

GUIDED PRACTICE

Convert.

1. 3 096 mL to L
   3 096 ÷ 1 000 = ▇
   3 096 mL = ▇ L

2. 9.25 t to kg
   9.25 × 1 000 = ▇
   9.25 t = ▇ kg

3. 798 mL to L
   798 ÷ 1 000 = ▇
   798 mL = ▇ L

FOCUS | Use MEASUREMENT and a CALCULATOR to study metric units of measurement.

PRACTICE

Choose the best unit of measure.

4. contents of a can of juice   5. mass of a shoe

6. length of a room   7. area of a field

8. contents of a gas tank   9. distance between two stores

10. contents of a 5-lb bag of flour   11. mass of an orange

12. mass of an elephant   13. capacity of a bathtub

Convert.

14. 752 mL = ▨ L   15. 8.5 L = ▨ mL   16. 15 672 mL = ▨ L

17. 6 043 kg = ▨ t   18. 3.5 t = ▨ kg   19. 8 639 g = ▨ kg

20. 4.1 kg = ▨ g   21. 52.6 kg = ▨ g   22. 482 mL = ▨ L

*23. 962 t = ▨ kg   *24. 62 mg = ▨ g   *25. 79 g = ▨ kg

MIXED PRACTICE
Maintaining and Reviewing Skills

Add or subtract.

26.	$426.45	27.	$4,681.05	28.	$750.00	29.	$1,572.68
	17.92		324.72		236.00		2,821.72
	+ 35.89		+ 506.14		+ 504.68		+ 623.56

30.	$1,000.00	31.	$2,704.95	32.	$35,900.00	33.	$867,953.00
	− 743.69		− 896.40		− 28,459.62		− 286,231.65

CHALLENGE

Solve. Use a calculator.

*34. A piece of computer paper has 2 tractor-feed guide strips. Each strip has 22 holes on it. How many full strips have to be collected to have a total of 1 million holes?

METRIC MEASURES
Of Capacity and Mass

Ruth bought some potatoes with a mass of 3.2 kilograms. How many grams is this?

Think: 1 000 g = 1 kg

3.2 × 1 000 = 3 200

There are 3 200 grams in 3.2 kilograms.

Frank purchased a bottle of juice marked 750 mL. What part of a liter is this?

Think: 1 000 mL = 1 L   750 ÷ 1 000 = 0.750

A bottle marked 750 mL is 0.75 L.

Rafael transported a shipment of wheat with a mass of 6.9 metric tons. How many kilograms is this?

Think: 1 000 kg = 1 t   6.9 × 1 000 = 6 900

The shipment of wheat had a mass of 6 900 kilograms.

PRACTICE

Complete.

1. 6 L = ■ mL

2. 7 640 kg = ■ t

3. 5 268 g = ■ kg

4. 7 kg = ■ g

5. 9.2 t = ■ kg

6. 5.5 L = ■ mL

7. 700 kg = ■ g

8. 800 kg = ■ t

9. 785 mL = ■ L

10. 9 642 mL = ■ L

11. 17 890 kg = ■ t

12. 25 g = ■ kg

MIXED PRACTICE
Maintaining and Reviewing Skills

Add or subtract.

13. 67,842 + 963

14. 17,090 − 4,362

15. $486.75 + $39.18

16. $5,624.32 + $8,305.29

17. $700 − $515.36

18. $2,000 − $79.50

FOCUS   Use MEASUREMENT to study metric units of measurement.

APPLICATION
Using Measurement

Volume is the number of cubic units that fit inside a figure.

A **cubic centimeter (cm³)** is a metric unit of volume. Another metric unit of volume is the **cubic meter (m³).**

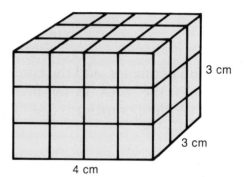

Cubic centimeter

To find the volume of the box in cubic centimeters, you can:

- Count the number of cubes
- Multiply the length (*l*), the width (*w*), and the height (*h*).

Formula for volume:

$$V = l \times w \times h$$
$$= 4 \times 3 \times 3$$
$$= 36 \text{ cm}^3$$

The volume of the box is 36 cm³.

Multiply to find the volume.

19.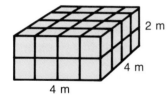
2 m
4 m
4 m

20.
TISSUES
5 cm
24 cm   12 cm

21.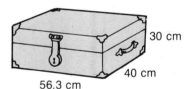
30 cm
40 cm
56.3 cm

22. *l* = 8 cm
w = 6 cm
h = 9 cm

23. *l* = 10 m
w = 3.4 m
h = 5 m

24. *l* = 20 cm
w = 1.4 cm
h = 30 cm

25. *l* = 25 m
w = 1.5 m
h = 2 m

26. *l* = 2.1 m
w = 1.6 m
h = 1m

27. *l* = 3.8 m
w = 0.9 m
h = 1.5 m

28. *l* = 16 cm
w = 12 cm
h = 1.8 cm

*29. *l* = 2 m
w = 89 cm
h = 1 m

30. How many boxes 4 cm long, 4 cm wide, and 4 cm high can fit into a box like the one at the right?

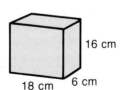
16 cm
18 cm   6 cm

Use MEASUREMENT to find the volume of a figure.

311

Using the Order of Operations

What is the formula for finding the perimeter of a rectangle?

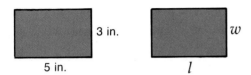

3 in.

5 in.

w

l

To find the perimeter, add the sum of the lengths of the sides. In the first rectangle above, the perimeter is 5 + 5 + 3 + 3 or 16 inches.

In the second rectangle, the length is represented by l, and the width is represented by w. The perimeter then is $l + l + w + w$, or $P = 2l + 2w$.

Use this formula for finding the perimeter of a rectangle where $l = 7$ and $w = 4$.

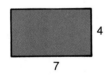

4

7

Method 1

$P = 2l + 2w$
$P = (2 \times 7) + (2 \times 4)$
$P = 14 + (2 \times 4)$
$P = 14 + 8$
$P = 22$

Notice that this method is correct, because it follows the rules for order of operations. (The same mathematical rules for order of operations hold for the computer's computations.)

Order of Operations

a. First perform any operations that are within parentheses.
b. Evaluate any powers.
c. Multiply and divide in order, from left to right.
d. Add and subtract in order, from left to right.

Examples:
- $A = 5 + 6 \times 7$
  First multiply, then add:
  $= 5 + 42$
- $B = 8 + 4(5)$
  $B = 8 + 20 = 28$
- $C = 15 - 2\wedge3$
  In computer work, we write $2\wedge3$ (or $2\uparrow3$ for some computers) to mean 2^3. Simplify exponents before subtracting.
  $C = 15 - 8$
  $C = 7$

CRITICAL THINKING

1. Find the value assigned to D:
   $D = 3 * (5 + 4) + 3\wedge4$

2. What value will the computer assign to Z if $X = 5$ and $Y = 10$?
   $Z = X * Y/Y * X$

3. Create an example in which the answer is correct even though the order of operations is not followed.

FOCUS | Use NUMBER skills and LOGIC to use the order of operations when programming in BASIC.

The Order of Operations Makes a Difference!

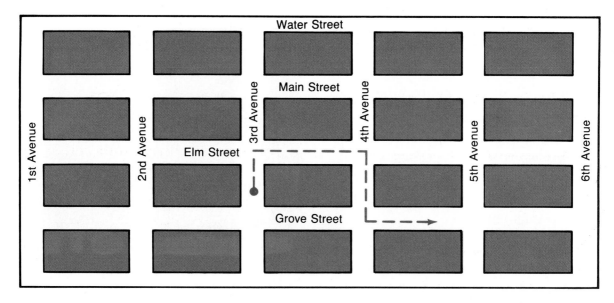

In the diagram above, a car is started on 3rd Avenue between Elm and Grove Streets. The driver makes the first right, turns right again, and then turns left. In the diagram below, a car starts from the same position, then turns left, right, and then right again. Notice that although both cars started from the same point and made two right turns and one left turn, they ended up in different locations. The reason for this is that they made the turns in different orders. Order is just as important in mathematics!

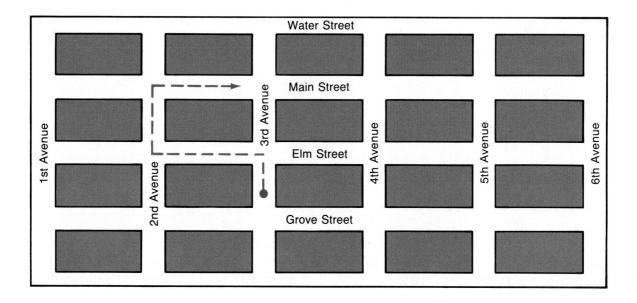

In Chapter 21 you formulated problems about a walkathon. To review, refer to pages 302 and 303.

1. What events can you think of, other than a walkathon that could benefit a charity?

To review metric measures of length, refer to page 304.

Convert.

2. 3.4 m = ▦ cm   **3.** 12 450 m = ▦ km   **4.** 18 cm = ▦ mm   **5.** 0.2 km = ▦ m

6. 13.5 cm = ▦ mm   **7.** 0.02 m = ▦ mm   **8.** 0.6 km = ▦ m   **9.** 7 km = ▦ m

10. 850 dm = ▦ m   **11.** 29 m = ▦ cm   **12.** 4.3 m = ▦ mm   **13.** 63 mm = ▦ cm

To review what you learned about metric measures of area, refer to page 306.

Find the area for each rectangle.

14. l = 90 cm
w = 80 cm

15. l = 18 m
w = 17 m

16. l = 12 m
w = 15 m

17. l = 17 km
w = 9 km

18. l = 8 mm
w = 21 mm

19. l = 13 cm
w = 12 cm

20. l = 7 km
w = 19 km

21. l = 18 mm
w = 11 mm

You learned about metric measures of capacity and mass. Refer to page 308.

Convert.

22. 684 mL = ▦ L   **23.** 9.3 L = ▦ mL   **24.** 84 t = ▦ kg   **25.** 720 mg = ▦ g

26. 6 kg = ▦ g   **27.** 8t = ▦ g   **28.** 7.58 g = ▦ kg   **29.** 4 785 mL = ▦ L

30. 310 mL = ▦ L   **31.** 4.7 kg = ▦ g   **32.** 11 L = ▦ mL   **33.** 4 000 mg = ▦ g

You learned about using the order of operations. To review, refer to pages 312 and 313.

34. Find the value assigned to b: $b = 5 \times (3 + 9) + 2^6$

| FOCUS | Review and test skills learned and practiced. |

Preparing for New Skills for Chapter 22

> **In the next chapter you will focus on**
>
> - formulating problems about helping an elderly neighbor.
> - multiplying decimals.
> - using patterns to multiply.
>
> - dividing decimals by whole numbers.
> - dividing decimals by decimals.
> - using metric measurement.
> - how math is used in music.

Multiplying and dividing decimals will be easier if you review multiplying and dividing with whole numbers. Study the examples.

Example 1:

```
      368
   ×   27
    2 576    7 × 368
    7 360   20 × 368
    9,936
```

Example 2:

```
      210
   ×  405
    1 050     5 × 210
   84 000   400 × 210
   85,050
```

Example 3:

```
        25
   36) 900
      − 72
       180
     − 180
```

Example 4:

```
       105
   42) 4410      Remember to place a
      − 42       zero in the quotient
       210       any time the remainder
     − 210       is less than the divisor.
```

Remember that you can multiply by 10, 100, or 1,000 just by moving the decimal point.

Example 5:

$$4.5 \times 100 = 4.50 = 450$$

Example 6:

$$0.354 \times 1,000 = 0.354 = 354$$

PRACTICE

Multiply or divide.

1. $23) \overline{920}$ **2.** 461×25 **3.** $82) \overline{8,692}$ **4.** 615×322 **5.** $75) \overline{22,500}$

6. 2.71×100 **7.** 0.3×10 **8.** $8.26 \times 1,000$ **9.** 23.007×100 **10.** $0.004 \times 1,000$

Review NUMBER skills in preparation for learning new skills.

FOCUS   Formulate problems using photo, data, and text.

22

Multiplication and Division With Decimals

DATA

Number of people at dinner 4

Ingredients:
Green beans
　　Cooking time: 20 min
　　Cost: $1.29 per pound

Chicken
　　Baking time: 45 min at 350°
　　Cost: $1.73 per pound

New potatoes
　　Cooking time: 15 min
　　Cost: $1.59 per pound

Salad
　　Lettuce: $1.09 per head
　　Tomatoes: $.69 per pound
　　Cucumbers: 5 for $1.00

Strawberries
　　Cost: $1.49 per pint

Melon
　　Cost: $2.49 each

Tomato juice
　　Cost: $.39 per 10-oz can

Helping an older person can be a rewarding and enjoyable experience. Tara and Joshua are cooking dinner for their neighbor, Mrs. Robinson, who just came home from the hospital. To make the meal more like a party, they have invited another neighbor, Mrs. Washington, to join them. Tara and Joshua know that a successful meal takes careful planning. They have to buy the right amount of food, find out how to cook it, and start each item at the right time so all the food gets done at once.

Is any experience necessary to plan and cook a meal? Does the data provide everything needed to prepare a dinner for four people? Estimate what such a meal will cost. What are some benefits that Tara and Joshua will derive from their activity?

By a Decimal

To multiply decimals, multiply as you do with whole numbers. Then write the decimal point in the product.

Multiplying Whole Numbers	Multiplying Decimals Learning Where to Write the Decimal Point		

$$253 \times 24$$

253	
× 24	
1 012	
5 060	
6,072	

253	0 places
× 2.4	+ 1 place
101 2	1 place
506 0	
607.2	

25.3	1 place
× 2.4	+ 1 place
10 12	2 places
50 60	
60.72	

2.53	2 places
× 2.4	+ 1 place
1 012	3 places
5 060	
6.072	

Number of digits to the right
of the decimal points

*The number of decimal places in the product is equal to the sum
of the number of decimal places in the factors.*

Multiply: 0.002×4.537

4.537	3 places
× 0.002	3 places
0.009074	6 places

Insert 2 zeros.

0.0361	4 places
× 0.0004	4 places
0.00001444	8 places

Insert 4 zeros.

Sometimes zeros must be written in the product.

GUIDED PRACTICE

Multiply.

1. 25.3 ←— 1 place
  × 2.6 ←— 1 place
  ←— 2 places

2. 4.37 ←— 2 places
  × 5.3 ←— 1 place
  ←— 3 places

3. 3.75 ←— 2 places
  × 0.75 ←— 2 places
  ←— 4 places

4. 0.26
  × 0.9

5. 165.1
  × 6.7

6. 4.008
  × 0.15

7. 0.765
  × 0.003

FOCUS | Use NUMBER skills to multiply decimals.

PRACTICE

Multiply.

8. $\begin{array}{r} 346 \\ \times\ 0.2 \\ \hline \end{array}$

9. $\begin{array}{r} 72.5 \\ \times\ \ \ 3 \\ \hline \end{array}$

10. $\begin{array}{r} 8.16 \\ \times\ \ \ 4 \\ \hline \end{array}$

11. $\begin{array}{r} 421 \\ \times\ 1.5 \\ \hline \end{array}$

12. $\begin{array}{r} 1.36 \\ \times\ 0.4 \\ \hline \end{array}$

13. $\begin{array}{r} 5.03 \\ \times\ 1.2 \\ \hline \end{array}$

14. $\begin{array}{r} 61.4 \\ \times\ 0.12 \\ \hline \end{array}$

15. $\begin{array}{r} 9.052 \\ \times\ \ \ \ 3 \\ \hline \end{array}$

16. $\begin{array}{r} 13.6 \\ \times\ 0.02 \\ \hline \end{array}$

17. $\begin{array}{r} 0.172 \\ \times\ \ \ \ 14 \\ \hline \end{array}$

18. $\begin{array}{r} 2.124 \\ \times\ \ \ 3.3 \\ \hline \end{array}$

19. $\begin{array}{r} 4.762 \\ \times\ \ 0.15 \\ \hline \end{array}$

20. $\begin{array}{r} 27.06 \\ \times\ \ 2.54 \\ \hline \end{array}$

21. $\begin{array}{r} 1.243 \\ \times\ 0.301 \\ \hline \end{array}$

22. $\begin{array}{r} 6.15 \\ \times\ 0.23 \\ \hline \end{array}$

23. $\begin{array}{r} 0.472 \\ \times\ 0.312 \\ \hline \end{array}$

24. $\begin{array}{r} 0.061 \\ \times\ 0.008 \\ \hline \end{array}$

25. $\begin{array}{r} 4.003 \\ \times\ 2.005 \\ \hline \end{array}$

26. $\begin{array}{r} 500 \\ \times\ 0.813 \\ \hline \end{array}$

27. $\begin{array}{r} 112 \\ \times\ 0.387 \\ \hline \end{array}$

28. $\begin{array}{r} 0.84 \\ \times\ 0.303 \\ \hline \end{array}$

29. $\begin{array}{r} 1.001 \\ \times\ \ \ 246 \\ \hline \end{array}$

30. $\begin{array}{r} 3.002 \\ \times\ \ \ 0.6 \\ \hline \end{array}$

31. $\begin{array}{r} 7.601 \\ \times\ \ \ 0.8 \\ \hline \end{array}$

32. $\begin{array}{r} 6.4 \\ \times\ 0.008 \\ \hline \end{array}$

33. 5.2×2.6

34. 0.747×90

35. 5.43×10

36. 35.7×0.134

37. 0.16×80

38. 77.5×0.294

39. 1.006×0.002

40. 0.307×2.18

41. 1.042×8.31

42. 0.0008×0.04

43. 2.877×0.4

44. 0.052×0.03

MIXED PRACTICE
Maintaining and Reviewing Skills

Multiply. Write answers in simplest terms.

45. $\frac{3}{4} \times \frac{3}{8}$

46. $7 \times \frac{3}{5}$

47. $\frac{2}{3} \times 3\frac{1}{5}$

48. $6 \times \frac{2}{3}$

49. $1\frac{1}{6} \times \frac{4}{7}$

50. $2\frac{3}{4} \times 1\frac{3}{5}$

51. $\frac{4}{5} \times 10\frac{1}{2}$

52. $7\frac{1}{2} \times \frac{2}{5}$

53. $5\frac{3}{10} \times 1\frac{1}{4}$

CHALLENGE

Find the next two missing numbers for each.

*54. 1, 0.5, 0.25, ■, ■

*55. 300, 3, 0.03, ■, ■

MULTIPLICATION OF DECIMALS
By 0.1, 0.01, and 0.001

- To multiply by 0.1, move the decimal point 1 place to the left.
- To multiply by 0.01, move the decimal point 2 places to the left.
- To multiply by 0.001, move the decimal point 3 places to the left.

$$546 \times 0.1 = 54.6 \qquad\qquad 546 \times 0.1 = 54.6$$

$$546 \times 0.01 = 5.46 \qquad\qquad 546 \times 0.01 = 5.46$$

$$546 \times 0.001 = 0.546 \qquad\qquad 546 \times 0.001 = 0.546$$

Sometimes zeros must be written in the product.

$$48 \times 0.1 = 4.8 \qquad\qquad 3.2 \times 0.1 = 0.32$$

$$48 \times 0.01 = 0.48 \qquad\qquad 3.2 \times 0.01 = 0.032$$

$$48 \times 0.001 = 0.048 \qquad\qquad 3.2 \times 0.001 = 0.0032$$

PRACTICE

Multiply. Write zeros if necessary.

1. 587 $\times 0.1$	**2.** 32.6 $\times 0.1$	**3.** 7.82 $\times 0.1$	**4.** 96.2 $\times 0.01$	**5.** 92.06 $\times 0.01$
6. 5.18 $\times 0.01$	**7.** 0.27 $\times 0.01$	**8.** 0.326 $\times 0.001$	**9.** 380.1 $\times 0.001$	**10.** 45.9 $\times 0.001$

11. 56.002×0.1 **12.** 502.3×0.01 **13.** 0.7×0.001

MIXED PRACTICE
Maintaining and Reviewing Skills

Divide.

14. $23\overline{)6,935}$ **15.** $42\overline{)2,753}$ **16.** $55\overline{)1,892}$ **17.** $98\overline{)1,253}$

18. $8\overline{)5,300}$ **19.** $90\overline{)79,394}$ **20.** $42\overline{)2,312}$ **21.** $17\overline{)8,429}$

FOCUS	Use NUMBER skills to multiply decimals.

APPLICATION
Using Patterns

Multiplying decimals is like multiplying whole numbers, except for the placement of the decimal point.

When you multiply **tenths** by **tenths**, the product is in **hundredths**.

$$0.1 \quad \times \quad 0.1 \quad = \quad 0.01$$

tenths × tenths = hundredths

When you multiply **tenths** by **hundredths**, the product is in **thousandths**.

$$0.1 \quad \times \quad 0.01 \quad = \quad 0.001$$

tenths × hundredths = thousandths

The number of decimal places in a product is equal to the sum of the number of decimal places in the factors.

Choose the place value for each product.

22. 0.3 × 0.5
    a. hundredths
    b. tenths

23. 1.14 × 1.2
    a. tenths
    b. thousandths

24. 25.6 × 120.33
    a. hundredths
    b. thousandths

25. 0.4 × 167.5
    a. hundredths
    b. thousandths

26. 25.4 × 35.6
    a. hundredths
    b. thousandths

27. 2.5 × 1.9
    a. tenths
    b. hundredths

28. 213.1 × 0.01
    a. tenths
    b. thousandths

29. 325.4 × 0.15
    a. hundredths
    b. thousandths

30. 248.1 × 3.2
    a. hundredths
    b. tenths

Choose the correct product.

31. 1.7 × 0.33
    a. 0.561
    b. 56.1

32. 20.2 × 1.11
    a. 224.22
    b. 22.422

33. 1.5 × 5.5
    a. 8.25
    b. 0.825

34. 4.5 × 0.05
    a. 0.225
    b. 0.0225

35. 0.98 × 0.02
    a. 1.96
    b. 0.0196

36. 1.36 × 0.03
    a. 0.0408
    b. 0.408

Use PATTERNS to multiply decimals.

DIVISION OF DECIMALS
By Whole Numbers

A package of paper party dishes has a mass of 43.2 grams. There are 16 paper dishes in each package. What is the mass of each dish?

Find: 43.2 ÷ 16

```
        2.7  ←—— Quotient
   16) 43.2  ←—— Dividend
       32
       11 2
       11 2
          0
```

Place the decimal point in the quotient directly above the decimal point in the dividend.

Then divide as if you were dividing whole numbers.

Each paper party dish had a mass of 2.7 grams.

Sometimes you must write one or more zeros in the quotient.

Find: 2.701 ÷ 73

```
        0.037
   73) 2.701
       2 19
        511
        511
          0
```

Sometimes you must write one or more zeros after the decimal point in the dividend in order to divide until there is a zero remainder.

Find: 32.7 ÷ 6

```
        5.45
    6) 32.70
       30
        2 7
        2 4
          30
          30
```

GUIDED PRACTICE

Divide. Watch for zeros in the quotient. You may have to write one or more zeros in the dividend.

```
        1.▮
1.  8) 15.2
        8
        7 2
```

```
         6.3▮
2.  15) 94.8
        90
         4 8
         4 5
```

```
        0.01▮
3.  24) 0.336
        24
         9
```

4. 5) 31.9   5. 4) 94.4   6. 78) 1.17   7. 54) 6.858

FOCUS Use NUMBER skills to divide decimals.

322

PRACTICE

Divide.

8. $5\overline{)12.60}$ **9.** $4\overline{)32.8}$ **10.** $7\overline{)28.77}$ **11.** $10\overline{)36.820}$ **12.** $41\overline{)17.425}$

13. $4\overline{)8.64}$ **14.** $2\overline{)38.7}$ **15.** $6\overline{)57.3}$ **16.** $4\overline{)33.7}$ **17.** $8\overline{)5.2}$

18. $3\overline{)22.65}$ **19.** $4\overline{)0.85}$ **20.** $8\overline{)20.76}$ **21.** $5\overline{)15.52}$ **22.** $8\overline{)249.6}$

23. $4\overline{)27.36}$ **24.** $5\overline{)47.3}$ **25.** $8\overline{)9.712}$ **26.** $6\overline{)1.344}$ **27.** $16\overline{)43.6}$

28. $15\overline{)16.2}$ **29.** $6\overline{)0.084}$ **30.** $97\overline{)12.61}$ **31.** $5\overline{)0.615}$ **32.** $7\overline{)23.03}$

33. $76\overline{)6.08}$ **34.** $7\overline{)101.64}$ **35.** $8\overline{)0.064}$ **36.** $41\overline{)2.1156}$ **37.** $32\overline{)19.2}$

38. $8.6 \div 40$ **39.** $2.92 \div 8$ **40.** $25.4 \div 8$

41. $5.1 \div 15$ **42.** $13.9 \div 4$ **43.** $177.3 \div 9$

MIXED PRACTICE
Maintaining and Reviewing Skills

Divide. Write answers in simplest terms.

44. $\dfrac{7}{8} \div \dfrac{15}{16}$ **45.** $\dfrac{3}{10} \div 6$ **46.** $\dfrac{3}{4} \div \dfrac{9}{10}$

47. $\dfrac{9}{10} \div \dfrac{8}{5}$ **48.** $2\dfrac{2}{3} \div \dfrac{5}{9}$ **49.** $1\dfrac{1}{2} \div 3\dfrac{1}{4}$

50. $8 \div 2\dfrac{2}{9}$ **51.** $2\dfrac{2}{3} \div \dfrac{3}{4}$ **52.** $7 \div 3\dfrac{6}{7}$

53. $\dfrac{1}{2} \div \dfrac{3}{20}$ **54.** $\dfrac{1}{2} \div \dfrac{4}{11}$ **55.** $\dfrac{5}{9} \div 5$

CHALLENGE

*56. What is the actual area of the room shown in this scale drawing?

1 cm = 4 m

DIVISION OF DECIMALS
Dividing by a Decimal

To divide by a decimal divisor, follow these steps:

- Multiply the divisor by the smallest power of ten, (10, 100, and so on) that will make the new divisor a whole number.
- Multiply the dividend by the same number (so that the quotient is not changed).
- Write the decimal point in the quotient directly above the decimal point in the new dividend.
- Divide as you would with whole numbers.

Find: $12.075 \div 2.3$

$$2.3)\overline{12.075}$$

Multiplying by 10 moves the decimal point one place to the right and makes the divisor a whole number.

$$
\begin{array}{r}
5.25 \\
2.3)\overline{12.075} \\
\underline{11\ 5} \\
57 \\
\underline{46} \\
115 \\
\underline{115}
\end{array}
$$

Check
$$
\begin{array}{r}
5.25 \\
\times\ 2.3 \\
\hline
1575 \\
1050 \\
\hline
12.075
\end{array}
$$

Find: $3.2 \div 0.125$

$$
\begin{array}{r}
25.6 \\
0.125)\overline{3.200}
\end{array}
$$
Sometimes zeros must be added in the dividend.

PRACTICE

Divide.

1. $0.5)\overline{18.45}$ **2.** $0.8)\overline{554.4}$ **3.** $0.9)\overline{19.233}$ **4.** $4.6)\overline{1,863}$ **5.** $0.37)\overline{0.34595}$

6. $0.03)\overline{2.751}$ **7.** $0.83)\overline{7.055}$ **8.** $0.004)\overline{0.380}$ **9.** $0.26)\overline{11.7}$ **10.** $8.4)\overline{0.5628}$

11. $0.06)\overline{195.24}$ **12.** $0.012)\overline{798.6}$ **13.** $5.05)\overline{10.1}$ **14.** $52.1)\overline{12.6603}$ **15.** $2.35)\overline{8.1075}$

MIXED PRACTICE
Maintaining and Reviewing Skills

Solve.

16. $\dfrac{5}{9} = \dfrac{a}{27}$ **17.** $\dfrac{4}{7} = \dfrac{32}{b}$ **18.** $\dfrac{11}{13} = \dfrac{44}{w}$ **19.** $\dfrac{100}{125} = \dfrac{n}{750}$ **20.** $\dfrac{7}{29} = \dfrac{d}{145}$

| FOCUS | Use NUMBER skills to divide decimals. |

324

APPLICATION
Using Measurement

These are commonly used units of **length** in the metric system.

meters (m)
kilometers (km)
centimeters (cm)
millimeters (mm)

1 km = 1 000 m	1 m = 0.001 km
1 m = 100 cm	1 cm = 0.01 m
1 m = 1 000 mm	1 mm = 0.001 m

To change to a smaller unit, multiply by 10, 100, and so on.

Express 3 km as meters.   Think: $\begin{cases} 3 \text{ km} = \blacksquare \text{ m} \\ 1 \text{ km} = 1\ 000 \text{ m} \\ 3 \text{ km} = 3 \times 1\ 000 \text{ m} \\ 3 \text{ km} = 3\ 000 \text{ m} \end{cases}$

To change to a larger unit, multiply by 0.1, 0.01, and so on.

Express 2 mm as meters.   Think: $\begin{cases} 2 \text{ mm} = \blacksquare \text{ m} \\ 1 \text{ mm} = 0.001 \text{ m} \\ 2 \text{ mm} = 2 \times 0.001 \text{ m} \\ 2 \text{ mm} = 0.002 \text{ m} \end{cases}$

Find each missing number.

21. 4 km = $\blacksquare$ m

22. 300 cm = $\blacksquare$ m

23. 4 000 mm = $\blacksquare$ m

24. 3 100 m = $\blacksquare$ km

25. 650 cm = $\blacksquare$ m

26. 2 400 mm = $\blacksquare$ m

27. 7 km = $\blacksquare$ m

28. 5 m = $\blacksquare$ mm

29. 200 m = $\blacksquare$ km

30. 6 m = $\blacksquare$ cm

31. 4 000 m = $\blacksquare$ km

32. 65 cm = $\blacksquare$ m

33. 616 cm = $\blacksquare$ m

34. 31 km = $\blacksquare$ m

35. 2 km = $\blacksquare$ m

36. 9 000 mm = $\blacksquare$ m

37. 7 000 cm = $\blacksquare$ m

38. 1.2 cm = $\blacksquare$ m

Tell if each names the same length. Write *yes* or *no*.

39. 5.4 m = 54 cm

40. 246 cm = 2.46 m

41. 0.4 m = 400 cm

42. 0.036 cm = 0.36 mm

43. 496 mm = 49.60 cm

44. 3 m = 3 000 mm

45. 2.5 m = 250 cm

46. 30 cm = 0.3 m

47. 8 km = 8 000 m

The Metronome

Many kinds of music have distinctive beats. Whenever music is written, the composer indicates that it should be performed at a specific pace or tempo. A number written at the beginning of the piece—120 for example—tells the performer that the piece should be played at a tempo of 120 beats per minute.

How fast is that? The metronome tells us. A **metronome** is a machine that beats out the time. When it is set at 120, it clicks 120 times every minute.

The mechanical metronome has a double pendulum. The rod in it that swings back and forth has a weight, called a *bob*, at each end, and a pivot in between. The upper bob, the only one you can see, can be moved up and down along a scale. Read the smallest number and the largest number on the scale. The largest number is closer to the pivot. The largest number also gives the faster tempo.

A long pendulum needs more time for a complete swing than a short pendulum. A short pendulum swings more times in a minute than a long one. With each swing of the pendulum, there is a click. The numbers on the scale tell us the number of clicks, or beats, per minute.

Some electronic metronomes not only click out the beats, but they can also be set to click more loudly for certain stressed beats.

Beethoven's "Eighth Symphony" is often called the "Metronome Symphony," because one part has a strong steady beat. Would you call rock music "metronome music"?

CRITICAL THINKING

1. When a metronome is set at 60, how many times does it click every minute? How much time is there between clicks, measured in fractions of a minute? measured in seconds?

2. When a metronome is set at 120, how many times does the pendulum click every minute? How many times does it click in one second? How much time is there between clicks?

3. Measure the pendulum from the pivot to the bob for the settings for 60 beats per minute and 120 beats per minute. For which setting is the pendulum longer? Is it twice as long?

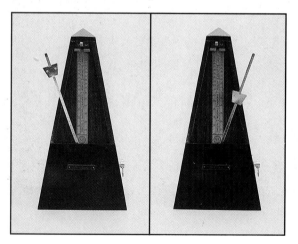

FOCUS | Use MEASUREMENT to understand how a metronome is used.

Symphony rehearsals insure that the many different beats will create a unified sound.

LOOKING BACK
Reviewing and Testing Chapter 22

In Chapter 22 you formulated problems about helping an elderly person. Refer to pages 316 and 317.

1. What factors could determine the types of food that are served at the dinner party?

You learned about multiplying a decimal by a decimal. To review, refer to page 318.

Multiply.

2. 4.836 × 3.8	**3.** 0.762 × 36.4	**4.** 8.752 × 0.87	**5.** 7.006 × 0.7	**6.** 58.42 × 36.17
7. 684 × 0.1	**8.** 0.85 × 0.72	**9.** 786 × 0.001	**10.** 517 × 0.01	**11.** 98.4 × 6.8

To review what you learned about dividing decimals by whole numbers, refer to page 322.

Divide.

12. 4)‾16.48   **13.** 9)‾118.8   **14.** 16)‾100.96   **15.** 23)‾70.173   **16.** 30)‾33.330

17. 7)‾29.12   **18.** 5)‾76.90   **19.** 42)‾122.22   **20.** 71)‾1.278   **21.** 22)‾0.154

You learned about dividing a decimal by a decimal. To review, refer to page 324.

Divide.

22. 0.9)‾185.4   **23.** 1.3)‾9.1   **24.** 8.9)‾41.207   **25.** 0.04)‾0.0728   **26.** 63.06)‾5.0448

27. 0.4)‾3.44   **28.** 0.5)‾3.15   **29.** 0.9)‾0.306   **30.** 4.2)‾5.502   **31.** 0.33)‾15.18

You learned about the metronome and its function in writing music. To review, refer to page 326.

32. If the metronome is set at 100, how many times does the pendulum click every minute? Every second?

FOCUS | Review and test skills learned and practiced.

LOOKING AHEAD
Preparing for New Skills for Chapter 23

In the next chapter you will focus on

- formulating problems about a thrift shop.
- writing ratios.
- identifying proportions.
- solving proportions.

- using a problem-solving strategy.
- using scale drawings.
- solving problems using proportion.
- using patterns in division.
- how math is used in keeping time.

It will be easier to work with proportions if you review solving equivalent fractions and simple equations. Study the examples.

Equivalent fractions name the same number.

Example 1:

$$\left.\frac{2}{4}, \frac{4}{8}, \frac{8}{16}, \frac{16}{32}\right\} \text{ equivalent fractions}$$

Each fraction names $\frac{1}{2}$.

Example 2:

$$\left.\frac{3}{9}, \frac{4}{12}, \frac{9}{27}, \frac{12}{36}\right\} \text{ equivalent fractions}$$

Each fraction names $\frac{1}{3}$.

You can use inverse operations to solve equations with an unknown.

Example 3:

$$3 \times n = 27$$
$$n = 27 \div 3$$
$$n = 9$$

Example 4:

$$n \div 6 = 7$$
$$n = 7 \times 6$$
$$n = 42$$

PRACTICE

Write an equivalent fraction for each.

1. $\frac{3}{4}$ **2.** $\frac{2}{3}$ **3.** $\frac{3}{7}$ **4.** $\frac{6}{10}$ **5.** $\frac{2}{9}$

Write an inverse equation. Then solve.

6. $3 \times a = 27$ **7.** $22 + z = 29$ **8.** $n \div 5 = 3$ **9.** $c - 11 = 17$

Review NUMBER skills and ALGEBRA in preparation for learning new skills.

FOCUS | Formulate problems using photo, data, and text.

23

Ratio and Proportion

DATA

Activity   Organizing Ms. Adams'
            Odd Odds-and-Ends
            Shop

Total pay for the job $200

Gail's share of the job $\frac{1}{2}$

Ben's share $\frac{1}{2}$

Quaye's share $\frac{1}{2}$ of Ben's share

Jill's share $\frac{1}{2}$ of Quaye's share

Max's share $\frac{1}{2}$ of Jill's share

Ben and Gail were in Ms. Adams' Odd Odds-and-Ends Shop, looking for an old jukebox for their "fifties" show. After two hours, Ben spotted the perfect jukebox. Unfortunately, it was under a bed and two tables, behind car doors and bedboards. "It will take days just to get it out," said Gail. "We might as well reorganize everything."

"Would you?" asked Ms. Adams. "I have been meaning to, but I've been busy. I will pay two hundred dollars.

Ben and Gail agreed to split the work and money. After two days' work, Ben realized he would need help; his computer class limited his work time. He offered "half the money" to Quaye, who shared the work with Jill, who was offered another half. Jill in turn asked her brother Max for help, promising half the money.

When the work was done, the $200 was divided among the five workers. Max said, "My half is less than Gail's. Something's wrong." Why is Max disappointed? Suggest how some hurt feelings might have been avoided.

Writing Ratios and Proportions

There are 3 sailboats and 5 motorboats docked at the town pier.

A **ratio** is a way to compare numbers. The *ratio* of sailboats to motorboats can be written as a fraction.

3 to 5 is equivalent to $\frac{3}{5}$.

5 to 3 is equivalent to $\frac{5}{3}$.

The ratio of 3 cans of peas for 89¢ can be written as a fraction.

3 for 89¢ is equivalent to $\frac{3}{89}$. ⟵ Number of cans ⟵ Total cost

The ratio of 5 pens for $1.98 can be written as a fraction.

Think: $1.98 is equivalent to 198¢.

5 for $1.98 is equivalent to $\frac{5}{198}$. ⟵ Number of pens ⟵ Total cost

A **proportion** is two equal ratios. To decide if two ratios form a proportion, use cross products to check for equivalence.

$\frac{3}{5} \overset{?}{=} \frac{6}{10}$ $\frac{3}{5} \diagup\!\!\!\!\diagdown \frac{6}{10}$ $3 \times 10 = 30$ $\frac{3}{5} = \frac{6}{10}$ Since the cross products are equal, the ratios form a proportion.
$5 \times 6 = 30$

GUIDED PRACTICE

Write ratios.

1. 8 to 15 $\frac{8}{\blacksquare}$

2. 4 for 50¢ $\frac{\blacksquare}{50}$

3. 6 for $1.49 $\frac{6}{\blacksquare}$

4. 3 to 107 $\frac{\blacksquare}{107}$

5. 14 out of 25

6. eleven to nine

7. 10 to 50

8. 9 for $2.00

Does each pair of ratios form a proportion?

9. $\frac{7}{8} = \frac{32}{28}$
$7 \times 28 = 196$
$8 \times 32 = \blacksquare$

10. $\frac{5}{6} = \frac{10}{12}$
$5 \times 12 = \blacksquare$
$6 \times 10 = \blacksquare$

11. $\frac{8}{9} = \frac{24}{27}$

12. $\frac{3}{159} = \frac{6}{477}$

FOCUS	Use NUMBER skills to write ratios and determine if ratios form a porportion

PRACTICE

Write ratios.

13. 4 to 5　　　　**14.** 8 to 11　　　　**15.** 9 to 8　　　　**16.** 1 to 6

17. four to six　　**18.** thirty to seven　**19.** five to ten　　**20.** two for fifty

21. 83 out of 100　**22.** 25 for $2　　　**23.** 10 for $10　　**24.** 225 to 98

25. $4 for 75　　　**26.** 3 to 1,001　　**27.** 203 to 100　　**28.** $7.25 each

Does each pair of ratios form a proportion?

29. $\frac{1}{2} = \frac{5}{10}$　　**30.** $\frac{25}{100} = \frac{1}{4}$　　**31.** $\frac{3}{8} = \frac{15}{40}$　　**32.** $\frac{2}{5} = \frac{50}{20}$

33. $\frac{19}{20} = \frac{39}{40}$　　**34.** $\frac{4}{99} = \frac{8}{198}$　　**35.** $\frac{3}{25} = \frac{9}{75}$　　**36.** $\frac{4}{79} = \frac{12}{158}$

37. $\frac{5}{10} = \frac{10}{150}$　　**38.** $\frac{2}{15} = \frac{6}{30}$　　**39.** $\frac{1}{17} = \frac{3}{51}$　　**40.** $\frac{50}{1} = \frac{200}{4}$

41. $\frac{79}{100} = \frac{237}{300}$　　**42.** $\frac{13}{39} = \frac{52}{156}$　　**43.** $\frac{3}{2} = \frac{30}{200}$　　**44.** $\frac{150}{100} = \frac{3}{2}$

MIXED PRACTICE
Maintaining and Reviewing Skills

Add, subtract, divide, or multiply.

45.　35,689
　　　+ 28,407

46.　926,841
　　　+ 378,045

47.　43,005
　　　− 18,654

48.　321,679
　　　− 214,501

49.　528
　　　× 42

50.　6,741
　　　× 89

51.　3,076
　　　× 190

52.　5,392
　　　× 378

53. $20\overline{)1,300}$　　**54.** $45\overline{)11,250}$　　**55.** $322\overline{)37,352}$　　**56.** $407\overline{)122,396}$

57. $32\overline{)2,816}$　　**58.** $66\overline{)26,408}$　　**59.** $129\overline{)23,617}$　　**60.** $200\overline{)124,800}$

CHALLENGE

Solve.

Iris earns $14 per week. She saves $4 per week.

****61.** What is the ratio of her savings to earnings?

****62.** What is the ratio of her earnings to savings?

RATIO AND PROPORTION

Solving Proportions

Dean used 3 bottles of fruit juice to serve 6 people. How many bottles are needed to serve 18 people?

Write a proportion.

People $\longrightarrow$ $\dfrac{6}{3} = \dfrac{18}{n}$ Let n stand for
Bottles $\longrightarrow$ number of bottles.

Use cross products to solve. $\dfrac{6}{3} \diagup\hspace{-1.2em}\diagdown \dfrac{18}{n}$

$$6 \times n = 3 \times 18$$
$$6 \times n = 54$$
$$\frac{6 \times n}{6} = \frac{54}{6} \qquad \text{(Divide both sides by 6.)}$$
$$n = 9$$

Dean needs 9 bottles of fruit juice.

Solve: $\dfrac{5}{a} = \dfrac{30}{36}$

Use cross products to solve. $\dfrac{5}{a} \diagup\hspace{-1.2em}\diagdown \dfrac{30}{36}$

$$5 \times 36 = a \times 30$$
$$180 = a \times 30$$
$$\frac{180}{30} = \frac{a \times 30}{30} \qquad \text{(Divide both sides by 30.)}$$
$$6 = a$$

PRACTICE

Solve these proportions.

1. $\dfrac{1}{2} = \dfrac{a}{4}$ **2.** $\dfrac{3}{5} = \dfrac{12}{b}$ **3.** $\dfrac{2}{c} = \dfrac{10}{40}$ **4.** $\dfrac{d}{7} = \dfrac{9}{21}$ **5.** $\dfrac{4}{10} = \dfrac{m}{30}$

6. $\dfrac{15}{x} = \dfrac{25}{50}$ **7.** $\dfrac{t}{100} = \dfrac{1}{4}$ **8.** $\dfrac{20}{4} = \dfrac{r}{1}$ **9.** $\dfrac{35}{w} = \dfrac{7}{14}$ **10.** $\dfrac{100}{p} = \dfrac{10}{1}$

11. $\dfrac{l}{4} = \dfrac{25}{2}$ **12.** $\dfrac{h}{49} = \dfrac{2}{98}$ **13.** $\dfrac{5}{2} = \dfrac{n}{20}$ **14.** $\dfrac{r}{8} = \dfrac{70}{80}$ **15.** $\dfrac{6}{t} = \dfrac{36}{54}$

MIXED PRACTICE
Maintaining and Reviewing Skills

Read each. Write *true*, *false*, or *open*.

16. $3 + 2 > 2 - 1$ **17.** $7.90 = 7.9$ **18.** $8 < 7$ **19.** $\dfrac{4}{9} = \dfrac{c}{36}$

20. $8^3 = 512$ **21.** $19 \times 10^3 = 1,900$ **22.** $7^6 = w$ **23.** $36 \times 10^4 = 360,000$

| FOCUS | Use NUMBER skills and ALGEBRA to solve proportions. |

APPLICATION
Using Measurement

Scale drawings are used to represent the actual dimensions of objects and distances.

Use a centimeter ruler to measure distances on the map.

According to the scale drawing, what is the actual distance from Stanton to the State park?

To find the actual dimensions on scale drawings follow these steps.:

- Measure the scale drawing.
- Set up a proportion using the scale measurements.
- Use cross products to solve.

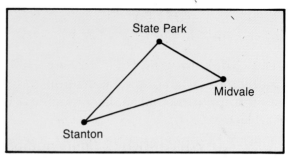

scale: 1 cm = 50 km

$$\frac{1}{50} = \frac{3}{n} \qquad \longleftarrow \text{ scale distance}$$
$$\longleftarrow \text{ actual distance}$$

$$1 \times n = 50 \times 3$$

$$1 \times n = 150$$

$$\frac{1 \times n}{1} = \frac{150}{1}$$

$$n = 150 \text{ km} \longleftarrow \text{ actual distance}$$

Use the map and your centimeter ruler to answer the following questions.

24. What is the actual distance between Stanton and Midvale?

25. What is the actual distance between Midvale and the State park?

26. How far would Jonathan drive if he started at Stanton, drove to the State Park, then drove to Midvale, and returned home to Stanton by the direct route?

27. How far would Rachel drive if she started at Midvale and drove to the State Park, then drove to Stanton and then to the State Park and then back to Midvale?

Use a centimeter ruler to make the following scale drawings.

28. Make a scale drawing of a soccer field whose length is 100 yards and whose width is 50 yards. Use the scale 1 in. = 10 yards.

29. Make a scale drawing of a swimming pool whose length is 25 meters and whose width is 10 meters. Use the scale 2 cm = 5 meters.

30. Make a scale drawing of a room. Give the scale measurements.

31. Make a scale drawing of a picnic table. Give the scale measurements.

Use MEASUREMENT to make a scale drawing.

Selecting a Strategy: Using Guess and Test

The five important steps to solving problems are READ, KNOW, PLAN, SOLVE, and CHECK. Guess and test can help you SOLVE and CHECK some kinds of problems. Each time you guess and test, you learn something new that makes your next guess better.

1. READ Which two 2-digit numbers made from the digits 1, 2, 3, 4, and 5, give the largest sum when added together? No single digit may be used more than once.

2. KNOW Ask yourself: What do I need to find out? Which two 2-digit numbers give the largest sum when added together?

Key facts: a. The two 2-digit numbers must be made from the digits 1, 2, 3, 4, and 5.

b. No digit may be used more than once.

3. PLAN Select a strategy: Try using guess and test. Keep trying combinations of 2-digit numbers until the largest sum is found.

4. SOLVE First guess. Guess two 2-digit numbers: 54, 32.

$54 + 32 = 86$

SOLVE Second guess. Guess two 2-digit numbers: 53, 42.

$53 + 42 = 95$

5. CHECK Test your guess. Ask yourself: Is 86 a reasonable sum? No, adding 5 and 3 in the tens place gives 80. If you change 3 to 4 and then add 5 and 4 in the tens place, you get 90. $90 > 80$.

CHECK Test again. Ask yourself: Is 95 a reasonable sum? Yes, 5 and 4 are the largest digits that can appear in the tens column. 2 and 3 are the largest digits that can appear in the ones column. Therefore, choosing 53 and 42 or 52 and 43 is correct.

FOCUS Use guess and test as part of the Five-Step PROBLEM-SOLVING Plan.

PRACTICE

Use guess and test to SOLVE each of the problems. Remember you may have to guess and test several times before you find a solution.

1. Which two 2-digit numbers made from the digits 5, 6, 7, and 8 give the largest sum when added together? No single digit may be used more than once.

2. Which 3-digit and 1-digit number made with the digits 3, 4, 5, and 6 give the largest product when multiplied together? No single digit may be used more than once.

3. Which two 3-digit numbers made from the digits 1, 2, 3, 4, 5, and 6 give the largest sum when added together? No single digit may be used more than once.

*4. Which 3-digit and 2-digit numbers made with the digits 1, 2, 3, 4, and 5 give the largest product when multiplied together? No single digit may be used more than once.

Use guess and test to determine what digits the letters stand for in each of the exercises below. (0 is zero in Exercise 7.)

5.
$$\begin{array}{r} 2B1 \\ \times\ \ \ 4 \\ \hline 8B4 \end{array}$$

6.
$$\begin{array}{r} BA \\ \times\ BA \\ \hline BAA \end{array}$$

7.
$$\begin{array}{r} A0A \\ \times\ \ \ A \\ \hline 2A2A \end{array}$$

8.
$$\begin{array}{r} A56 \\ \times\ \ \ A \\ \hline 51A \end{array}$$

9.
$$\begin{array}{r} AB \\ \times\ \ B \\ \hline A01 \end{array}$$

10. $B2B \div B = 10B$

11. $BB4 \div B = 11B$

12. $12A \div A = 2A$

13.
$$\begin{array}{r} 21A \\ \times\ \ \ 4 \\ \hline 84A \end{array}$$

14.
$$\begin{array}{r} AAA \\ \times\ \ \ A \\ \hline 277A \end{array}$$

15.
$$\begin{array}{r} 1B1 \\ \times\ \ \ B \\ \hline B4B \end{array}$$

16.
$$\begin{array}{r} AB \\ \times\ \ B \\ \hline 189 \end{array}$$

*17.
$$\begin{array}{r} BA2 \\ \times\ \ \ A \\ \hline 972 \end{array}$$

Class Project

Form a group with several of your classmates. Bring a container filled with some item such as pennies, paper clips, marbles, or beans to class. Count how many items are in the container and write the number on a piece of paper. Then exchange containers with another group and estimate the number of items in the container you receive. Do not open the container to make your estimates. At the end of the week, compare estimates and find which group was the closest.

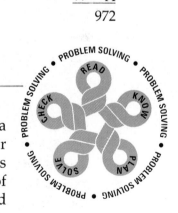

Using Proportions to Solve Problems

Enrique is baking rolls. The recipe calls for 2 cups of flour for 36 rolls. How many cups will he need to make 144 rolls?

Start with a ratio.

$\dfrac{2}{36}$ ←— Cups
←— Rolls

Set up a proportion.

$\dfrac{2}{36} = \dfrac{n}{144}$ ←— Cups
←— Rolls

Use cross products to solve.

$\dfrac{2}{36} \times \dfrac{n}{144}$

$$2 \times 144 = 36 \times n$$
$$288 = 36 \times n$$
$$\dfrac{288}{36} = \dfrac{36 \times n}{36} \qquad \text{(Divide both sides by 36.)}$$
$$8 = n$$

Enrique needs 8 cups of flour to make 144 rolls.

Betina bought 3 cans of water chestnuts for $2.98. How much will 6 cans cost?

Think: $2.98 = 298 cents   Ratio: $\dfrac{3}{298}$ Proportion: $\dfrac{3}{298} = \dfrac{6}{x}$ ←— Cans
←— Cost

Use cross products to solve. $\dfrac{3}{298} \times \dfrac{6}{x}$

$$3 \times x = 298 \times 6$$
$$3 \times x = 1,788$$
$$\dfrac{3 \times x}{3} = \dfrac{1,788}{3} \qquad \text{(Divide both sides by 3.)}$$
$$x = 596 \text{ cents, or } \$5.96$$

GUIDED PRACTICE

Solve.

1. 2 jars for 99¢
   How much for 4 jars?
   $\dfrac{2}{99} = \dfrac{4}{x}$ ←— Jars
   ←— Cost

2. 5 pens for $1.98
   How much for 15 pens?
   $\dfrac{5}{198} = \dfrac{15}{t}$ ←— Pens
   ←— Cost

3. 55 km in 3 hours
   How far in 6 hours?

4. 75 km in 4 hours
   How long to travel 300 km?

5. 7 m of silk for 2 dresses
   How many meters for 6 dresses?

6. $25 for 3 dinners
   How much for 12 dinners?

| FOCUS | Use NUMBER skills and ALGEBRA to solve word problems involving proportions. |

PRACTICE

Write a proportion.
Solve.

7. 3 tennis balls for $2.98
How much for 6 tennis balls?

8. 12 balloons for 89¢
How much for 72 balloons?

9. 75¢ per hour rental
How much for 4 hours?

10. 39 beads on a necklace
How many beads on 5 necklaces?

11. 500 sheets in 2 tablets
How many sheets in 6 tablets?

12. 6 cans for $2.89
How much for 18 cans?

13. 8 tires for 2 cars
How many tires for 10 cars?

14. 35 miles per gallon of gas
How many miles for 20 gallons?

15. 1,100 ft per second
How many feet in 4 seconds?

16. 14 days in 2 weeks
How many days in 8 weeks?

17. 5 cm per 100 km
How many kilometers for 15 cm?

18. 1,000 miles in 3 days
How many days for 9,000 miles?

19. 3 kg of meat for 10 patties
How many patties from 9 kg?

20. 2 kg of cheese for 15 people
How much cheese for 45 people?

21. 72 pens per carton
How many cartons for 432 pens?

22. 36 eggs in 2 cartons
How many eggs in each carton?

23. 24 pigeons in 4 coops
How many pigeons in each?

24. 12 oz for 55¢
How many ounces for $2.75?

MIXED PRACTICE
Maintaining and Reviewing Skills

Multiply or divide.

25. $71 \times 1,000$ **26.** $5.42 \div 100$ **27.** $0.9 \div 1,000$ **28.** 0.77×10 **29.** $0.004 \times 1,000$

30. $6.3 \div 100$ **31.** $89.41 \div 1,000$ **32.** 100×27.63 **33.** $67 \div 1,000$ **34.** 0.0086×10

35. 100×417 **36.** $0.625 \div 100$ **37.** $0.9 \times 1,000$ **38.** $1,000 \times 0.006$ **39.** $46.8 \div 1,000$

CHALLENGE

Solve.

*40. A computer printer prints 3.5 lines in 5 seconds. How many lines does it print per minute?

RATIO AND PROPORTION
Using Proportions to Solve Problems

Below is a list of items that Mr. Cho bought in the produce department.

1 lb of onions
2 heads of lettuce
1 cucumber
4 bags of radishes
4 bunches of carrots
12 tomatoes
2 lb of spinach
1 bunch of celery
2 peppers

PRICE LIST	
Carrots	2 for 98¢
Spinach	69¢ lb
Celery	2 for 88¢
Cucumbers	3 for 75¢
Radishes	2 for 60¢
Lettuce	95¢ each
Onions	3 lb for 69¢
Tomatoes	6 for 78¢
Peppers	4 for $1.00

How much did Mr. Cho pay for 12 tomatoes?

Solve: $\dfrac{6}{78} = \dfrac{12}{n}$

$6 \times n = 78 \times 12$

$6 \times n = 936$

$\dfrac{6 \times n}{6} = \dfrac{936}{6}$ (Divide both sides by 6.)

$n = 156$

Mr. Cho paid $1.56 for 12 tomatoes.

PRACTICE

Solve.

1. $\dfrac{3}{45} = \dfrac{1}{r}$ **2.** $\dfrac{69}{3} = \dfrac{t}{6}$ **3.** $\dfrac{s}{10} = \dfrac{20}{50}$ **4.** $\dfrac{9}{v} = \dfrac{3}{4}$ **5.** $\dfrac{3}{5} = \dfrac{x}{100}$

6. $\dfrac{5}{n} = \dfrac{45}{63}$ **7.** $\dfrac{6}{8} = \dfrac{y}{40}$ **8.** $\dfrac{13}{11} = \dfrac{t}{22}$ **9.** $\dfrac{m}{42} = \dfrac{1}{6}$ **10.** $\dfrac{n}{100} = \dfrac{10}{1,000}$

MIXED PRACTICE
Maintaining and Reviewing Skills

Which property of multiplication is shown?

11. $19 \times w = 0$ **12.** $27 \times t = 27$ **13.** $(c \times d) \times e = c \times (d \times e)$

14. $25 \times 67 = 67 \times 25$ **15.** $0 \times 346 = 0$ **16.** $1 \times 87 = 87$

FOCUS	Use NUMBER skills and ALGEBRA to solve word problems involving proportions.

APPLICATION

Using Customary Units

The table below shows how customary units of length are related.

12 inches (in.) = 1 foot (ft) 3 feet (ft) = 1 yard (yd)	36 inches (in.) = 1 yard (yd) 5,280 feet (ft) = 1 mile (mi) 1,760 yards (yd) = 1 mile (mi)

2 ft = ■ in.

Write and solve a proportion.

Feet $\longrightarrow$ $\dfrac{2}{■} = \dfrac{1}{12}$
Inches $\longrightarrow$

$2 \times 12 = ■ \times 1$

$24 = ■ \times 1$

$24 = ■$

2 ft = 24 in.

12 ft = ■ yd

Write and solve a proportion.

Feet $\longrightarrow$ $\dfrac{12}{■} = \dfrac{3}{1}$
Yards $\longrightarrow$

$12 \times 1 = ■ \times 3$

$12 = ■ \times 3$

$4 = ■$

12 ft = 4 yd

Complete.

17. 4 ft = ■ in. **18.** 108 in. = ■ ft **19.** 2 mi = ■ yds **20.** 84 in. = ■ ft

21. 2 yd = ■ in. **22.** 27 ft = ■ yd **23.** 5 yd = ■ ft **24.** 3 mi = ■ ft

25. 79 in. = ■ ft ■ in. **26.** 325 ft = ■ yds ■ ft **27.** 17 ft = ■ yd ■ ft

Using Customary Units

The table below shows how customary units of capacity and weight are related.

8 fluid ounces (fl oz) = 1 cup (c) 2 cups (c) = 1 pint (pt) 2 pints (2 pt) = 1 quart (qt)	2 quarts (qt) = 1 half gallon $\left(\frac{1}{2} \text{ gal}\right)$ 4 quarts (qt) = 1 gallon (gal) 16 ounces (oz) = 1 pound (lb)

Complete.

28. 80 oz = ■ lb **29.** 4 lb = ■ oz **30.** 45 lb = ■ oz **31.** 32 oz = ■ lb

32. 4 c = ■ fl oz **33.** 6 qt = ■ pt **34.** 5 pt = ■ c **35.** 4 gal = ■ qt

36. 46 oz = ■ lb ■ oz **37.** 78 oz = ■ lb ■ oz **38.** 65 oz = ■ lb ■ oz

Use MEASUREMENT to convert customary units of measure.

Ancient Timekeeping

Clocks and watches are so common today that we sometimes take them for granted. The first "clock" dates back to about 3500 B.C. It was called a **gnomon**. The gnomon was a vertical stick or a pillar that cast a shadow on a numbered scale to show the hour.

The sundial developed from the principle of the gnomon. From ancient Egypt to the sixteenth century, sundials of all shapes were used to tell time. For the sundial to work properly, it had to align to the Earth's axis. That meant the gnomon (still the instrument used to cast a shadow), had to be adjusted depending on the sundial's location on Earth. At the equator, the gnomon had to be horizontal to point in the right direction. At the north pole, it had to point straight up. Another problem with the sundial was that it needed daylight to be read.

As early as 1400 B.C. the ancients began to invent other timekeeping devices. The most popular of these was the candle clock and the water clock, or clepsydra. The candle clock used burning wax to show the passage of time. Evenly spaced pellets were fit into the wax and as the candle burned down, the pellets dropped. The water clock consisted of a bowl with measure markings on the side and a hole in the bottom. The bowl was filled to the brim at twilight each day. As the water dripped out at a constant rate, the level of the water showed how much time had passed. In ancient Rome, attorneys used a clepsydra to time their speeches.

CRITICAL THINKING

1. Defend or deny this statement: A sundial with a gnomon pointing up would be equally accurate at the equator and the north pole.

2. If there are 12 evenly spaced measures on a clepsydra which takes 8 hours to empty, how much time has passed when the water has dropped 3 units from the top?

3. What problems do you see with the candle clock?

FOCUS Use MEASUREMENT to understand and appreciate ancient timekeeping devices.

This Roman sundial still keeps time as long as the sun shines. What time is it?

LOOKING BACK
Reviewing and Testing Chapter 23

In Chapter 23 you formulated problems about workers in a thrift shop. To review, refer to page 331 for data.

1. Did each of the workers get paid a "fair share" for the amount of work they did?

You learned about writing ratios and proportions. To review, refer to page 332.

Write a ratio.

2. 7 to 4

3. 87 out of 100

4. 3 to 5

5. 9 out of 300

Does each pair of ratios form a proportion? Write *yes* or *no*.

6. $\frac{7}{9} = \frac{14}{18}$

7. $\frac{10}{15} = \frac{20}{150}$

8. $\frac{6}{8} = \frac{54}{72}$

9. $\frac{14}{15} = \frac{84}{90}$

10. $\frac{2}{7} = \frac{5}{28}$

Use the Five-Step Problem-Solving Plan to solve this problem. Refer to page 336.

11. Which two 2-digit numbers made with the digits 3, 4, 5, 6, and 7 give the largest product when multiplied together? No single digit may be used more than once.

To review what you learned about using proportions to solve problems, refer to page 338.

Write a proportion. Solve.

12. 5 cans for $2.65
How much for 15 cans?

13. 27 miles per gallon of gas
How many miles for 15 gallons?

14. 45 yards for $5.15
How much for 315 yards?

15. 4 footballs for $18.50
How much for 6 balls?

You learned about ancient time-keeping devices. To review, refer to page 342.

16. There are 12 evenly-spaced marks on a clepsydra. If it takes 9 hours to empty, how much time has passed when the third mark is reached?

FOCUS | Review and test skills learned and practiced.

LOOKING AHEAD
Preparing for New Skills for Chapter 24

In the next chapter you will focus on

- formulating problems about a boating event.
- finding the outcomes of an experiment.
- finding the probability of an event.
- finding sample spaces using tree diagrams.
- using probability to predict outcomes.
- how math is used in technology.

It will be easier to learn about probability if you study the following examples.

Barbara has 4 blue marbles and 6 red marbles.

Example 1:

The ratio of blue marbles to red marbles is

$$4:6, \text{ or } \frac{4}{6}, \text{ or } \frac{2}{3}.$$

Example 2:

The ratio of blue marbles to total marbles is

$$4:10, \text{ or } \frac{4}{10}, \text{ or } \frac{2}{5}.$$

Solve for *n*.

Example 3:

$$\frac{1}{2} = \frac{n}{12}$$
$$1 \times 12 = 2 \times n$$
$$12 = 2 \times n$$
$$\frac{12}{2} = \frac{2 \times n}{2}$$
$$6 = n$$

Example 4:

$$\frac{n}{12} = \frac{5}{4}$$
$$n \times 4 = 12 \times 5$$
$$n \times 4 = 60$$
$$\frac{n \times 4}{4} = \frac{60}{4}$$
$$n = 15$$

PRACTICE

There are 4 orange beads, 3 white beads, and 7 blue beads in a box. Write each ratio.

1. blue beads to orange beads

2. white beads to total beads

Solve for *n*.

3. $\frac{5}{6} = \frac{n}{18}$

4. $\frac{7}{n} = \frac{21}{9}$

5. $\frac{4}{8} = \frac{3}{n}$

6. $\frac{n}{4} = \frac{20}{8}$

Review NUMBER skills in preparation for learning new skills.

FOCUS   Formulate problems using photo, data, and text.

CHAPTER 24

Probability

DATA

Boat name	Snoozer Cruiser
Boat's "hull"	Double bed
Boat's "sails"	Bedsheets
Captain's position	Asleep
Finish-line position	7th

Boats made from bedframes? Rafts made from rubber tubes? Sailboats made from styrofoam? What is all this? It's the Fool's Rules Regatta, of course.

Imagine a race in which none of the boats look like boats and everyone gets cheered, whether they sink or sail. The Fool's Rules Regatta has only one rule for what boats can look like: they can look like anything.

There are two other important rules in this race. Entrants may not bring their boats to the race. They bring materials and tools with them and assemble their boats on the beach half an hour before the race begins. The other rule is that all entrants must wear life preservers.

The accent in this race is not on sleekness and speed. What matters is the originality of the design of the boat. The craft shown here is not exactly an America's Cup winner, but it did finish the race.

Think of all the things lying around your house that could be turned into a boat. What would make the boat float? What could be used for the sail? Remember, the boat is not supposed to sink. So try to design a foolish boat that might finish.

Outcomes

This spinner is divided into 4 equal sections. In one spin, what is the chance of getting red?

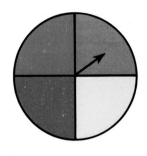

There are 4 sections, so there are 4 **possible outcomes.** All of the outcomes are *equally likely*. Only 1 section is red. Getting red is a **favorable outcome**.

To find the probability of getting red, use this formula.

Possible Outcomes: blue (B), green (G), red (R), yellow (Y)

$$\text{Probability} = \frac{\text{number of favorable outcomes}}{\text{number of possible outcomes}} = \frac{1}{4}$$

The chance of getting red is 1 in 4 or 1 out of 4. The **probability** (*P*) of getting red is $\frac{1}{4}$.

This spinner is divided into 6 equal sections. In one spin, what is the probability of getting a 2 or a 4?

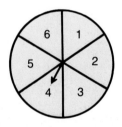

There are 6 sections, so there are 6 *equally likely* outcomes. Two sections are numbered two or four, therefore there are 2 **favorable outcomes**.

Possible Outcomes: one, two, three four, five, six

$$\text{Probability} = \frac{\text{number of favorable outcomes}}{\text{number of possible outcomes}} = \frac{2}{6} = \frac{1}{3}$$

The chance of getting a 2 or a 4 is 1 in 3, or 1 out of 3. The **probability** (*P*) of getting a 2 or a 4 is $\frac{1}{3}$.

GUIDED PRACTICE

You spin the spinner one time.

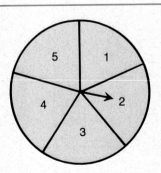

1. How many favorable outcomes are there for getting a 2 or a 3?

2. How many possible outcomes are there?

FOCUS Use PROBABILITY to predict outcomes.

PRACTICE

List all the possible outcomes.

3. 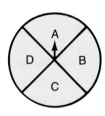   **4.** 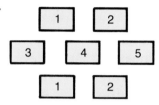   **5.**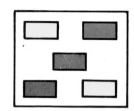

Spin the spinner one time. Give the probability of each.

6. 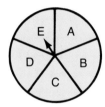   **7.** 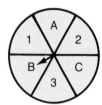   **8.**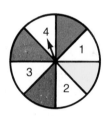

Give the probability of the spinner stopping on

9. red.   **10.** 3.

11. yellow or blue.   ***12.** 2, 4, or 1.

MIXED PRACTICE
Maintaining and Reviewing Skills

Write the prime factorization of each composite number.
Write prime if the number is prime.

13. 55   **14.** 167   **15.** 68   **16.** 59

17. 105   **18.** 91   **19.** 73   **20.** 43

21. 100   **22.** 19   **23.** 84   **24.** 234

CHALLENGE

Sammy will choose one letter of the alphabet at random.
What is the probability of choosing each of the following?

*25. a vowel   ***26.** a letter in his first name

PROBABILITY
Outcomes

The spinner at the right is divided into 8 equal sections. In one spin, what is the chance of getting blue?

There are 8 sections, so there are 8 equally likely outcomes. Since 2 sections are blue, there are 2 **favorable outcomes.** It is *more likely* that the spinner will stop on blue than the other possible outcomes.

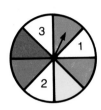

To find **probability** (*P*) use this formula.

Probability $= \frac{\text{number of favorable outcomes}}{\text{number of possible outcomes}} = \frac{2}{8}$ or $\frac{1}{4}$

The chance of getting blue is 1 in 4, or 1 out of 4.
The **probability** (*P*) of getting blue is $\frac{1}{4}$.

PRACTICE

List the possible outcomes for each. Then give the probability of getting each outcome if you have only one try.

1.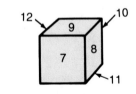

2.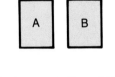

3.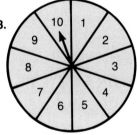

Paula will select one digit from 0 through 9 at random. What is the probability for each of the following?

4. 6 or 7   **5.** an odd number   **6.** 5   **7.** a number < 3

MIXED PRACTICE
Maintaining and Reviewing Skills

Round each to the nearest hundredth and thousandth.

8. 3.2064   **9.** 9.0093   **10.** 6.3452   **11.** 23.4862

12. 5.3827   **13.** 21.7559   **14.** 4.2176   **15.** 4.9995

FOCUS | Use PROBABILITY to predict outcomes.

APPLICATION
Using Ratio and Proportion

Proportions can be used to find the number of times an outcome can be expected to occur.

In one spin, the chance of getting the letter B is 1 out of 4. The probability is $\frac{1}{4}$. How many times can you expect to get the letter B in 8 spins?

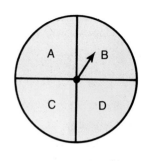

First write a proportion; then use cross products to solve.

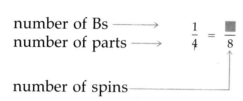

$$\text{number of Bs} \longrightarrow \quad \frac{1}{4} = \frac{\blacksquare}{8}$$

number of parts $\longrightarrow$

number of spins

Cross Products

$$1 \times 8 = 4 \times \blacksquare$$
$$8 = 4 \times \blacksquare$$
$$8 \div 4 = \blacksquare$$
$$2 = \blacksquare$$

You can expect to get 2 Bs in 8 spins.

Write the number of As you can expect to get for each number of spins given.

16. 3 spins

17. 6 spins

18. 4 spins

19. 4 spins

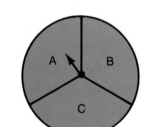

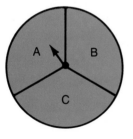

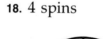

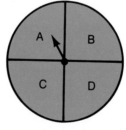

20. 10 spins

21. 10 spins

22. 12 spins

23. 12 spins

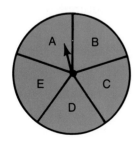

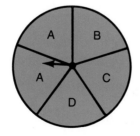

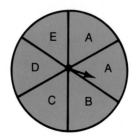

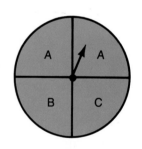

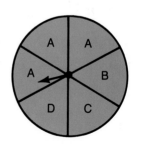

Use NUMBER skills to predict probability by writing ratios and proportions.

Sample Space

Bart has two spinners. One has the colors red and yellow on it. The other has the numbers 1, 2, and 3 on it. Each spinner is divided into equal sections.

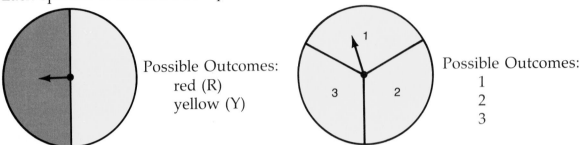

Possible Outcomes:
red (R)
yellow (Y)

Possible Outcomes:
1
2
3

What are the possible outcomes if Bart spins each spinner once?

Use a tree diagram to show all the possible outcomes. A **sample space** is a complete list of all the possible outcomes.

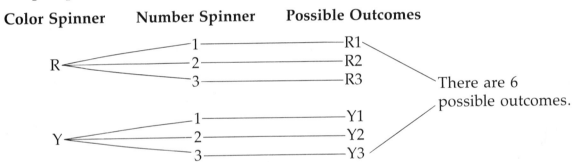

Color Spinner   Number Spinner   Possible Outcomes

R — 1 — R1
— 2 — R2
— 3 — R3

There are 6 possible outcomes.

Y — 1 — Y1
— 2 — Y2
— 3 — Y3

The sample space consists of 6 possible outcomes.

GUIDED PRACTICE

Copy and complete the tree diagram showing all the possible outcomes for tossing a coin and spinning the spinner.

1.

H — R, Y, G, W   T — R, ■, ■, ■

2. List the possible outcomes.

HR, HY, HG, HW, ■, ■, ■, ■

| FOCUS | Use PROBABILITY to determine sample space. |

PRACTICE

Make a tree diagram to show the sample space for each.

3. An outcome consists of one letter followed by one number. Use the letters J, K, L, M, N and the numbers 1, 2, 3.

4. An outcome consists of one number followed by one color. Use the numbers 2, 4, 6 and the colors yellow, green, and blue.

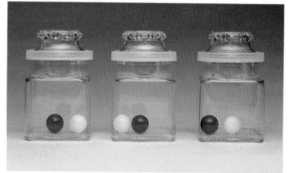

For the following, assume you pick one marble from each jar without looking.

5. There are 3 jars. Each jar has 1 white and 1 black marble. Make a tree diagram to show all the possible outcomes.

6. How many possible outcomes are there?

7. What is the probability of picking at least 2 black marbles?

8. What is the probability of picking 2 white marbles and 1 black marble?

9. What is the probability of picking 3 black marbles?

10. What is the probability of picking at least 2 white marbles?

11. What is the probability of picking at least 1 white marble?

MIXED PRACTICE
Maintaining and Reviewing Skills

List in order from least to greatest.

12. 39,389; 39,892; 39,382; 39,983

13. 54,923; 54,932; 54,239; 54,329

14. 800,528; 800,825; 800,258; 800,852

15. 760,166; 670,661; 670,616; 760,661

16. 74,577; 74,757; 77,754; 74,775

17. 610,016; 601,106; 610,610; 601,016

CHALLENGE

Toss a penny, then a dime; which outcome (H) heads or (T) tails is *more likely* to occur? (Hint: P = probability)

*18. $P(T)$ or $P(TT)$

*19. $P(TT)$ or $P(HH)$

*20. $P(H)$ or $P(HH)$

PROBABILITY
Sample Space

What are the possible outcomes if one card is picked from each pair of cards?

You can use a tree diagram to show all the possible outcomes. A **sample space** is a list of all the possible outcomes.

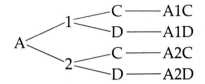 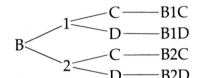 The tree diagram shows that there are 8 possible outcomes in the sample space.

PRACTICE

Suppose you pick one card from each set. Copy and complete the tree diagram. Then use it to answer the following questions.

1. List all the possible outcomes.

2. What is the probability of getting YY?

3. What is the probability of getting at least one X?

4. What is the probability of getting ZY?

5. What is the probability of getting XX, YY, or ZZ?

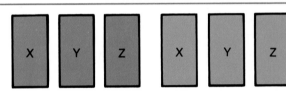

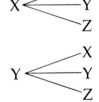

MIXED PRACTICE
Maintaining and Reviewing Skills

Multiply.

6.   3.48
    × 0.58
	7. 5.6
	    × 0.56
		8. 5.31
		    × 6.37
			9. 47.2
			    × 0.108
				10. 24.06
				    × 0.075

11. 0.5125×80 **12.** 3.86×0.57 **13.** 24.96×0.075

FOCUS   Use PROBABILITY to determine sample space.

APPLICATION
Using Probability

Probabilities can be used to determine the number of times an event will occur. This is called the *probable outcome.*

If you toss a coin 50 times, you can find the probable outcome for the number of times tails will occur.

Multiply the probability of one outcome by the number of trials to find the probable outcome.

Probability of one outcome	$\frac{1}{2} \times 50 = 25$	Number of trials

The probable number of times tails will occur in 50 tosses is 25.

Determine the probability of each of the following events.

14. The number of times a star will occur in 27 spins.

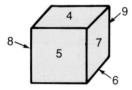

15. The number of times a star will occur in 63 spins.

16. The number of times 4 will be on top in 12 tosses.

17. The number of times an odd number will occur in 50 spins.

18. The number of times a letter will occur in 24 spins.

19. The number of times a star will occur in 120 spins.

Use PROBABILITY to determine probable outcomes.

Writing a Basic Program

In order to have the computer solve a problem, we must go through the following steps:

The Analysis—This is the step in which the algorithm is developed.

The Plan—In this step, we outline what the **computer** must do in order to solve the problem.

The Planned Output—This is the step in which we plan how the screen will look when we run the program.

The Program—In this step, the plan is translated into computer statements. The program is coded.

Use the steps above to write a computer program that will find the average of three numbers.

The Analysis

In order to develop an algorithm for finding the average of three numbers, it would be helpful to look at an actual example: *Find the average of 40, 50, and 60.* To do this, we must add the numbers and divide the sum by 3. Why is it incorrect to say that the average will be 40 + 50 + 60/3 ? The / tells the computer to divide. (Notice that the order of operations tells us that the division must be done first. This means that 40 + 50 + 60/3 or 40 + 50 + 20 = 110.) The average should fall in between the smallest and largest numbers. To correct this, we must use parentheses so that the addition is done first. Thus, the average is (40 + 50 + 60)/3 or 150/3 or 50.

To write the algorithm for finding the average, use A for the first number, B for the second, and C for the last. AV will stand for the average.

The Plan

1. Tell the computer the three numbers: A, B, and C.
2. The computer will calculate AV = (A + B + C)/3.
3. The computer will print the result.

The Planned Output

FINDING THE AVERAGE
—BY KIM
(skip a line)
WHAT ARE THE THREE NUMBERS?
?40, 50, 60
THE AVERAGE IS 50

The Program

```
10   PRINT "FINDING THE AVERAGE"
20   PRINT "—BY KIM"
30   PRINT
40   PRINT "WHAT ARE THE THREE
     NUMBERS?"
50   INPUT A, B, C
60   AV = (A + B + C)/3
70   PRINT "THE AVERAGE IS"; AV
80   END
```

CRITICAL THINKING

1. Where and how was the algorithm used in the plan? the program?

2. What is the purpose of the PRINT statement in line 30?

FOCUS | Use LOGIC to write a computer program to find the average of three numbers.

How many people are in this group? To estimate an answer count the number of people in the highlighted grids at the top, middle, and bottom of the page.

Find the average number of people of the three grids.

Multiply this average times the total number of square inches in the grid (42).

This will give you an estimate of the whole group. Think how much faster this is than counting hundreds of heads!

LOOKING BACK
Reviewing and Testing Chapter 24

In Chapter 24 you formulated problems about the Fool's Rules Regatta. To review, refer to pages 346 and 347.

1. What factors should be considered before construction of a boat begins?

To review probability, refer to page 348.

List all the possible outcomes. Then give the probability of each if the spinner is spun only one time.

2.

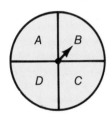

3.

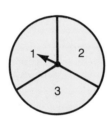

4.

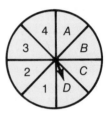

Give the probability of each, if the spinner is spun only one time.

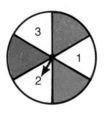

5. blue

6. 2

7. blue, red, or 1

8. green or 3

To review sample space, refer to page 352.

Make a tree diagram to show all the possible outcomes. An outcome consists of one letter followed by one number.

9. Use the letters R, G, Y, B, and the numbers 2, 4, 6, 8.

You learned about writing a program to find the average of three numbers. To review, refer to page 356.

10. What changes would you make in coding the program if a fourth number, 30, were included in the average?

FOCUS | Review and test skills learned and practiced.

LOOKING AHEAD
Preparing for New Skills for Chapter 25

In the next chapter you will focus on

- **formulating problems about water conservation.**
- **identifying the parts of a circle.**
- **finding the circumference of a circle.**
- **finding the area of a circle.**
- **recognizing and drawing lines of symmetry.**
- **how math is used in consumer education.**

Learning about parts of a circle and area of a circle will be easier if you review naming angles and finding the area of a rectangle. Study the examples.

An angle is formed by two rays that have the same endpoint.

Example 1:

Name the angle and its sides.

$\angle GHI$ or $\angle IHG$

sides: $\overrightarrow{HG}$ and $\overrightarrow{HI}$

Example 2:

Name the angle and its sides.

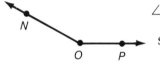

$\angle NOP$ or $\angle PON$

sides: $\overrightarrow{ON}$ and $\overrightarrow{OP}$

Use this formula to find the area of a rectangle:
Area $(A) = $ length $(l) \times$ width (w)

Example 3:

3 in. ▢ 4 in.

$A = l \times w$
$A = 4 \times 3$
$A = 12 \text{ in}^2$

Example 4:

12 mm ▢ 7 mm

$A = l \times w$
$A = 12 \times 7$
$A = 84 \text{ mm}^2$

PRACTICE

Name each angle and its sides.

1.

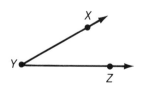

2.

3.

Find the area of each rectangle using the given measures.

4. $l = 13$ in., $w = 8$ in. **5.** $l = 15$ yd, $w = 15$ yd **6.** $l = 6$ cm, $w = 5$ cm

Review GEOMETRY in preparation for learning new skills.

Write the letter of the correct answer.

What is the equivalent decimal?

1. $\frac{4}{5}$ **A.** 0.75   **B.** 0.8   **C.** 0.88   **D.** 0.50

2. $\frac{22}{25}$ **E.** 0.44   **F.** 0.22   **G.** 0.88   **H.** 1.02

3. $\frac{8}{11}$ **A.** $0.\overline{72}$ **B.** 0.75   **C.** 0.72   **D.** $0.\overline{7}$

What is the equivalent fraction or mixed number?

4. 0.175   **E.** $\frac{7}{40}$ **F.** $\frac{17}{5}$ **G.** $\frac{175}{100}$ **H.** $\frac{1}{175}$

5. 0.72   **A.** $\frac{3}{4}$ **B.** $\frac{36}{10}$ **C.** $\frac{18}{25}$ **D.** $\frac{3}{8}$

6. 8.35   **E.** $\frac{800}{35}$ **F.** $8\frac{7}{20}$ **G.** $8\frac{35}{50}$ **H.** $\frac{8}{35}$

7. 2.375   **A.** $2\frac{3}{10}$ **B.** $2\frac{1}{3}$ **C.** $2\frac{3}{8}$ **D.** $\frac{23}{100}$

Round to the nearest hundredth.

8. 9.724   **E.** 9.70   **F.** 9.72

         G. 9.73   **H.** 9.74

9. 6.335   **A.** 6.33   **B.** 6.35

         C. 6.00   **D.** 6.34

Which is a correct statement?

10. **E.** 2.73 < 2.75   **F.** 2.65 > 2.74

     G. 2.37 > 2.73   **H.** 2.60 = 2.060

11. **A.** 8.728 = 8.720   **B.** 8.722 > 7.822

     C. 8.782 > 9.671   **D.** 8.728 < 8.727

12. **E.** 0.3354 > 0.4353   **F.** 0.3481 > 1.3480

     G. 0.0354 = 0.3540   **H.** 0.2355 > 0.0586

Add or subtract.

13. $\begin{array}{r} 1.739 \\ + 1.422 \\ \hline \end{array}$ **A.** 3.161   **B.** 2.961   **C.** 3.251   **D.** 3.171

14. $\begin{array}{r} 3.08 \\ + 5.265 \\ \hline \end{array}$ **E.** 9.265   **F.** 8.423   **G.** 8.270   **H.** 8.345

15. $\begin{array}{r} 23.645 \\ + 13.486 \\ \hline \end{array}$ **A.** 10.131   **B.** 37.131   **C.** 26.239   **D.** 36.231

16. $\begin{array}{r} 6.28 \\ - 4.39 \\ \hline \end{array}$ **E.** 1.89   **F.** 1.67   **G.** 2.67   **H.** 2.89

17. $\begin{array}{r} 8.34 \\ - 0.775 \\ \hline \end{array}$ **A.** 8.215   **B.** 7.565   **C.** 7.665   **D.** 7.656

18. $\begin{array}{r} \$9.95 \\ - 3.79 \\ \hline \end{array}$ **E.** $6.16   **F.** $6.56   **G.** $5.96   **H.** $13.74

Multiply or divide.

19. $\begin{array}{r} 21.6 \\ \times \quad 10 \\ \hline \end{array}$ **A.** 216.0   **B.** 2.16   **C.** 21.60   **D.** 0.216

20. $\begin{array}{r} 0.528 \\ \times \quad 100 \\ \hline \end{array}$ **E.** 52.8   **F.** 5.28   **G.** 528   **H.** 0.0528

21. $\begin{array}{r} 0.0394 \\ \times \quad 1,000 \\ \hline \end{array}$ **A.** 3.94   **B.** 39.4   **C.** 0.394   **D.** 394

22. $16.23 \div 10$ **E.** 0.1623   **F.** 162.3   **G.** 1.623   **H.** 162.30

23. $320.3 \div 10^3$ **A.** 3.203   **B.** 0.03203   **C.** 32.035   **D.** 0.3203

FOCUS   Review concepts and skills taught in Chapters 17–24.

Convert.

24. 2.5 km = ■ m

    E. 2 500 m   **F.** 0.25 m

    G. 25 000 m   **H.** 25 m

25. 500 mL = ■ L

    A. 0.50 L   **B.** 50 L

    C. 5 L   **D.** 0.5 L

26. 8 t = ■ kg

    E. 40 kg   **F.** 80 kg

    G. 8 000 kg   **H.** 4 000 kg

27. 750 mm = ■ cm

    A. 7.5 cm   **B.** 75 cm

    C. 750 cm   **D.** 7 500 cm

Multiply or divide.

28. 12.53   **E.** 100.24   **F.** 1,002.40
$\underline{\times\quad 8}$ **G.** 96.53   **H.** 10.024

29. 9.062   **A.** 15.13354   **B.** 1.5133
$\underline{\times\ 1.67}$ **C.** 15.13244   **D.** 1,513.35

30. 5.16   **E.** 38.757   **F.** 38.007
$\underline{\times\ 7.5}$ **G.** 30.70   **H.** 38.7

31. 8) 39.2   **A.** 4.09   **B.** 49

     C. 4.9   **D.** 4.8

32. 6) 5.346   **E.** 0.891   **F.** 0.8091

     G. 8.901   **H.** 89.01

33. 22) 90.86   **A.** 43.1   **B.** 41.30

     C. 4.13   **D.** 5.1

Which proportions are true? Use cross products to check.

34. E. $\frac{3}{6} = \frac{10}{18}$ **F.** $\frac{3}{6} = \frac{11}{22}$

    G. $\frac{5}{6} = \frac{10}{18}$ **H.** $\frac{3}{6} = \frac{5}{6}$

35. A. $\frac{3}{4} = \frac{80}{100}$ **B.** $\frac{50}{80} = \frac{3}{4}$

    C. $\frac{3}{4} = \frac{45}{60}$ **D.** $\frac{30}{100} = \frac{3}{4}$

Use a proportion to solve each problem.

36. If 3 records cost $9.96, how much will 2 records cost?

    E. $6.64 **F.** $12.23 **G.** $5.94 **H.** $6.32

37. If there are 5,280 feet in one mile, how many feet are in 3 miles?

    A. 1,760 ft   **B.** 15,840 ft

    C. 16,000 ft   **D.** 3,520 ft

Give the probability for each outcome if the spinner is spun only 1 time.

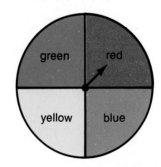

38. red

    E. $\frac{1}{3}$ **F.** $\frac{2}{3}$ **G.** $\frac{4}{4}$ **H.** $\frac{1}{4}$

39. red or blue

    A. $\frac{3}{4}$ **B.** $\frac{1}{2}$ **C.** $\frac{4}{1}$ **D.** $\frac{2}{2}$

40. red, blue, or yellow

    E. $\frac{3}{4}$ **F.** $\frac{1}{4}$ **G.** $\frac{1}{2}$ **H.** 1

FOCUS | Formulate problems using photo, data, and text.

25

Circles

DATA

Rate of wasted water
  1 qt per hour
  24 qt (6 gal) per day
  42 gal per week
  168 gal per month
  2,190 gal per year

Dimensions of possible pool
Length	25 ft
Width	10 ft
Depth	5 ft
Volume	1,250 ft³
	(about 2,500 gal)

Helpful measures and information
  Volume = $l \times w \times d$
  4 qt = 1 gal
  1 gal measures 0.5 ft³

"You really should fix that faucet," Sidney said to Kevin as they sat in Kevin's kitchen.

"It's not dripping that much," said Kevin. He tightened the handle. "Is that better?"

"It's still dripping. We have to watch it. Wasted drops add up."

"A few drops can't add up to much," insisted Kevin.

"You'd be surprised. If you'll get a quart jar, we could experiment and see how those drops add up."

Kevin got an empty, one-quart juice jar. Sidney set it under the faucet. After an hour, the jar was full. "Do you want a drink?" asked Kevin.

"Very funny," said Sidney. "But you'd better pour this into something bigger."

Kevin poured the water into the bath tub. It only made a thin, broken puddle. "It'll take forever to fill this tub."

What are Sidney and Kevin in the process of discovering? What do the photo and data suggest? Predict some possible results of their argument.

Identify Parts of a Circle

A **circle** is a set of points in a plane that are all the same distance from the given point called the **center**. It is a **closed curve.**

$\overline{LM}$ is a **radius**. A radius is a line segment with one endpoint at the center of the circle and the other endpoint on the circle. All radii of the same circle are equal. (*Radii* is plural for radius.)

$\overline{RS}$ is a **chord.** A chord is a line segment with endpoints on a circle.

$\overline{NP}$ is a **diameter.** A diameter is a chord that passes through the center of the circle. The length of a diameter in a circle is twice the length of a radius in the circle.

$\overset{\frown}{VW}$ is an **arc.** An arc is a part of a circle that lies between any two points on the circle.

$\angle LMN$ is a **central angle.** The vertex of a central angle is the center of a circle.

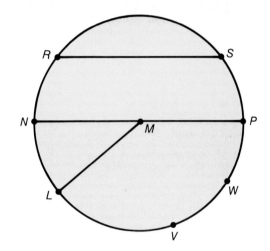

GUIDED PRACTICE

Use Circle C to answer the following.

1. $\overline{AB}$ is a chord. Name three more chords.

2. $\overline{EB}$ is a diameter. The measure of $\overline{EB}$ is 4 cm. Name another diameter and give its measure.

3. $\overline{CB}$ is a radius. The measure of $\overline{CB}$ is 2 cm. Name three other radii and give their measures.

4. $\overset{\frown}{AB}$ is an arc. $\overset{\frown}{AD}$ is also an arc. Name three other arcs.

5. $\angle ACB$ is a central angle. Name three other central angles.

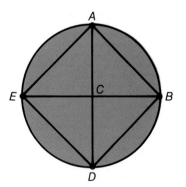

| FOCUS | Use GEOMETRY to identify parts of a circle. |

PRACTICE

Use Circle *F* to help you answer Exercises 6–13.

6. Name the diameters shown.

7. Name the radii.

8. Name the chords.

9. Name five arcs.

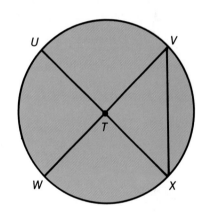

If the measure of $\overline{GK}$ is 8 m

10. What is the measure of $\overline{GF}$?

11. What is the measure of $\overline{FH}$?

12. What is the measure of $\overline{LH}$?

13. If the measure of $\overline{LF}$ is 4 m, what is the measure of $\overline{FK}$?

Use Circle *T* to help you answer Exercises 14–17.

14. Why is $\overline{VX}$ not a diameter?

15. Why is $\overline{UX}$ not a radius?

If the measure of $\overline{TX}$ is 2.5 cm

16. What is the measure of $\overline{UT}$?

17. What is the measure of $\overline{WV}$?

MIXED PRACTICE
Maintaining and Reviewing Skills

Multiply.

18. $\frac{22}{7} \times 14$ 19. $\frac{22}{7} \times 6$ 20. $\begin{array}{r} 3.14 \\ \times6 \\ \hline \end{array}$ 21. $\begin{array}{r} 8.25 \\ \times 3.14 \\ \hline \end{array}$

CHALLENGE

Write which circle has a longer radius.

*22. Circle *A:* *d* = 80 cm
   Circle *B:* *r* = 0.5 m

*23. Circle *X:* *r* = 0.85 m
   Circle *Y:* *d* = 150 cm

CIRCLES
Finding the Circumference of a Circle

The distance around a quarter is 7.53 centimeters. The distance around a circle is its **circumference.**

There is a relationship between the circumference and the diameter of any circle.

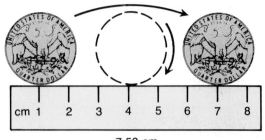

7.53 cm

Coin	Circumference (C)	Diameter (d)	C ÷ d (nearest hundredth)
penny	5.96 cm	1.9	3.14
nickel	6.59 cm	2.1	3.14
dime	5.65 cm	1.8	3.14
quarter	7.53 cm	2.4	3.14

The rounded quotient 3.14 is the same for all circles. The Greek letter π (pi) is the symbol for this quotient. The symbol π is approximately equal to 3.14 or $\frac{22}{7}$. To find the circumference of a circle use:

$$\frac{C}{d} = \pi \quad \text{or} \quad C = \pi \times d$$

A diameter of a circle is twice as long as a radius of the circle. To find the circumference you can also use:

$$C = 2 \times \pi \times r$$

PRACTICE

Find the circumference of each circle. Use the radius (r) or diameter (d) given. Use 3.14 for π.

1. d = 17 cm   **2.** r = 28 in.   **3.** r = 15 mm   **4.** d = 6.6 cm   **5.** d = 10 cm

6. r = 6 ft   **7.** d = 2.4 km   **8.** d = 3 m   **9.** r = 12 m   **10.** r = 28 cm

MIXED PRACTICE
Maintaining and Reviewing Skills

Write each number in standard form.

11. 3.14×5^2 **12.** 3.14×8^2 **13.** 4×10^6 **14.** 0.25×4^4 **15.** 0.005×10^5

FOCUS | Use GEOMETRY to find the circumference of a circle.

APPLICATION

Using Geometry

Use a compass to draw a circle with a radius of 2 centimeters.

- Draw a line segment that is exactly the length of the given radius.

- Place the compass point at one endpoint of the line segment and the pencil at the other endpoint.

- Swing the compass around to construct the circle.

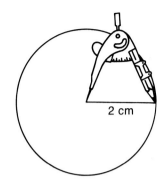

2 cm

Using a protractor follow these steps to construct a central angle with a measure of 45°. Use the circle you have already constructed.

- Place the center mark of the protractor on the center of the circle.

- Line up the base of the protractor with the radius of the circle.

- Draw a point on the circumference of the circle at the 45° mark. Then draw a line from the center of the circle to the 45° mark.

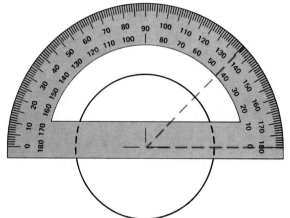

Draw each circle below. Use the radius or diameter given. Then give the circumference for each. Use 3.14 for π.

16. $r = 3$ cm
17. $r = 4$ in.
18. $r = 5$ cm
19. $r = 1$ in.

20. $r = 8$ cm
21. $r = 10$ mm
22. $r = 3\frac{1}{2}$ in.
23. $r = 2.5$ cm

24. $d = 10$ cm
25. $d = 16.8$ cm
26. $d = 15$ cm
27. $d = 14$ cm

For each of the following exercises, draw a circle and construct a central angle with the measure given.

28. $m\angle = 30°$
29. $m\angle = 90°$
30. $m\angle = 60°$
31. $m\angle = 10°$

Use GEOMETRY to draw a circle and construct a central angle.

CIRCLES
Finding the Area of a Circle

The interior of a circle can be separated into eight equal parts.

These equal parts can be arranged to form this figure.

The arcs of each part can be "straightened" to form a parallelogram.

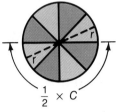

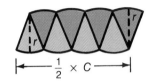

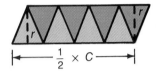

Each of these three figures has the same area. To find the area of the circle, find the area of the parallelogram.

Area of parallelogram = base × height

$$A = b \times h$$

$$\text{base} = \frac{1}{2} \times C \qquad \text{height} = r \text{ (height of parallelogram)}$$

$$\text{base} = \frac{1}{2} \times (2 \times \pi \times r)$$

$$\text{base} = \pi \times r$$

To find the area of a circle substitute $\pi \times r$ for the base and r for the height.

$$A = b \times h$$
$$A = (\pi \times r) \times r \qquad (r \times r = r^2)$$
$$A = \pi \times r^2$$

Since the area of the parallelogram is the same as the area of the circle, then the formula for finding the area of a circle is: $A = \pi \times r^2$.

GUIDED PRACTICE

Find each missing factor. Then solve to find the area of each circle. Use 3.14 for π.

1. $r = 2$ cm $A = 3.14 \times \blacksquare \times 2$

2. $r = 6$ m $A = \blacksquare \times 6 \times 6$

Find each missing factor. Then solve to find the area of each circle. Use $\frac{22}{7}$ for π.

3. $r = 14$ mm $A = \frac{22}{7} \times 14 \times \blacksquare$

4. $r = 7$ cm $A = \frac{\blacksquare}{\blacksquare} \times 7 \times \blacksquare$

| FOCUS | Use GEOMETRY to find the area of a circle. |

PRACTICE

Find the area of each circle. Use 3.14 for π.

5. $r = 15$ cm   **6.** $r = 12$ m   **7.** $r = 4$ in.   **8.** $r = 3$ ft

9. $r = 9$ yd   **10.** $r = 2$ mi   **11.** $r = 8$ km   **12.** $r = 18$ mm

13. $r = 6$ m   **14.** $r = 2.4$ km   **15.** $r = 7$ in.   **16.** $r = 5$ in.

Find the area of each circle. Use $\frac{22}{7}$ for π.

17. $d = 14$ cm   **18.** $d = 28$ mm   **19.** $d = 42$ in.   **20.** $d = 70$ km

21. $d = 140$ ft   **22.** $d = 210$ mm   **23.** $d = 21$ mi   **24.** $d = 35$ yd

25. $d = 105$ cm   **26.** $d = 56$ m   **27.** $d = 7$ km   **28.** $d = 63$ m

MIXED PRACTICE
Maintaining and Reviewing Skills

Find the circumference of each circle. Use 3.14 for π.

29. $d = 4$ cm   **30.** $d = 6$ mm   **31.** $r = 14$ ft   **32.** $r = 12$ cm

33. $r = 5$ in.   **34.** $r = 3$ in.   **35.** $d = 7$ m   **36.** $d = 8$ cm

Find the circumference of each circle. Use $\frac{22}{7}$ for π.

37. $r = 7$ m   **38.** $d = 56$ in.   **39.** $r = 14$ ft   **40.** $d = 28$ yd

41. $d = 63$ in.   **42.** $r = 21$ ft   **43.** $d = \frac{14}{11}$ cm   **44.** $d = \frac{7}{11}$ m

CHALLENGE

*45. A circular island is surrounded by a reef. What is the area of the island?

*46. What is the area of the reef? (Hint: subtract the area of the smaller circle from the area of the larger one.)

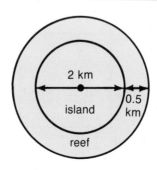

CIRCLES
Finding the Area of a Circle

Find the area of this circle. Use 3.14 for π. Round your answer to the nearest tenth.

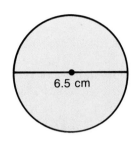

6.5 cm

First find the radius. The length of the radius is one-half the length of the diameter.

$$\text{So, } r = \frac{1}{2} \times 6.5$$
$$r = 0.5 \times 6.5$$
$$r = 3.25$$

Then use the radius to find the area. Round your answer to the nearest tenth.

$$A = \pi \times r^2$$
$$A = 3.14 \times 3.25^2$$
$$A = 3.14 \times 3.25 \times 3.25$$
$$A = 33.16625$$
$$A = 33.2$$

The area of the circle is about 33.2 cm².

PRACTICE

The measure of a radius or diameter of a circle is given. Find the area. Round your answers to the nearest tenth. Use 3.14 for π.

1. $r = 4.6$ m

2. $r = 3.2$ mm

3. $r = 2.15$ m

4. $r = 4.75$ cm

5. $d = 9$ cm

6. $d = 12.6$ m

7. $d = 15$ m

8. $d = 21$ km

* 9. $r = 5.01$ cm

*10. $r = 3.42$ m

*11. $r = 7.01$ mm

*12. $r = 0.35$ cm

MIXED PRACTICE
Maintaining and Reviewing Skills

Find the area of each figure.

13.

2 m

6 m

14.

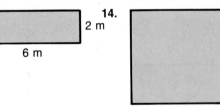

8 mm

15.

8 m

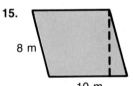

10 m

16.

12 in.

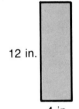

4 in.

| FOCUS | Use GEOMETRY to find the area of a circle. |

APPLICATION
Using Symmetry

A figure has line **symmetry** if it can be folded so that one part exactly matches the other part. The fold line is a line of **symmetry.**

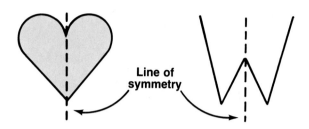

Line of symmetry

Each of these figures is symmetric.

Some figures have more than one line of symmetry.

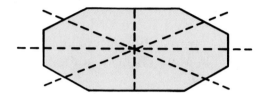

Some figures have no lines of symmetry.

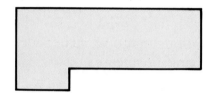

Is each figure symmetric? Write *yes* or *no.*

17. 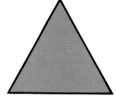   **18.**    **19.**    **20.**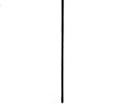

Copy each figure. Draw all lines of symmetry.

21.   **22.**   **23.**   **24.**

Complete each drawing to make a symmetric figure.   Answers may vary.

25.    **26.**   **27.**   **28.**

Use GEOMETRY to recognize and draw lines of symmetry.

MATH IN CONSUMER EDUCATION

Banking

Banks have existed in one form or another for thousands of years. Every town or village had a person who would do the same things that banks do: save people's money for them, lend them money when they need it, and handle transactions for people. Today, banks have grown to be big corporations that offer many services to people and businesses.

The first bank in the United States was started in 1782. Now there are more than 15,000 banks all across the country.

Banks provide a safe place to keep money. In fact, they encourage us to save money by paying us interest. This kind of account is called a savings account. In a savings account, you may deposit or withdraw your money. The money you save earns interest. Banks usually pay about 5% interest every year.

Banks lend money to people and allow them to pay it back in small amounts over a period of time. Not many people have enough money to buy a new car, or a house, and pay for it all at once. They can get a loan from a bank, and pay a little bit to the bank every month. They have to pay the bank interest on the loan, generally around 10%.

At your request banks will transfer your money to another person or business. This type of account is called a checking account. A checking account allows you to pay for things with a piece of paper—a check—so you don't have to carry large amounts of money with you. You just have to make sure that you have enough money in your account to cover the check. A check register is used to record all checking account transactions. The check register below shows some typical transactions.

ENTER ALL TRANSACTIONS THAT AFFECT YOUR ACCOUNT BALANCE			DEBITS			CREDITS		
ITEM NO OR CODE	DATE	DESCRIPTION OF TRANSACTION	PAYMENT OR WITHDRAWAL	√ T	FEE	DEPOSIT OR INTEREST	BALANCE	
							531	18
616	9/3	Realty Associates (rent)	389 00				389	00
							142	18
	9/6	Deposit				203 14	203	14
							345	32
616	9/3	Rock Insurance	58 00				58	00
							287	32
618	9/6	Electric	49 17				49	17
							238	15

Maintaining a checking account is easy. In fact, most banking is easy. You just need to add or subtract every time you put money in or take it out.

CRITICAL THINKING

1. How can a bank help you start a business?

2. If you wanted to put money away for college, what kind of account should you get? What will happen to your money if you leave it in the account?

3. Compare a checking account and a savings account.

FOCUS | Use NUMBER skills to learn practical aspects of banking.

Banking from the home is now possible through the use of computers and modems.

LOOKING BACK
Reviewing and Testing Chapter 25

In Chapter 25 you formulated problems about water conservation. To review, refer to page 363 for data.

1. If the bathtub held 20 gallons of water, how long would it take to fill?

To review the parts of a circle, refer to page 364.

Use circle *A* to answer questions 2–5.

2. Name the diameters.

3. Name the radii.

4. Name the chords.

5. Name five arcs.

6. If the measure of $\overline{FC}$ is 10 cm, what is the measure of $\overline{AC}$? $\overline{EB}$? $\overline{EA}$?

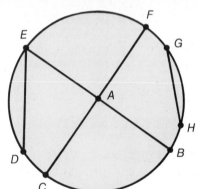

To review circumference and area of a circle, refer to pages 366 and 368.

Find the circumference of each circle, given the diameter or radius. Use 3.14 for π.

7. $d = 13$ km   8. $r = 3$mm   9. $d = 5$ mm   10. $r = 8$ m   11. $d = 4$ cm

Find the area of each circle given the diameter or radius. Use 3.14 for π.

12. $d = 30$ ft   13. $r = 10$ in.   14. $r = 8$ mi   15. $d = 4$ ft   16. $r = 9$ yd

To review consumer education in banking refer to page 372.

17. Your checkbook balance is $200. If you write checks for $15.85, $84.20, and $12.26, what is your balance?

| FOCUS | Review and test skills learned and practiced. |

LOOKING AHEAD
Preparing for New Skills for Chapter 26

> **In the next chapter you will focus on**
> - **formulating problems about time lapse photography.**
> - **writing ratios as fractions or percents.**
> - **writing percents as fractions or decimals.**
> - **constructing a circle graph.**
> - **using a problem-solving strategy.**
> - **finding a percent of a number.**
> - **how math is used in geography.**

Working with percents will be easier if you review writing fractions in simplest terms and writing decimal equivalents of fractions. Study the examples.

Example 1: $\frac{3}{12} = \frac{3 \div 3}{12 \div 3} = \frac{1}{4}$

Example 2: $\frac{10}{50} = \frac{10 \div 10}{50 \div 10} = \frac{1}{5}$

You can write a fraction with a denominator of 100 as a decimal.

Example 3: $\frac{15}{100} = 0.15$

Example 4: $\frac{3}{100} = 0.03$ Write a zero in the tenths place.

To change any fraction to a decimal, divide the numerator by the denominator.

Example 5: $\frac{3}{4}$ $\quad 4)\overline{3.00} \quad 0.75 \quad -28 \quad 20 \quad -20$

Example 6: $\frac{7}{20}$ $\quad 20)\overline{7.00} \quad 0.35 \quad -60 \quad 1\,00 \quad -1\,00$

PRACTICE

Write each fraction in simplest terms.

1. $\frac{28}{49}$
2. $\frac{36}{50}$
3. $\frac{25}{40}$
4. $\frac{56}{63}$
5. $\frac{14}{16}$
6. $\frac{15}{21}$

Write the decimal equivalent of each fraction.

7. $\frac{21}{100}$
8. $\frac{78}{100}$
9. $\frac{8}{100}$
10. $\frac{9}{20}$
11. $\frac{14}{50}$
12. $\frac{1}{100}$

Review NUMBER skills in preparation for learning new skills.

FOCUS   Formulate problems using photo, data, and text.

CHAPTER 26

Meaning of Percent and Percent of a Number

DATA

Activity   Making a time-lapse film

Days of filming	60
Frames shot per day	12
Total frames shot	720
Projection speed	24 frames per second

Actual length of film 30 seconds

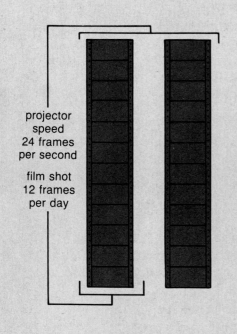

projector
speed
24 frames
per second

film shot
12 frames
per day

Katia, Willis, and Joy made a film to accompany their report on tropisms.*

"Our film," Katia told the class, "shows phototropism, the effect that light has on the way a plant grows. We made time-lapse film to speed things up."

"We planted 3 seeds in pots by the window," said Willis. "When the first shoots appeared, we began to film them, and continued for the next 60 days. Instead of filming the plants all day long, we only took 12 frames each day."

"And now we're going to project our phototropism film at a rate of twenty-four frames per second."

Jackie, a girl in the class, grinned and raised her hand. "Will there be an intermission? Sixty days is a long time."

"No intermission," said Willis. He turned off the lights and Katia turned on the projector.

"Wow," said Jackie. "That was fast."

Why was she surprised? Why was the film so short? What problems may arise using time lapse films?

Ratios, Fractions, and Percents

Percent means "per hundred." It can be thought of as a ratio of parts to one hundred.

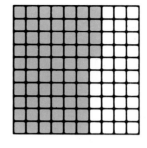

As a ratio $\rightarrow$ 63 out of 100

As a fraction $\rightarrow \frac{63}{100}$

As a percent $\rightarrow 63\%$

42 out of 100 are shaded

$\frac{42}{100} \rightarrow$ fraction

$42\% \rightarrow$ percent

75 out of 100 are shaded

$\frac{75}{100} \rightarrow$ fraction

$75\% \rightarrow$ percent

Here are ratios written as fractions and as percents.

29 out of 100 $\frac{29}{100} = 29\%$ 1 out of 5 $\frac{1}{5} = \frac{1 \times 20}{5 \times 20} = \frac{20}{100} = 20\%$

80 out of 100 $\frac{80}{100} = 80\%$ 2 out of 4 $\frac{2}{4} = \frac{2 \times 25}{4 \times 25} = \frac{50}{100} = 50\%$

4 out of 100 $\frac{4}{100} = 4\%$ 166 to 100 $\frac{166}{100} = 166\%$

GUIDED PRACTICE

Write each ratio as a fraction and as a percent.

1. 71 out of 100

$\frac{71}{100} = \blacksquare$

2. 8 out of 100

$\frac{\blacksquare}{100} = \blacksquare$

3. 3 out of 5

$\frac{3}{5} = \frac{\blacksquare}{100} = \blacksquare$

4. 257 to 100

$\frac{\blacksquare}{100} = \blacksquare$

Write each percent as a fraction.

5. $40\% = \frac{40}{100} = \frac{\blacksquare}{\blacksquare}$ **6.** $50\% = \frac{\blacksquare}{100} = \frac{\blacksquare}{\blacksquare}$ **7.** $7\% = \frac{\blacksquare}{100}$ **8.** $75\% = \frac{\blacksquare}{100} = \frac{\blacksquare}{\blacksquare}$

Write each percent as a fraction in simplest terms.

9. 47% **10.** 33% **11.** 20% **12.** 125%

FOCUS   Use NUMBER skills to convert equivalent ratios, fractions, and percents.

PRACTICE

What percent of each square is shaded?

13. 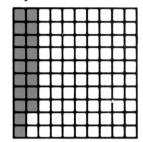   **14.** 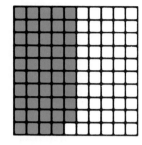   **15.**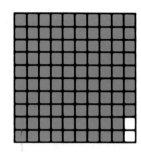

Write each ratio as a percent.

16. 49 out of 100   **17.** 6 out of 100   **18.** 4 out of 100

19. 89 out of 100   **20.** 238 to 100   **21.** 200 to 100

22. 1 out of 2   **23.** 3 out of 4   **24.** 30 out of 50

25. 7 out of 10   **26.** 1 out of 25   **27.** 20 out of 20

Write each percent as a fraction in simplest terms.

28. 49%   **29.** 62%   **30.** 70%   **31.** 11%   **32.** 85%

33. 3%   **34.** 1%   **35.** 146%   **36.** 319%   **37.** 225%

MIXED PRACTICE
Maintaining and Reviewing Skills

Write the decimal for each.

38. eight tenths

39. sixteen hundredths

40. nine and one-tenth

41. twenty-six and four-tenths

42. four and fifty-four hundredths

43. eleven and one-hundredth

44. nineteen and nine-tenths

45. two and seven-hundredths

CHALLENGE

Solve.
Joanne shaded 0.4 of a 10-by-10 square.

*46. Write a decimal in hundredths for the shaded part.

*47. Write a decimal for the part not shaded.

PERCENT
Fractions, Decimals, and Percents

Here are ratios written as fractions, decimals, and percents.

Ratio	Fraction	Decimal	Percent
35 out of 100	$\frac{35}{100}$	0.35	35%
9 out of 100	$\frac{9}{100}$	0.09	9%
4 out of 10	$\frac{4}{10}$	0.40	40%
1 out 20	$\frac{1}{20}$	0.05	5%
23 out of 50	$\frac{23}{50}$	0.46	46%

PRACTICE

Change fractions and decimals to percents.

1. $\frac{15}{100}$ **2.** $\frac{4}{100}$ **3.** $\frac{64}{100}$ **4.** $\frac{93}{100}$ **5.** $\frac{438}{100}$

6. 0.72 **7.** 0.59 **8.** 0.06 **9.** 0.8 **10.** 3.89

Change percents to fractions in simplest terms.

11. 23% **12.** 30% **13.** 1% **14.** 259% **15.** 302%

Change percents and fractions to decimals.

16. 51% **17.** $\frac{3}{4}$ **18.** $\frac{7}{10}$ **19.** 2% **20.** 501%

21. 80% **22.** $\frac{1}{2}$ **23.** 16% **24.** 11% **25.** $\frac{3}{50}$

MIXED PRACTICE
Maintaining and Reviewing Skills

Multiply or divide.

26. $\begin{array}{r} 572 \\ \times\ 0.15 \\ \hline \end{array}$ **27.** $\begin{array}{r} 28 \\ \times\ 0.6 \\ \hline \end{array}$ **28.** $\begin{array}{r} \$45.96 \\ \times\ 0.25 \\ \hline \end{array}$ **29.** $\begin{array}{r} \$79.90 \\ \times\ 0.30 \\ \hline \end{array}$ **30.** $\begin{array}{r} \$245.50 \\ \times\ 0.06 \\ \hline \end{array}$

31. $0.8\overline{)20.24}$ **32.** $0.16\overline{)3.952}$ **33.** $0.02\overline{)758.36}$ **34.** $3.6\overline{)292.86}$ **35.** $0.9\overline{)0.0243}$

FOCUS Use NUMBER skills to convert equivalent fractions, decimals, and percents.

APPLICATION
Using Statistics

A **circle graph** is often used to show data given in percents. The greater the percent, the greater the area on the graph.

Tina made a circle graph to show how she spent her time one day.

What percent of the day does each part of the circle represent?

36. sleeping and eating

37. school, club, and homework

38. playing

39. chores

40. other

41. What percent of the day does the whole graph show?

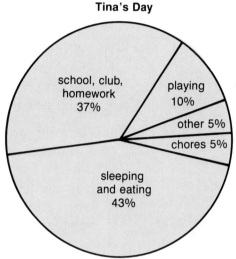

Tina's Day

school, club, homework 37%

playing 10%

other 5%

chores 5%

sleeping and eating 43%

Tina made another circle graph to show her classmates' favorite kind of books.

Use the circle graph below to answer these questions.

42. What percent of the students prefer mystery books?

43. What kind of book did 10% of Tina's classmates prefer?

44. What kind of book was the least favorite?

45. Which kind of book was more popular than mystery?

46. Which two kinds of books were less popular than nonfiction?

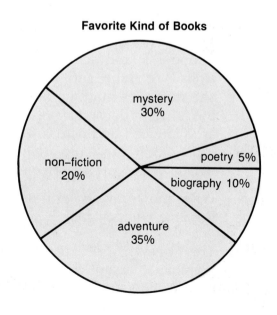

Favorite Kind of Books

mystery 30%

poetry 5%

non-fiction 20%

biography 10%

adventure 35%

Use STATISTICS to read and interpret a circle graph.

Selecting a Strategy: Using Logic

Logic is a strategy that helps you PLAN what to do. When using logic, look for clues that point to a solution.

1. READ Willie, John, and Rosalina all have jobs after school: mowing lawns, painting signs, and delivering groceries. Willie's sister likes her sign painting job, and John doesn't have a lawn mower. Which job does each person have?

2. KNOW Ask yourself: What do I need to find out? Which jobs do Willie, John, and Rosalina have?

Key facts:
a. The jobs are mowing, painting, and delivering.
b. Willie's sister likes her sign painting job.
c. John doesn't have a lawn mower.

3. PLAN Select a strategy: Try using logic. Make a chart to organize the clues. At the top, write an initial to stand for each person. Along the side, write a letter to stand for each job: M = mowing; D = delivering; P = painting. Use a √ for yes and an X for no in the appropriate boxes.

4. SOLVE Fill in the chart with Xs and √s. Willie's sister must be Rosalina. She likes to paint signs. Put a √ under R and across from P. Put a X across from P for John and Willie. If Rosalina paints, she does not mow or deliver. Put Xs in these boxes. John doesn't have a lawn mower so put an X under J and across from M. Look at your chart. John can only deliver (put a √). That means Willie cannot deliver and must mow.

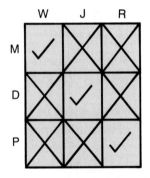

Willie mows lawns, John delivers groceries, and Rosalina paints signs.

5. CHECK The answer is reasonable because each possibility, except the ones in the answer, has been eliminated.

| FOCUS | Use logic as part of the Five-Step PROBLEM–SOLVING Plan. |

PRACTICE

Use logic to help PLAN and SOLVE each problem. Look for clues to help you.

1. Tony, Martha, and George have different hobbies. One likes to draw, one likes to build model ships, and one likes to collect stamps. Use the clues to find which hobby goes with which person.
   a. George has never seen a model ship.
   b. Tony thinks Martha's stamp albums are interesting.

2. Charlie, Maria, Tom, and Betty are the names of Joe's father, mother, sister, and brother. Use the clues to find how each person is related to Joe.
   a. Joe is older than Maria.
   b. Maria is older than Charlie.

3. Three brothers (Larry, Robert, and Eliot) and three sisters (Peggy, Bonnie, and Sandy) played chess. Each brother played against a different sister. Use the clues to find each pair of opponents.
   a. Eliot did not play Bonnie.
   b. Bonnie did not play Robert.
   c. Robert watched Sandy win against his brother.

4. José, Barbara, and Nancy each like a different sport. One likes basketball, one likes swimming, and one likes running. Use the clues to find out which person likes which sport.
   a. José doesn't like the water.
   b. Nancy likes to watch José take foul shots.
   c. If Barbara could, she would run all day.

5. This number is larger than 7, but less than a dozen. It has two digits and reads the same backward and forward. What is the number?

6. This number is an even number between 20 and 40. It has two digits that add up to 9. What is the number?

7. Joe types twice as fast as Betty, but only half as fast as Lori. If Joe types 30 words a minute, how fast do Betty and Lori type?

8. Bob walked half as far as Allen, but twice as far as Larry. If Larry walked 10 miles, how far did Bob and Allen walk?

Class Project

Work with a few of your classmates. Write your own logic problems. Be sure to give enough clues. Then exchange your problems with another group and solve the problems you receive. When you finish, check with the group that wrote the problems to see if they agree with your answers.

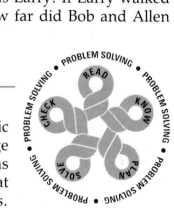

Finding a Percent of a Number

During a 4-game tournament, the team scored a total of 260 points. Malcolm scored 15% of the points. How many points did he score?

Find 15% of 260.

Change the percent to a decimal.   Think: 15% = 0.15.

$$\begin{array}{r} \text{Multiply:} \quad 260 \\ \times\ 0.15 \\ \hline 13\ 00 \\ 26\ 00 \\ \hline 39.00 \end{array}$$

Malcolm scored 39 points.

A basketball team won 80% of their games. If they played 15 games, how many games did they win?

Find 80% of 15.

Change the percent to a decimal.   Think: 80% = 0.80 = 0.8.

$$\begin{array}{r} \text{Multiply:} \quad 15 \\ \times\ 0.8 \\ \hline 12.0 \end{array}$$

The team won 12 games.

Remember that multiplying decimals is like multiplying whole numbers. The number of decimal places in the product is equal to the sum of the decimal places in the factors.

GUIDED PRACTICE

Change each percent to a decimal and solve.

1. 15% of 260

$$\begin{array}{r} 260 \\ \times\ 0.15 \end{array}$$

2. 25% of $600

$$\begin{array}{r} \$600 \\ \times\ 0.25 \end{array}$$

3. 75% of 48

$$\begin{array}{r} 48 \\ \times\ 0.75 \end{array}$$

4. 60% of 520

$$\begin{array}{r} 520 \\ \times\ 0.6 \end{array}$$

5. 32% of $795

6. 4% of $963

7. 1% of 2,587

8. 90% of $5,462

FOCUS	Use NUMBER skills to find a percent of a number.

PRACTICE

Change each percent to a decimal and solve.

9. 10% of 90

10. 25% of 200

11. 50% of 300

12. 75% of 480

13. 35% of 700

14. 8% of 900

15. 90% of 640

16. 15% of 320

17. 5% of 740

18. 75% of 400

19. 30% of 120

20. 36% of 125

21. 5% of $860

22. 15% of $450

23. 45% of $3,000

MIXED PRACTICE
Maintaining and Reviewing Skills

Copy and complete the chart.

	Ratio	Fraction	Decimal	Percent
24.	37 out of 100	$\frac{37}{100}$	0.37	■
25.	7 out of 20	$\frac{7}{20}$	■	■
26.	150 to 100	■	■	■
27.	306 to 100	■	■	■
28.	49 out of 50	■	■	■
29.	3 out of 20	■	■	■

CHALLENGE

*30. Look at this list of numbers. Circle the prime numbers. What percent of the numbers are prime numbers?

*31. Make your own list of numbers so that 60% of the numbers are prime numbers.

1	7	23	3	14
11	8	21	15	19
16	6	13	27	33
12	4	37	24	18

PERCENT
Finding a Percent of a Number

Janell bought a $79.50 coat for 20% off the original price. How much did she save?

Find 20% of $79.50.

$$\begin{array}{r} 79.50 \\ \times \quad 0.2 \\ \hline 15.900 \end{array}$$ ◄——— Write 20% as 0.2

20% of 79.50 is 15.90

Janell saved $15.90.

Find 138% of 523.

$$\begin{array}{r} 523 \\ \times\ 1.38 \\ \hline 41\ 84 \\ 156\ 90 \\ \underline{523\ 00} \\ 721.74 \end{array}$$ ◄——— Write 138% as 1.38

138% of 523 is 721.74

PRACTICE

Change each percent to a decimal and solve.

1. 25% of 80
2. 30% of 120
3. 35% of 70
4. 18 % of 240

5. 75% of $695
6. 8% of $735
7. 52% of 126
8. 3% of 245

9. 4% of 257
10. 75% of 95
11. 17% of 1,204
12. 40% of 320

13. 138% of 523
14. 125% of 80
15. 12% of $248.50
16. 175% of $455.40

MIXED PRACTICE
Maintaining and Reviewing Skills

Does each pair of ratios form a proportion? Write *yes* or *no*.

17. $\dfrac{25}{100} = \dfrac{12}{48}$
18. $\dfrac{50}{100} = \dfrac{45}{90}$
19. $\dfrac{20}{100} = \dfrac{50}{125}$
20. $\dfrac{5}{100} = \dfrac{3}{60}$

21. $\dfrac{2}{50} = \dfrac{10}{250}$
22. $\dfrac{4}{5} = \dfrac{80}{200}$
23. $\dfrac{6}{7} = \dfrac{54}{81}$
24. $\dfrac{3}{23} = \dfrac{6}{36}$

| FOCUS | Use NUMBER skills to find a percent of a number. |

APPLICATION
Using a Calculator

A calculator is particularly helpful in finding a percent of a number because it places the decimal point properly.

What is 5% of $135?

Key: 135 $\boxed{\times}$ 5 $\boxed{\%}$ $\boxed{=}$ 6.75

On some calculators you do not need to key $\boxed{=}$ after $\boxed{\%}$.

When finding percent of money, be sure to include the $ sign in your answer.

Find	*Key*	
25. 12% of 248	248 $\boxed{\times}$ 12 $\boxed{\%}$ $\boxed{=}$	▉
26. 24% of 590	590 $\boxed{\times}$ 24 $\boxed{\%}$ $\boxed{=}$	▉
27. 47% of 649	649 $\boxed{\times}$ 47 $\boxed{\%}$ $\boxed{=}$	▉
28. 3% of 704	704 $\boxed{\times}$ 3 $\boxed{\%}$ $\boxed{=}$	▉
29. 33% of $795	795 $\boxed{\times}$ 33 $\boxed{\%}$ $\boxed{=}$	▉
30. 15% of $2,085	2,085 $\boxed{\times}$ 15 $\boxed{\%}$ $\boxed{=}$	▉
31. 2% of $4,098	4,098 $\boxed{\times}$ 2 $\boxed{\%}$ $\boxed{=}$	▉
32. 1% of $59	59 $\boxed{\times}$ 1 $\boxed{\%}$ $\boxed{=}$	▉
33. 209% of 83	83 $\boxed{\times}$ 209 $\boxed{\%}$ $\boxed{=}$	▉
34. 73.5% of 98	98 $\boxed{\times}$ 73.5 $\boxed{\%}$ $\boxed{=}$	▉

35. What is 45% of $236?

36. What is 18% of $527?

37. What is 5% of $843?

38. What is 137% of $425?

39. What is 99% of 2,000?

40. What is 3.5% of 100?

41. What is 280% of 32?

42. What is 300% of 12.4?

43. What is 225% of 7.2?

44. What is 19% of 3,300?

45. What is 29% of 2,788?

46. What is 2% of $82,760.50?

47. What is 225% of 12?

48. What is 7.25% of $12,500?

Use a CALCULATOR to find a percent of a number.

Computing Distances

Maps show many things. They show land, rivers, directions, locations, and cities. One important fact contained in maps is the distance from one place to another.

In the United States, distance is measured in miles. One mile is equal to 5,280 feet in length.

Most countries use the metric system which measures distance in kilometers. One kilometer (km) is equal to about $\frac{5}{8}$ of one mile (mi).

Maps can be made in any size. Small maps may show the whole world; large maps may show the streets of a city. It is therefore important that the scale to which a map is drawn appears on each map. The scale shows how much of the distance on the map is the same as a certain land measure.

Some maps also show a number scale which is written as a ratio. If the scale is 1 to 5,000, usually written as 1:5,000, this means that 1 inch on the map is equal to 5,000 inches (416 feet, 8 inches). It could also mean that 1 centimeter is equal to 5 000 centimeters (50 meters). Look at this map scale.

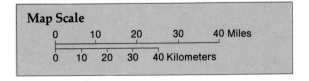

Using a strip of paper that has a straight edge, you can mark off the scale on a map to find out how far it is from one place to another.

If you wanted to find out how far it is from San Francisco to San José on a map like the one below, you might mark off the scale on a strip of paper and place it on the map to estimate the distance between the points.

If you had a longer distance, you might move the strip of paper every 25 or 40 miles.

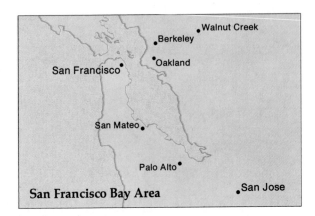

CRITICAL THINKING

1. How is the distance represented on a map explained on the map?

2. What is the unit of land measure used in the United States?
   What is the unit of measure used in most countries?

3. Why is it necessary for each map to have a scale on it?

FOCUS — Use MEASUREMENT to determine distance on a map.

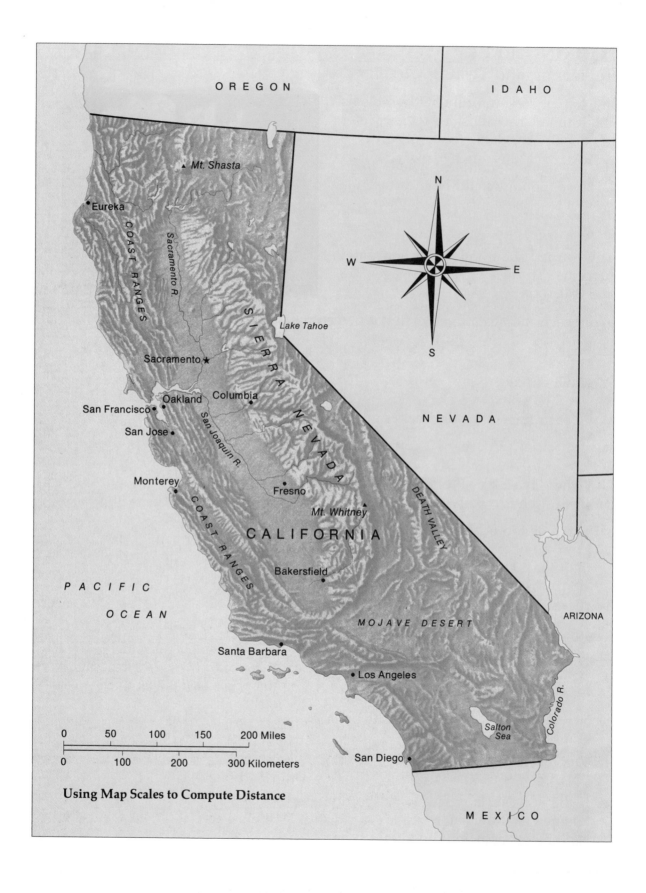

OREGON

IDAHO

▲ Mt. Shasta

•Eureka

COAST RANGES

Sacramento R.

SIERRA

Lake Tahoe

Sacramento ★

NEVADA

Oakland Columbia

San Francisco•

San Joaquin R.

San Jose•

NEVADA

Monterey•

COAST RANGES

Fresno•

DEATH VALLEY

Mt. Whitney ▲

CALIFORNIA

PACIFIC

OCEAN

Bakersfield•

MOJAVE DESERT

ARIZONA

Santa Barbara•

•Los Angeles

Colorado R.

Salton Sea

0   50   100   150   200 Miles

0   100   200   300 Kilometers

San Diego•

Using Map Scales to Compute Distance

MEXICO

LOOKING BACK
Reviewing and Testing Chapter 26

In Chapter 26 you formulated problems about time-lapse films. To review, refer to page 377 for data.

1. Give some examples where time-lapse filming would be most useful.

You learned about ratios, fractions, and percents. To review, refer to pages 378 and 380.

Write each ratio as a fraction and a percent.

2. 4 out of 5

3. 4 out of 100

4. 85 out of 100

5. 47 out of 100

6. 308 to 100

7. 3 out of 100

Write each fraction or decimal as a percent.

8. 0.44

9. $\frac{75}{100}$

10. 0.9

11. $\frac{2}{5}$

Use the Five–Step Problem–Solving Plan to solve this problem. Refer to page 382.

12. Three children had a total of 6 sea shells. One had an even number less than 5. The second had 1 shell less than that. How many shells did the third child have?

To review finding a percent of a number, refer to page 384.

Change each percent to a decimal and solve.

13. 12% of 80

14. 45% of 300

15. 72% of 80

16. 5% of 125

17. 37% of 175

18. 95% of 600

19. 50% of 700

20. 40% of 60

21. 98% of 50

You learned about computing distances on a map. To review, refer to pages 388 and 389.

22. If the scale on a map shows 1 centimeter for every 17 kilometers, how far apart are two cities if they are 4 centimeters apart on the map?

| FOCUS | Review and test skills learned and practiced. |

LOOKING AHEAD

Preparing for New Skills for Chapter 27

In the next chapter you will focus on

- formulating problems about a party.
- finding a percent of a number.
- finding what percent one number is of another.
- interpreting a circle graph.
- finding a number when a percent of it is known.
- how math is used in music.

Working with percents will be easier if you review writing percents as fractions and solving proportions. Study the examples.

Example 1:

$$56\% = \frac{56}{100} = \frac{56 \div 4}{100 \div 4} = \frac{14}{25}$$

Example 2:

$$195\% = \frac{195}{100} = 1\frac{95}{100} = 1\frac{19}{20}$$

To solve a proportion, first find the cross products. Then solve the equation that results.

Example 3:

$$\frac{7}{5} = \frac{14}{b}$$
$$7 \times b = 5 \times 14$$
$$7 \times b = 70$$
$$\frac{7 \times b}{7} = \frac{70}{7} \quad \textbf{Divide by 7.}$$
$$b = 10$$

Example 4:

$$\frac{a}{16} = \frac{3}{8}$$
$$a \times 8 = 16 \times 3$$
$$a \times 8 = 48$$
$$\frac{a \times 8}{8} = \frac{48}{8} \quad \textbf{Divide by 8.}$$
$$a = 6$$

PRACTICE

Write each percent as a fraction in simplest terms.

1. 45%   **2.** 75%   **3.** 18%   **4.** 180%   **5.** 125%

Solve each proportion.

6. $\dfrac{c}{20} = \dfrac{15}{100}$ **7.** $\dfrac{18}{100} = \dfrac{36}{d}$ **8.** $\dfrac{a}{5} = \dfrac{16}{20}$ **9.** $\dfrac{4}{w} = \dfrac{12}{27}$

10. $\dfrac{9}{n} = \dfrac{18}{100}$ **11.** $\dfrac{21}{7} = \dfrac{t}{6}$ **12.** $\dfrac{a}{8} = \dfrac{3}{2}$ **13.** $\dfrac{25}{100} = \dfrac{5}{r}$

Review NUMBER skills in preparation for learning new skills.

FOCUS   Formulate problems using photo, data, and text.

27

Percent

DATA

Number of students	143
Number of invited guests	12

Party supplies and prices

Case of soda	$12.00
cans per case	24
ounces per can	12
Package of 30	
6-oz plastic cups	$1.09
Package of 100	
paper plates	$2.99
Package of 100	
paper napkins	$1.19
Bag of 50 plastic forks	$1.59
Balloons	$0.25 each
helium-filled	$1.25 each
Twelve-foot rolls of crepe	
paper streamers	$0.98 each

Possible gifts and prices:

Radio/cassette player	$129
Camping equipment	$174
Exercise equipment	$149

"I think we're ready," said Jim, tacking up the last piece of crepe paper. "Let's get everyone together and turn out the lights."

The students at Northbrook School were giving a farewell party for their science teacher, Mr. Alvarez, who was retiring at the end of the year.

For several months, Jim and a committee of students had been planning the party, collecting money for a gift, buying the food and decorations, and arranging with the principal to keep Mr. Alvarez at an "important meeting" while they decorated the cafeteria. As a special surprise, Jim's committee had located people who had been in Mr. Alvarez's class at Northbrook many years ago and invited them to join in the celebration.

What are some good reasons for giving a party at school? What plans and preparations are necessary? How far ahead should plans be made? Plan an imaginary (or real) party, make a list of things that must be done, and indicate the best way to do them.

Finding What Percent One Number Is of Another

Elbert took a math test with a total of 40 problems. He did 32 of the problems correctly. What percent of the problems did he do correctly?

What percent of 40 is 32?

$$\frac{n}{100} = \frac{32}{40}$$ Write a proportion.

$$40 \times n = 100 \times 32$$ Use cross products.

$$40 \times n = 3,200$$ Multiply.

$$\frac{40 \times n}{40} = \frac{3,200}{40}$$ Divide.

$$n = 80$$

Elbert did 80% of the problems correctly.

What percent of 50 is 77?

$$\frac{n}{100} = \frac{77}{50}$$ Write a proportion.

$$50 \times n = 100 \times 77$$ Use cross products.

$$50 \times n = 7,700$$ Multiply.

$$\frac{50 \times n}{50} = \frac{7,700}{50}$$ Divide.

$$n = 154$$

77 is 154% of 50.

GUIDED PRACTICE

Solve.

1. What percent of 48 is 36?

$$\frac{x}{100} = \frac{36}{48}$$

2. What percent of 150 is 30?

$$\frac{x}{100} = \frac{30}{150}$$

3. What percent of 10 is 15?

$$\frac{x}{100} = \frac{15}{10}$$

4. What percent of 96 is 24?

$$\frac{x}{100} = \frac{24}{96}$$

5. What percent of 25 is 3?

6. What percent of 60 is 15?

FOCUS   Use NUMBER skills to find what percent one number is of another.

PRACTICE

Solve.

7. What percent of 10 is 5?

8. What percent of 80 is 20?

9. What percent of 100 is 37?

10. What percent of 2 is 8?

11. What percent of 16 is 4?

12. What percent of 200 is 40?

13. What percent of 96 is 72?

14. What percent of 500 is 10?

15. What percent of 360 is 90?

16. What percent of 360 is 18?

17. What percent of 50 is 123?

18. What percent of 75 is 150?

19. What percent of 10 is 95?

20. What percent of 25 is 42?

*21. What percent of 4,500 is 45?

*22. What percent of 4,500 is 4,950?

MIXED PRACTICE
Maintaining and Reviewing Skills

Write the equivalent fraction.

23. 0.25
24. 0.50
25. 0.30
26. 0.80
27. 0.20

28. 0.75
29. 0.60
30. 0.125
31. 0.40
32. 0.625

33. 0.66
34. 0.70
35. 0.88
36. 0.375
37. 0.10

38. 0.15
39. 0.22
40. 0.07
41. 0.95
42. 0.01

CHALLENGE

Use a calculator to find percents.

What percent of 192 is 48?

Think: "is" divided by "of".   48 ÷ 192

Key: 48 $\div$ 192 $=$

See: 0.25   0.25 = 25%   48 is 25% of 192

43. What percent of 720 is 180?

44. What percent of 7,800 is 2,106?

45. What percent of 3,690 is 1,291.5?

46. What percent of $650 is $97.50?

47. What percent of 900 is 45?

48. What percent of $1,800 is $36?

Use a CALCULATOR to find percents.

PERCENT
Finding What Percent One Number Is of Another

What percent of 64 is 16?

$$\frac{n}{100} = \frac{16}{64} \qquad \text{Write a proportion.}$$

$$64 \times n = 100 \times 16 \qquad \text{Use cross products.}$$

$$64 \times n = 1,600 \qquad \text{Multiply.}$$

$$\frac{64 \times n}{64} = \frac{1,600}{64} \qquad \text{Divide.}$$

$$n = 25$$

16 is 25% of 64.

PRACTICE

Solve.

1. What percent of 12 is 9?

2. What percent of 90 is 36?

3. What percent of 50 is 10?

4. What percent of 120 is 30?

5. What percent of 72 is 36?

6. What percent of 80 is 20?

7. What percent of 375 is 75?

8. What percent of 125 is 5?

9. What percent of 370 is 37?

10. What percent of 360 is 18?

11. What percent of 12 is 18?

12. What percent of 85 is 51?

13. What percent of 36 is 9?

14. What percent of 70 is 28?

15. What percent of 4,800 is 240?

16. What percent of 15 is 45?

MIXED PRACTICE
Maintaining and Reviewing Skills

Divide.

17. $0.25\overline{)36.00}$

18. $0.6\overline{)12.00}$

19. $0.75\overline{)24.00}$

20. $0.9\overline{)36.00}$

21. $0.4\overline{)48.00}$

22. $0.15\overline{)60.00}$

23. $0.3\overline{)72.00}$

24. $0.75\overline{)450.00}$

25. $0.9\overline{)72.00}$

26. $0.45\overline{)117.00}$

27. $0.05\overline{)3.00}$

28. $0.01\overline{)70.00}$

29. $0.25\overline{)525.00}$

30. $0.30\overline{)990.00}$

31. $0.90\overline{)81.00}$

32. $0.05\overline{)95.00}$

FOCUS | Use NUMBER skills to find what percent one number is of another.

APPLICATION
Using Statistics

The monthly income for the Carr family is $3,600. They made a circle graph to show their budget.

How much has the Carr family budgeted for savings?

What is 5% of $3,600?

$$\begin{array}{r} \$3,600 \\ \times \quad 0.05 \\ \hline \$180.00 \end{array}$$ Write the percent as a decimal.
Place the decimal point in the product.

The Carr family budgets $180.00 a month for savings.

Carr Family Monthly Budget

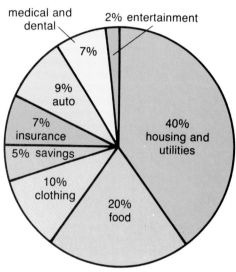

Copy the circle graph. Write in the amount the Carr family has budgeted for each of the following:

33. Housing and Utilities

34. Food

35. Clothing

36. Medical and Dental

37. Entertainment

38. Insurance

39. Automobile

40. Make a circle graph showing what part of your week is spent for each of the following activities. Put in both the percents and the hours.
Remember: a week has 168 hours.

    A. Sleeping   B. Attending school   C. Doing homework
    D. Doing chores   E. Washing and dressing   F. Eating
    G. Free time

41. Write a paragraph explaining how you figured out the amount of time spent for each item listed in Exercise 40. List the steps that you followed to construct your circle graph.

Use STATISTICS to interpret a circle graph.

Finding a Number When a Percent of It Is Known

Mr. Salim paid $120 for a topcoat that was on sale. This was 75% of the original price. What was the original price of the topcoat?

75% of what number is 120?

$$\frac{75}{100} = \frac{120}{n}$$ Write a proportion.

$$75 \times n = 100 \times 120$$ Use cross products.

$$75 \times n = 12{,}000$$ Multiply.

$$\frac{75 \times n}{75} = \frac{12{,}000}{75}$$ Divide.

$$n = 160$$

75% of 160 is 120.

The original price of the topcoat was $160.

78 is 130% of what number?

$$\frac{78}{n} = \frac{130}{100}$$ Write a proportion.

$$78 \times 100 = 130 \times n$$ Use cross products.

$$7{,}800 = 130 \times n$$ Multiply.

$$\frac{7{,}800}{130} = \frac{130 \times n}{130}$$ Divide.

78 is 103% of 60.

GUIDED PRACTICE

Solve.

1. 10% of what number is 15?

$$\frac{10}{100} = \frac{15}{x}$$

2. 80 is 125% of what number?

$$\frac{80}{x} = \frac{125}{100}$$

3. 42 is 75% of what number?

4. 20% of what number is 30?

5. 50% of what number is 95?

6. 36 is 75% of what number?

| FOCUS | Use NUMBER skills to find a number when a percent of it is known. |

PRACTICE

Solve.

7. 50% of what number is 5?

8. 25 is 10% of what number?

9. 89 is 25% of what number?

10. 25% of what number is 10?

11. 40% of what number is 20?

12. 62 is 40% of what number?

13. 15 is 25% of what number?

14. 75% of what number is 12?

15. 210 is 75% of what number?

16. 270 is 75% of what number?

17. 50 is 10% of what number?

18. 40% of what number is 168?

19. 30% of what number is 45?

20. 15% of what number is 9?

21. 60% of what number is 15?

22. 8 is 32% of what number?

23. 90% of what number is 45?

24. 25% of what number is 32?

25. 12% of what number is 24?

26. 7 is 35% of what number?

27. 245 is 35% of what number?

*28. $12\frac{1}{2}$% of what number is 36?

MIXED PRACTICE
Maintaining and Reviewing Skills

Solve. Use related sentences.

29. $n + 15 = 25$

30. $s - 18 = 63$

31. $54 - t = 12$

32. $384 + a = 400$

33. $14 \times m = 42$

34. $k \times 11 = 176$

35. $297 + b = 987$

36. $21 \times k = 441$

37. $488 - d = 201$

38. $13 \times a = 169$

39. $267 - n = 188$

40. $b + 173 = 229$

41. $n + 25 = 103$

42. $z \times 22 = 374$

43. $75 - a = 56$

CHALLENGE

Solve.

*44. An antique dealer received $33.75 commission for selling a quilt. If the dealer's commission was 15% of the selling price, what was the selling price?

PERCENT

Finding a Number When a Percent of It Is Known

75% of what number is 108?

$$\frac{75}{100} = \frac{108}{n}$$ Write a proportion.

$$75 \times n = 100 \times 108$$ Use cross products.

$$75 \times n = 10,800$$ Multiply.

$$\frac{75 \times n}{75} = \frac{10,800}{75}$$ Divide.

$$n = 144$$

75% of 144 is 108

PRACTICE

Solve.

1. 36 is 30% of what number?

2. 8 is 40% of what number?

3. $9 is 15% of what number?

4. $24 is 75% of what number?

5. $70 is 25% of what number?

6. $45 is 150% of what number?

7. $30 is 60% of what number?

8. $9 is 60% of what number?

9. 50 is 125% of what number?

10. 38 is 50% of what number?

11. 20 is 25% of what number?

12. 27 is 30% of what number?

13. Toni bought a lawn mower for $450. This was 75% of the original price. What was the original price of the lawn mower?

14. Nathan earned $75 one week. This was 150% of what he earned the week before. How much had he earned the week before?

MIXED PRACTICE

Maintaining and Reviewing Skills

Solve.

15. What is 35% of $212?

16. What is 60% of $480?

17. What is 10% of $80.50?

18. What is 25% of $250?

19. What percent of $24 is $18?

20. What percent of 50 is 48?

FOCUS   Use NUMBER skills to find a number when a percent of it is known.

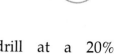
Solve.

21. With an 18% discount, Marion saved $9.72 on a weight set. What was the original price of the set?

22. Alan bought a drill at a 20% discount. He saved $15.99. What was the original price of the drill?

23. Mr. Brodsky bought a stereo system. The original price was $750. It was on sale for 75% of the original price. How much did Mr. Brodsky pay for the stereo system?

24. Norman bought a baseball glove on sale. He paid $12 for it. This was 50% less than the original price of the glove. What was the original price of the baseball glove?

25. Diedra purchased some video tapes for her home recorder. She paid $36 for tapes that originally cost $48. What percent of the original price did Diedra pay for the video tapes?

26. Clara Sue had a tape deck installed in her car. She received a 30% discount on the tape deck, which originally cost $90. How much did Clara Sue pay for the tape deck?

27. Herman purchased a set of luggage for $175. It was marked down from the original price of $200. What percent of the original price did Herman pay?

28. Marvin took advantage of a 40% discount sale and purchased a new lawn mower. How much did he save on a lawn mower that had an original price of $420?

29. Carmen bought a new coat at a sale and saved $45. The original price of the coat was $150. What percent of the original price did Carmen pay for the coat?

30. Steve paid $96 for a drum set that was originally priced at $120. What percent of the original price did Steve save by buying the drum set on sale?

31. Ann bought a bike that cost $200. It went on sale and was discounted 10%. Her employee discount was 10% off the sale price. How much did she pay for the bike?

32. Beth bought a new dress. The dress was marked 40% off. The original price of the dress was $48. How much did Beth save? How much did she pay for the dress?

33. Miriam bought a coat originally marked at $150. It had two markdowns. First it was reduced by 25%. Then it was marked down from that price 10%. How much did Miriam pay for the coat?

34. An art dealer received an $84 commission for selling an oil painting. The commission was 16% of the original selling price. How much did the painting sell for?

Use NUMBER skills to solve percent problems.

401

Chance and Music

Writing music seems to be a very creative activity, but is it really? Two hundred years ago the great composer Wolfgang Mozart made up a game designed to enable anyone to write a dance, without knowledge of music.

Mozart's idea is like the one used to program computers to write music.

Mozart wrote out a group of dances. Each of the measures of the dances was numbered. First the player threw a number cube. The numbers that appeared on several throws were added and then matched to the measures of the dances. The player would continue to roll the number cube and choose the measures until the new dance had been written.

In 1957, the ILLIAC computer at the University of Illinois was programmed to write a set of musical pieces. Different rules were given to the computer for each piece. The output depended partly on what the rules told it to do and partly on chance.

The computer's music wasn't easy to listen to, but it held great fascination for the computer programmers because it proved that a computer could be programmed to write original music.

Here is how chance and rules can teach us to write a piece of music. This is how Mozart's game works.

Suppose that instead of a number cube you use two coins, a penny, and a nickel. Let the outcome of the coin toss tell you which measure of music to use. List all the possible outcomes.

head, head   head, tail
tail, head   tail, tail

We have four possible outcomes. Each of the four is equally likely. So we need four measures of music written in three-quarter time and numbered to match the outcomes of tossing the coins.

Now, toss the coins and write your dance. But do not be surprised if your composition has the same measures occur twice in a row or if all the measures turn out to be the same!

CRITICAL THINKING

1. You are about to choose the first measure of your dance by tossing a coin. You don't want to begin with a dotted note. What is the likelihood of a measure without a dotted note being chosen?

2. Toss your coins to compose the rhythm of an eight-measure dance.

3. In what ways was Mozart's writing of the dances like the work of a computer programmer?

FOCUS | Use PROBABILITY to compose music.

At the age of five, Wolfgang Amadeus Mozart (1756–1791) was beginning to compose minuets and other musical pieces.

Jazz musician Herbie Hancock composes some of his music with a computer and a synthesizer.

LOOKING BACK
Reviewing and Testing Chapter 27

In Chapter 27 you formulated problems about a party. To review, refer to page 393 for data.

1. What was the cost for each can of soda?

To review what you learned about finding what percent one number is of another, refer to pages 394–396.

Solve.

2. What percent of 25 is 15?

3. What percent of 80 is 24?

4. What percent of 180 is 27?

5. What percent of 180 is 9?

6. What percent of 800 is 168?

7. What percent of 450 is 324?

To review what you learned about circle graphs, refer to page 397.

There are 1,200 movies filmed each year. Look at the graph and determine the number of each type of movie that is filmed.

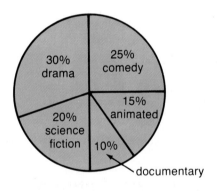

8. Animated

9. Drama

10. Science Fiction

11. Comedy

12. Documentary

To review what you learned about finding a number when a percent of it is known, refer to page 398.

13. 20% of what number is 80?

14. 42% of what number is 84?

15. 15% of what number is 135?

16. 140% of what number is 560?

You learned about chance and music. To review, refer to page 402.

17. What is the probability of having two notes in the first measure of your dance?

FOCUS | Review and test skills learned and practiced.

LOOKING AHEAD
Preparing for New Skills for Chapter 28

In the next chapter you will focus on

- formulating problems about school supplies.
- ordering integers.
- finding the opposite of an integer.
- locating integers in a grid.
- adding integers with like signs.
- how math is used in health.

Working with integers will be easier if you review locating whole numbers on a number line and comparing whole numbers. Study the examples.

Example 1:

Locate 3 and 5.

Example 2:

Locate 11 and 25.

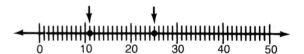

Use > or < to compare numbers. Remember the greater number is always farther to the right on the number line.

Example 3:

$$25 > 11$$

Example 4:

$$76{,}321 < 76{,}592$$

PRACTICE

Tell which number is represented by the given letter.

1. *A*   **2.** *B*   **3.** *C*   **4.** *D*

Draw a number line like the one above on a separate sheet of paper. Locate each of the following numbers.

5. 8   **6.** 12   **7.** 21   **8.** 26

Compare. Use > or <.

9. 21 ● 12   **10.** 35 ● 48   **11.** 102 ● 120   **12.** 1,351 ● 1,349

Review NUMBER skills in preparation for learning new skills.

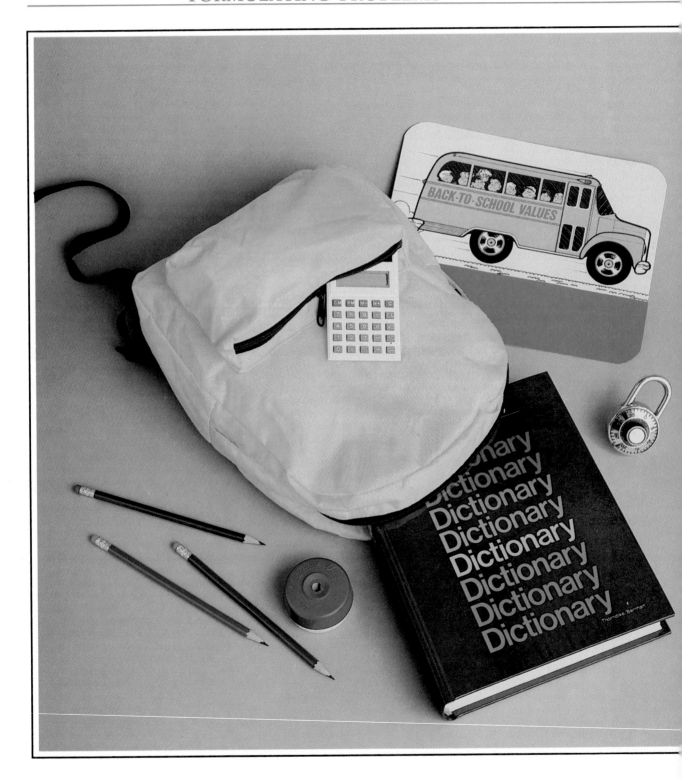

CHAPTER **28**

Compare and Order Integers and Addition With Like Signs

DATA

WHITEHALL & SONS

Item	Regular Price	Discount
Dictionary	$ 4.95	10%
Lock	$ 5.95	10%
Calculator	$19.99	15%
Knapsack	$15.00	10%
Sharpener	$ 5.00	50%

S.J. GREEN & CO.

Item	Regular Price	Discount
Dictionary	$ 4.95	10%
Lock	$ 5.95	15%
Calculator	$18.00	10%
Knapsack	$17.50	10%
Sharpener	$ 4.00	20%

MAXWELL'S

Item	Regular Price	Discount
Dictionary	$ 4.95	20%
Lock	$ 6.99	30%
Calculator	$22.50	25%
Knapsack	$21.99	25%
Sharpener	$ 4.50	30%

One day Joanne heard her mother say that she had almost enough money saved to buy a small home computer for the family to use. But with school starting soon, she would have to wait until she bought Joanne's school supplies. Then she could buy the computer.

Joanne noticed that several stores were having back-to-school sales. She decided to compare prices of school supplies at the different stores. Then she could buy each item she needed at the store with the lowest price. Joanne figured that by shopping carefully she might save enough money so that her mother would not have to wait to buy the computer. Her list included a pocket dictionary, lock, calculator, knapsack, and pencil sharpener.

Try to predict where Joanne will buy her school supplies. Will she make all her purchases at one store? Are there any considerations when shopping other than prices?

Comparing and Ordering

Whole numbers and their opposites are called **integers**. On a horizontal number line, points to the **right** of zero are **positive** and points to the **left** of zero are **negative**.

The integer ⁻2 is read *negative two*. It names the point 2 units to the left of zero. Its opposite is ⁺2.

The integer ⁺5 is read *positive five*. It names the point 5 units to the right of zero. Its opposite is ⁻5.

The **greater** of two integers is always the one farther to the **right** on a number line.

Compare ⁺8 and ⁺2. The integer ⁺8 is farther to the right than the ⁺2.

Therefore ⁺8 > ⁺2.

Compare ⁻6 and ⁻4. The integer ⁻4 is farther to the right than the ⁻6.

Therefore ⁻4 > ⁻6.

Order these integers from least to greatest:

⁻6, ⁺8, 0, ⁻8, ⁺4.

To list integers in order, think of them as they appear on a number line.

The integers in order are ⁻8, ⁻6, 0, ⁺4, ⁺8.

GUIDED PRACTICE

1. Which integer is farther to the right on the number line, ⁺3 or ⁻6? Which integer is greater?

2. Which integer is farther to the right on the number line, ⁻7 or ⁻1? Which integer is greater?

3. Which integer is farther to the right on the number line, 0 or ⁺4. Which integer is greater?

FOCUS | Use NUMBER skills to compare and order integers.

PRACTICE

Write the opposite integer for each.

4. $^+7$ **5.** $^+13$ **6.** $^-9$ **7.** $^-17$ **8.** $^+21$

9. $^-19$ **10.** $^-1$ **11.** $^+29$ **12.** $^+40$ **13.** $^-33$

Compare each pair of integers. Use > or <.

14. $^+13 \bullet ^+14$ **15.** $^+15 \bullet ^-6$ **16.** $0 \bullet ^-5$ **17.** $^-8 \bullet ^+6$

18. $0 \bullet ^+6$ **19.** $^+39 \bullet ^-39$ **20.** $^-12 \bullet ^-10$ **21.** $^+15 \bullet ^-21$

22. $^-5 \bullet ^+1$ **23.** $^+14 \bullet ^-13$ **24.** $^+15 \bullet ^-16$ **25.** $^-40 \bullet ^-3$

26. $^+1 \bullet ^-1$ **27.** $^-8 \bullet ^-18$ **28.** $^+35 \bullet ^-4$ **29.** $^-12 \bullet ^-1$

30. $^-16 \bullet ^+14$ **31.** $^-32 \bullet ^+33$ **32.** $^-21 \bullet ^+24$ **33.** $^-10 \bullet 0$

List in order from least to greatest.

34. $^+8, ^-10, ^-4, ^+1, ^+3$ **35.** $^-12, ^-5, ^+10, ^+9, ^-2$ **36.** $^-3, ^+2, ^-1, ^+5, ^-6$

37. $^-7, ^+2, ^+4, 0, ^-1$ **38.** $^-4, ^+2, ^-7, 0, ^+8$ **39.** $^+6, ^-6, ^+4, ^-3, ^-7$

MIXED PRACTICE

Write the integers that replace a and b on each number line.

40.

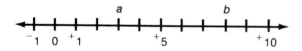

41.

42.

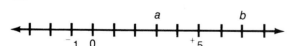

43.

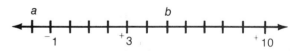

44.

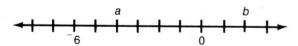

45.

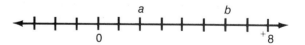

CHALLENGE

46. How many integers are there between $^-9$ and $^+12$?

INTEGERS
Comparing and Ordering

On a horizontal number line, integers to the **right** of zero are **positive** and integers to the **left** of zero are **negative**. Zero is neither positive nor negative.

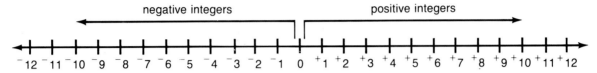

The integers on the number line are in order from least to greatest. The integer farther to the right on the number line is greater.

Compare $^-9$ and $^-7$.

The integer $^-7$ is farther to the right. Therefore it is greater than $^-9$. $^-9 < {}^-7$

Compare $^+4$ and $^+7$.

The integer $^+7$ is farther to the right. Therefore it is greater than $^+4$. $^+4 < {}^+7$

PRACTICE

Compare the integers. Use > or <.

1. $^+5$ ● $^-1$
2. $^-8$ ● $^-3$
3. 0 ● $^+9$
4. $^+15$ ● $^+51$

5. $^-14$ ● $^+2$
6. 0 ● $^-12$
7. $^+23$ ● $^+24$
8. $^-14$ ● $^-17$

9. $^+27$ ● $^+20$
10. $^-1$ ● $^+1$
11. $^+19$ ● $^+9$
12. $^-21$ ● $^-19$

List the integers in order from least to greatest.

13. $^+15,\ ^-30,\ ^-5,\ 0,\ ^-25,\ ^+35$

14. $^+4,\ ^-18,\ ^-7,\ 0,\ ^+6,\ ^-2$

15. $^+9,\ ^-25,\ 0,\ ^+16,\ ^-2,\ ^-18$

16. $^+19,\ ^-22,\ 0,\ ^-1,\ ^+11,\ ^-6$

MIXED PRACTICE
Maintaining and Reviewing Skills

Tell which addition or multiplication property each represents.

17. $c + d = d + c$

18. $(r + s) + t = r + (s + t)$

19. $a \times b = b \times a$

20. $a \times (b + c) = (a \times b) + (a \times c)$

21. $a \times (b \times c) = (a \times b) \times c$

22. $a + 0 = a$

FOCUS Use NUMBER skills to compare and order integers.

410

APPLICATION

Using Algebra

An ordered pair of integers can be used to locate points on a grid.

Ordered Pair **Location**
(4, 5)   4 units right
                   5 units up

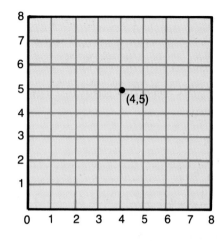

The perpendicular number lines on a grid are axes which divide the grid into 4 sections or **quadrants**. The **axes'** point of intersection (0, 0) is the **origin**. Each ordered pair of integers is a set of coordinates for a point.

The **first** integer or **coordinate** tells how many units to move **left** or **right**. The **second** coordinate tells how many units to move **up** or **down**.

Ordered Pair   **Location**
(4, 4)   4 units right
                   4 units up
(⁻2, 5)   2 units left
                   5 units up
(⁻5, ⁻2)   5 units left
                   2 units down
(4, ⁻3)   4 units right
                   3 units down

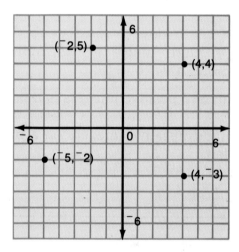

A point on a grid can be named by a capital letter or the coordinate.

Give the point named by each ordered pair.

23. (3, 5)   **24.** (⁻2, 4)   **25.** (⁻3, ⁻1)

Give the coordinates for each.

26. B   **27.** C   **28.** E

Graph each point on a 4-quadrant graph.

29. (4, ⁻4)   **30.** (⁻5, 3)   **31.** (⁻2, ⁻6)

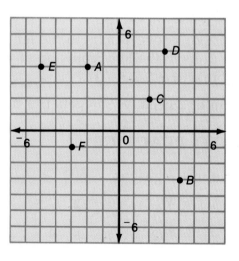

Use ALGEBRA to graph points with integers.

With Like Signs

Toni collected sports stickers. He bought 4 stickers on Monday. On Tuesday he bought 4 more stickers. How many stickers in all did he buy?

To add positive integers on a number line you move to the right.

Add: $^+4 + {}^+4$

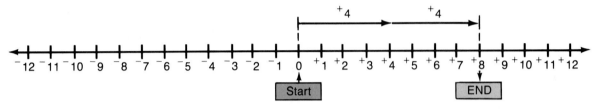

Start at zero. Move 4 units to the right and from there move 4 more units to the right. You stop at $^+8$. Therefore $^+4 + {}^+4 = {}^+8$.

The sum of 2 positive integers is a positive integer.

To add negative integers on a number line you move to the left.

Add: $^-4 + {}^-7$

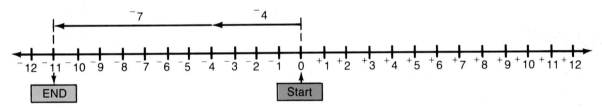

Start at zero. Move 4 units to the left and from there move 7 more units to the left. You stop at $^-11$. Therefore $^-4 + {}^-7 = {}^-11$.

The sum of 2 negative integers is a negative integer.

GUIDED PRACTICE

Find the missing signs.

1. $^-2 + {}^-4 = \blacksquare 6$

2. $^+7 + {}^+7 = \blacksquare 14$

3. $^-6 + {}^-1 = \blacksquare 7$

4. $^-6 + {}^-6 = \blacksquare 12$

5. $^-9 + {}^-10 = \blacksquare 19$

6. $^+9 + {}^+5 = \blacksquare 14$

| FOCUS | Use NUMBER skills to add integers. |

PRACTICE

Add.

7. $^+4 + {}^+3$ 8. $^-3 + {}^-1$ 9. $^+5 + {}^+8$ 10. $^-5 + {}^-11$

11. $^-4 + {}^-5$ 12. $^+6 + {}^+6$ 13. $^-3 + {}^-8$ 14. $^+12 + {}^+8$

15. $^+5 + {}^+9$ 16. $^-2 + {}^-1$ 17. $^-10 + {}^-20$ 18. $^-8 + {}^-15$

19. $^-7 + {}^-12$ 20. $^-25 + {}^-8$ 21. $^+18 + {}^+50$ 22. $^+25 + {}^+25$

23. $^-11 + {}^-9$ 24. $^+9 + {}^+8$ 25. $^-9 + {}^-8$ 26. $^+14 + {}^+7$

27. $^-18 + {}^-6$ 28. $^+17 + {}^+12$ 29. $^-14 + {}^-2$ 30. $^-10 + {}^-8$

31. $^-50 + {}^-25$ 32. $^+35 + {}^+15$ 33. $^-40 + {}^-60$ 34. $^+50 + {}^+49$

MIXED PRACTICE
Maintaining and Reviewing Skills

Round each to the nearest hundredth.

35. 2.573   36. 1.869   37. 25.714   38. 35.007   39. 0.198

40. 4.357   41. 5.382   42. 0.066   43. 28.934   44. 0.616

Round each to the nearest thousandth.

45. 2.9546   46. 8.7120   47. 5.9175   48. 0.0308   49. 5.2416

50. 7.0659   51. 0.6007   52. 0.9999   53. 1.9995   54. 17.7983

Write an addition number sentence using positive and negative integers. Then solve.

55. Tracy made 9 banners in one day. The next day she made 12 more banners. How many banners did she make in all?

56. The Kingpins bowling team lost 4 games. Then they lost 3 other games. How many games did the Kingpins lose in all?

CHALLENGE

*57. Use + or − signs between digits to make the number sentence true. Hint: You may not have to put a sign between each digit.

     9   8   7   6   5   4   3   2   1 = 100

ADDITION OF INTEGERS
With Like Signs

In the first play the Kickers lost 4 yards. In the next play they lost 8 more yards. How many yards did the Kickers lose in the first two plays?

To add negative integers move left.　　　To add positive integers move right.

Add: $^-4 + \,^-8$

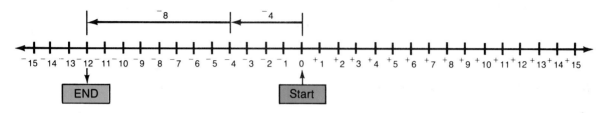

Start at zero. A negative 4 means a move 4 units to the left. Then from that point move 8 more units to the left. You stop at $^-12$. Therefore $^-4 + \,^-8 = \,^-12$.

The sum of 2 positive integers is a positive integer. The sum of 2 negative integers is a negative integer.

PRACTICE

Add.

1. $^-6 + \,^-9$　　　**2.** $^-6 + \,^-2$　　　**3.** $^-7 + \,^-8$　　　**4.** $^+9 + \,^+12$

5. $^-1 + \,^-1$　　　**6.** $^-3 + \,^-4$　　　**7.** $^-4 + \,^-4$　　　**8.** $^-1 + \,^-5$

9. $0 + \,^-8$　　　**10.** $^-13 + \,^-6$　　　**11.** $^-25 + \,^-15$　　　**12.** $^+38 + \,^+17$

13. $^-18 + \,^-7$　　　**14.** $^+14 + \,^+2$　　　**15.** $^+31 + \,^+21$　　　**16.** $^-64 + 0$

17. $^-16 + \,^-8$　　　**18.** $0 + \,^+10$　　　**19.** $^-1 + \,^-11$　　　**20.** $^-17 + \,^-7$

MIXED PRACTICE
Maintaining and Reviewing Skills

Add or subtract.

21. $7\frac{2}{4} + 8\frac{1}{5}$　　　**22.** $9\frac{2}{3} - 6\frac{1}{3}$　　　**23.** $17\frac{2}{5} - 13$　　　**24.** $14 + 9\frac{2}{3}$

25. $15 - 6\frac{4}{7}$　　　**26.** $25 - 4\frac{6}{9}$　　　**27.** $6\frac{2}{3} + 4\frac{1}{4}$　　　**28.** $4\frac{2}{7} - 2\frac{1}{3}$

FOCUS　Use NUMBER skills to add integers.

414

APPLICATION
Using Algebra

Whole numbers and their opposites can be used to represent many situations.

Situation:
Mary was 3 inches taller. $^+3$

Opposite Situation:
Mary was 3 inches shorter. $^-3$

Situation:
Jim went down 4 steps. $^-4$

Opposite situation:
Jim went up 4 steps, $^+4$

Write the integer for each situation.

24. The temperature dropped 10°.

25. The kite rose 75 meters.

26. Miguel spent $6.

27. The team won by 5 points.

28. It was one hour before class.

29. The bird dove 10 meters.

30. The hole was 1 meter deep.

31. Jose gained 3 kilograms.

32. The anchor dropped 50 feet.

33. Eric earned $20.

34. Sue walked up 2 floors.

35. He made a $9 profit.

36. It was 9° cooler.

37. The ball rolled 6 feet backward.

38. Susan spent $100.

39. The roots reached 9 feet below ground.

Write the opposite situation and its integer.

40. The team won by 9 points.

41. Tim bought 7 plants.

42. The city is 32 miles north.

43. He walked 5 feet to the right.

44. Ted ran 2 hours after lunch.

45. It is 11° warmer.

46. Shorten the hem 2 inches.

47. Ann opened 6 boxes.

48. It was eleven seconds before liftoff.

49. They lost by 18 points.

50. They used 75 liters of gas.

51. The clock was ahead 1 hour.

Use ALGEBRA to find opposite integers.

Heart Rate

Do you ever wonder why you feel your heart beating faster while you run or play ball?

This happens because, during exercise, your heart works harder. It actually beats more times per minute than when you are doing such things as walking, studying, or listening to music.

The heart is a muscle that expands as blood flows into it and contracts as it pumps blood away from it. Veins carry blood to the heart while arteries carry blood from the heart to other parts of the body. As the heart contracts, it pumps blood through the arteries causing them to swell. The regular swelling of the arteries caused by the heart contracting is called the pulse.

You can feel your pulse by placing your forefinger and middle finger on the inside of your wrist. You should feel a regular rhythmical beat. If you count how many times you feel this regular beat in 15 seconds and then multiply this number by 4, you can find how many times your heart beats per minute. This is your heart rate.

Heart rate = Number of heart beats in 15 seconds × 4

Try calculating your heart rate at different times of the day. See whether or not you always get the same number.

Look at the chart that follows. It shows examples of Bill's heart rate. Bill is a healthy twelve year old.

Bill's Heart Beats per Minute	
Walking	72
Eating lunch	80
Playing	100
Running	120
Studying	76
Sleeping	68

Keep in mind that your heart rate can be different than Bill's. He is only an example. Remember, people are different.

CRITICAL THINKING

1. Explain how the heart works.

2. What is the pulse?

3. Compare Bill's heart rate while he is running and while he is sleeping.

4. Why do you suppose Bill's heart rate is higher during the day than either the morning or evening?

FOCUS | Use NUMBER skills to learn about heart rate.

Cross-country skiing can provide an excellent cardio-vascular workout.

LOOKING BACK

Reviewing and Testing Chapter 28

In Chapter 28 you formulated problems about shopping for school supplies. To review, refer to pages 406 and 407.

1. Think about the supplies you would need when you return to school. Make a list.

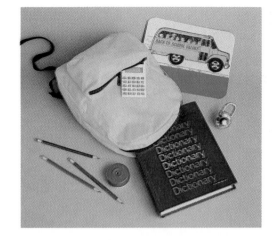

To review what you learned about comparing and ordering integers, refer to page 408.

Write the opposite integer for each.

2. $^-6$ **3.** $^+8$ **4.** $^+12$ **5.** $^-7$

Compare each pair of integers. Use < or >.

6. $^+11 \bullet ^+7$ **7.** $^-8 \bullet ^-10$ **8.** $^+6 \bullet ^-3$ **9.** $^-1 \bullet 0$

10. $^+4 \bullet ^-3$ **11.** $^-7 \bullet ^+7$ **12.** $^+16 \bullet ^+19$ **13.** $^-4 \bullet ^-7$

List in order from least to greatest.

14. $^-6, ^+1, ^-4, ^+9, ^-8$ **15.** $0, ^+7, ^+1, ^-1, ^+4$

You learned about the addition of integers with like signs. Refer to page 412.

Add.

16. $^+4 + ^+3$ **17.** $^-6 + ^-3$ **18.** $^-7 + ^-6$ **19.** $^+8 + ^+2$

20. $^-14 + ^-12$ **21.** $^+11 + 0$ **22.** $^-9 + ^-4$ **23.** $^+26 + ^+14$

24. $^+8 + ^+9$ **25.** $^+7 + ^+26$ **26.** $^-16 + ^-11$ **27.** $^-14 + 0$

28. $^-14 + ^-14$ **29.** $^+9 + ^+7$ **30.** $^-11 + ^-13$ **31.** $^-26 + ^-6$

You learned about computing your heart rate. To review, refer to page 416.

32. If you heart beats 56 times in 30 seconds, what is your heart rate?

FOCUS   Review and test skills learned and practiced.

LOOKING AHEAD

Preparing for New Skills for Chapter 29

In the next chapter you will focus on

- formulating problems about a movie sound track.
- adding integers with unlike signs.
- graphing a line.
- using a problem-solving strategy.

- subtracting integers with like signs.
- subtracting integers with unlike signs.
- how math is used in geography.

Adding and subtracting integers will be easier if you review plotting integers on a grid. Study the examples.

Example 1:

$^+5 + {}^+2 = {}^+7$

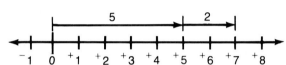

Example 2:

$^-3 + {}^-6 = {}^-9$

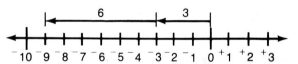

To graph a point, use the first coordinate to move left or right; use the second coordinate to move up or down.

Example 3:

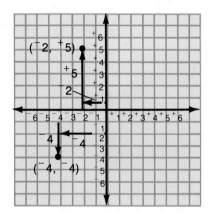

Example 4:

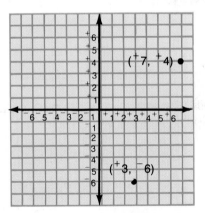

PRACTICE

Add.

1. $^+6 + {}^+5$

2. $^-7 + {}^-9$

3. $^-3 + {}^-11$

4. $^+36 + {}^+58$

Draw a four-quadrant graph on grid paper. Graph each point.

5. $(^+2, {}^+3)$

6. $(^+2, {}^-3)$

7. $(^-1, {}^+7)$

8. $(^-4, {}^-3)$

Review NUMBER skills and ALGEBRA in preparation for learning new skills.

FOCUS   Formulate problems using a photo, data, and text.

Addition and Subtraction of Integers With Like and Unlike Signs

DATA

Goal To make a 22 minute 10 second movie soundtrack

Cassette playing time

	Minutes	Seconds
Ali	3	15
	3	00
	7	20
	4	18
	2	10
	6	02
Total	26	05
Lin	6	00
	3	25
	6	55
	4	45
	2	25
	3	05
Total	26	35
Zack	4	15
	6	15
	4	10
	5	45
	3	25
	2	35
Total	26	25

Zack, Lin, and Ali have made a film that runs for exactly 22 minutes and 10 seconds. Now they are ready for the final step. They will be adding a soundtrack.

The filmmakers each have a different idea of exactly what songs to use, so they have each recorded a cassette to go with the film. Together they will view the film to see how it works with each of the three cassettes. Then they will vote for one.

Each person taped six songs, from records, to make the cassettes. No one was able to match the film time exactly. They voted anyway and chose Zack's cassette. Lin was not sure they could use Zack's cassette. Ali was confident that they could, even though they would have to solve a few problems.

What problems could Ali have been considering? How can these problems be solved? Is there a likelihood of getting a finished soundtrack to match the desired length?

With Unlike Signs

While playing Spello, Terry gained 8 points for using most of her letters to make a word. At the end of the game, Terry lost 3 points for not using all her letters. What was her total gain or loss at Spello?

Think: Gained 8 points $^+8$
Lost 3 points $^-3$

To add positive integers on a number line move right.
To add negative integers on a number line move left.

Add: $^+8 + {}^-3$

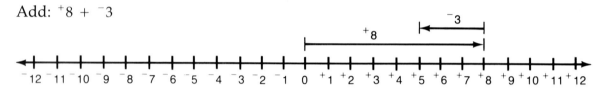

Start at zero. Move 8 units to the right to show $^+8$. From that point move 3 units to the left to show $^-3$. You stop at $^+5$. Therefore $^+8 + {}^-3 = {}^+5$.

Add: $^-7 + {}^+4$

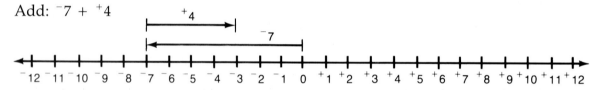

Start at zero. Move 7 units to the left to show $^-7$. From that point move 4 units to the right to show $^+4$. You stop at $^-3$. Therefore $^-7 + {}^+4 = {}^-3$.

GUIDED PRACTICE

Add. Use the number line to help.

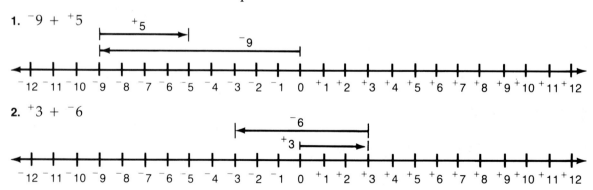

1. $^-9 + {}^+5$

2. $^+3 + {}^-6$

| FOCUS | Use NUMBER skills to add integers. |

PRACTICE

Add.

3. ⁻4 + ⁺1

4. ⁺9 + ⁻3

5. ⁺3 + ⁻5

6. ⁺5 + ⁻2

7. ⁻6 + ⁺4

8. ⁺7 + ⁻3

9. ⁺2 + ⁻9

10. ⁺9 + ⁻7

11. ⁻9 + ⁺9

12. ⁻8 + ⁺3

13. ⁺6 + ⁻12

14. ⁻4 + ⁺2

15. ⁻18 + ⁺12

16. ⁻3 + ⁺10

17. ⁻5 + ⁺9

18. ⁻9 + ⁺2

19. ⁻4 + ⁺11

20. ⁺5 + ⁻2

21. ⁻3 + ⁺4

22. ⁻3 + ⁺5

23. ⁻7 + ⁺3

24. ⁺3 + ⁻5

25. ⁻8 + ⁻4

26. ⁺8 + ⁻3

27. ⁺5 + ⁻5

28. ⁻14 + ⁺8

29. ⁺3 + ⁻11

30. ⁻9 + ⁺15

Write an addition sentence for each number line.

31.

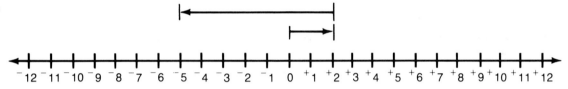

32.

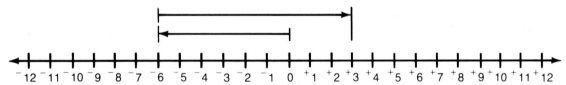

MIXED PRACTICE
Maintaining and Reviewing Skills

Solve.

33. $(5 - 3) + (25 \div 5) = t$

34. $(47 - 9) - (5 \times 2) = c$

35. $(9 - 2) + (8 - 3) = s$

36. $(49 \div 7) \times (64 \div 8) = t$

37. $(26 + 20) - (36 \div 9) = d$

38. $(72 \div 8) \times (100 \div 10) = a$

CHALLENGE

Give the next three numbers in the sequence.

*39. ⁺2, ⁻2, ⁺4, ⁻4, ⁺8, ⁻8, ■, ■, ■

ADDITION OF INTEGERS
With Unlike Signs

In his first turn at a board game, Steven moved ahead 9 spaces. In his next turn, he moved back 4 spaces. What was the total gain or loss after two turns?

Think: 9 spaces ahead $^+9$
4 spaces back $^-4$

Add: $^+9 + {}^-4$

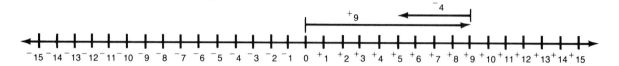

Start at zero. Move 9 units to the right to show $^+9$. From that point move 4 units to the left to show $^-4$. You stop at $^+5$.

Therefore $^+9 + {}^-4 = {}^+5$.

Steven gained 5 spaces after two turns.

PRACTICE

Add.

1. $^-2 + {}^+6$
2. $^-5 + {}^+8$
3. $^+2 + {}^-7$
4. $^+5 + {}^-2$

5. $^+10 + {}^-6$
6. $^+9 + {}^-12$
7. $^+15 + {}^-15$
8. $^-7 + {}^+9$

9. $^-15 + {}^+10$
10. $^-23 + {}^+8$
11. $^+4 + {}^-10$
12. $^+7 + {}^-14$

13. $^-18 + {}^+17$
14. $^-12 + {}^+7$
15. $^-20 + {}^+35$
16. $^-8 + {}^+16$

17. $^-12 + {}^+9$
18. $^+9 + {}^-15$
19. $^-8 + {}^+8$
20. $^-1 + {}^+1$

MIXED PRACTICE
Maintaining and Reviewing Skills

Add.

21. $^+85 + {}^+72$
22. $^-6 + {}^-14$
23. $^-9 + {}^-32$
24. $^+24 + {}^+6$

25. $^-70 + {}^-19$
26. $^-50 + {}^-75$
27. $^-110 + {}^-150$
28. $^-150 + {}^-100$

29. $^+155 + {}^+45$
30. $^-230 + {}^-100$
31. $^-1 + {}^-526$
32. $^+125 + {}^+50$

FOCUS | Use NUMBER skills to add integers.

APPLICATION

Using Algebra

Use these ordered pairs to graph points in the first quadrant. Connect the points with a ruler to form a line. Remember the first coordinate tells how many units to move *left* or *right*. The second coordinate tells how many units to move *up* or *down*.

(x, y)
$(^+3, \ ^+7)$
$(^+2, \ ^+5)$
$(^+1, \ ^+3)$
$(0, \ ^+1)$

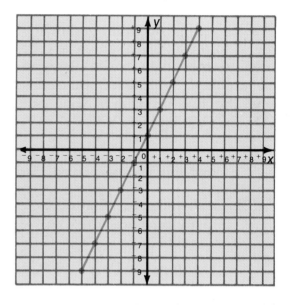

To extend the line into the third quadrant, use negative numbers to continue the sequence.

(x, y)
$(^-1, \ ^-1)$
$(^-2, \ ^-3)$
$(^-3, \ ^-5)$
$(^-4, \ ^-7)$

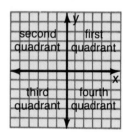

Look at the line on the graph.
Tell if each ordered pair forms a point on the line. Write *yes* or *no*.

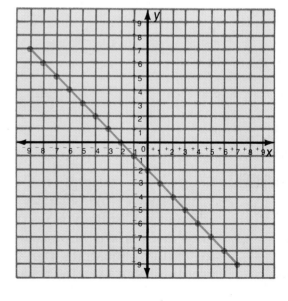

33. $(^+5, \ ^+4)$ **34.** $(^-2, 0)$

35. $(^+4, \ ^-6)$ **36.** $(^+3, \ ^+4)$

37. $(^+1, \ ^-3)$ **38.** $(^-4, \ ^-5)$

39. $(^-6, \ ^+5)$ **40.** $(^-7, \ ^+5)$

41. $(0, \ ^-1)$ **42.** $(^+7, \ ^-9)$

43. $(^-8, \ ^+5)$ **44.** $(^-4, \ ^+2)$

45. $(^-8, \ ^+6)$

Use ALGEBRA to graph coordinate pairs.

Choosing Strategies

There are several strategies that can be used to solve problems: using a diagram, finding a pattern, making a list, using a formula, using guess and test, and using logic. Sometimes more than one strategy can be used to solve the same problem. Whichever strategy is used, remember to follow the five problem solving steps: READ, KNOW, PLAN, SOLVE, and CHECK.

1. READ — If 8 people enter a singles competition, how many matches will be played to determine a winner?

2. KNOW — Ask yourself: What do I need to find out? How many matches must be played to determine a winner?

Key facts: a. There are 8 people playing.

b. The 8 people are playing singles competition.

3. PLAN — Select a strategy: Try using a diagram or finding a pattern.

4. SOLVE — Using a diagram

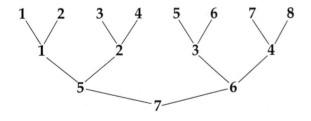

Finding a pattern
  2 people ⟶ 1 match
  4 people ⟶ 3 matches
  6 people ⟶ 5 matches
  8 people ⟶ 7 matches

The rule is: The number of matches that must be played is one less than the number of people playing them.

Using either strategy, 7 matches will have to be played to determine a winner.

5. CHECK — Review each strategy once again. Ask yourself: Is the answer the same as well as reasonable, when either strategy is used? The answer is the same and reasonable since both the diagram and the pattern illustrate the number of matches necessary to determine a winner.

FOCUS | Choose a strategy as part of the Five-Step PROBLEM–SOLVING Plan.

PRACTICE

Select a strategy to solve each problem. Show your work. Remember to READ, KNOW, PLAN, SOLVE, and CHECK.

1. Eight teams are going to play in a tournament. Each team will play every other team once. How many games will be played?

2. Complete the pattern below. Then write the rule that describes the pattern. 0.15, 0.18, 0.21, ■, ■, 0.30

3. How many ways can you give change, using bills only, from a $100 bill for a $78 dollar purchase?

4. What two single-digit numbers have a sum of 5 and a product of 4?

5. Mr. Grover drove 700 miles in 3 days. He drove half the distance the first day. He drove half the remaining distance the second day. How far did Mr. Grover drive the third day to complete the trip?

6. A frame shaped like an equilateral triangle has a base of 11 inches and is 9.5 inches high. What is the area of the frame? What is its perimeter?

7. Which two 2-digit numbers made from the digits 3, 4, 5, and 6 give the largest sum when added together? No single digit may be used more than once.

8. There are 6 people in a room. Each person says hello to every other person once. How many times will you hear the word *hello*?

9. Tom, Mark, and Joan each have a different pet. One pet is a dog, one is a cat, and one is a bird. Joan doesn't like cats. Mark thinks Tom is too crazy about cats. Joan cleans her bird's cage every day. Who owns which pet?

10. Sal, Marla, Bonnie, and Craig were seeing who could do the most push-ups. Sal did half as many as Marla. Craig did half as many as Sal. Bonnie did twice as many as Marla. Who won the push-up contest? Who came in last?

Class Project

Work with a few of your classmates and select a problem that is interesting to everyone. For example, you might want to find out how the desks in the classroom can be rearranged so that friends can sit together and also be able to do their work better. See if you can find more than one way to solve the problem your group chooses. Which strategy would be the best one to use? Why?

With Like Signs

In a science lab students worked with ions which had a charge of ⁻4. During an experiment the ions lost 2 negative charges. What was the charge of the ions then?

Subtract: ⁻4 − ⁻2

You can use a number line to subtract integers. Subtracting an integer is the same as adding its opposite.

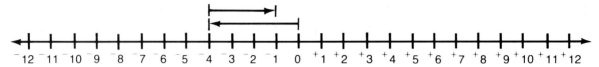

Start at zero. Move 4 units to the left to show ⁻4. From that point move in the direction which is the **opposite** of ⁻2. Move 2 units to the **right** to show ⁺2. You stop at ⁻2.
Therefore ⁻4 − ⁻2 = ⁻4 + ⁺2 = ⁻2

The charge of the ions was ⁻2.

Subtract: ⁺12 − ⁺5

Start at zero. Move 12 units to the right to show ⁺12. From that point move in the direction which is the opposite of ⁺5. Move 5 units to the left to show ⁻5. You stop at ⁺7.

Therefore ⁺12 − ⁺5 = ⁺12 + ⁻5 = ⁺7.

GUIDED PRACTICE

Subtract. Use the number line to help.

1. ⁻3 − ⁻5

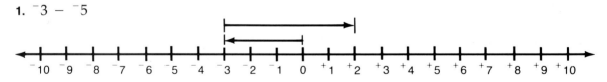

2. ⁺3 − ⁺4

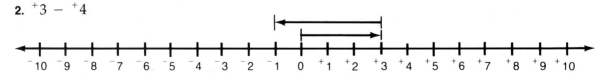

FOCUS | Use NUMBER skills to subtract integers.

PRACTICE

Subtract.

3. $^+6 - {}^+3$

4. $^-11 - {}^-4$

5. $^+2 - {}^+9$

6. $^-11 - {}^-7$

7. $^+13 - {}^+3$

8. $^-2 - {}^-8$

9. $^+6 - {}^+7$

10. $^-2 - {}^-2$

11. $^+8 - {}^+9$

12. $^-3 - {}^-8$

13. $^-3 - {}^-10$

14. $^-6 - {}^-5$

15. $^+10 - {}^+7$

16. $^-8 - {}^-9$

17. $^-14 - {}^-7$

18. $^+7 - {}^+8$

19. $^-18 - {}^-9$

20. $^+3 - {}^+9$

21. $^+8 - {}^+6$

22. $^+4 - {}^+4$

23. $^-2 - {}^-9$

24. $^-13 - {}^-14$

25. $^+14 - {}^+6$

26. $^+18 - {}^+11$

Write a subtraction sentence to match the arrows on the number line.

27.

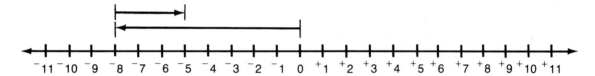

MIXED PRACTICE
Maintaining and Reviewing Skills

Find each percent.

28. What is 25% of 40?

29. What is 12% of 150?

30. What is 30% of 50?

31. What is 50% of 40?

32. What is 10% of 600?

33. What is 20% of 300?

CHALLENGE

Use integers to make each sentence true.

*34. $x + {}^+1 = {}^+25$

*35. $^-4 - n = 0$

*36. $^-8 + a = 0$

*37. $x + x = {}^-6$

SUBTRACTION OF INTEGERS
With Like and Unlike Signs

To subtract an integer add its opposite.

Subtract: $^+3 - {}^-5$

Start at zero. Move 3 units to the right to show $^+3$. From that point move in the direction which is the **opposite** of $^-5$. Move 5 units to the right to show $^+5$. You stop at $^+8$. Therefore $^+3 - {}^-5 = {}^+3 + {}^+5 = {}^+8$.

Subtract: $^+4 - {}^+6$

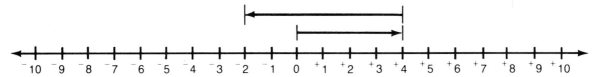

Start at zero. Move 4 units to the right to show $^+4$. From that point move in the direction which is the **opposite** of $^+6$. Move 6 units to the left to show $^-6$. You stop at $^-2$. Therefore $^+4 - {}^+6 = {}^+4 + {}^-6 = {}^-2$.

PRACTICE

Subtract.

1. $^-12 - {}^-4$ **2.** $^+8 - {}^-7$ **3.** $^+6 - {}^-10$ **4.** $^+14 - {}^+9$

5. $^-4 - {}^+5$ **6.** $^+7 - {}^-4$ **7.** $^+2 - {}^+9$ **8.** $^-15 - {}^+13$

9. $^-7 - {}^+21$ **10.** $^-6 - {}^+1$ **11.** $^+2 - {}^-10$ **12.** $^-8 - {}^+7$

MIXED PRACTICE
Maintaining and Reviewing Skills

Compare. Use >, <, or =.

13. 0.08 ●   **14.** 0.04 ● 0.44   **15.** 7 ● 4.75   **16.** 6.4 ● 6.359

17. 0.50 ●   **18.** 184.808 ● 4.88   **19.** 0.737 ● 0.733   **20.** 5.09 ● 5.091

FOCUS | Use NUMBER skills to subtract integers.

APPLICATION
Using Algebra

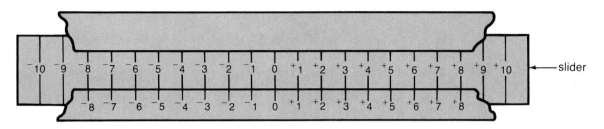

Make a cardboard model of the slide rule. Use it to add or subtract integers.

Add: $^+4 + {}^-3$

■ Look at the first integer. ($^+4$). Move the slider so that the zero of the slider is above the first integer of the exercise.

■ Look at the second integer. ($^-3$) Find it on the slider. Do not move the slider.

■ Read the number on the ruler below the second integer. This is the sum. ($^+1$)

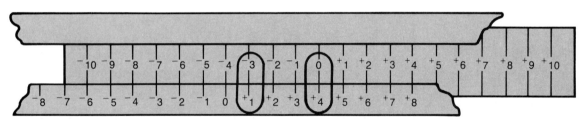

Therefore $^+4 + {}^-3 = {}^+1$

To subtract on a slide rule rewrite the exercise using addition.

$$^+2 - {}^+4 \text{ means } {}^+2 + {}^-4 \qquad {}^+3 - {}^-5 \text{ means } {}^+3 + {}^+5$$

Use your slide rule to do these exercises.

21. $^+3 + {}^-5$ 22. $^+2 + {}^-5$ 23. $^-3 + {}^-4$

24. $^+6 + {}^+2$ 25. $^-6 + {}^+4$ 26. $^+1 + {}^-5$

27. $^+3 - {}^+5$ 28. $^+4 - {}^-3$ 29. $^-2 - {}^-4$

30. $^-8 - {}^+1$ 31. $^-3 - {}^-3$ 32. $^+5 - {}^+5$

Use ALGEBRA to add and subtract integers on a slide rule.

Numbers That Show Direction

As people began to explore the Earth, they developed a way to pinpoint places. They wanted to know exactly where they were, where they had been, and where they were going.

To map the huge sphere of the Earth, the navigators and explorers made up a series of imaginary lines.

Some of the lines go north and south. Some lines go east and west. Any point on the Earth can be located by where the north-south and east-west lines meet. The lines that go from the North Pole to the South Pole are called **lines of longitude** or **meridians**.

The line around the middle is the **equator**. It is equidistant from each pole and divides the Earth in half.

The lines parallel to the equator are called **parallels of latitude**. They are evenly spaced above and below the equator.

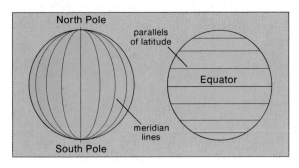

The circular Earth is divided into 360 equal parts called **degrees**. The symbol for degree is °. Each degree is divided into 60 minutes and each minute into 60 seconds.

All places above, or north of, the equator have a positive (+) latitude; places below, or south of, the equator have a negative (−) latitude.

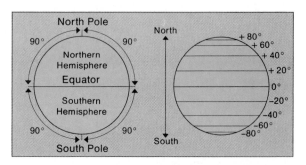

The meridian passing through Greenwich, England, is marked 0° and called the **prime meridian**. Every meridian east of it is positive (+) and every meridian west of it is negative (−).

Numbers like +40 or −30 are called **directed numbers** or signed numbers, because they show direction and have a + or − sign. Zero (0) is the only directed number that has no sign.

CRITICAL THINKING

1. How do the meridians differ from the parallels?

2. Where is the equator?

3. What is the difference between latitudes +60° and −60°?

FOCUS   Use MEASUREMENT to learn about longitude and latitude.

This photograph of an "earthrise" was taken on the NASA Apollo 10 manned spaceflight, which orbited the moon.

LOOKING BACK

Reviewing and Testing Chapter 29

In Chapter 29 you formulated problems about a movie. To review, refer to page 421 for data.

1. How might the filmmakers use Zack's cassette without eliminating one entire song?

To review addition of integers with unlike signs, refer to pages 422 and 424.

Add.

2. $^+6 + {}^-3$ **3.** $^+7 + {}^-8$ **4.** $^-9 + {}^+11$ **5.** $^-12 + {}^+14$ **6.** $^-17 + {}^+9$

7. $^-10 + {}^+10$ **8.** $^-12 + {}^+9$ **9.** $^+8 + {}^-14$ **10.** $^+15 + {}^-13$ **11.** $^+4 + {}^-13$

Write an addition sentence for each number line.

12.
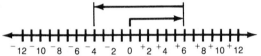

13.
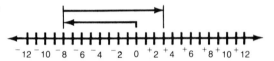

Use the Five-Step Problem-Solving Plan to choose a strategy and solve the problem. Refer to page 426.

14. A painter has 8 pints of red paint, 6 pints of yellow paint, and 4 pints of blue. She mixed $\frac{1}{4}$ of the red and some of the yellow to make orange. Then she used $\frac{1}{3}$ of the remaining red paint and some blue to make purple. What fraction of the red paint was left?

You learned about subtraction of integers with like and unlike signs. To review, refer to pages 428 and 430.

Subtract.

15. $^+5 - {}^+2$ **16.** $^+2 - {}^+4$ **17.** $^-14 - {}^+1$ **18.** $^+18 - {}^+12$ **19.** $^+11 - {}^-17$

20. $^-26 - {}^+14$ **21.** $^+14 - {}^-11$ **22.** $^+6 - {}^+9$ **23.** $^-16 - {}^+12$ **24.** $^+13 - {}^-12$

To review geography, refer to page 432.

25. If a place on Earth has a latitude of $^+50°$ and a longitude of $^-20°$, where is it in respect to the equator and Greenwich?

| FOCUS | Review and test skills learned and practiced. |

LOOKING AHEAD
Preparing for New Skills for Chapter 30

In the next chapter you will focus on

- formulating problems about building an igloo.
- multiplying integers with like and unlike signs.
- finding patterns.

- using a problem-solving strategy.
- dividing integers with like and unlike signs.
- using front-end estimation.
- how math is used in technology.

Learning to multiply and divide integers will be easier if you review multiplication of basic facts and related sentences for multiplication and division. Study the examples.

Each division sentence has a related multiplication sentence.

Example 1:

A related multiplication sentence for $6 \div 3 = 2$ is $2 \times 3 = 6$

Example 2:

A related multiplication sentence for $12 \div 6 = 2$ is $2 \times 6 = 12$

Example 3:

A related multiplication sentence for $20 \div 5 = \blacksquare$ is $\blacksquare \times 5 = 20$

PRACTICE

Find each product.

1. 8×9 **2.** 5×7 **3.** 9×4 **4.** 6×7

5. 2×9 **6.** 4×7 **7.** 6×3 **8.** 8×5

9. 3×7 **10.** 9×5 **11.** 3×8 **12.** 4×5

Write a related multiplication sentence for each division sentence.

13. $15 \div 3 = 5$ **14.** $24 \div 8 = 3$ **15.** $90 \div 10 = 9$ **16.** $64 \div 8 = 8$

17. $20 \div 4 = 5$ **18.** $21 \div 7 = 3$ **19.** $45 \div 9 = 5$ **20.** $63 \div 7 = 9$

21. $54 \div 6 = \blacksquare$ **22.** $56 \div 8 = \blacksquare$ **23.** $81 \div 9 = \blacksquare$ **24.** $5 \div 5 = \blacksquare$

Review NUMBER skills in preparation for learning new skills.

FOCUS | Formulate problems using photo, text, and data.

30

Multiplication and Division With Integers

DATA

Building material	Snow
Number of doors	1
Number of windows	1
Window material	Ice
Diameter	10 feet
Height	5 feet
Circumference	31 feet, 5 inches
Building time for one person	1 hour, 30 minutes

A traditional house, as most Americans know it, is a structure consisting of many building materials—wood, brick, stone, metal, glass, plastic—fashioned into a limitless variety of products that builders of various trades must know how to use. With a wide variety of tools, carpenters construct the frame, but only after bricklayers have finished the foundation.

The Eskimos of Canada, however, live in snowhouses built of two materials, snow and ice. They build these houses themselves, using one basic tool—the ivory snow knife.

If this seems a simple task, consider that the Eskimos must know what *kind* of snow to use. It must be just right, neither too hard nor too soft.

Looking at the shape of the traditional snowhouse, suggest some other decisions an Eskimo must make before beginning construction. Using the specifications given in the data, predict some problems that might occur during construction of a snowhouse.

With Like and Unlike Signs

Shares of a certain stock company rose 2 points each day for 5 days. What was the total gain or loss of the stock after 5 days?

You can use repeated addition to solve this problem.

$$^+2 + {^+2} + {^+2} + {^+2} + {^+2} = {^+10}$$

You can use multiplication as a shortcut to addition.

$$^+5 \times {^+2} = {^+10}$$

Number of days ⟋   ⟍ Number of points

There was a ten-point gain in the stock.

Multiply: $^+2 \times {^+3}$
The product of two positive integers is positive.

$$^+2 \times {^+3} = {^+6}$$

Multiply: $^-2 \times {^-3}$
The product of two negative integers is positive.

$$^-2 \times {^-3} = {^+6}$$

Multiply: $^-2 \times {^+3}$
The product of a positive integer and a negative integer is negative.

$$^-2 \times {^+3} = {^-6}$$
$$^+2 \times {^-3} = {^-6}$$

Multiply: $0 \times {^+2}$
The product of zero and either a positive or negative integer is zero.

$$0 \times {^+2} = 0$$
$$0 \times {^-2} = 0$$

Here are the rules for multiplying integers.
- If two integers have like signs, their product is positive.
- If two integers have unlike signs, their product is negative.
- If any integer is multiplied by zero, the product is zero.

GUIDED PRACTICE

Write whether each product is positive (+) or negative (−).

1. $^+5 \times {^+4} = \blacksquare 20$

2. $^+9 \times {^-1} = \blacksquare 9$

3. $^+3 \times {^+5} = \blacksquare 15$

4. $^-3 \times {^+7} = \blacksquare 21$

5. $^-6 \times {^-6} = \blacksquare 36$

6. $^+4 \times {^-3} = \blacksquare 12$

| FOCUS | Use NUMBER skills and a CALCULATOR to multiply integers. |

PRACTICE

Multiply.

7. $^+6 \times {}^+3$

8. $^+8 \times {}^+9$

9. $^-7 \times {}^-3$

10. $^-7 \times {}^-8$

11. $^+5 \times {}^-4$

12. $^+8 \times {}^+6$

13. $^-10 \times {}^-10$

14. $^-4 \times {}^+9$

15. $^+9 \times 0$

16. $^+6 \times {}^+5$

17. $^-8 \times {}^-2$

18. $^-6 \times {}^+4$

19. $^+9 \times {}^+4$

20. $^-7 \times 0$

21. $^-4 \times {}^+10$

22. $^+8 \times {}^-8$

23. $^+1 \times {}^+7$

24. $^-4 \times {}^+2$

25. $^-9 \times {}^+9$

26. $^-3 \times {}^-4$

27. $0 \times {}^+6$

28. $^+2 \times {}^-9$

29. $^+2 \times {}^+2$

30. $^+8 \times {}^-9$

31. $^-9 \times {}^+3$

32. $^-2 \times {}^+6$

33. $^+5 \times {}^+5$

*34. $(^+2 \times {}^+3) \times {}^-5$

*35. $(^+4 \times {}^-4) \times {}^-2$

*36. $(^+5 \times 0) \times {}^+3$

MIXED PRACTICE
Maintaining and Reviewing Skills

Add or subtract.

37. $^+6 + {}^+4$

38. $^-8 - {}^+6$

39. $0 - {}^-8$

40. $^-8 + {}^+4$

41. $^-15 - {}^-9$

42. $^-3 + {}^-9$

43. $^-5 + {}^+8$

44. $^-7 - {}^-2$

45. $^+2 + {}^-11$

46. $^-8 + 0$

47. $^+5 - {}^+3$

48. $^+3 + {}^-7$

CHALLENGE

Solve. Use a calculator.

*49. If a certain stock loses 3 points on each of 5 days and then gains 2 points on the next day, what is the total gain or loss at the end of 6 days?

MULTIPLICATION
With Like and Unlike Signs

A certain stock lost 3 points each day for 3 days. What was the total loss or gain of the stock?

You can use multiplication to solve this problem.

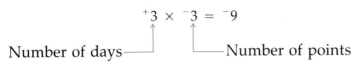

$$^+3 \times {}^-3 = {}^-9$$

Number of days ———┘   └——— Number of points

There was a nine-point loss in the stock.

The product of two integers with unlike signs is negative.

$$^-2 \times {}^+4 = {}^-8 \qquad {}^+2 \times {}^-4 = {}^-8$$

The product of two integers with like signs is positive.

$$^+2 \times {}^+4 = {}^+8 \qquad {}^-2 \times {}^-4 = {}^+8$$

The product of zero and any integer is zero.

$$0 \times {}^+2 = 0 \qquad {}^-4 \times 0 = 0$$

PRACTICE

Multiply.

1. $^+7 \times {}^-4$
2. $^-8 \times {}^-5$
3. $^-3 \times {}^+8$
4. $^-10 \times 0$
5. $^+3 \times {}^-6$
6. $^+10 \times {}^+5$
7. $^-9 \times {}^+6$
8. $^+9 \times {}^+11$
9. $^-5 \times {}^+6$
10. $^+4 \times {}^-4$
11. $0 \times {}^+5$
12. $^+8 \times {}^+3$
13. $^+7 \times {}^+5$
14. $^+6 \times {}^+6$
15. $^+6 \times {}^+7$

MIXED PRACTICE
Maintaining and Reviewing Skills

Find the greatest common factor for each pair.

16. 5 and 20
17. 8 and 12
18. 6 and 20
19. 8 and 9
20. 6 and 48
21. 9 and 15
22. 8 and 10
23. 4 and 5
24. 12 and 14

| FOCUS | Use NUMBER skills to multiply integers. |

APPLICATION
Using Patterns and Functions

In order to complete a number sequence you must find a **rule**.

Complete this sequence.

$$^-8, \ ^-6, \ ^-4, \ ^-2, \ 0, \ ^+2, \ ^+4, \ \blacksquare, \ \blacksquare, \ \blacksquare$$

Study two numbers at a time. Work from left to right. Find the relationship between $^-8$ and $^-6$, then $^-6$ and $^-4$, and so on. The rule is to add $^+2$ to each number.

The next numbers in the sequence are $^+6$, $^+8$, and $^+10$.

Complete each sequence. Write the rule, then give the next 3 numbers.

25. Sequence: $^-22, \ ^-19, \ ^-16, \ ^-13, \ ^-10, \ ^-7, \ ^-4, \ \blacksquare, \ \blacksquare, \ \blacksquare$

26. Sequence: $^+3, \ ^+5, \ ^-10, \ ^-8, \ ^+16, \ ^+18, \ ^-36, \ \blacksquare, \ \blacksquare, \ \blacksquare$

27. Sequence: $^-16, \ ^-14, \ ^-15, \ ^-13, \ ^-14, \ ^-12, \ ^-13, \ \blacksquare, \ \blacksquare, \ \blacksquare$

28. Sequence: $^+12, \ ^+8, \ ^+4, \ 0, \ ^-4, \ ^-8, \ ^-12, \ \blacksquare, \ \blacksquare, \ \blacksquare$

29. Sequence: $0, \ ^-6, \ ^-1, \ ^-7, \ ^-2, \ ^-8, \ ^-3, \ \blacksquare, \ \blacksquare, \ \blacksquare$

30. Sequence: $^+2, \ ^-4, \ ^+8, \ ^-16, \ ^+32, \ \blacksquare, \ \blacksquare, \ \blacksquare$

31. Sequence: $^-20, \ ^-15, \ ^-10, \ ^-5, \ 0, \ ^+5, \ ^+10, \ ^+15, \ \blacksquare, \ \blacksquare, \ \blacksquare$

32. Sequence: $^+8, \ ^-8, \ ^+8, \ ^-8, \ ^+8, \ ^-8, \ ^+8, \ \blacksquare, \ \blacksquare, \ \blacksquare$

*33. Sequence: $^-8, \ ^-7, \ ^-9, \ ^+27, \ ^+28, \ ^+26, \ ^-78, \ \blacksquare, \ \blacksquare, \ \blacksquare$

Use PATTERNS AND FUNCTIONS to complete number sequences.

With Like and Unlike Signs

Paula has 12 goldfish. She puts 3 goldfish in each glass bowl. How many bowls does she need?

You can use division to solve this problem.

$$\text{Dividend} \quad \text{Divisor} \qquad \text{Quotient}$$
Divide: $^+12 \div ^+3 = \blacksquare \longleftarrow$ Number of bowls
In all ⎯⎯↑ ⎿⎯In each bowl

To divide integers use a related multiplication equation.

$$\blacksquare \times ^+3 = ^+12 \longleftarrow \text{In all}$$
Number of bowls ⎯↑ ⎿⎯In each bowl

The quotient of two positive integers is positive.
Therefore $^+12 \div ^+3 = ^+4$.
Paula needs 4 bowls.

Divide: $^-12 \div ^-3$
The quotient of two negative integers is positive.
Therefore $^-12 \div ^-3 = ^+4$

Divide: $^-12 \div ^+3$
The quotient of a positive integer and a negative integer is negative.
Therefore $^-12 \div ^+3 = ^-4$
$^+12 \div ^-3 = ^-4$

Divide: $0 \div 6$
Zero divided by any integer, except zero, is zero.
Division by zero is impossible.
Therefore $0 \div ^+6 = 0$
$0 \div ^-6 = 0$

■ If two integers have like signs, their quotient is positive.
$+ \div + = +$
$- \div - = +$

■ If two integers have unlike signs, their quotient is negative.
$+ \div - = -$
$- \div + = -$

GUIDED PRACTICE

Write whether each quotient is positive ($+$) or negative ($-$).

1. $^+15 \div ^-3 = \blacksquare 5$ **2.** $^+6 \div ^+2 = \blacksquare 3$ **3.** $^-10 \div ^+5 = \blacksquare 2$ **4.** $^-9 \div ^-3 = \blacksquare 3$

| FOCUS | Use NUMBER skills to divide integers. |

Divide.

5. $^+18 \div {}^+6$ 6. $^-12 \div {}^-4$ 7. $^-45 \div {}^+5$

8. $^+36 \div {}^-3$ 9. $^-63 \div {}^-9$ 10. $^+88 \div {}^-8$

11. $^+27 \div {}^-9$ 12. $^-20 \div {}^+4$ 13. $^+36 \div {}^-4$

14. $^-21 \div {}^+3$ 15. $^+28 \div {}^-4$ 16. $^-56 \div {}^+7$

17. $^+30 \div {}^-6$ 18. $^+25 \div {}^-5$ 19. $^+16 \div {}^+4$

20. $^+32 \div {}^+4$ 21. $^-40 \div {}^-4$ 22. $^+55 \div {}^+11$

23. $^-54 \div {}^+6$ 24. $^+33 \div {}^-3$ 25. $^-64 \div {}^+8$

26. $^+70 \div {}^+10$ 27. $^+72 \div {}^+6$ 28. $^+40 \div {}^+8$

29. $^+50 \div {}^+5$ 30. $^-48 \div {}^+4$ 31. $^+60 \div {}^-10$

32. $^+81 \div {}^+9$ 33. $^-108 \div {}^-12$ 34. $^-96 \div {}^+8$

MIXED PRACTICE
Maintaining and Reviewing Skills

Complete. Write an equal ratio for each.

35. $\dfrac{4}{9} = \dfrac{12}{\blacksquare}$ 36. $\dfrac{12}{14} = \dfrac{\blacksquare}{7}$ 37. $\dfrac{3}{10} = \dfrac{12}{\blacksquare}$

38. $\dfrac{5}{6} = \dfrac{\blacksquare}{36}$ 39. $\dfrac{12}{32} = \dfrac{\blacksquare}{8}$ 40. $\dfrac{35}{42} = \dfrac{\blacksquare}{6}$

41. $\dfrac{4}{5} = \dfrac{12}{\blacksquare}$ 42. $\dfrac{3}{5} = \dfrac{\blacksquare}{40}$ 43. $\dfrac{5}{9} = \dfrac{\blacksquare}{36}$

44. $\dfrac{\blacksquare}{4} = \dfrac{3}{12}$ 45. $\dfrac{4}{7} = \dfrac{\blacksquare}{14}$ 46. $\dfrac{9}{10} = \dfrac{27}{\blacksquare}$

CHALLENGE

Find the rule. Write the next 3 numbers.

*47. 16, 32, $^-8$, $^-16$, 4, $\blacksquare$, $\blacksquare$, $\blacksquare$

DIVISION OF INTEGERS
With Like and Unlike Signs

To find the quotient of two integers, use a related multiplication equation.

Divide:

$$^+15 \div {}^+3 = \blacksquare \leftarrow \text{Number of groups}$$

Number in all ⟶ ⟵ Number in each group

Find the missing factor.

Multiply:

$$\blacksquare \times {}^+3 = {}^+15 \leftarrow \text{Number in all}$$

Number of groups ⟶ ⟵ Number in each group

$^+5 \times {}^+3 = {}^+15$; Therefore $^+15 \div {}^+3 = {}^+5$.

The quotient of two integers with like signs is positive.

$$^+15 \div {}^+3 = {}^+5 \qquad {}^-15 \div {}^-3 = {}^+5$$

The quotient of two integers with unlike signs is negative.

$$^-15 \div {}^+3 = {}^-5 \qquad {}^+15 \div {}^-3 = {}^-5$$

Zero divided by any integer, except zero, is zero.
Division by zero is impossible.

$$0 \div {}^+3 = 0 \qquad 0 \div {}^-3 = 0$$

PRACTICE

Divide.

1. $^-42 \div {}^+7$
2. $^+35 \div {}^+5$
3. $^-48 \div {}^-6$

4. $^+44 \div {}^-4$
5. $^-60 \div {}^+12$
6. $^-90 \div {}^+9$

7. $^+49 \div {}^+7$
8. $^+72 \div {}^-8$
9. $^+84 \div {}^-7$

10. $^-80 \div {}^+10$
11. $^+66 \div {}^+11$
12. $^-120 \div {}^+10$

MIXED PRACTICE
Maintaining and Reviewing Skills

Complete.

13. $3 \text{ km} = \blacksquare \text{ m}$
14. $1 \text{ m} = \blacksquare \text{ km}$
15. $\blacksquare \text{ mm} = 14 \text{ m}$

16. $\blacksquare \text{ m} = 3\,000 \text{ mm}$
17. $\blacksquare \text{ cm} = 0.08 \text{ m}$
18. $5 \text{ m} = \blacksquare \text{ cm}$

| FOCUS | Use NUMBER skills to divide integers. |

444

APPLICATION
Using Front-End Estimation

Rounding is one strategy to help you estimate. **Front-end estimation** is another. Front-end estimation involves two steps. First, perform the operation on the front-end digits, the most important digits. Then look at the rest of the digits in each number and **adjust** your estimate.

Estimate the sum.

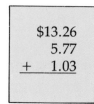

$13.26
  5.77
+ 1.03

First, add the digits in the front end.

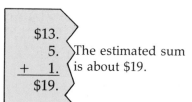

$13.
  5.
+ 1.
────
$19.

The estimated sum is about $19.

Then look at the rest of the digits. Adjust your estimate, if necessary.

$13.26 ─ Since this is about
  5.77   another $1, adjust
+ 1.03 ─ the estimate **up**.
────
$19.   Estimate: **about $20**

Here are two examples for finding differences.

Estimate the difference: 9,387 − 4,809.

Front-end digits: 9 − 4 = 5

The difference is about 5,000.

Rest of the digits: Since 387 < 809, adjust the estimate **down**.

Estimate: **less than 5,000**

Estimate the difference: $7.50 − $3.29.

Front-end digits: $7 − $3 = $4

The difference is about $4.

Rest of the digits: Since 50 > 29, adjust the estimate **up**.

Estimate: **more than $4**

Choose the best estimate.

19.   28.99 ┐─about $1   a. about $37
            2.49 ┤─about $1   b. about $38
         + 7.48 ┘   c. about $39

20.   8,923   a. about 7,000
        − 1,798   b. more than 7,000
                   c. less than 7,000

Estimate each sum or difference, using front-end estimation.

21. 629 − 388   **22.** 875 + 129   **23.** 5,098 − 4,129   **24.** $8.07 + $8.19

25. 9,800 − 2,699   **26.** $35.55 + $8.55   **27.** $15.00 − $13.28   **28.** 8,968 + 5,995

Estimate to see if the answer is reasonable. Write *yes* or *no*.

29. 6,126 − 3,298 = 3,828   **30.** 398 + 699 = 987   **31.** $8.00 − $6.38 = $1.62

Use front-end ESTIMATION to estimate sums and differences.

Programming Computers

Assume that you have to complete the following addition exercises:

1. $^+14$
    $^+21$
    $+ ^-4$

2. $^-22$
    $^+17$
    $^-4$
    $+ ^+18$

3. $^+104$
    $^-217$
    $^-506$
    $^-222$
    $+ ^+108$

4. $^-45$
    $^-111$
    $^+80$
    $^-43$
    $+ ^+77$

After doing these exercises, it would be helpful to have the correct answers so that you could check your work!

Let us write a program for adding integers so that we can use it to check the examples above. (Which of the exercises is the longest?) Since the third and fourth exercises involve the addition of five integers, be sure to allow for this in the computer program. Of course, if the exercise has fewer than five numbers, zeros can be entered for the missing numbers.

Enter five integers. The computer will add them and print out their sum.

The Analysis

While we have only worked with positive numbers on our MATH IN TECHNOLOGY pages, the programs we have written will work with negative numbers as well.

We are entering five numbers. Use the memory cell names A, B, C, D, and E. Their sum, S, is calculated by $S = A + B + C + D + E$.

The Plan

1. Enter the five integers (including zeros if there are fewer than five).
2. Calculate $S = A + B + C + D + E$.
3. Print S.
4. There are no more steps.

The Planned Output

CHECKING HOMEWORK—ADDING INTEGERS
ENTER FIVE INTEGERS TO BE ADDED
? $^-3$, 4, $^-2$, $^-8$, 0
THE SUM IS $^-9$
DID YOU GET THAT FOR THE ANSWER?
IF SO—VERY GOOD
IF NOT—TRY AGAIN

The Program

```
10   PRINT "CHECKING HOMEWORK
     —ADDING INTEGERS"
20   PRINT "ENTER FIVE INTEGERS
     TO BE ADDED"
30   INPUT  A, B, C, D, E
40   S = A + B + C + D + E
50   PRINT "THE SUM IS "; S
60   PRINT "DID YOU GET THAT FOR
     THE ANSWER?"
70   PRINT "IF SO—VERY GOOD"
80   PRINT "IF NOT—TRY AGAIN"
90   END
```

CRITICAL THINKING

1. What changes would you make in the program to add up to 7 integers? (Hint: change 3 lines)

2. How could the program be changed to *subtract* one integer from another?

FOCUS | Use LOGIC to program a computer to work with integers.

446

The vertical line shows positive/negative direction in five foot increments.

LOOKING BACK
Reviewing and Testing Chapter 30

In Chapter 30 you formulated problems about building a snowhouse. To review, refer to page 437 for data.

1. If the diameter is 10 ft, what is the area of the floor inside the circular snowhouse. Use 3.14 for π.

You learned about multiplying with like and unlike signs. To review, refer to page 438.

Multiply.

2. $^+7 \times {}^+3$

3. $^-8 \times {}^-4$

4. $^-6 \times {}^+5$

5. $^-9 \times {}^-8$

6. $^+12 \times {}^+11$

7. $^+14 \times {}^-10$

8. $^-11 \times {}^-4$

9. $^-17 \times {}^+6$

10. $^-26 \times {}^+14$

11. $^+11 \times {}^+11$

12. $^+18 \times {}^-13$

13. $^-8 \times {}^-12$

To review what you learned about dividing integers with like and unlike signs, refer to page 442.

Divide.

14. $^+24 \div {}^+4$

15. $^-81 \div {}^-9$

16. $^+72 \div {}^-6$

17. $^-99 \div {}^-9$

18. $^-135 \div {}^-9$

19. $^+56 \div {}^+4$

20. $^-84 \div {}^+7$

21. $^+126 \div {}^-3$

22. $^-153 \div {}^-9$

23. $^-85 \div {}^-5$

24. $^+105 \div {}^+7$

25. $^+96 \div {}^-6$

To review what you learned about front-end estimation, refer to page 445.

Choose the better estimate. Write the letter.

26. 47,272 a. about 55,000
    + 8,926 b. about 56,000

27. 6,672 a. more than 6,000
    − 726 b. less than 6,000

You learned about programming computers. To review, refer to page 446.

28. If the program were changed to multiply two integers, what would line 40 say?

FOCUS | Review and test skills learned and practiced.

LOOKING AHEAD
Preparing for New Skills for Chapter 31

In the next chapter you will focus on

- formulating problems about a bicycle.
- writing algebraic notation.
- using variables in algebraic notation.
- writing equations and inequalities.
- using front-end estimation.
- how math is used in sports.

It will be easier to write an equation or inequality from a word sentence by reviewing some mathematical symbols. Study the examples.

Example 1:

4 + 5   four plus five
    or
    the sum of four and five

Example 2:

4 × 5   four times five
    or
    the product of four and five

Example 3:

8 − 4   eight minus four
    or
    the difference between eight and four

Example 4:

12 ÷ 3   twelve divided by three
    or
    the quotient of twelve divided by three

Example 5:

8 > 2   eight is greater than two

Example 6:

3 + 2 < 6   the sum of three and two is less than six

PRACTICE

Write in words.

1. $4 + 8$
2. $8 - 2$
3. 15×2
4. $20 \div 5$
5. $\frac{8}{2}$
6. $19 + 11$
7. 6×2
8. $9 + 13$
9. $6 < 9$
10. $13 < 24$
11. $88 > 33$
12. $19 > 10$
13. $3 + 4 < 9$
14. $5 + 6 > 10$
15. $21 < 15 \times 2$
16. $3 \div 1 < 5$

Review NUMBER skills in preparation for learning new skills.

CHAPTER 31

Math Expressions and Equations

DATA

The high-wheeler

Invented in 1869

Front wheels	48–52 inches
Back wheels	24–26 inches
Weight	44–55 pounds
Good touring speed	$14\frac{1}{2}$ mph

The chain drive

Invented in 1885

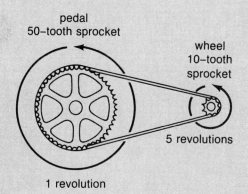

pedal
50–tooth sprocket

wheel
10–tooth sprocket

5 revolutions

1 revolution

Many people who see drawings or photographs of the high-wheeler shown here think it is one of the earliest bicycles, possibly one of the first invented. Actually, the bicycle had been around for nearly a century when the first high-wheeler—also known as the ordinary, the pennyfarthing, or the goo—was built in France in 1869. (Earlier bikes tended to have wheels that were the same size.)

The high-wheeler was considered the last word in progress but not a practical means of transportation. It was primarily a plaything of the rich. Riding manuals for the high-wheeler instructed owners to concentrate on looking ahead. This was more important than looking to either side. The reason: the high-wheeler had no brakes.

Still, this strange bike was very popular and was manufactured in great numbers, especially in England. It made the world aware of the bicycle. The end came for the high-wheeler with the invention of the chain drive in 1885.

Suggest some possible problems that the riders faced.

ALGEBRA
Expressions

To solve a problem, word phrases must be changed into mathematical symbols. The mathematical expression can also be called **algebraic notation**.

Joanna's collection of 4 dolls increased by 5.———→Word phrase
Think: "Increased by" means addition.
Write: 4 + 5 ———→ Algebraic notation

Study these examples:

Word Phrase	Think	Algebraic Notation
Jane's age of 12 plus 6	*plus* means addition	6 + 12 or 12 + 6
Jim's height of 68 in. decreased by 7	*decreased by* means subtraction	68 − 7
36 apples shared equally among 3 friends	*shared equally* means division	36 ÷ 3 or $\frac{36}{3}$
two times the baby's weight of 12 lb.	*times* means multiplication	2 × 12 or 12 × 2
Jason's age of 14 less 7	*less* means subtraction	14 − 7

GUIDED PRACTICE

Look for word clues to determine the correct operation.
Write in algebraic notation.

1. the sum of 7 and 6

2. the product of 9 and 8

3. the difference of 36 minus 32

4. the quotient of 28 divided by 7

increased by, more, plus, sum, total **+**

decreased by, difference, less, minus **−**

divided by, shared equally, quotient **÷**

multiplied by, times, product **×**

FOCUS | Use ALGEBRA to interpret mathematical expressions.

452

PRACTICE

Write in algebraic notation. Look for clues in the word phrases to determine the correct operations.

5. the sum of 35 and 8

6. seven less than 20

7. fifty-six shared equally among 7

8. $12 equally divided among 6 people

9. ten times the cost of $2

10. the total of 13 and 30

11. $15 more than $75

12. the quotient of 49 divided by 7

13. the product of 15 and 24

14. eighteen decreased by 10

15. the result of subtracting 4 from 12

16. twelve less than 15

17. the total of $8, $10, and $15

18. the number 47 minus 16

19. the product of 30 and 4.5

20. two and two-thirds as much as 5

21. the result of dividing 27 by 0.9

22. the difference between $5\frac{1}{2}$ and $2\frac{3}{4}$

MIXED PRACTICE
Maintaining and Reviewing Skills

Add, subtract, multiply, or divide decimals.

23. 3.6×4.9 **24.** $12 \div 0.4$ **25.** $1.5 \div 0.5$ **26.** $3.78 - 2.95$ **27.** $12 + 0.302$

28. $4.726 + 17.93$ **29.** 2.7×5.81 **30.** $18 - 0.329$ **31.** $6.25 \div 2.5$ **32.** $1 - 0.009$

33. $35.873 + 89.08$ **34.** 2.5×27.63 **35.** $5.1 - 3.326$ **36.** 0.35×0.28 **37.** $0.08 \div 4$

CHALLENGE

Write the algebraic notation for these mixed operation word phrases. Then find the result.

38. five more than the sum of 3 and 4

39. the product of 10 and the difference between 10 and 2

40. the product of 6 and 9 plus the product of 5 and 3

ALGEBRA
Expressions

A **variable** is a symbol that stands for an unknown number. A letter is usually used to represent the variable.

Word Phrase	Algebraic Notation
the sum of 9 and a number n	$9 + n$ or $n + 9$
fifty divided by some number, t	$50 \div t$ or $\frac{50}{t}$
John's age a subtracted from 30	$30 - a$
the product of 5 and the width w	$5 \times w$ or $w \times 5$
a number n minus 18	$n - 18$

PRACTICE

Write in algebraic notation. Use a letter of your choice where needed.

1. 14 minus 7

2. the product of 9 and 13

3. 18 divided by 2

4. the sum of 6 and 1

5. three more than a number n

6. two less than a number t

7. the product of 6 and r

8. some number n times 5

9. a number s decreased by 3

10. from 13 subtract a number d

11. some number m divided by 9

12. the quotient of n divided by 6

13. a number q is subtracted from 30

14. the product of c and 15

15. the sum of a number and 100

16. the product of 17 and a number

17. some number times 48

18. nine subtracted from a number

19. twelve increased by a number

20. some number divided by 14

FOCUS Use ALGEBRA to interpret mathematical expressions with variables.

454

Using Measurement

The measurements for dimensions of figures are often given using variables. For example the rectangle below has a length of 5x and a width of x.

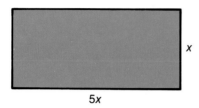

5x

x

To find the perimeter of this rectangle, substitute the length (5x) and the width (x) in the formula $P = 2l + 2w$.

$$P = 2l + 2w$$
$$P = 2(5x) + 2(x)$$
$$P = 10x + 2x$$
$$P = 12x$$

The perimeter of the rectangle is 12x.

Copy and complete the chart below. For each value of x find the length, width, or perimeter. Use $P = 12x$. The first one is done for you.

	x	length l 5x	width w x	perimeter P 12x
21.	2 in.	10 in.	2 in.	24 in.
22.	4	20	▪	48
23.	10	50	10	▪
24.	17	▪	17	204
25.	9	▪	9	▪
26.	11	55	11	▪
27.	25	▪	▪	300
28.	37	▪	▪	▪

Use MEASUREMENT to find dimensions of a figure.

Writing Equations and Inequalities

You can write an **equation** from a word sentence. Use an equal sign (=).

Word sentence	Equation
The sum of 8 and 9 *is* 17.	8 + 9 = 17
Four less than 16 is *equal* to 12.	16 − 4 = 12

You can write an **inequality** from a word sentence. Use the signs: is greater than (>) or is less than (<).

Word sentence	Inequality
Ten divided by 2 *is less than* 6.	10 ÷ 2 < 6
The product of 2 and 10 *is greater than* 17.	2 × 10 > 17

GUIDED PRACTICE

Translate the word sentences into equations or inequalities.
Look for clue words to tell the difference.

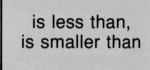

is, is equal to, is as much as	is more than, is greater than	is less than, is smaller than
=	>	<

1. Twenty and 5 is equal to 25.

2. Eight decreased by 2 is equal to 6.

3. Eight less than 10 is 2.

4. Nine and 6 is more than 10.

5. Nine multiplied by 6 is equal to 54.

FOCUS | Use ALGEBRA to write equations and inequalities.

PRACTICE

Write an equation or an inequality. Use >, <, or =.

6. Twenty less 12 is equal to 8.

7. The product of 6 and 8 is 48.

8. Eight minus 6 is 2.

9. Fifty more than 2 is equal to 52.

10. Eight minus 6 is less than 5.

11. Forty less 11 is equal to 29.

12. The result of 15 divided by 5 is equal to 3.

13. Nineteen increased by 5 is greater than 21.

14. Twelve times 4 is more than 36.

15. Twelve more than 6 equals 18.

16. The cost of 10 books at $2 each is $20.

17. Twelve rolls shared equally among 6 people is 2 rolls each.

*18. Three times as many students as parents went to a class concert. There were 375 students and 125 parents.

*19. There are 23 sandwiches on a platter. Fifteen of them are egg salad. Eight are tuna salad.

MIXED PRACTICE
Maintaining and Reviewing Skills

Solve using order of operations.

20. $(25 - 5) \div 4$

21. $4 \times (4 + 3)$

22. $3 \times 2 + 3 \times 5$

23. $(2 \times 2)^2 - 8$

24. $(18 \div 6) \times (2 + 1)$

25. $22 - (100 \div 5)$

26. $1 + 8 \div 2 - 5$

27. $25 - 8 \times 2$

28. $(15 - 6) + (22 - 9)$

29. $5 \div (5 \times 10)$

30. $3^2 \times 2 - 7$

31. $4 \times 8 \div 4 + 4$

CHALLENGE

Write an equation or inequality.

*32. Ben is twice as old as the sum of Jessie's and Bill's ages. Jessie is 12. Bill is 10. Ben is 44.

*33. Nanci's earnings divided by 2 is more than the sum of $5 and Cathy's earnings. Nanci earned $30. Cathy earned $9.

ALGEBRA
Writing Equations and Inequalities

When a word sentence includes an unknown number, use a *variable* to write an equation or inequality.

Word sentence	Algebraic Notation
Four more than Lynn's age a is 9.	$4 + a = 9$
The product of 6 and the length t is 42.	$6 \times t = 42$
A certain number divided by 3 is equal to 19.	$n \div 3 = 19$ (variables)
A number decreased by 5 is less than 3.	$x - 5 < 3$ (inequality)

PRACTICE

Write an equation or inequality. Use the letter of your choice where needed.

1. A number r decreased by 10 is equal to 14.

2. The product of the number b and 12 is 96.

3. Grampa's age 90 divided by this number is equal to 3.

4. Forty-four decreased by a certain number is equal to 1.

5. Seventeen more than a number is less than 80.

6. Eighteen times n dollars gives the total price of $90.

7. The product of 5 and a number is more than 10.

*8. Twelve is less than the sum of a number and 6.

MIXED PRACTICE
Maintaining and Reviewing Skills

Write each number in two ways so that it will be given as a fraction in simplest terms, as a decimal, and as a percent.

9. 17%

10. $\dfrac{57}{100}$

11. 75%

12. 0.25

13. $\dfrac{11}{100}$

14. $\dfrac{4}{5}$

15. $\dfrac{1}{100}$

16. $\dfrac{3}{100}$

17. 50%

18. $\dfrac{27}{100}$

19. 5%

20. 0.1

21. 0.09

22. $\dfrac{3}{10}$

23. 0.6

FOCUS	Use ALGEBRA to write equations and inequalities.

458

APPLICATION
Using Front-End Estimation

Here is how to use front-end estimation to estimate products.

Estimate 4 × 324.

Multiply the front-end digits.	Look at the other digits.	Add the products.	Adjust the estimate, if necessary.
Think of 4 × 300.	Think of 4 × 20.		Since 24 was rounded down, the estimate, 1,280, is too small. Adjust up. Estimate: *more than 1,280*

$$\begin{array}{r} 324 \\ \times\ \ \ 4 \\ \hline 1,200 \end{array} \qquad \begin{array}{r} 20 \\ \times\ \ 4 \\ \hline 80 \end{array} \qquad \begin{array}{r} 1,200 \\ +\ \ \ \ 80 \\ \hline 1,280 \end{array}$$

To estimate $7\overline{)6,804}$, find how many digits are in the quotient and find the first digit.

$$?\ \blacksquare\blacksquare\blacksquare \qquad\qquad ?\ \blacksquare\blacksquare \qquad\qquad 9\ \blacksquare\blacksquare$$
$$7\overline{)6,804} \qquad\qquad 7\overline{)6,804} \qquad\qquad 7\overline{)6,804}$$

Since 7 > 6, the first digit is not in the thousands place.

$7\overline{)68}$ is about 9 The quotient has three digits. The first digit is 9.

The quotient is more than 900. It is less than 1,000. Estimate: *between 900 and 1,000*

Write the better estimate.

24. $\begin{array}{r} 6,487 \\ \times\ \ \ \ \ \ \ 5 \\ \hline \end{array}$ **a.** less than 32,500 **b.** more than 32,500

25. $3\overline{)7,541}$ **a.** between 2,000 and 3,000 **b.** between 200 and 300

Estimate each product or quotient.

26. 3 × 934 **27.** 3 × 547 **28.** 6 × 4,889 **29.** 7 × 9,946

30. $7\overline{)569}$ **31.** $3\overline{)847}$ **32.** $2\overline{)9,909}$ **33.** $6\overline{)5,007}$

34. 8 × 7,086 **35.** $7\overline{)1,111}$ **36.** 9 × 693 **37.** $9\overline{)8,430}$

Estimate to see if the answer is reasonable. Write *yes* or *no*.

38. 8 × 449 $\stackrel{?}{=}$ 3,592 **39.** 7 × 433 $\stackrel{?}{=}$ 4,951 **40.** 4,008 ÷ 8 $\stackrel{?}{=}$ 51

41. 6 × 8,009 $\stackrel{?}{=}$ 4,854 **42.** 858 ÷ 3 $\stackrel{?}{=}$ 286 **43.** 6,213 ÷ 3 $\stackrel{?}{=}$ 271

Use front-end ESTIMATION to estimate products and quotients.

Baseball

Did you ever go to a baseball game or watch one on television? Do you remember hearing numbers like .250, .300 or .400? These numbers stand for players' batting averages. Do you realize that nearly every part of the game is explained using statistics?

Batting averages are the most widely used statistic in baseball. A batting average is a ratio of the number of hits a player gets to the number of times that player is at bat. It is expressed as a decimal rounded to the thousandth.

A player batting .300, for example, has had 3 hits for every 10 times at bat. To find a batting average, you can use this formula.

$$\text{Batting average} = \frac{\text{number of hits}}{\text{number of times at bat}}$$

A batting average of .300 is very good.

Baseball Standings			
American League East			
Team	W	L	Pct.
Toronoto	91	54	.628
New York	86	60	.589
Baltimore	78	67	.538
Detroit	75	70	.517
Boston	73	73	.500
Milwaukee	64	81	.441
Cleveland	54	94	.365

There are statistics to express a team's standing, its wins and losses, and its percentage of the number of games won to the number of games played.

W stands for the number of games won so far during the season. **L** stands for the number of games lost. To find the number of games a team has played, add the numbers in the won and lost columns.

The percentage, **Pct.**, is always expressed as a decimal rounded to the thousandth. It is a ratio of the number of games won to the number of games played. The higher the decimal number, the higher the team's standing in the league. The first-place team has the highest percentage while the last-place team has the lowest percentage.

Other baseball statistics, all expressed as percentages, are a player's fielding average, a player's success in stealing bases, a pitcher's won-and-lost record, and a player's on-base average.

CRITICAL THINKING

1. List five ways that percentage statistics are used in baseball.

2. Explain why a team with the most wins may not have the highest percentage (Pct.) in the league.

FOCUS | Use STATISTICS to study numbers in baseball.

Pete Rose, first baseman/manager of the Cincinnati Reds, holds the record for the most hits in the history of baseball.

LOOKING BACK
Reviewing and Testing Chapter 31

In Chapter 31 you formulated problems about a bicycle. To review, refer to page 451 for data.

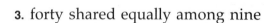

1. If the diameter of a front wheel is 48 in. and the diameter of the back wheel is 24 in., what is the difference in the circumference of the two wheels? Use 3.14 for π.

To review what you learned about algebraic notation, refer to pages 452 and 454.

Write in algebraic notation.

2. thirty decreased by 12

3. forty shared equally among nine

4. the total of 17 and 29

5. the product of eleven and six

6. sixteen increased by b

7. the product of seven and t

8. the quotient of c divided by ten

9. five subtracted from x

You learned about writing equations and inequalities. Refer to page 456.

Write each as an equation or inequality.

10. six minus two is less than five

11. eighteen less 12 is equal to six

12. five increased by a number is greater than seven

13. fifty divided by this number is equal to 10

To review what you learned about front-end estimation, refer to page 459.

Choose the better estimate. Write the letter.

14. $3{,}948 \times 6$ a. less than 24,000
    b. more than 24,000

15. $4\overline{)4{,}622}$ a. between 1,000 and 2,000
    b. between 100 and 200

You learned about using statistical percentages in baseball. To review, refer to page 460.

16. If team A's record is 106 wins and 56 losses, what is their percentage?

FOCUS | Review and test skills learned and practiced.

LOOKING AHEAD
Preparing for New Skills for Chapter 32

In the next chapter you will focus on

- **formulating problems about a vacation.**
- **constructing line segments and angles.**
- **bisecting a line segment.**
- **constructing congruent triangles.**
- **graphing congruent triangles.**
- **how math is used in technology.**

Constructing line segments, angles, and triangles will be easier if you review naming angles and graphing ordered pairs. Study the examples.

Example 1:

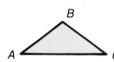

This angle is $\angle S$, or $\angle RST$, or $\angle TSR$.

Example 2:

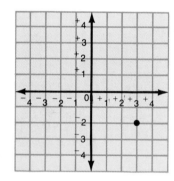

The angles in this triangle are $\angle BAC$, $\angle ABC$, and $\angle BCA$.

The example below shows how to graph a point.

Example 3: Graph: ($^+3$, $^-2$)

The first coordinate tells how many spaces to move left or right. The second tells how many spaces to move up or down.

The ordered pair ($^+3$, $^-2$) tells you to move 3 places to the right and 2 places down.

PRACTICE

Name the angles in each figure.

1.
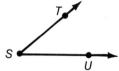

2.
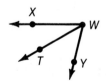

3.
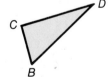

4.

Draw a four-quadrant grid on graph paper. Graph each point.

5. ($^-3$, $^-4$)   **6.** ($^+3$, $^-5$)   **7.** ($^-1$, $^+6$)   **8.** ($^+2$, $^+5$)

Review GEOMETRY and ALGEBRA in preparation for learning new skills.

FOCUS | Formulate problems using photo, data, and text.

32

Geometric Constructions

DATA

Price Family Account Book

18 days	1,857.6 miles traveled
Sleeping accommodations	$471.54
Meals	$325.31
Gasoline (108 gallons)	$114.94
Oil, greasing, and other car services	$25.00
Automobile tolls	$10.90
Refreshments and incidentals	$50.90

The Price family went on a special summer vacation. They traveled by car from their home in Des Moines, Iowa, to Florida.

They kept a careful record of their expenses and a diary of the places they visited. They made a budget for 28 days because Mr. and Mrs. Price had four weeks of vacation time. They planned to spend $2,500.

The data given represents the money the Prices spent after 18 days. Would they stay within their budget with 10 more days to go? Could they have cut expenses? How? Are there other expenses that might have been necessary? Try to suggest some ways the Prices might have reduced expenses.

Constructing Line Segments and Angles

Congruent figures have the same length or measure. The symbol ≅ means "is congruent to."

Construct a line segment congruent to $\overline{AB}$.

 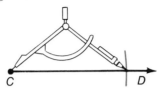 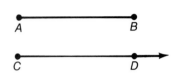

Step 1: Draw a ray. Label the endpoint C.
Step 2: Open the compass to the length of $\overline{AB}$.
Step 3: With the compass point at point C, use the same opening and draw an arc that intersects the ray. Label the point D. $\overline{CD} \cong \overline{AB}$

Construct an angle congruent to ∠STU.

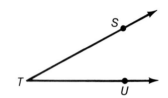

Step 1: Draw a ray. Label the endpoint P.

Step 2: Drawn an arc through ∠STU.

Step 3: With the compass at point P, use the same opening and draw an arc that intersects your ray. Label the intersection point R.

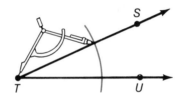 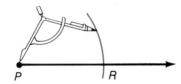

Step 4: Adjust the compass and measure the opening of ∠STU where the arc intersects the rays.

Step 5: With the same compass opening and point R as the center, drawn an arc. Label the point of intersection point Q.

Step 6: Draw a ray from point P through point Q. ∠STU ≅ ∠QPR.

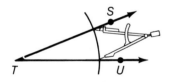 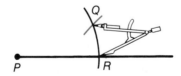 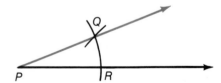

GUIDED PRACTICE

Trace each figure. Then use a compass to construct a congruent figure.

1.

2.

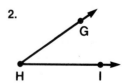

FOCUS | Use GEOMETRY to construct line segments and angles.

PRACTICE

Trace each figure. Then use a compass to construct a congruent figure.

3.

4.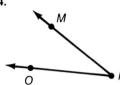

5.

6.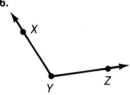

Use a ruler to draw each segment given. Then construct a congruent figure.

7. 4 cm   **8.** 6 cm   **9.** 8 cm   **10.** 11 cm

Use a protractor to draw an angle with each given measure. Then use a compass to construct a congruent angle.

11. 45°   **12.** 80°   **13.** 50°   **14.** 75°

MIXED PRACTICE
Maintaining and Reviewing Skills

Use one word from each row to describe each triangle.

Row A: right, acute, obtuse   Row B: scalene, equilateral, isosceles

15.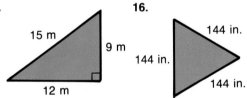

16.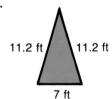

17.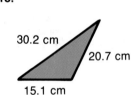

18.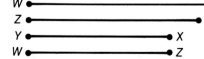

CHALLENGE

*19. Use a compass and a protractor to construct a figure with the angle and line segment measures given. Then identify the polygon formed.

m∠ZWX = 60°   m∠WXY = 60°   m∠XYZ = 120°   m∠YZW = 120°

W •——————————————————• X
Z •———————————————• Y
Y •——————————————• X
W •————————————• Z

GEOMETRY

Constructing Line Segments and Angles

A compass and straightedge are used to construct congruent line segments and angles.

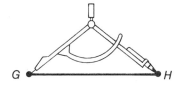 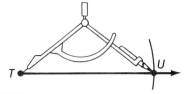

Congruent segments have the same length. $\overline{GH} \cong \overline{TU}$

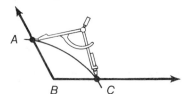 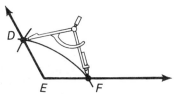

Congruent angles have the same measure. $\angle ABC \cong \angle DEF$

PRACTICE

Trace each figure. Then use a compass to construct a congruent figure.

1.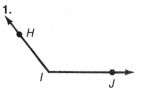

2.

3.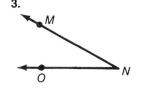

4.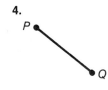

5. Draw a 10-centimeter line segment. Then use a compass to construct a congruent line segment.

* 6. Use a protractor to draw an angle that is half the measure of a right angle. Then use a compass to construct a congruent angle.

MIXED PRACTICE
Maintaining and Reviewing Skills

Write each expression.

7. The product of 12 and 16

8. The result of dividing 49 by 7

9. The sum of 28 and 19

10. Forty-three decreased by 8

11. The quotient of 60 divided by 10

12. Seven multiplied by ten

FOCUS | Use GEOMETRY to construct line segments and angles.

APPLICATION
Using Geometry

To **bisect** a line segment means to divide it into two congruent parts.

You can use a compass and a straightedge to construct a **perpendicular bisector** of a segment. A perpendicular bisector bisects a line segment while forming right angles with the given line segment.

Step 1: Open the compass more than half the length of QR. With point Q as the center, draw an arc as shown.

Step 2: With the same compass opening and point R as the center, draw an arc. Label the intersection points S and T.

Step 3: Draw $\overleftrightarrow{ST}$. Label the intersection or midpoint of $\overline{QR}$ and $\overleftrightarrow{ST}$ point U. $\overleftrightarrow{ST}$ is the perpendicular bisector of $\overline{QR}$. $\overline{QU} \cong \overline{UR}$.

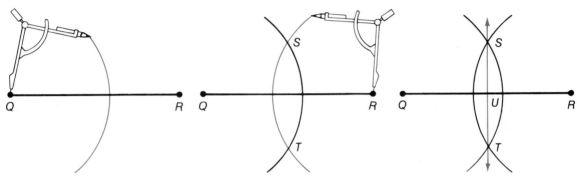

Trace each line segment. Then use a compass and a straightedge to construct the perpendicular bisector.

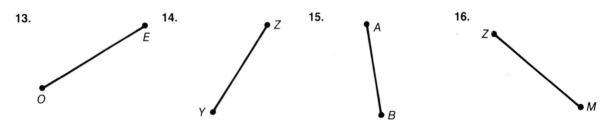

13.　　　　14.　　　　15.　　　　16.

17. Draw a line segment that measures 6 centimeters. Label the endpoints M and N. Construct a perpendicular bisector, $\overline{OP}$. Label the midpoint Q. Is $\overline{MQ} \cong \overline{QN}$?

*18. Trace the triangle below. Then construct the perpendicular bisector of each side.

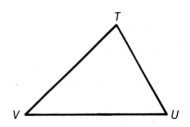

Use GEOMETRY to construct perpendicular bisectors of line segments.

Constructing Congruent Triangles

Congruent triangles are triangles that have the same size and shape.

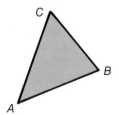

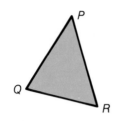

$$\triangle ABC \cong \triangle PQR$$

$\angle A \cong \angle P$	$\overline{AB} \cong \overline{PQ}$
$\angle B \cong \angle Q$	$\overline{BC} \cong \overline{QR}$
$\angle C \cong \angle R$	$\overline{AC} \cong \overline{PR}$

Construct a triangle congruent to $\triangle HIJ$ using the three sides of the given triangle, $\overline{HI}$, $\overline{IJ}$, and $\overline{JH}$.

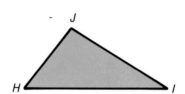

Step 1: Draw a ray. Label the endpoint S. Construct $ST \cong HI$.

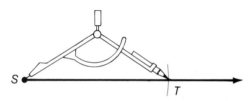

Step 2: Open the compass to the length of $\overline{IJ}$. With the same compass opening, and point T as the center, draw an arc.

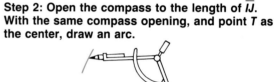

Step 3: Open the compass to the length of $\overline{HJ}$. With the same compass opening and point S as the center, draw an arc. Label the intersection R.

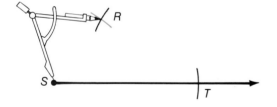

Step 4: Connect the points to form $\overline{SR}$ and $\overline{TR}$. $\triangle STR \cong \triangle HIJ$.

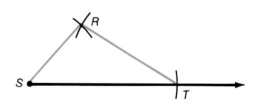

GUIDED PRACTICE

$\triangle LMN \cong \triangle EDF$. Use the congruent triangles to answer the following.

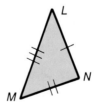

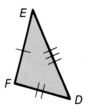

1. $\overline{LN} \cong$ ▉

2. $\overline{DE} \cong$ ▉

3. $\angle N \cong$ ▉

4. $\angle E \cong$ ▉

FOCUS Use GEOMETRY to construct congruent triangles.

PRACTICE

Use the congruent triangles to complete each exercise.

5. $\angle D \cong \blacksquare$

6. $\overline{FD} \cong \blacksquare$

7. If $\angle F = 55°$, $\angle \blacksquare = 55°$

8. If $\overline{DE} = 10$ in., $\overline{JK} = \blacksquare$

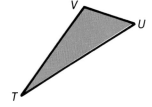
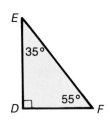
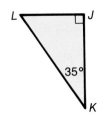

Trace each triangle. Then use a compass and a straightedge to construct a congruent triangle.

9.

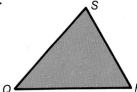

10.

11.

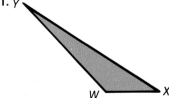

MIXED PRACTICE
Maintaining and Reviewing Skills

Write each expression.

12. A number b minus 26

13. Six times a number n

14. Fifteen added to a number a

15. The product of 9 and a number z

16. A number x divided by 6

17. A number y decreased by 11

CHALLENGE

Use rectangle $QRST$ to answer the following.

*18. List the pairs of congruent triangles.

*19. Which angles are congruent to $\angle QTS$?

*20. The measure of $\angle TUS$ is $\blacksquare$ and is equal to the measure of $\angle \blacksquare$.

*21. The measure of $\angle URQ$ is $\blacksquare$ and is equal to the measure of $\angle \blacksquare$.

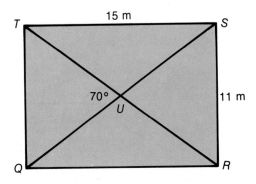

GEOMETRY

Constructing Congruent Triangles

Steve needs to draw a triangle congruent to the one shown. He constructs a triangle congruent to △*XYZ* using the sides $\overline{XY}$, $\overline{YZ}$, and $\overline{XZ}$.

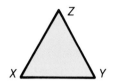

Step 1: Draw a ray.
Label the endpoint *M*.
Construct $\overline{MN} \cong \overline{XY}$.

Step 2: Open the compass to the length of $\overline{YZ}$.
With the same compass opening, and point *N* as the center, draw an arc.

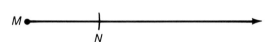

Step 3: Open the compass to the length of $\overline{XZ}$.
With the same compass opening and point *M* as the center, draw an arc. Label the intersection *O*.

Step 4: Connect the points to form $\overline{MO}$ and $\overline{NO}$.

△*MNO* ≅ △*XYZ*

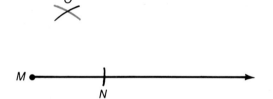

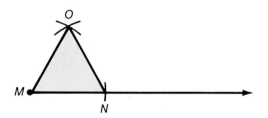

If three sides of one triangle are congruent to the corresponding sides of another triangle, the triangles are congruent.

PRACTICE

Trace each triangle. Then use a compass and a straightedge to construct a congruent triangle.

1.
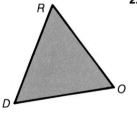

2.
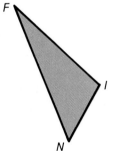

3.
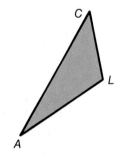

4.
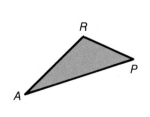

FOCUS Use GEOMETRY to construct congruent triangles.

MIXED PRACTICE

Maintaining and Reviewing Skills

Use circle F to answer the following.

5. Name a chord.

6. Name the diameter.

7. Name two radii.

8. Name two arcs.

9. Name a central angle.

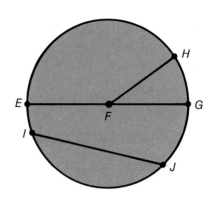

APPLICATION

You can use ordered pairs to draw a triangle congruent to $\triangle ABC$. Notice the graph below.

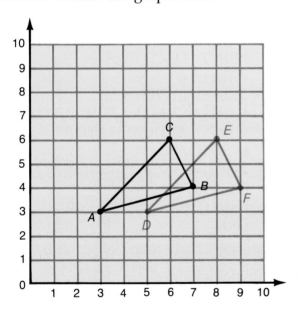

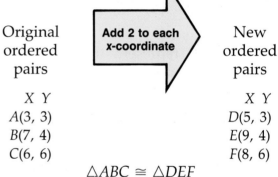

Original ordered pairs

Add 2 to each x-coordinate

New ordered pairs

X	Y
$A(3, 3)$
$B(7, 4)$
$C(6, 6)$

X	Y
$D(5, 3)$
$E(9, 4)$
$F(8, 6)$

$$\triangle ABC \cong \triangle DEF$$

$\triangle DEF$ is located 2 units to the right of $\triangle ABC$.

Use graph paper to complete the following.

10. Draw $\triangle XYZ$ using these ordered pairs: $X(10,4)$, $Y(3,3)$, and $Z(3,8)$. Subtract 2 from each x-coordinate and list the new ordered pairs. Locate the points and connect them to make a new triangle. Is the new triangle congruent to $\triangle XYZ$?

*11. Draw $\triangle CDE$ using the ordered pairs $C(1,5)$, $D(6,9)$, and $E(10,4)$. Then draw a congruent triangle 2 units down. List the ordered pairs of the new triangle.

Use GEOMETRY and ALGEBRA to graph congruent triangles.

How Does the Computer Deal With Fractions?

If your computer does not use fractions, how would you enter $\frac{1}{2}$?

One approach is to enter two numbers, the numerator and the denominator of the fraction. The following program will give useful results.

Enter the numerator and the denominator of a fraction. Print out the decimal equivalent of the fraction.

The Analysis

We will represent the numerator and denominator with the letters N and D. After entering these values, the computer will calculate F = N/D. To find the decimal equivalent of a fraction, divide the numerator by the denominator. For example, to find the decimal equivalent of 5/8 divide:

$$8)\overline{5.000} \quad 0.625$$

By writing F = N/D, the results will be found the same way we did above.

The Plan
1. Enter the values of N and D.
2. Computer will find F = N/D.
3. Print out the results.
4. End.

The Planned Output
FRACTIONS AND DECIMALS
ENTER THE NUMERATOR
AND DENOMINATOR

? 4,8
4/8 = 0.5

The most difficult part in getting this output printed is the last line. The values N, D, and F will be printed, but in between, we will print the symbols "/" and "=". Remember that all symbols that appear in between quotes will be printed as well as the numerical values of N, D, and F.

The Program
```
10   PRINT "FRACTIONS AND"
15   PRINT "DECIMALS"
20   PRINT
30   PRINT "ENTER THE"
35   PRINT "NUMERATOR AND THE"
36   PRINT "DENOMINATOR"
40   INPUT N
50   INPUT D
60   F = N/D
70   PRINT N; "/"; D ; "="; F
80   END
```

CRITICAL THINKING

1. Are there any values that should not be entered for N or D? Explain.

2. What will be the output for the following when input in the program above?

   a. 3, 4   b. 3, 5   c. 1, 8

FOCUS | Use LOGIC to write a computer program to change fractions to decimals.

Here is a program for renaming fractions. Read each line carefully. Try entering and running it on your computer.

```
10    PRINT "RENAMING FRACTIONS": PRINT
20    PRINT "ENTER NUMERATOR FIRST, THEN DENOMINATOR"
30    INPUT N
40    INPUT D
50    FOR P = N TO 2 STEP - 1
60    IF N/P = INT (N/P) THEN 80
70     GOTO 90
80    IF D/P = INT (D/P) THEN 120
90    NEXT P
100   PRINT N;"/";D; " IS ALREADY IN SIMPLEST TERMS"
110   GOTO 150
120   NN = N/P: REM NEW NUMERATOR
130   ND = D/P: REM NEW DENOMINATOR
140   PRINT "THIS FRACTION RENAMED IN SIMPLEST TERMS IS ";NN;"/";ND
      END
```

Here are three outputs from this program:

```
RUN
RENAMING FRACTIONS

ENTER NUMERATOR FIRST , THEN DENOMINATOR
?25
?75
THIS FRACTION RENAMED IN SIMPLEST TERMS IS 1/3
```

```
RUN
RENAMING FRACTIONS

ENTER NUMERATOR FIRST , THEN DENOMINATOR
?16
?18
THIS FRACTION RENAMED IN SIMPLEST TERMS IS 8/9
```

```
RUN
RENAMING FRACTIONS

ENTER NUMERATOR FIRST , THEN DENOMINATOR
?37
?40
37/40 IS ALREADY IN SIMPLEST TERMS
```

Reviewing and Testing Chapter 32

In Chapter 32 you formulated problems about a budget. To review, refer to page 465 for data.

1. What was the average price the Smiths paid for a gallon of gasoline? Round to the nearest hundredth.

You learned about constructing line segments and angles. To review, refer to pages 466 and 468.

Trace each figure. Then construct a congruent figure.

2.

3.

4.

5.

To review bisecting line segments and constructing congruent triangles, refer to pages 469 and 470.

Trace each line segment. Then use a compass to construct a perpendicular bisector.

6.

7.

8.

Trace each triangle. Then use a compass and a straightedge to construct a congruent triangle.

9.

10.

11.

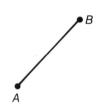

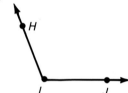

You have learned computer programming. To review, refer to the program on page 474.

12. What will the output be for the following input?

    a. 2,5   **b.** 7, 8   **c.** 1, 10   **d.** 20, 40

FOCUS	Review and test skills learned and practiced.

LOOKING AHEAD
Preparing for Next Year

This year you focused on

NUMBER SKILLS	PROBABILITY AND STATISTICS
MEASUREMENT	ALGEBRA
GEOMETRY	LOGIC
PATTERNS AND FUNCTIONS	

It will be easier for you to get a good start next year if you keep your math skills sharp while you are not at school. Here are a few suggestions for things to do on your vacation that will help you stay mathematically powerful.

NUMBER SKILLS
Look through some newspapers for the greatest numbers you can find. Can you find a number greater than one million? Greater than one billion? Write the numbers down and what they represent.

MEASUREMENT
Write down everything you eat in one day and estimate the size of the serving. Then get a book that tells about calories and measure the number of calories you ate that day. Was it more than you needed?

GEOMETRY
Many structures are made up of geometric shapes that form different angles. Look for and keep a list of structures that have different geometric shapes and angles.

PATTERNS AND FUNCTIONS
Look for various wallpaper prints in stores or in your home. Do you see any repeating or symmetrical patterns? Design your own wallpaper using repeating patterns.

PROBABILITY AND STATISTICS
What is your favorite activity? Keep a record of the time spent on one activity every day for a week. Then make a bar graph to show how many hours each day you actually spend on the activity. (Round your times to the nearest half hour.)

ALGEBRA
Decide on something you really want to buy and find out how much it costs. Do you have enough money? If not, then write an equation to find out how much more money you need. Use this formula to write the equation: Cost of item − amount you have = x (amount you need).

LOGIC
Write some logic statements about a day that is coming up. For instance, "If it is raining on Tuesday, I will go to the movies," or, "If I don't have to babysit, I will call my best friend." Then, if the conditions are met, do what you planned.

Preparing for next year.

Write the letter of the correct answer.

Use circle D to answer the questions.

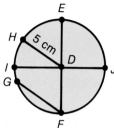

1. Which line segment is a diameter?

A. $\overline{DJ}$ **B.** $\overline{EF}$ **C.** $\overline{GF}$ **D.** $\overline{HD}$

2. Which line segment is a radius?

E. $\overline{EF}$ **F.** $\overline{IJ}$ **G.** $\overline{GF}$ **H.** $\overline{HD}$

3. Find the area of circle D. Use 3.14 for π.

   A. 15.7 cm^2 **B.** 78.5 cm^2

   C. 31.4 cm^2 **D.** 70.5 cm^2

Which is the equivalent percent?

4. 71 out of 100   **E.** 36%   **F.** 7%

                  G. 71%   **H.** 29%

5. 33 out of 100   **A.** 33%   **B.** 6%

                  C. 66%   **D.** 67%

Choose the equivalent fraction.
Simplify if possible.

6. 48%   **E.** $\frac{48}{50}$ **F.** $\frac{12}{25}$

         G. $\frac{24}{100}$ **H.** $\frac{96}{100}$

7. 61%   **A.** $\frac{61}{100}$ **B.** $\frac{61}{50}$

       C. $\frac{6}{10}$ **D.** $\frac{30}{100}$

Solve.

8. What percent of 80 is 20?

   E. 40%   **F.** 20%   **G.** 25%   **H.** 50%

9. What is 30% of 120?

   A. 40   **B.** 12   **C.** 26   **D.** 36

10. What percent of 100 is 15?

   E. 115%   **F.** 55%   **G.** 30%   **H.** 15%

11. 10% of what number is 6?

   A. 66   **B.** 60   **C.** 40   **D.** 160

12. What is 8% of $320?

   E. $256   **F.** $40   **G.** $400   **H.** $328

Which inequality is true?

13. A. $^-8 < {}^+8$ **B.** $^-8 > {}^+8$

     C. $^+8 < {}^+8$ **D.** $^-8 < {}^-8$

14. E. $^+6 < {}^+5$ **F.** $^-6 < {}^+5$

     G. $^-6 > {}^-5$ **H.** $^+6 < {}^-5$

15. A. $0 > {}^-16$ **B.** $0 > {}^+10$

     C. $0 < {}^-10$ **D.** $0 > 0$

Add.

16. $^+6 + {}^+7$ **E.** $^-13$ **F.** $^+1$

                 G. $^-1$ **H.** $^+13$

17. $^-12 + {}^-9$ **A.** $^-3$ **B.** $^+21$

                 C. $^-21$ **D.** $^+3$

FOCUS   Review concepts and skills taught in Chapters 25–32.

Add or subtract.

18. $^{+}8 + ^{-}6$ **E.** $^{-}14$ **F.** $^{+}14$

                      G. $^{+}2$ **H.** $^{-}2$

19. $^{-}4 + ^{+}5$ **A.** $^{+}1$ **B.** $^{-}9$

                      C. $^{-}5$ **D.** $^{+}9$

20. $^{+}15 + ^{-}23$ **E.** $^{-}38$ **F.** $^{+}38$

                      G. $^{+}8$ **H.** $^{-}8$

21. $^{+}16 - ^{+}15$ **A.** $^{-}1$ **B.** $^{+}31$

                      C. $^{+}1$ **D.** $^{+}3$

22. $^{-}9 - ^{-}5$ **E.** $^{-}4$ **F.** $^{+}14$

                      G. $^{-}14$ **H.** $^{+}4$

23. $^{+}19 - ^{+}20$ **A.** $^{-}39$ **B.** $^{-}1$

                      C. $^{+}1$ **D.** $^{+}1$

Multiply or divide.

24. $^{+}5 \times ^{-}4$ **E.** $^{+}20$ **F.** $^{+}2$

                      G. $^{-}9$ **H.** $^{-}20$

25. $^{-}6 \times ^{-}3$ **A.** $^{+}18$ **B.** $^{-}18$

                      C. $^{-}9$ **D.** $^{-}3$

26. $^{-}8 \times ^{+}4$ **E.** $^{-}12$ **F.** $^{-}4$

                      G. $^{+}32$ **H.** $^{-}32$

27. $^{-}6 \times ^{-}5$ **A.** $^{-}35$ **B.** $^{+}30$

                      C. $^{-}30$ **D.** $^{-}25$

28. $^{-}16 \div ^{-}4$ **E.** $^{+}4$ **F.** $^{+}8$

                      G. $^{-}4$ **H.** $^{-}12$

29. $^{+}48 \div ^{-}6$ **A.** $^{-}16$ **B.** $^{-}8$

                      C. $^{+}8$ **D.** $^{+}4$

Choose the algebraic notation.

30. sixty-four shared equally among 8

     E. $64 \div 8$ **F.** $64 - 8$

     G. $64 + 8$ **H.** $8 \div 64$

31. the product of 15 and 31

     A. $31 - 15$ **B.** $31 \div 15$

     C. 15×31 **D.** $15 + 31$

32. the difference of 100 minus 22

     E. 100×22 **F.** $22 - 100$

     G. $22 \div 100$ **H.** $100 - 22$

33. some number b divided by 5

     A. $10 \div 5$ **B.** $b \div 5$

     C. $5 \div 6$ **D.** $b \times 5$

34. five times 6 is more than 28

     E. $5 + 28 > 6$ **F.** $5 - 6 = 28$

     G. $5 + 6 < 28$ **H.** $5 \times 6 > 28$

35. 81 divided by 3 is less than 30

     A. $81 \times 3 > 30$ **B.** $81 \div 30 < 3$

     C. $81 \div 3 < 30$ **D.** $81 \times 3 < 30$

Find the congruent angle.

36.

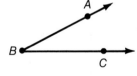

   E.   **F.**

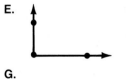

   G.   **H.**

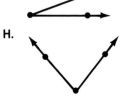

Write the letter of the correct answer.

Round to the nearest tenth.

1. 6.86
- **A.** 6.8
- **B.** 6.6
- **C.** 6.9
- **D.** 8.0

2. 8.15
- **E.** 8.2
- **F.** 8.1
- **G.** 8.25
- **H.** 8.0

3. 0.76
- **A.** 0.75
- **B.** 0.8
- **C.** 1.0
- **D.** 0.6

Round to the nearest hundredth.

4. 5.233
- **E.** 5.24
- **F.** 5.3
- **G.** 5.20
- **H.** 5.23

5. 11.008
- **A.** 11.08
- **B.** 11.00
- **C.** 11.01
- **D.** 11.050

6. 9.999
- **E.** 9.99
- **F.** 9.98
- **G.** 10.0
- **H.** 10.99

Which is a true statement?

7.
- **A.** 8.93 > 8.94
- **B.** 8.8 < 8.92
- **C.** 8.90 = 8.89
- **D.** 8.83 > 8.92

8.
- **E.** 5.500 < 5.498
- **F.** 5.381 < 5.292
- **G.** 5.481 > 4.581
- **H.** 5.481 = 4.581

9.
- **A.** 1.228 < 1.225
- **B.** 0.228 > 0.0096
- **C.** 1.228 = 1.028
- **D.** 0.228 < 0.099

10.
- **E.** 9.31 = 9.3100
- **F.** 9.301 > 9.31
- **G.** 9.31 < 9.3100
- **H.** 9.103 > 9.301

11.
- **A.** 2.602 > 26
- **B.** 2.602 = 26.02
- **C.** 26.20 < 26.02
- **D.** 26.02 > 2.602

Add or subtract.

12.
$$\begin{array}{r} 4.88 \\ + 2.27 \\ \hline \end{array}$$
- **E.** 6.61
- **F.** 7.61
- **G.** 6.15
- **H.** 7.15

13.
$$\begin{array}{r} 9.698 \\ + 2.34 \\ \hline \end{array}$$
- **A.** 12.380
- **B.** 12.038
- **C.** 12.388
- **D.** 11.13

14.
$$\begin{array}{r} 0.587 \\ + 0.698 \\ \hline \end{array}$$
- **E.** 1.115
- **F.** 1.285
- **G.** 0.111
- **H.** 12.850

15.
$$\begin{array}{r} \$18.25 \\ - \quad 7.98 \\ \hline \end{array}$$
- **A.** $26.23
- **B.** $26.27
- **C.** $10.27
- **D.** $10.23

16.
$$\begin{array}{r} 28.61 \\ - \quad 6.853 \\ \hline \end{array}$$
- **E.** 21.763
- **F.** 35.463
- **G.** 21.757
- **H.** 21.463

17.
$$\begin{array}{r} 13.626 \\ - \quad 9.7 \\ \hline \end{array}$$
- **A.** 3.926
- **B.** 23.326
- **C.** 3.900
- **D.** 3.984

Multiply or divide.

18.
$$\begin{array}{r} 13.6 \\ \times \quad 5.9 \\ \hline \end{array}$$
- **E.** 81.2
- **F.** 802.40
- **G.** 80.24
- **H.** 81.04

19.
$$\begin{array}{r} 5.382 \\ \times \quad 1.6 \\ \hline \end{array}$$
- **A.** 8.6
- **B.** 8.6221
- **C.** 0.8611
- **D.** 8.6112

20. $6\overline{)20.4}$
- **E.** 3.4
- **F.** 34
- **G.** 4.3
- **H.** 3.5

21. $12\overline{)50.52}$
- **A.** 5.01
- **B.** 4.21
- **C.** 4.021
- **D.** 4.251

22. $3\overline{)6.204}$
- **E.** 2.068
- **F.** 2.7
- **G.** 20.68
- **H.** 2.680

FOCUS | Review concepts and skills taught in Chapters 17–32.

Convert.

23. 100 mm = ■ cm

    A. 1 cm   **B.** 1 000 cm

    C. 10 cm   **D.** 100 000 cm

24. 2 500 g = ■ kg

    E. 25 000 kg   **F.** 25 kg

    G. 0.25 kg   **H.** 2.5 kg

25. 2 100 mL = ■ L

    A. 0.21 mL   **B.** 2.1 L

    C. 210 mL   **D.** 21.1 L

26. 4 km = ■ m

    E. 400 000 m   **F.** 4 000 m

    G. 0.4 m   **H.** 40 000 m

Which proportions are true? Use cross products to check.

27. A. $\dfrac{18}{24} = \dfrac{2}{3}$ **B.** $\dfrac{6}{10} = \dfrac{18}{24}$

    C. $\dfrac{6}{10} = \dfrac{3}{4}$ **D.** $\dfrac{3}{4} = \dfrac{18}{24}$

28. E. $\dfrac{5}{6} = \dfrac{100}{120}$ **F.** $\dfrac{5}{6} = \dfrac{25}{36}$

    G. $\dfrac{5}{6} = \dfrac{15}{24}$ **H.** $\dfrac{5}{6} = \dfrac{2}{3}$

29. A. $\dfrac{2}{7} = \dfrac{6}{10}$ **B.** $\dfrac{2}{7} = \dfrac{14}{49}$

    C. $\dfrac{2}{7} = \dfrac{20}{14}$ **D.** $\dfrac{2}{7} = \dfrac{14}{35}$

Use a proportion to solve.

30. There are 60 minutes in one hour. How many minutes are in a day?

    E. 720   **F.** 1,720 **G.** 144   **H.** 1,440

Solve.

31. What is 40% of $200?

    A. $500 **B.** $80 **C.** $125 **D.** $240

32. What percent of 30 is 6?

    E. 50% **F.** 25% **G.** 20% **H.** 6%

33. What percent of 200 is 72?

    A. 36% **B.** 144% **C.** 7.2% **D.** 18%

34. What percent of 3,000 is 75?

    E. 12.5% **F.** 7.5% **G.** 2.5% **H.** 25%

35. 25% of what number is 90?

    A. 190 **B.** 21 **C.** 270 **D.** 360

36. 60% of what number is 6?

    E. 160 **F.** 10 **G.** 100 **H.** 16

Add or subtract.

37. $^{+}9 + {}^{+}6$ **A.** $^{+}15$ **B.** $^{+}3$

                 C. $^{+}16$ **D.** $^{-}15$

38. $^{+}10 + {}^{-}4$ **E.** $^{+}6$ **F.** $^{+}14$

                 G. $^{-}6$ **H.** $^{-}14$

39. $^{-}11 - {}^{+}12$ **A.** $^{-}23$ **B.** $^{-}1$

                 C. $^{+}23$ **D.** $^{+}1$

40. $^{-}21 + {}^{+}8$ **E.** $^{-}12$ **F.** $^{+}12$

                 G. $^{-}29$ **H.** $^{-}13$

41. $^{+}8 - {}^{+}18$ **A.** $^{-}26$ **B.** $^{+}16$

                 C. $^{-}10$ **D.** $^{+}10$

42. $^{-}13 + {}^{+}21$ **E.** $^{+}8$ **F.** $^{+}18$

                 G. $^{-}8$ **H.** $^{-}16$

EXTRA PRACTICE

(pages 18–19) Write in standard form.

1. ten thousand, three hundred fourteen

2. thirteen thousand, two hundred seventy

3. sixty-five thousand, one hundred seven

4. three hundred thousand, nine hundred forty

5. ten million, six thousand, eight hundred twenty

6. thirty-three million, nine hundred thousand, fifty-six

7. two hundred million, eighteen thousand, eighty-one

8. four billion, one hundred thousand, ninety-nine

(pages 24–25) Round to the nearest billion.

9. 1,347,100,789

10. 6,804,634,814

11. 5,498,175,000

12. 996,500,458

13. 8,601,431,000

14. 5,500,000,000

(pages 34–35) Compare. Use >, <, or =.

1. 168 $<$ 257

2. 6,205 $<$ 7,000

3. 13,298 $>$ 1,399

4. 9,089 $<$ 9,713

5. 13,538 $<$ 13,539

6. 21,000 $>$ 2,100

7. 56,493 $<$ 65,492

8. 116,884 $<$ 116,885

9. 450,032 $>$ 41,767

10. 628,012 $=$ 628,012

11. 7,845,461 $>$ 794,546

12. 12,500,651,000 $>$ 12,700

(pages 38–39) Write in standard form.

13. 2^6

14. 5^3

15. 6^3

16. 10^0

17. 8^2

18. 6^2

19. 2^7

20. 15^0

21. 4×5^2

22. 2×4^5

23. $4^3 \times 2$

24. $3^3 \times 4$

25. 6×7^2

26. $8^3 \times 8$

27. $0^6 \times 8$

28. 10×5^3

29. $10^4 \times 4$

30. 20×6^4

31. $9^6 \times 10$

32. $10^{10} \times 7^0$

(pages 48–49) Solve.

1. $63 \div 7 - 6 = n$
2. $13 + (4 \times 6) = d$
3. $3 \times 2 + 20 \div 2 = a$

4. $3 + 49 \div 7 = h$
5. $25 + 18 \div 6 - 12 = b$
6. $103 \times (18 \div 9) = f$

7. $84 \div 6 \times 7 + 1 = n$
8. $19 + 2 \times 3 \div 6 = t$
9. $31 - 4^2 + 3 = x$

10. $(3 + 2)^2 - 2 \times 5 = m$
11. $8 + 2 \times 3^2 - 6 = a$
12. $14 - 8 \times 6^0 = d$

13. $3^3 \div (10 - 7) \times 1^3 = e$
14. $(2^2 - 1^2)^2 - 9 = k$
15. $13^0 \div (2 - 1)^3 = b$

(pages 52–53) Write an inverse sentence and solve.

16. $8 + a = 15$
17. $2 + x = 27$
18. $n \times 4 = 24$
19. $a \div 8 = 9$

20. $n - 54 = 36$
21. $11 \times b = 88$
22. $t \div 8 = 9$
23. $g - 29 = 60$

24. $z \times 6 = 42$
25. $y \div 9 = 4$
26. $18 + t = 30$
27. $c \div 7 = 8$

28. $b \div 5 = 9$
29. $8 \times t = 48$
30. $38 + k = 47$
31. $g - 19 = 25$

(pages 62–63) Add.

1.
$$216 + 173$$
364

2.
$$28 + 186$$
214

3.
$$1,094 + 305$$
1,399

4.
$$2,342 + 5,077$$
7,419

5.
$$79 + 6,542$$
6,621

6.
$$363 \\ 19 \\ + 107$$

7.
$$712 \\ 138 \\ + 275$$

8.
$$1,937 \\ 818 \\ + 66$$

9.
$$13,133 \\ 4,785 \\ + 10,601$$

10.
$$11 \\ 11,000 \\ + 8,718$$
19,729

(pages 68–69) Subtract.

11.
$$86 - 32$$

12.
$$157 - 48$$

13.
$$1,244 - 955$$

14.
$$9,345 - 6,835$$

15.
$$16,753 - 863$$

16.
$$297 - 136$$

17.
$$928 - 397$$

18.
$$4,369 - 1,829$$

19.
$$2,136 - 1,984$$

20.
$$48,910 - 15,487$$

EXTRA PRACTICE

(pages 78–79) Find all the factors for each number.

1. 3   **2.** 12   **3.** 13   **4.** 15   **5.** 18

6. 32   **7.** 35   **8.** 64   **9.** 75   **10.** 81

11. 125   **12.** 130   **13.** 169   **14.** 189   **15.** 187

(pages 82–83) Complete each prime factorization. Then express each answer in exponential form.

16. $72 = 2 \times 2 \times 2 \times \blacksquare \times \blacksquare = \blacksquare$ **17.** $132 = 3 \times \blacksquare \times \blacksquare \times 11 = \blacksquare$

18. $225 = 3 \times 3 \times \blacksquare \times \blacksquare = \blacksquare$ **19.** $189 = 7 \times \blacksquare \times \blacksquare \times \blacksquare = \blacksquare$

20. $216 = \blacksquare \times \blacksquare \times \blacksquare \times 3 \times 3 \times 3 = \blacksquare$ **21.** $400 = \blacksquare \times \blacksquare \times 2 \times 2 \times 2 \times 2 = \blacksquare$

22. $340 = \blacksquare \times \blacksquare \times 5 \times \blacksquare = \blacksquare$ **23.** $10,550 = \blacksquare \times 5 \times 5 \times \blacksquare = \blacksquare$

(pages 94–95) Multiply.

1. $\begin{array}{r} 38 \\ \times\ 3 \\ \hline \end{array}$	**2.** $\begin{array}{r} 216 \\ \times\ 6 \\ \hline \end{array}$	**3.** $\begin{array}{r} 157 \\ \times\ 14 \\ \hline \end{array}$	**4.** $\begin{array}{r} 324 \\ \times\ 25 \\ \hline \end{array}$	**5.** $\begin{array}{r} 297 \\ \times\ 118 \\ \hline \end{array}$
6. $\begin{array}{r} 179 \\ \times\ 39 \\ \hline \end{array}$	**7.** $\begin{array}{r} 212 \\ \times\ 175 \\ \hline \end{array}$	**8.** $\begin{array}{r} 681 \\ \times\ 405 \\ \hline \end{array}$	**9.** $\begin{array}{r} 234 \\ \times\ 91 \\ \hline \end{array}$	**10.** $\begin{array}{r} 852 \\ \times\ 711 \\ \hline \end{array}$
11. $\begin{array}{r} 394 \\ \times\ 261 \\ \hline \end{array}$	**12.** $\begin{array}{r} 794 \\ \times\ 131 \\ \hline \end{array}$	**13.** $\begin{array}{r} 811 \\ \times\ 247 \\ \hline \end{array}$	**14.** $\begin{array}{r} 721 \\ \times\ 52 \\ \hline \end{array}$	**15.** $\begin{array}{r} 526 \\ \times\ 397 \\ \hline \end{array}$

(96–98) Divide.

16. $7\overline{)3,052}$ **17.** $4\overline{)2,724}$ **18.** $8\overline{)1,632}$ **19.** $3\overline{)1,430}$ **20.** $16\overline{)2,160}$

21. $23\overline{)4,863}$ **22.** $58\overline{)4,930}$ **23.** $86\overline{)3,698}$ **24.** $32\overline{)1,090}$ **25.** $44\overline{)13,538}$

26. $92\overline{)44,436}$ **27.** $87\overline{)11,489}$ **28.** $17\overline{)8,993}$ **29.** $66\overline{)8,996}$ **30.** $57\overline{)56,373}$

(pages 106–107) Multiply.

| 1. | 264
 × 12 | 2. | 2,531
 × 37 | 3. | 5,576
 × 208 | 4. | 2,285
 × 449 | 5. | 3,012
 × 216 |

1. 264   **2.** 2,531   **3.** 5,576   **4.** 2,285   **5.** 3,012
    × 12   × 37   × 208   × 449   × 216

6. 405   **7.** 519   **8.** 272   **9.** 9,855   **10.** 4,931
   × 133   × 180   × 272   × 111   × 3,148

11. 7,957   **12.** 1,912   **13.** 2,711   **14.** 3,821   **15.** 3,651
    × 293   × 486   × 77   × 13   × 789

(pages 110–111) Divide.

16. $56\overline{)10,752}$ **17.** $43\overline{)17,833}$ **18.** $38\overline{)26,144}$ **19.** $76\overline{)50,699}$

20. $48\overline{)10,080}$ **21.** $116\overline{)74,588}$ **22.** $368\overline{)272,688}$ **23.** $424\overline{)179,796}$

24. $576\overline{)52,450}$ **25.** $701\overline{)75,007}$ **26.** $214\overline{)147,550}$ **27.** $888\overline{)270,840}$

(pages 122–123) Find the (GCF) greatest common factor.

1. 12 and 15   **2.** 10 and 45   **3.** 11 and 22   **4.** 13 and 35   **5.** 63 and 24

6. 20 and 70   **7.** 42 and 77   **8.** 16 and 80   **9.** 75 and 100   **10.** 48 and 104

11. 9, 24, and 66   **12.** 16, 32, and 56   **13.** 12, 44, and 96   **14.** 18, 54, and 180

15. 11, 55, and 121   **16.** 26, 39, and 65   **17.** 20, 80, and 220   **18.** 75, 120, and 150

(pages 128–129) Find the (LCM) least common multiple.

19. 6 and 8   **20.** 6 and 9   **21.** 4 and 5   **22.** 10 and 12   **23.** 3 and 15

24. 2 and 17   **25.** 10 and 15   **26.** 10 and 16   **27.** 3 and 51   **28.** 4 and 11

29. 2, 5, and 6   **30.** 3, 4, and 18   **31.** 4, 5, and 10   **32.** 2, 6, 9, and 12

33. 2, 3, and 9   **34.** 2, 5, and 7   **35.** 4, 9, and 27   **36.** 4, 8, 20, and 32

EXTRA PRACTICE

(pages 138–139) Find the missing numerator or denominator.

1. $\dfrac{3}{5} = \dfrac{\blacksquare}{10}$ 2. $\dfrac{4}{6} = \dfrac{\blacksquare}{15}$ 3. $\dfrac{2}{4} = \dfrac{\blacksquare}{12}$ 4. $\dfrac{3}{8} = \dfrac{\blacksquare}{24}$

5. $\dfrac{8}{12} = \dfrac{32}{\blacksquare}$ 6. $\dfrac{6}{6} = \dfrac{13}{\blacksquare}$ 7. $\dfrac{7}{10} = \dfrac{21}{\blacksquare}$ 8. $\dfrac{12}{60} = \dfrac{\blacksquare}{10}$

9. $\dfrac{14}{28} = \dfrac{\blacksquare}{4}$ 10. $\dfrac{3}{15} = \dfrac{15}{\blacksquare}$ 11. $\dfrac{32}{36} = \dfrac{\blacksquare}{9}$ 12. $\dfrac{2}{24} = \dfrac{1}{\blacksquare}$

13. $\dfrac{3}{21} = \dfrac{\blacksquare}{7}$ 14. $\dfrac{18}{33} = \dfrac{6}{\blacksquare}$ 15. $\dfrac{8}{72} = \dfrac{\blacksquare}{18}$ 16. $\dfrac{9}{12} = \dfrac{\blacksquare}{72}$

(pages 142–143) Find the equivalent fractions with like denominators. Use the LCD.

17. $\dfrac{1}{2}$ and $\dfrac{4}{5}$ 18. $\dfrac{1}{3}$ and $\dfrac{3}{6}$ 19. $\dfrac{5}{8}$ and $\dfrac{1}{6}$ 20. $\dfrac{3}{9}$ and $\dfrac{5}{6}$

21. $\dfrac{2}{3}$ and $\dfrac{3}{7}$ 22. $\dfrac{1}{4}$ and $\dfrac{1}{5}$ 23. $\dfrac{3}{10}$ and $\dfrac{4}{15}$ 24. $\dfrac{7}{12}$ and $\dfrac{8}{9}$

25. $\dfrac{2}{7}$ and $\dfrac{2}{5}$ 26. $\dfrac{2}{4}$ and $\dfrac{2}{6}$ 27. $\dfrac{3}{4}, \dfrac{1}{3},$ and $\dfrac{5}{6}$ 28. $\dfrac{3}{5}, \dfrac{2}{8},$ and $\dfrac{16}{20}$

(pages 152–153) Add. Write your answers in simplest terms.

1. $\dfrac{3}{6}$
  $+\dfrac{2}{6}$

2. $\dfrac{5}{10}$
  $+\dfrac{3}{10}$

3. $\dfrac{2}{4}$
  $+\dfrac{1}{3}$

4. $3\dfrac{1}{4}$
  $+2\dfrac{3}{4}$

5. $1\dfrac{4}{5}$
  $+2\dfrac{2}{3}$

6. $\dfrac{1}{3} + \dfrac{2}{4} + \dfrac{5}{12}$ 7. $\dfrac{2}{5} + \dfrac{3}{4} + \dfrac{6}{10}$ 8. $\dfrac{7}{8} + \dfrac{2}{3} + \dfrac{5}{6}$ 9. $\dfrac{7}{12} + \dfrac{8}{9} + \dfrac{3}{6}$

(pages 158–159) Subtract. Write your answers in simplest terms.

10. 2
   $-1\dfrac{1}{4}$

11. $3\dfrac{5}{7}$
   $-2\dfrac{3}{7}$

12. $6\dfrac{4}{9}$
   $-4\dfrac{1}{3}$

13. $14\dfrac{3}{5}$
   $-10\dfrac{5}{6}$

14. $22\dfrac{2}{3}$
   $-8\dfrac{3}{7}$

15. $8\dfrac{2}{3} - 3\dfrac{2}{5}$ 16. $11\dfrac{2}{6} - 9\dfrac{2}{3}$ 17. $\dfrac{13}{15} - \dfrac{23}{60}$ 18. $2\dfrac{5}{9} - 1\dfrac{4}{5}$ 19. $12\dfrac{7}{10} - 7\dfrac{4}{6}$

(pages 168–169) Find the area of each rectangle.

1.
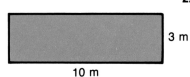
3 m

10 m

2.
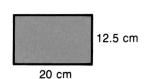
12.5 cm

20 cm

3.

18 ft

6 ft

4. $l = 12$ in.
$w = 5$ in.

5. $l = 15$ cm
$w = 10$ cm

6. $l = 13$ ft
$w = 7$ ft

7. $l = 35$ mm
$w = 20$ mm

(pages 172–173) Find the area of each parallelogram.

8.
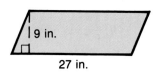
9 in.

27 in.

9.
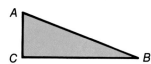
6 cm

18 cm

10.
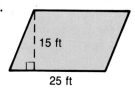
15 ft

25 ft

11. $b = 5$ cm
$h = 9$ cm

12. $b = 8$ in.
$h = 12$ in.

13. $b = 13$ m
$h = 13$ m

14. $b = 3$ km
$h = 8$ km

(pages 182–183) Use your protractor to find the measure of each angle.

1. m∠A =
   m∠B =
   m∠C =

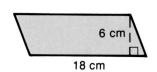

2. m∠D =
   m∠E =
   m∠F =

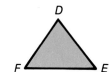

3. Is △ABC a right triangle, an obtuse triangle, or an acute triangle?

4. Is △DEF a right triangle, an obtuse triangle, or an acute triangle?

(pages 186–187) Find the measures of the angles for each parallelogram.

5.

6.

65°

EXTRA PRACTICE

(pages 196–197) Find the mean and median for each exercise.

1. 36, 51, 75, 58, 62, 72

2. 21, 29, 25, 19, 31, 25

3. 35, 42, 71, 40, 76, 42

4. 119, 150, 98, 163, 117, 109

5. 85, 184, 111, 131, 92, 153

6. 118, 27, 123, 112, 104, 122

7. 289, 215, 213, 268, 272, 273

8. 313, 94, 100, 53, 426, 52

(pages 202–203) Copy and complete the frequency table using the test scores below. Then find the range and mode.

Test Scores: 95, 80, 88, 95, 97, 80, 95, 81, 97, 81, 98, 95, 80, 98

9. Range: ■

10. Mode: ■

Score	Tally	Frequency
80					
81		2
	I	
		4
98		

(pages 212–213) Multiply. Write your answers in simplest terms.

1. $\frac{2}{3} \times \frac{1}{2}$

2. $\frac{2}{4} \times \frac{3}{5}$

3. $\frac{4}{5} \times \frac{3}{10}$

4. $\frac{1}{4} \times \frac{8}{9}$

5. $\frac{1}{5} \times \frac{10}{12}$

6. $\frac{5}{6} \times \frac{18}{25}$

7. $\frac{1}{2} \times \frac{6}{7}$

8. $\frac{7}{8} \times \frac{48}{49}$

9. $\frac{1}{3} \times \frac{2}{4} \times \frac{1}{2}$

10. $\frac{2}{5} \times \frac{10}{12} \times \frac{3}{4}$

11. $\frac{1}{5} \times \frac{2}{5} \times \frac{3}{5}$

12. $\frac{4}{9} \times \frac{3}{8} \times \frac{16}{24}$

(pages 218–219) Divide. Write your answers in simplest terms.

13. $6 \div \frac{2}{3}$

14. $7 \div \frac{3}{5}$

15. $\frac{4}{5} \div \frac{1}{5}$

16. $\frac{5}{8} \div \frac{2}{4}$

17. $\frac{9}{15} \div \frac{9}{3}$

18. $\frac{5}{12} \div \frac{5}{6}$

19. $\frac{13}{14} \div \frac{6}{7}$

20. $30 \div \frac{5}{6}$

21. $48 \div \frac{8}{9}$

22. $\frac{8}{15} \div \frac{4}{5}$

23. $\frac{4}{6} \div 3$

24. $\frac{8}{9} \div 4$

(pages 226–227) Multiply. Write your answers in simplest terms.

1. $\frac{12}{10} \times \frac{2}{3}$ 2. $2\frac{1}{2} \times \frac{3}{4}$ 3. $3\frac{1}{3} \times \frac{2}{3}$ 4. $4\frac{2}{8} \times \frac{8}{17}$

5. $3\frac{4}{5} \times \frac{10}{8}$ 6. $\frac{5}{6} \times 2\frac{2}{5}$ 7. $\frac{6}{9} \times 1\frac{3}{15}$ 8. $12\frac{1}{3} \times \frac{3}{4}$

9. $2\frac{1}{4} \times 3\frac{1}{2}$ 10. $5\frac{7}{8} \times 5\frac{1}{3}$ 11. $\frac{1}{2} \times \frac{3}{4} \times 2\frac{2}{3}$ 12. $1\frac{2}{5} \times 3\frac{6}{10} \times \frac{1}{4}$

(pages 230–231) Divide. Write your answers in simplest terms.

13. $4\frac{1}{3} \div \frac{1}{3}$ 14. $\frac{3}{4} \div 1\frac{2}{16}$ 15. $3\frac{5}{10} \div \frac{2}{5}$ 16. $\frac{12}{15} \div 1\frac{2}{3}$

17. $15\frac{4}{5} \div \frac{9}{10}$ 18. $11\frac{2}{6} \div \frac{34}{60}$ 19. $6\frac{1}{2} \div 2\frac{3}{4}$ 20. $3\frac{1}{5} \div 1\frac{4}{10}$

21. $8\frac{2}{3} \div 1\frac{4}{9}$ 22. $14\frac{3}{10} \div 2\frac{3}{30}$ 23. $22\frac{1}{2} \div 1\frac{4}{5}$ 24. $6\frac{1}{4} \div 5\frac{5}{9}$

(pages 244–245) Write as decimals. Use the bar for repeating decimals.

1. $\frac{2}{5}$ 2. $\frac{6}{10}$ 3. $\frac{5}{6}$ 4. $\frac{2}{9}$ 5. $\frac{17}{20}$

6. $\frac{13}{16}$ 7. $\frac{18}{25}$ 8. $\frac{30}{33}$ 9. $\frac{43}{200}$ 10. $\frac{15}{18}$

11. $\frac{8}{12}$ 12. $\frac{18}{45}$ 13. $\frac{1}{20}$ 14. $\frac{7}{11}$ 15. $\frac{34}{450}$

(pages 250–251) Write as fractions or mixed numbers. Simplify if possible.

16. 0.20 17. 0.75 18. 0.16 19. 0.48 20. 0.35

21. 0.80 22. 0.144 23. 0.360 24. 0.17 25. 0.175

26. 4.75 27. 6.35 28. 10.65 29. 20.020 30. 18.050

31. 21.95 32. 9.120 33. 13.575 34. 5.1600 35. 6.7520

EXTRA PRACTICE

(pages 260–261) Round to the nearest tenth.

1. 5.28   **2.** 9.84   **3.** 13.65   **4.** 0.793   **5.** 31.060

Round to the nearest hundredth.

6. 9.363   **7.** 2.755   **8.** 14.006   **9.** 32.692   **10.** 8.888

Round to the nearest thousandth.

11. 4.3418   **12.** 11.9015   **13.** 38.40063   **14.** 16.5554   **15.** 0.00090

(page 264–265) Compare. Use >, <, or =.

16. 7.389 ● 7.413   **17.** 10.6 ● 10.5   **18.** 13.74 ● 13.47   **19.** 0.3 ● 0.30

20. 21.873 ● 21.872   **21.** 3.356 ● 3.3651   **22.** 85.252 ● 8.595   **23.** 6.7043 ● 6.8042

(pages 274–275) Add.

1.   0.14 $+$ 0.25   **2.**   0.64 $+$ 0.13   **3.**   0.87 $+$ 0.06   **4.**   3.38 $+$ 1.65   **5.** $12.56 $+$ 5.75

6.   0.957 $+$ 0.463   **7.**   2.6 $+$ 6.35   **8.**   5.009 $+$ 8.3   **9.** $44.82 $+$ 66.59   **10.**   2.393 $+$ 8.76

11. 0.34 + 0.28   **12.** 1.49 + 3.61   **13.** 8.95 + 2.1   **14.** 9.17 + 18.9

15. 295.08 + 12.75   **16.** 15.24 + 15.477   **17.** 27.98 + 11.86   **18.** 31.312 + 0.9

(pages 278–279) Subtract.

19.   8.74 $-$ 5.53   **20.**   20.38 $-$ 9.59   **21.**   12.32 $-$ 4.6   **22.**   48.8 $-$ 26.03   **23.**   51.694 $-$ 18.89

24.   16.05 $-$ 8.346   **25.** $101.85 $-$ 75.98   **26.**   31.3 $-$ 29.781   **27.**   0.2 $-$ 0.193   **28.**   36.6 $-$ 14.767

29. 9.38 − 2.19   **30.** 11.08 − 4.4   **31.** 86.15 − 17.98   **32.** 94.899 − 7.21

33. 42.76 − 19.29   **34.** 76.04 − 47.98   **35.** 13.798 − 2.807   **36.** 862 − 14.029

(pages 288–289) Multiply.

1. $\begin{array}{r} 31.4 \\ \times\ \ 10 \\ \hline \end{array}$	**2.** $\begin{array}{r} 4.28 \\ \times\ \ 10 \\ \hline \end{array}$	**3.** $\begin{array}{r} 0.913 \\ \times\ \ 10 \\ \hline \end{array}$	**4.** $\begin{array}{r} 1.706 \\ \times\ \ 10 \\ \hline \end{array}$	**5.** $\begin{array}{r} 0.099 \\ \times\ \ 10 \\ \hline \end{array}$
6. $\begin{array}{r} 25.9 \\ \times\ 100 \\ \hline \end{array}$	**7.** $\begin{array}{r} 0.181 \\ \times\ 100 \\ \hline \end{array}$	**8.** $\begin{array}{r} 2.075 \\ \times\ 100 \\ \hline \end{array}$	**9.** $\begin{array}{r} 18.001 \\ \times\ 100 \\ \hline \end{array}$	**10.** $\begin{array}{r} 0.007 \\ \times\ 100 \\ \hline \end{array}$
11. $\begin{array}{r} 4.17 \\ \times\ 1{,}000 \\ \hline \end{array}$	**12.** $\begin{array}{r} 28.832 \\ \times\ 1{,}000 \\ \hline \end{array}$	**13.** $\begin{array}{r} 0.6543 \\ \times\ 1{,}000 \\ \hline \end{array}$	**14.** $\begin{array}{r} 0.002 \\ \times\ 1{,}000 \\ \hline \end{array}$	**15.** $\begin{array}{r} 0.5685 \\ \times\ 1{,}000 \\ \hline \end{array}$

16. 9.1×10^3 **17.** 35.06×10^2 **18.** 0.381×10^5 **19.** 0.972×10^3

20. 4.873×10^4 **21.** 27.84×10^3 **22.** 0.0029×10^5 **23.** 892.13×10^2

(pages 294–295) Divide.

24. $51.4 \div 10$ **25.** $7.83 \div 10$ **26.** $0.621 \div 10$ **27.** $16.03 \div 10$

28. $27.1 \div 100$ **29.** $272.6 \div 100$ **30.** $300.04 \div 100$ **31.** $2{,}029 \div 100$

32. $185 \div 1{,}000$ **33.** $1.38 \div 1{,}000$ **34.** $5{,}847 \div 10^3$ **35.** $166 \div 10^4$

36. $842.7 \div 10^3$ **37.** $28.32 \div 10^2$ **38.** $52.27 \div 10^3$ **39.** $895.7 \div 10^3$

(pages 304–305) Convert metric measures of length.

1. $7 \text{ m} = \blacksquare \text{ cm}$ **2.** $10 \text{ cm} = \blacksquare \text{ mm}$ **3.** $7.5 \text{ km} = \blacksquare \text{ m}$ **4.** $4 \text{ m} = \blacksquare \text{ cm}$

5. $3\ 841 \text{ m} = \blacksquare \text{ km}$ **6.** $0.75 \text{ m} = \blacksquare \text{ cm}$ **7.** $0.16 \text{ km} = \blacksquare \text{ m}$ **8.** $800 \text{ mm} = \blacksquare \text{ cm}$

9. $0.049 \text{ m} = \blacksquare \text{ mm}$ **10.** $6\ 565 \text{ mm} = \blacksquare \text{ m}$ **11.** $1\ 000 \text{ cm} = \blacksquare \text{ km}$ **12.** $0.486 \text{ km} = \blacksquare \text{ m}$

13. $19.1 \text{ m} = \blacksquare \text{ cm}$ **14.** $250 \text{ mm} = \blacksquare \text{ m}$ **15.** $1.25 \text{ m} = \blacksquare \text{ cm}$ **16.** $5\ 658 \text{ mm} = \blacksquare \text{ m}$

(pages 308–309) Convert metric units of capacity and mass.

17. $5\ 658 \text{ mg} = \blacksquare \text{ kg}$ **18.** $2.8 \text{ t} = \blacksquare \text{ kg}$ **19.** $10\ 183 \text{ mg} = \blacksquare \text{ g}$ **20.** $308 \text{ t} = \blacksquare \text{ kg}$

21. $8\ 314 \text{ mL} = \blacksquare \text{ L}$ **22.** $35 \text{ mg} = \blacksquare \text{ g}$ **23.** $5\ 000 \text{ g} = \blacksquare \text{ t}$ **24.** $9.5 \text{ L} = \blacksquare \text{ mL}$

25. $43.210 \text{ L} = \blacksquare \text{ mL}$ **26.** $4.2 \text{ kg} = \blacksquare \text{ mg}$ **27.** $256 \text{ mg} = \blacksquare \text{ g}$ **28.** $8\ 289 \text{ mg} = \blacksquare \text{ g}$

29. $128.7 \text{ t} = \blacksquare \text{ kg}$ **30.** $789 \text{ g} = \blacksquare \text{ t}$ **31.** $87 \text{ mg} = \blacksquare \text{ g}$ **32.** $23.2 \text{ mL} = \blacksquare \text{ L}$

EXTRA PRACTICE

(pages 318–319) Multiply.

1. $\quad 21.8$ $\underline{\times\ \ 0.4}$	**2.** $\quad 52.7$ $\underline{\times\ \ 1.4}$	**3.** $\quad 5.76$ $\underline{\times\ \ 0.8}$	**4.** $\quad 2.53$ $\underline{\times\ \ 5.4}$	**5.** $\quad 8.41$ $\underline{\times\ 10.7}$
6. $\quad 0.724$ $\underline{\times\ \ 2.3}$	**7.** $\quad 26.31$ $\underline{\times\ \ 9.05}$	**8.** $\quad 3.863$ $\underline{\times\ 2.751}$	**9.** $\quad 10.308$ $\underline{\times\ \ \ 9.2}$	**10.** $\quad 30.50$ $\underline{\times\ \ 1.00}$

11. 3.85×2.5 **12.** 0.74×30.3 **13.** 3.892×6.57 **14.** 0.368×0.54 **15.** 12.0×2.500

(pages 322–323) Divide.

16. $5 \overline{) 13.90}$ **17.** $8 \overline{) 34.56}$ **18.** $10 \overline{) 81.323}$ **19.** $23 \overline{) 35.88}$ **20.** $4 \overline{) 24.94}$

21. $3 \overline{) 29.463}$ **22.** $16 \overline{) 86.384}$ **23.** $31 \overline{) 26.257}$ **24.** $48 \overline{) 4.08}$ **25.** $94 \overline{) 4.606}$

(pages 324–325)

26. $0.5 \overline{) 3.25}$ **27.** $0.9 \overline{) 0.117}$ **28.** $0.2 \overline{) 0.0042}$ **29.** $4.6 \overline{) 42.78}$ **30.** $5.2 \overline{) 5.6524}$

31. $0.8 \overline{) 34.56}$ **32.** $2.3 \overline{) 35.88}$ **33.** $0.4 \overline{) 24.94}$ **34.** $0.3 \overline{) 29.463}$ **35.** $3.1 \overline{) 26.257}$

(pages 332–333) Write each ratio as a fraction.

1. 7 to 13   **2.** twenty to eight   **3.** 10 for $12   **4.** 61 to 100

Does each pair of ratios form a proportion? Write *yes* or *no*.

5. $\dfrac{4}{8} = \dfrac{1}{2}$ **6.** $\dfrac{10}{30} = \dfrac{9}{36}$ **7.** $\dfrac{7}{12} = \dfrac{28}{48}$ **8.** $\dfrac{2}{8} = \dfrac{8}{16}$

9. $\dfrac{23}{25} = \dfrac{92}{100}$ **10.** $\dfrac{4}{13} = \dfrac{12}{39}$ **11.** $\dfrac{3}{7} = \dfrac{45}{56}$ **12.** $\dfrac{66}{120} = \dfrac{11}{20}$

(pages 338–339) Write a proportion. Solve.

13. 3 oranges for $1.00
     How much for 5 oranges?

14. 12 eggs per carton $\dfrac{12}{1} =$
     How many cartons for 204 eggs?

15. 55 miles per hour
     How much time for 341 miles?

16. 5 gallons of gas for $9.25
     How much for 12 gallons?

(pages 348–349) List all the possible outcomes. Then give the probability of each if the spinner is spun only 1 time.

1.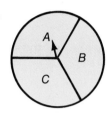

2.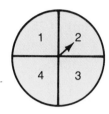

3.

4.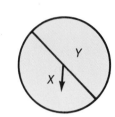

Give the probability for each outcome if the spinner is spun only 1 time.

5. B

6. 2

7. 4, B, or 2

8. 1, 2, 3, or 4

9. A, B, C, D, or 3

10. 1, B, A, 2, 4, or D

(pages 352–353)

11. Make a tree diagram to show the sample space for each. An outcome consists of one letter followed by one number. Use the letters R and B and the numbers 3, 5, and 8.

(pages 364–365)

Use circle M to answer the questions below.

1. Name the diameters shown.

2. Name the radii.

3. Name the chords.

4. Name five arcs.

5. If the measure of $\overline{QP}$ is 10 cm, what is the measure of:
$\overline{ON}$ $\overline{MO}$ $\overline{MP}$

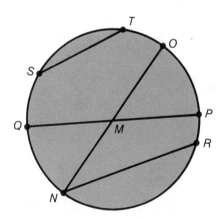

(pages 368–369) Find the area of each circle. Use 3.14 for π.

6. $r = 3$ cm

7. $r = 18$ ft

8. $r = 21$ mm

9. $r = 16$ km

EXTRA PRACTICE

(pages 378–379) Write each ratio as a percent.

1. 52 out of 100   **2.** 9 out of 100   **3.** 73 out of 100   **4.** 100 to 100

5. 20 out of 50   **6.** 6 out of 10   **7.** 13 out of 25   **8.** 15 to 20

Write each percent as a fraction. Simplify, if possible.

9. 34%   **10.** 75%   **11.** 9%   **12.** 2%   **13.** 10%

14. 12%   **15.** 40%   **16.** 113%   **17.** 160%   **18.** 350%

(pages 384–385) Change percents to decimals and solve.

19. 32% of 100   **20.** 79% of 300   **21.** 60% of 210   **22.** 19% of 150

23. 4% of 628   **24.** 20% of 90   **25.** 75% of 8   **26.** 85% of 250

27. 20% of $200.00   **28.** 9% of $96.00   **29.** 0.5% of $300.00   **30.** 12.3% of 165

(pages 394–395) Solve.

1. What percent of 20 is 5?   **2.** What percent of 90 is 45?

3. What percent of 200 is 66?   **4.** What percent of 50 is 13?

5. What percent of 25 is 24?   **6.** What percent of 20 is 17?

7. What percent of 10 is 6?   **8.** What percent of 35 is 70?

9. What percent of 72 is 72?   **10.** What percent of 8 is 72?

(pages 398-399) Solve.

11. 10% of what number is 9?   **12.** 150% of what number is 30?

13. 25% of what number is 55?   **14.** 40% of what number is 120?

15. 75% of what number is 210?   **16.** 25% of what number is 4?

17. 60% of what number is 90?   **18.** 12% is what number is 9?

(pages 408–409) Write the opposite integer for each.

1. $^+5$ **2.** $^+9$ **3.** $^-24$ **4.** $^-30$ **5.** $^+44$

6. $^-51$ **7.** $^-69$ **8.** $^+84$ **9.** $^+162$ **10.** $^-306$

11. $^+25$ **12.** $^-31$ **13.** $^+97$ **14.** $^-124$ **15.** $^+1$

Compare each pair of integers. Use > or <.

16. $^+18$ ● $^+19$ **17.** $^+12$ ● $^-13$ **18.** 0 ● $^-4$ **19.** $^-17$ ● $^+36$

20. $^-48$ ● $^+8$ **21.** $^+4$ ● $^-4$ **22.** $^-15$ ● $^-16$ **23.** $^+43$ ● $^-55$

24. $^+27$ ● $^-4$ **25.** $^-84$ ● $^-41$ **26.** $^+204$ ● $^-204$ **27.** $^+72$ ● $^+85$

(pages 412–413) Add.

28. $^+5 + {}^+6$ **29.** $^-2 + {}^-3$ **30.** $^+7 + {}^+15$ **31.** $^-23 + {}^-19$

32. $^+50 + {}^+32$ **33.** $^-45 + {}^-66$ **34.** $^+10 + {}^+110$ **35.** $^-30 + {}^-30$

36. $^+136 + {}^+258$ **37.** $^-305 + {}^-106$ **38.** $^+525 + {}^+444$ **39.** $^-625 + {}^-376$

40. $^+97 + {}^+248$ **41.** $^-43 + {}^-9$ **42.** $^+326 + {}^+428$ **43.** $^+24 + {}^+59$

(pages 422–423) Add.

1. $^-5 + {}^+2$ **2.** $^+8 + {}^-6$ **3.** $^-4 + {}^+10$ **4.** $^+9 + {}^-11$

5. $^-14 + {}^-1$ **6.** $^+20 + {}^-20$ **7.** $^-18 + {}^+6$ **8.** $^+3 + {}^-13$

9. $^-6 + {}^+16$ **10.** $^+7 + {}^-30$ **11.** $^-15 + {}^+45$ **12.** $^+1 + {}^-21$

13. $^-28 + {}^+24$ **14.** $^+72 + {}^-18$ **15.** $^+36 + {}^-9$ **16.** $^-241 + {}^+64$

(pages 428–429) Subtract.

17. $^-9 - {}^-5$ **18.** $^+18 - {}^+12$ **19.** $^-3 - {}^-12$ **20.** $^+7 - {}^+11$

21. $^-22 - {}^-13$ **22.** $^+28 - {}^+17$ **23.** $^-8 - {}^-16$ **24.** $^+10 - {}^+20$

25. $^-13 - {}^-22$ **26.** $^+50 - {}^+55$ **27.** $^-63 - {}^-36$ **28.** $^+75 - {}^+75$

29. $^+83 - {}^-41$ **30.** $^-24 - {}^+27$ **31.** $^+73 - {}^-21$ **32.** $^-58 - {}^-214$

The Five-Step Problem-Solving Plan

1. READ   Do I understand the meaning of each word in the problem?

2. KNOW   What is the question? What key facts do I need? The **key facts** are the facts I need to solve the problem.

3. PLAN   Which strategy should I choose? Which operation(s) should I use?

4. SOLVE   Carry out the plan. Will an equation help to solve the problem? What is my answer?

5. CHECK   Why is my answer reasonable? Does it answer the question?

Multiplication/Division Table

	0	1	2	3	4	5	6	7	8	9	10	11	12
0	0	0	0	0	0	0	0	0	0	0	0	0	0
1	0	1	2	3	4	5	6	7	8	9	10	11	12
2	0	2	4	6	8	10	12	14	16	18	20	22	24
3	0	3	6	9	12	15	18	21	24	27	30	33	36
4	0	4	8	12	16	20	24	28	32	36	40	44	48
5	0	5	10	15	20	25	30	35	40	45	50	55	60
6	0	6	12	18	24	30	36	42	48	54	60	66	72
7	0	7	14	21	28	35	42	49	56	63	70	77	84
8	0	8	16	24	32	40	48	56	64	72	80	88	96
9	0	9	18	27	36	45	54	63	72	81	90	99	108
10	0	10	20	30	40	50	60	70	80	90	100	110	120
11	0	11	22	33	44	55	66	77	88	99	110	121	132
12	0	12	24	36	48	60	72	84	96	108	120	132	144

Table of Symbols

Symbol	Meaning	Symbol	Meaning
+	plus	3^2	exponent
−	minus	∟	right angle
×	times; multiplied by	$\angle XYZ$	angle XYZ
÷	divided by	$m\angle QRS$	measure of angle QRS
=	is equal to	$\overset{\frown}{AB}$	arc AB
≠	is not equal to	$\overset{\leftrightarrow}{AB}$	line AB
≅	is congruent to	$\overline{AB}$	line segment AB
~	is similar to	$\overset{\rightarrow}{AB}$	ray AB
≈	is approximately equal to	%	percent
‖	is parallel to	$0.\overline{4}$	repeating decimal
⊥	is perpendicular to	π	pi; 3.14
>	is greater than	°	degrees
<	is less than	^+x	positive integer x
( )	parentheses mean "do this operation first."	^-x	negative integer x
		$\lvert x \rvert$	absolute value of x

Estimation Strategies

Rounding Round the numbers and approximate an answer.

29,462 →	29,000	3,792 → 3,800	632 → 600	19) 8,417
+ 7,839 →	+ 8,000	− 837 → − 800	× 87 → × 90	400
	37,000	3,000	54,000	20) 8,000

Front-End Estimation To estimate sums, differences, and products, first perform the operation on the front-end digits. Then look at the rest of the digits in each number and adjust your estimate.

Add: 7,817 + 8,198

Add the front-end digits.

$$
\begin{array}{c}
7,817 \\
+\ 8,198 \\
\hline
\end{array}
\qquad
\begin{array}{c}
7,817 \\
+\ 8,198 \\
\hline
15,
\end{array}
$$
The estimate is about 15,000.

Look at the other digits.
Adjust your estimate, if necessary.

$$
\begin{array}{c}
7,\boxed{817} \\
+8,\boxed{198}
\end{array}
$$ →about 1,000
So adjust the estimate up.
Estimate: **about 16,000**

Subtract: 8,286 − 3,389

Front-end digits: 8 − 3 = 5 The difference is about 5,000. Other digits: Since 286 < 389, adjust the estimate, 5,000, down. Estimate: **less than 5,000**

Subtract: 51,601 − 7,299

Front-end digits: 51 − 7 = 44 The difference is about 44,000. Other digits: Since 601 > 299, adjust the estimate, 44,000, up. Estimate: **more than 44,000**

Multiply: 9 × 8,417

Multiply the front-end digits.
9 × 8,000.

$$
\begin{array}{c}
8,417 \\
\times\ \ \ \ \ 9 \\
\hline
\end{array}
\qquad
\begin{array}{c}
8,000 \\
\times\ \ \ \ 9 \\
\hline
72,000
\end{array}
$$

Look at the other digits.
9 × 400.

$$
\begin{array}{c}
400 \\
\times\ \ \ 9 \\
\hline
3,600
\end{array}
$$

Add the products.

$$
\begin{array}{c}
72,000 \\
+\ 3,600 \\
\hline
75,600
\end{array}
$$

Adjust the estimate, if necessary. Since 417 was rounded down, the estimate, 75,600, is too small. Adjust up. Estimate: **more than 75,600**

To estimate a quotient, find how many digits are in the quotient and find the first digit. Divide: 7,126 ÷ 9

? ■■■
9) 7,126

Since 9 > 7, the first digit is not in the thousands place.

?■■
9) 7,126

9) 71 is about 7. The quotient has 3 digits. The first digit is 7.

7■■
9) 7,126

The quotient is more than 700. It is less than 800. Estimate: **between 700 and 800**

Period	Billions			Millions			Thousands			Ones								
Number	6	5	2	9	1	8	5	4	3	6	7	9	2	1	3	5	3

Place: Hundreds, Tens, Ones (Billions) | Hundreds, Tens, Ones (Millions) | Hundreds, Tens, Ones (Thousands) | Hundreds, Tens, Ones (Ones) | Tenths | Hundredths | Thousandths | Ten-thousandths | Hundred-thousandths

Number	Place	Value
6	hundred billions	600,000,000,000
5	ten billions	50,000,000,000
2	billions	2,000,000,000
9	hundred millions	900,000,000
1	ten millions	10,000,000
8	millions	8,000,000
5	hundred thousands	500,000
4	ten thousands	40,000
3	thousands	3,000
6	hundreds	600
7	tens	70
9	ones	9
2	tenths	0.2
1	hundredths	0.01
3	thousandths	0.003
5	ten-thousandths	0.0005
3	hundred-thousandths	0.00003

Time Measurements

1 second (s)	=	0.0000116 day
1 minute (min)	=	0.0006944 day
1 hour (h)	=	3,600 seconds
	=	0.0417 day
1 day (d)	=	86,400 seconds
	=	1,440 minutes
1 decade	=	10 years
1 score	=	20 years
1 century	=	100 years
1 millenium	=	1,000 years

Metric System Prefixes

Prefix	Symbol	Place	Value
mega-	M	one million	1 000 000
kilo-	k	one thousand	1 000
hecto-	h	one hundred	100
deka-	da	ten	10
deci-	d	one tenth	0.1
centi-	c	one hundredth	0.01
milli-	m	one thousandth	0.001
micro-	μ	one millionth	0.000001
nano-	n	one billionth	0.000000001

Table of Metric Measures

Length

1 centimeter (cm)	=	10 millimeters (mm)

1 decimeter (dm) = $\begin{cases} 100 \text{ millimeters} \\ 10 \text{ centimeters} \end{cases}$

1 meter (m) = $\begin{cases} 1\ 000 \text{ millimeters*} \\ 100 \text{ centimeters} \\ 10 \text{ decimeters} \end{cases}$

1 kilometer (km)	=	1 000 meters

Area

1 square meter (m^2) = $\begin{cases} 100 \text{ square decimeters } (dm^2) \\ 10\ 000 \text{ square centimeters } (cm^2) \end{cases}$

Volume

1 cubic centimeter (cm^3)	=	1 000 cubic millimeters (mm^3)

1 cubic decimeter (dm^3) = $\begin{cases} 1\ 000 \text{ cubic centimeters } (cm^3) \\ 1 \text{ liter } (L) \end{cases}$

1 cubic meter (m^3)	=	1 000 000 cubic centimeters

Capacity

1 liter (L) = $\begin{cases} 1\ 000 \text{ milliliters } (mL) \\ 1\ 000 \text{ cubic centimeters } (cm^3) \end{cases}$

Mass

1 gram (g)	=	1 000 milligrams (mg)
1 kilogram (kg)	=	1 000 grams
1 metric ton (t)	=	1 000 kilograms

Temperature

Water freezes at 0 degrees Celsius (0°C).
Water boils at 100 degrees Celsius (100°C).

* According to the United States Metric Association, spaces are used instead of commas in metric measurement.

Table of Customary Measures

Length

1 foot (ft)	=	12 inches (in.)
1 yard (yd)	=	{ 3 feet 36 inches
1 mile (mi)	=	{ 1,760 yards 5,280 feet

Area

1 square foot (ft^2)	=	144 square inches (in^2)
1 square yard (yd^2)	=	9 square feet
1 acre	=	4,840 square yards

Volume

1 cubic foot (ft^3)	=	1,728 cubic inches (in^3)
1 cubic yard (yd^3)	=	27 cubic feet

Capacity

1 cup (c)	=	8 fluid ounces (fl oz)
1 pint (pt)	=	{ 16 fluid ounces 2 cups
1 quart (qt)	=	{ 32 fluid ounces 4 cups 2 pints
1 gallon (gal)	=	{ 128 fluid ounces 16 cups 8 pints 4 quarts

Weight

1 pound (lb)	=	16 ounces (oz)
1 ton (t)	=	2,000 pounds

Temperature

Water freezes at 32 degrees Fahrenheit (32°F).
Water boils at 212 degrees Fahrenheit (212°F).

Table of Geometric Figures and Formulas

Two-dimensional figures

 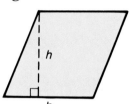 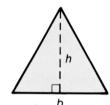 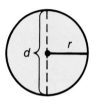

Rectangle
Perimeter =
$s_1 + s_2 + s_3 + s_4$
or $2(l + w)$
Area = $l \times w$

Parallelogram
Perimeter =
$s_1 + s_2 + s_3 + s_4$
or $2(l + w)$
Area = $b \times h$

Triangle
Perimeter =
$s_1 + s_2 + s_3$
Area = $\frac{1}{2} \times b \times h$

Circle
Circumference =
$\pi \times d$
Area = $\pi \times r^2$

Triangles

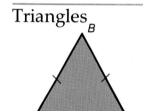 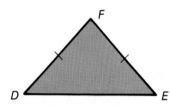 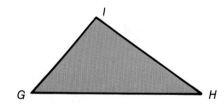

Equilateral: all sides are congruent

Isosceles: at least two sides are congruent

Scalene: no sides are congruent

Three-dimensional figures

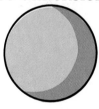 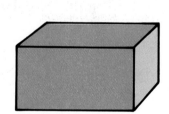

Sphere

Cube

Rectangular prism

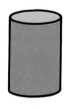  

Cylinder

Square pyramid

Cone

acute angle An angle that measures more than 0° but less than 90°.

acute triangle A triangle with three acute angles.

addend A number that is to be added. In 2 + 3 = 5, 2 and 3 are addends.

addition property of zero The sum of 0 and any number is that same number. $a + 0 = a$

adjacent angles Two angles that have a common side. $\angle ABC$ and $\angle CBD$ are adjacent angles.

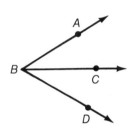

algorithm A step-by-step procedure for solving a problem.

angle A figure formed by two rays with a common endpoint.

arc A part of the circumference of a circle.

area The number of square units needed to cover a surface.

associative property of addition Changing the grouping of addends does not change the sum. $(a + b) + c = a + (b + c)$

associative property of multiplication Changing the grouping of factors does not change the product. $(a \times b) \times c = a \times (b \times c)$

average See *mean.*

BASIC A computer language. BASIC stands for **B**eginner's **A**ll-purpose **S**ymbolic **I**nstruction **C**ode.

binary A system of writing numbers that uses only the digits 0 and 1. The binary system is used in computers.

bisect Divide a figure into two congruent parts.

central angle An angle with its vertex at the center of a circle. $\angle XYZ$ is a central angle of circle Y.

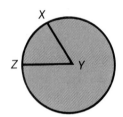

chord A line segment with endpoints on a circle.

circle A figure that has all points the same distance from a given point called the center.

circumference The distance around a circle.

coding the program Translating a plan for solving a problem into computer statements.

commutative property of addition Changing the order of the addends does not change the sum. $a + b = b + a$

commutative property of multiplication Changing the order of the factors does not change the product. $a \times b = b \times a$

complementary angles Two angles for which the sum of their measures is 90°.

composite number A number greater than 1 that has more than two factors.

computer plan The list of steps to follow in order to solve a problem. The first step in programming a computer.

computer program Step-by-step plan telling the computer what to do. It is written in computer language such as BASIC, Pascal, or COBOL.

congruent Figures with the same size and shape are congruent. Angles with the same measure are congruent.

coordinate axes Two perpendicular number lines that divide a plane and are used to graph ordered pairs.

coordinates The numbers of an ordered pair that indicate the location of a point on a plane.

cross products In the proportion $\frac{2}{3} = \frac{4}{6}$, 2×6 and 3×4 are the cross products.

cube (figure) A solid figure with six congruent square faces. (numeration) A number raised to the third power.

cylinder A solid figure with two bases that are congruent circles.

data A collection of facts.

decagon A polygon with ten sides.

decimal A number with place values based on ten. The following are decimals: 587 6.9 13.05

degree (angle) A unit for measuring angles. (temperature) A unit for measuring temperature.

denominator The bottom number in a fraction. It names the total number of equal parts. In $\frac{2}{3}$, 3 is the denominator.

diagonal A line segment that connects two vertices of a figure but is not a side or edge of the figure.

diameter A line segment with endpoints on a circle and passing through the center of the circle.

difference The result of subtracting one number from another.

distributive property The product of a number and a sum can be written as the sum of two products.
$$a \times (b + c) = (a \times b) + (a \times c)$$

dividend The number that is divided by another number. In $63 \div 9$ or $9\overline{)63}$, 63 is the dividend.

divisible One number is divisible by another number when there is no remainder after division. The number 6 is divisible by 2 since $6 \div 2 = 3$ and there is no remainder.

divisor A number by which another number is divided. In $63 \div 7$ or $7\overline{)63}$, 7 is the divisor.

END A command which must be the last statement of every computer program. This tells the computer that no other instructions will be coming.

equation A mathematical sentence using an equal sign ($=$). A statement that two expressions are equal.

equilateral triangle A triangle with three congruent sides.

equivalent fractions Two or more fractions that have the same value.

even number A whole number that is divisible by 2. Any whole number that has a ones digit of 0, 2, 4, 6, or 8.

exponent The number that shows how many times the base is used as a factor. In 5^3, the exponent is 3. The base 5 is used as a factor 3 times: $5^3 = 5 \times 5 \times 5 = 125$.

expression A combination of symbols such as numbers, letters, operation signs and parentheses that represents a number.

factor A number that is to be multiplied. In $4 \times 6 = 24$, 4 and 6 are factors.

fraction A number expressed in the form $\frac{a}{b}$.

frequency table An ordered listing of data and of the number of times each item occurred.

function A rule that assigns any given number in one set with exactly one corresponding number in another set.

greatest common factor (GCF) The greatest number that is a factor of two or more numbers. The greatest common factor of 24 and 32 is 8.

hard copy A permanent record of output, for example a computer printout.

hexagon A polygon with six sides.

improper fraction A fraction that has a numerator greater than or equal to the denominator.
Examples: $\frac{4}{4}$ or $\frac{7}{3}$.

inequality A mathematical sentence using an inequality symbol, such as $<$, $>$, or $\neq$.

INPUT A command that tells the computer to stop and wait for data to be entered.

integers The positive whole numbers, their opposites, and zero . . ., -3, -2, -1, 0, 1, 2, 3, . . .

intersecting lines Two lines that have a point in common.

inverse operation An operation that undoes another operation. Addition and subtraction are inverse operations. Multiplication and division are inverse operations.

isosceles triangle A triangle with two congruent sides.

kilogram (kg) The basic unit of mass in the metric system.

least common denominator (LCD) The least common multiple of the denominators of two or more fractions.

least common multiple (LCM) The least number that is not zero and is the multiple of two or more numbers. The least common multiple of 4 and 6 is 12.

line A straight path of points that goes on endlessly in two directions.

line segment A part of a line with two endpoints.

liter (L) The basic unit of capacity in the metric system.

Logo   A simple computer language that uses graphics on the screen.

mean   The average of a set of numbers. The sum of a set of numbers divided by the number of addends.

median   The middle number in a set of data which has been arranged in order. When there are two middle numbers, the median is their average.

memory   The place in which the computer stores information such as programs and data.

meter (m)   The basic unit of length in the metric system.

midpoint   The point that divides a line segment into two congruent parts.

mixed number   A number expressed as a whole number and a fraction.

mode   The item or items that occurs most frequently in a set of data.

multiple   A multiple of a number is the product of that number and a whole number.

multiplication property of one   The product of 1 and any number is the number itself. $a \times 1 = a$

multiplication property of zero   The product of 0 and any number is 0. $a \times 0 = 0$

negative number   A number that is less than zero.

numerator   The top number in a fraction. It names the number of parts being considered. In $\frac{2}{3}$, 2 is the numerator.

obtuse angle   An angle that measures more than 90° but less than 180°.

obtuse triangle   A triangle with one obtuse angle.

octagon   A polygon with eight sides.

odd number   A whole number that is not divisible by 2. Any whole number that has a ones digit of 1, 3, 5, 7, or 9.

order of operations   When there is more than one operation and parentheses are used, first do what is inside the parentheses. Next, multiply and divide from left to right. Then add and subtract from left to right.

ordered pair   A pair of numbers that names a point on a plane.

origin   The point of intersection of the x-axis and the y-axis. Its coordinates are (0, 0).

outcome   A possible result in a probability experiment.

output   The result of the program produced by the computer.

parallel lines   Two straight lines in a plane that do not intersect.

parallelogram   A quadrilateral with opposite sides congruent and parallel.

Pascal   A computer language that is more structured than BASIC.

pentagon   A polygon with five sides.

percent (%)   Per hundred. It gives the ratio of a number to 100.

perimeter   The sum of the lengths of the sides of a polygon.

perpendicular bisector   A line that passes through the midpoint of a given line segment and is perpendicular to it.

ndicular lines Two lines that ...and form four right angles.

pi (π) The ratio of the circumference to the diameter in any circle. Its value is approximately 3.14 or $\frac{22}{7}$.

place value The value assigned to a digit in a number because of its position. Each place denotes a value of 10 times the place to its right.

planned output Steps in a program that arrange how the output will appear on the screen.

polygon A closed figure in a plane made up of line segments.

positive number A number that is greater than 0.

power A number expressed as a base and an exponent. 2^4 is the fourth power of 2. $2^4 = 16$.

prime factorization A number expressed as the product of prime numbers.

prime number A number greater than 1 that has exactly two factors, 1 and the number itself.

PRINT A command that tells the computer to display a certain output.

probability The chance that a given event will occur.

product The result of multiplying two numbers.

program See *computer program*.

proportion An equation stating that two ratios are equivalent.
Example: $\frac{3}{5} = \frac{6}{10}$.

protractor An instrument used to measure angles.

quadrant The x- and y-axes divide the coordinate plane into four regions called quadrants.

quadrilateral A polygon with four sides.

quotient The number you get when one number is divided by another. In $56 \div 8$ or $8\overline{)56}$, the quotient is 7.

radius A line segment from the center of a circle to any point on the circle.

range The difference between the greatest number and the least number of a set of data.

ratio A comparison of two numbers, usually expressed as a fraction.

ray A part of a line with one endpoint and extending without end in the other direction.

reciprocals Two numbers that have a product of 1. The fractions $\frac{2}{3}$ and $\frac{3}{2}$ are reciprocals since $\frac{2}{3} \times \frac{3}{2} = \frac{6}{6} = 1$.

rectangle A parallelogram with four right angles.

regular polygon A polygon with all sides congruent and all angles congruent.

relatively prime Two or more numbers that have a greatest common factor of 1. Example: 9 and 11.

remainder The number left over after a division is completed.
Example:

$$7 \overline{)\,64} \quad \begin{array}{r} 9 \text{ R1} \leftarrow \text{Remainder} \\ -63 \\ \hline 1 \end{array}$$

repeating decimal A decimal in which one or more digits repeat without end. Examples: $0.333 \ldots$, or $0.\overline{3}$, $0.123123123 \ldots$, or $0.\overline{123}$.

right angle An angle that measures $90°$.

right triangle A triangle with one right angle.

RUN A command that tells the computer to execute a program.

sample space A list of all possible outcomes of a given situation.

scale drawing A drawing that represents a real object. The measures shown on the drawing are proportional to actual measures of the object.

scalene triangle A triangle with no congruent sides.

scientific notation A number written as a number between 1 and 10 multiplied by a power of ten.
Example: $1,060 = \underbrace{1.06 \times 10^3}_{\text{scientific notation}}$

sequence A set of numbers written in order, usually according to a pattern.

simplest terms A fraction is in simplest terms when the only common factor of the numerator and the denominator is 1. A mixed number is in simplest terms when the fraction part is less than 1 and is in simplest terms.

square A rectangle with four congruent sides and four right angles.

straight angle An angle that measures $180°$.

sum The result of adding two numbers.

supplementary angles Two angles for which the sum of their measures is $180°$.

symmetry A figure has symmetry, if, when folded along a central line, the two parts match exactly.

terminating decimal A decimal which has a definite number of decimal places. Examples: 0.2, 0.1005, 0.0000007

trapezoid A quadrilateral with only one pair of parallel sides.

triangle A polygon with three sides.

twin primes Two prime numbers that differ by 2, such as 11 and 13.

variable A letter used to represent an unknown number.

vertex A point that two rays of an angle have in common. The common point of any two sides in a polygon.

volume The number of cubic units needed to fill a space.

whole number Any of the numbers 0, 1, 2, 3, . . .

A

Addition
  with calculator,
  of decimals, 274–277
  estimating sums, 64, 445, 497
  of fractions and mixed numbers, 152–155
  of integers, 412–414, 419, 422–424, 431
  in magic squares, 99
  mental addition, 27
  properties of, 53, 65, 97
  of whole numbers, 27, 62–64, 271
Algebra, 5, 13
  applications, 51, 65, 95, 109, 411, 415, 425, 431
  equations, 48–49, 51–54, 109, 329, 435, 456–458
  exponential expressions, 45
  exponents, 38–41, 48–50, 75, 82–84
  expressions, 45, 48–50, 89, 449, 452–454
  formula for area of a circle, 293, 368–370, 501
  formula for area of irregular figures, 171, 175
  formula for area of a parallelogram, 172–175, 293, 501
  formula for area of a rectangle, 168–172, 174-175, 292–293, 359, 501
  formula for area of a triangle, 170–172, 174–175, 293, 501
  formula for circumference of a circle, 501
  formula for perimeter of a parallelogram, 501
  formula for perimeter of a rectangle, 455, 501
  formula for perimeter of a triangle, 501
  formula for volume of a rectangular prism, 363
  graphing a line on a grid, 425
  graphing linear equations, 161, 425
  graphing ordered pairs of integers on a grid, 411, 419
  grid, 161, 411, 419, 425, 463, 473
  inequalities, 449, 456–458
  inverse equations, 52–54
  inverse operations, 45, 52–54
  order of operations, 48–50, 89, 312–313

Algebra (*continued*)
  ordered pairs, 161, 411, 419, 425, 463, 473
  parentheses, 48–50
  power, 48–50, 75
  properties of addition, 53, 65, 97
  properties of multiplication, 95, 97, 109
  solving proportions, 334, 338–341, 345, 391, 394–396, 398–401
  true, false, and open sentences, 49, 51, 306
  variables, 51, 454–455, 458
Angles
  classifying, 182–185
  complementary, 187
  exterior, 183
  measuring, 179, 182–183
  naming, 182–183, 359, 463
  of polygons, 186–189
  straight, 182
  supplementary, 187
  vertex of, 182
Applications. *See* Problem-solving applications.
Area
  of a circle, 293, 368–370, 501
  of an irregular figure, 171, 175
  of a parallelogram, 172–175, 293, 501
  of a rectangle, 168–172, 174–175, 292–293, 359, 501
  of a triangle, 170–172, 174–175, 293, 501
Associative property
  of addition, 53, 65
  of multiplication, 95, 109
Average, 47, 196–199, 460. *See also* Mean.
Axis of a grid, 411

B

Banking, 277, 281, 372–373
Bar graph, 37, 199
Base-Two (binary) number system, 41
Binary (base-two) number system, 41

C

Calculator
  applications, 81, 253, 263, 309, 387

Calculator (*continued*)
  changing fractions to decimals, 253, 263
  finding factors of numbers, 81
  finding integer sums and differences, 43
  finding a percent of a number, 387
  finding products of whole numbers, 83
  finding what percent one number is of another, 395
  identifying prime numbers, 81
Calendars, 79, 273
Capacity, 77, 298, 308–310, 341
Centimeter, 304–307, 499
  cubic, 311, 499
  square, 168–175, 306, 499
Circle
  arc, 364–365, 466–469
  area of, 293, 368–370, 501
  center, 364, 367
  central angle of, 364, 367
  chord, 364–365
  circumference of, 366, 369, 501
  construction of, 367
  diameter, 364–367, 369–370
  pi (π), 366, 368–370
  radius, 364–370
Circle graph, 381, 397
Circumference, 366, 369
Class projects. *See* Projects.
Common Factor, 145. *See also* Greatest common factor.
Commutative property
  of addition, 53, 65, 97
  of multiplication, 95, 97, 109
Comparing and ordering
  decimals, 264–267
  fractions, 142–144
  integers, 408–410
  money amounts, 267
  whole numbers, 34–36, 135, 257, 405
Composite numbers, 78–84, 117
Computer
  algorithms, 176–177, 220, 356
  BASIC, 86–87, 220, 268–269, 356, 446–447
  calculating area of a rectangle, 220
  END, 220
  flowcharts, 87
  FORTRAN, 86
  and fractions, 474–475
  input, 268–269
  INPUT, 220
  and integers, 446–447
  languages, 86–87, 220

Computer (*continued*)
  Logo, 86
  Math in technology, 86–87,
    176–177, 220–221, 268–269,
    312–313, 356–357, 446–447,
    474–475
  memory, 86
  order of operations, 312–313
  output, 268–269, 356
  PASCAL, 86
  plan, 176–177, 356
  planned output, 356
  PRINT, 86–87, 220, 268–269,
    356, 446–447
  program, 86–87, 220, 268–269,
    356, 446–447, 474–475
  RUN, 86–87, 220
Congruence, 466–468, 470–473
Construction
  of a circle, 367
  of a congruent angle, 466–468
  of a congruent figure, 466–468
  of a congruent triangle, 470–472
  of a congruent line segment,
    466–468
  of a perpendicular bisector, 469
Coordinate graph. *See* Grid.
Critical thinking, 28–29, 42–43,
  56–57, 72–73, 86–87, 100–101,
  114–115, 132–133, 146–147, 162–
  163, 176–177, 190–191, 206–207,
  220–221, 234–235, 254–255,
  268–269, 282–283, 298–299, 312–
  313, 326–327, 342–343, 356–357,
  372–373, 388–389, 402–403,
  416–417, 432–433, 446–447,
  460–461, 474–475. *See also* Math
  in content.
Cross products, 138–140
Cube 282–283, 501
Cubic centimeter, 311, 499
Cubic foot, 341, 363, 500
Cubic inch, 341, 500
Cubic meter, 311, 499
Cup, 341, 500
Customary units of area
  square foot, 150–151, 168–175,
    210–211, 500
  square inch, square mile, square
    yard, 168–175, 500
Customary units of capacity
  convert units, 341, 500
  cup, ounce, pint, quart, 341, 500
  gallon, 77, 341, 363, 500
Customary units of length
  convert units, 341, 500
  foot, 137, 150–151, 210–211,
    341, 500
  inch, 341, 455, 500
  mile, 77, 100, 303, 341, 500
  yard, 341, 500
Customary units of volume
  convert units, 341,500
  cubic foot, 341, 363, 500

Customary units of volume
(*continued*)
  cubic inch, 341, 500
  cubic yard, 341, 500
Customary units of weight
  convert units, 341, 500
  ounce, pound, 341, 500
Customary units of temperature
  degrees Fahrenheit, 273, 500

D

Data bank, 496–501
Decimals
  addition of, 274–277
  applications, 277, 281
  changing fractions and mixed
    numbers to decimals, 244–
    247, 263, 375
  changing decimals to fractions
    and mixed numbers, 250–251,
    253
  comparing and ordering, 264–
    267
  convert metric measures, 291,
    297
  decimal-fraction equivalents, 252
  division of, 294–295, 297, 301,
    322–324
  estimate products of, 290, 296
  multiplication of, 288–289, 291,
    301, 315, 318–321, 325
  place value of, 271
  repeating, 244–246
  rounding, 260–263, 267, 285
  sequences of, 295
  subtraction of, 278–281
  terminating, 244–247
Decimeter, 304, 499
Degree (angular), 179, 182–183,
  185
Degree (temperature)
  Celsius, 298, 499
  Fahrenheit, 273, 500
Denominator, 138–140, 142–144
Diameter, 364–367, 369–370
Distributive property of
  multiplication, 109
Dividend, 96
Divisibility patterns, 113, 125, 203
Division
  basic facts table, 496
  with calculator, 81
  with decimals, 294–295, 297,
    301, 322–324
  divisibility patterns, 113, 125,
    203
  estimating quotients, 96, 98,
    296, 459, 497
  with fractions and mixed
    numbers, 216–219, 223, 230–
    232

Division (*continued*)
  of integers, 442–444
  in magic squares, 99
  with money,
  of whole numbers, 96–98, 103,
    110–112, 237, 315
Divisor, 96

E

Electricity
  kilowatt, kilowatt-hour, watt,
    254
Endpoints, 182, 406
Equation, 51–54, 109, 329, 456–
  458
Equivalent fractions, 138–140,
  142–144, 149, 161, 329
Estimation
  applications
    with decimals, 260–263, 290,
      296
    with fractions, 159, 215
    with measurement, 71, 304
    with money, 445
    with statistics and probability,
      7, 199, 397
    with whole numbers, 24–26,
      64, 71, 83
  to check for reasonable answers,
    22–23, 66–67, 71, 126–127,
    155–157, 200–201, 219, 248–
    249, 292–293, 336–337, 382–
    383, 445, 459
  strategies
    clustering and adjusting,
      445
    compatible numbers, 497
    front-end estimation, 445, 459,
      497
    range, 96, 98, 459
    rounding to find differences,
      71, 83, 497
    rounding to find products, 93,
      215, 290, 296, 497
    rounding to find quotients,
      96, 98, 110–111, 296, 459,
      497
    rounding to find sums, 64, 83,
      159, 445, 497
Evaluating information, 37, 55,
  66–67, 85
Expanded notation, 18–20, 31
Exponential notation, 31, 38–41,
  45, 82–84
Exponents, 38–41, 48–50, 75, 82–
  84
Expressions, 45, 48–50, 89, 449,
  452–454
Extra practice, 482–495

, 78–84, 117
..tor tree, 82–84
Flowchart, 87
Foot, 137, 150–151, 210–211, 341, 500
   cubic, 341, 363, 500
   square, 150–151, 168–175, 210–211, 500
Formulas
   area of a circle, 293, 368–370, 501
   area of irregular figures, 171, 175
   area of parallelogram, 172–175, 293, 501
   area of a rectangle, 168–172, 174–175, 292–293, 359, 501
   area of a triangle, 170–172, 174–175, 293, 501
   circumference of a circle, 501
   perimeter of a parallelogram, 501
   perimeter of a rectangle, 455, 501
   perimeter of a triangle, 501
   volume of a rectangular prism, 363
Formulating Problems
   age differences, 224–225
   building a snowhouse, 436–437
   crocodile breeding in Kenya, 104–105
   daily schedule, 16–17
   diving for silver ingots, 90–91
   flight schedules, 60–61
   floor plan, 210–211
   flying a hot-air balloon, 120–121
   Fool's Rules Regatta, 346–347
   forest fires, 194–195
   fuel economy of motor vehicles, 76–77
   helping an elderly person, 316–317
   high-wheeler bicycles, 450–451
   Marlboro Milers, 46–47
   movies and sound tracks, 420–421
   opinion poll, 258–259
   ordering in a restaurant, 166–167
   painting a room, 150–151
   planning activities for young children, 286–287
   planning a party, 392–393
   schedules, 180–181
   school orientation, 242–243
   shopping for school supplies, 406–407
   soap box cars, 136–137
   taking a trip, 272–273
   television viewing schedule, 32–33

Formulating problems (continued)
   time-lapse films, 376–377
   vacation budget, 464–465
   walkathon, 302–303
   water conservation, 362–363
   workers in a thrift shop, 330–331
Fractions and mixed numbers
   addition of, 152–155
   changing decimals to, 250–251, 253
   changing, to decimals, 244–247, 263, 375
   changing percents to, 391
   comparing and ordering, 142–144
   and computers, 474–475
   cross products, 138–140
   decimal-fraction equivalents, 252
   denominator, 138–140, 142–144
   division of, 216–219, 223, 230–232
   equivalent fractions, 138–140, 142–144, 149, 161, 329
   exploring density of fractions, 233
   geometric sequences of, 261
   improper fractions, 209, 223
   least common denominator (LCD), 142–144, 149
   mixed numbers, 209, 223
   multiplication of, 165, 212–215, 223, 226–228
   numerator, 138–140, 142–144
   on a number line, 160
   reciprocals, 214
   sequences of, 129, 217, 231, 261
   in simplest terms, 124–125, 145, 149, 209, 237, 375
   subtraction of, 158–160
Frequency table, 202–205
Front-end estimation, 445, 459, 497

G

Gallon, 77, 341, 363, 500
GCF (greatest common factor) 122–125, 145, 149
Geometry, 5, 9
   angles, 179, 182–183, 185, 359, 463, 466–468
   angles of polygons, 186–189
   applications, 161, 185, 189, 367, 469
   arc, 364–365, 466–469
   area, 168–175, 292–293, 298, 359, 368–370, 501
   circle, 293, 364–370, 501
   classifying angles, triangles, 182–185

Geometry (continued)
   closed curve, 364
   compass, 466–469
   complementary angles, 187
   congruence, 466–468, 470–473
   constructing a circle, 367
   constructing congruent angles, 466–468
   constructing congruent figures, 466–468
   constructing congruent triangles, 470–472
   constructing congruent line segments, 466–468
   constructing perpendicular bisectors, 469
   cube, 282–283, 501
   decagon, 188
   degree (angular), 179, 182–183, 185
   diagonal, 234–235
   exterior angle, 183
   grid, 161, 411, 419, 425, 463, 473
   hexagon, 188
   irregular figures, 171, 175
   line, 425
   line segment, 364–365, 367, 466–468
   measuring angles with a protractor, 179, 182–183
   octagon, 188
   parallelogram, 165, 172–175, 186–187, 293, 501
   pentagon, 188
   perimeter, 455, 501
   pi (π), 366, 368–370
   polygon, 186–189, 292–293
   protractor, 179, 182–183
   pyramids, 56–57
   quadrilaterals, 186–187, 189
   ray, 466–468
   rectangle, 165, 168–172, 174–175, 186, 189, 206–207, 292–293, 359, 455, 501
   rectangular prism, 363, 501
   square, 186, 189, 234–235
   straight angle, 182
   supplementary angles, 187
   symmetry, 371
   tangram puzzle, 234–235
   trapezoid, 186
   triangle, 165, 170–172, 174–175, 182–185, 189, 293, 470–473, 501
   vertex of angles, 182
   volume, 311, 341, 363, 499–500
Geometric patterns—tessellation, 132–133
Geometric sequences, 261, 331
Golden ratio, 206–207
Gram, 291, 298, 308–310
Graphs
   bar graph, 37, 199

Graphs (continued)
    circle graph, 381, 397
    line graph, 205
Greatest common factor (GCF), 122–125, 145, 149
Grid, 161, 411, 419, 425, 463, 473

H

Hexagon, 188
Hour, 155, 498

I

Identity property
    of one (multiplication), 109
    of zero (addition), 53
Improper fractions, 209, 223
Inch, 341, 455, 500
    cubic, 341, 500
    square, 168–175, 500
Inequalities, 449, 456–458
Integers
    addition of, 412–414, 419, 422–424, 431
    comparing and ordering, 408–410
    division of, 442–444
    graph ordered pairs of integers on a grid, 411, 419
    multiplication of, 438–440
    negative, 408–411, 425
    on a number line, 408–411, 428–431
    positive, 408–411
    sequences of, 423, 441, 443
    subtraction of, 428–431
Inverse operations, 45, 52–54
Irregular figures, 171, 175

K

Kilogram, 291, 308–310, 499
Kilometer, 121, 297, 304–307, 325, 500
    cubic, 499
    square, 168–175, 306, 499
Kilowatt, kilowatt-hour, 254

L

Languages, computer
    COBOL, FORTRAN, Logo, Pascal, 86
    BASIC, 86–87, 220, 268–269, 356, 446–447

Languages, computer (continued)
    Least common denominator (LCD), 142–144, 149
    Least common multiple (LCM), 128–130, 135, 142–144, 149
    Length
        customary units, 77, 100, 137, 150–151, 210–211, 303, 341, 455, 500
        metric units, 121, 297–298, 304–307, 325, 499
Line, 425
Line graph, 205
Line segment, 364–365, 367, 466–468
Line of symmetry, 371
Logic, 4, 12
    algorithm, 176–177, 220, 356
    applications, 99, 233
    determine whether a fraction is in simplest terms, 145
    exploring density of fractions, 233
    finding rules describing number patterns, 200–201
    flowchart, 87
    game of nim, 114–115
    guess and test, 336–337
    magic square, 99
    making predictions based on information, data, 17, 47, 91, 105
    order of operations, 48–50, 89, 312–313
    problem solving, 382–383
    true, false, and open sentences, 49, 51, 306
Logo, 86
Looking ahead, 31, 45, 59, 75, 89, 103, 117, 135, 149, 165, 177, 193, 209, 223, 237, 257, 271, 285, 301, 315, 329, 345, 359, 375, 391, 405, 419, 435, 449, 463, 477
Looking back, 30, 44, 58, 74, 88, 102, 116, 134, 148, 164, 178, 192, 208, 222, 236, 256, 270, 284, 300, 314, 328, 344, 358, 374, 390, 404, 418, 434, 448, 462, 476

M

Maps, 72–73, 100–101, 335, 388–389
Math in content
    architecture, 42–43
    art, 132–133
    cartography, 72–73, 100–101
    consumer education, 190–191, 372–373
    games, 114–115, 234–235, 282–283
    geography, 388–389, 432–433

Math in content (continued)
    health, 416–417
    history of mathematics, 146–147, 342–343
    music, 326–327, 402–403
    science, 162–163, 254–255, 298–299
    social studies, 56–57, 206–207
    sports, 28–29, 460–461
    technology, 86–87, 176–177, 220–221, 268–269, 312–313, 356–357, 446–447, 474–475
Math strands, 5. *See also* Algebra; Geometry; Logic; Measurement; Number skills; Patterns and Functions; Statistics and Probability.
Mean, 47, 196–199, 460. *See also* Average.
Measurement, 5, 8. *See also* Customary measurement and Metric measurement.
    of angles using a protractor, 179, 182–183
    applications, 171, 175, 247, 291, 307, 311, 325, 335, 341, 455
    in electricity, 254
    finding foreign currency exchange rates, 291
    Solving problems, 307
    of time, 17, 33, 47, 61, 155, 215, 225, 247, 273, 317, 342–343, 421
Median, 196–198
Memory, computer, 86
Mental arithmetic. *See also* Estimation.
    applications, 291, 297
    converting metric measures, 291, 297
    dividing decimals, 297
    dividing by multiples of ten, 103, 297
    divisibility rules, 124–125
    finding 3-digit sums and differences, and 4-digit products, 27
    in measurement, 304
    multiplying by multiples of ten, 103
    meter, 121, 297–298, 304–307, 325, 499
    cubic, 311, 499
    square, 168–175, 298, 306, 499
Metric units of area
    square centimeter, 168–175, 306, 499
    square dekameter, 306
    square kilometer, 168–175, 306
    square meter, 168–175, 298, 306, 499
    square millimeter, 168–175, 306
Metric units of capacity
    liter, 298, 308–310, 499

its of capacity (continued)
, 308–310, 499
s of length
..meter, 304–307, 325, 499
converting units, 325, 499
decimeter, 304, 499
dekameter, 297, 304, 306
hectometer, 297, 304
kilometer, 121, 297, 304–307, 325, 499
meter, 121, 297–298, 304–307, 325, 499
millimeter, 304–306, 325, 499
Metric units of mass
converting units, 291, 499
dekagram, hectogram, 291
gram, 291, 298, 308–310, 499
kilogram, 291, 308–310, 499
metric ton, 308–310, 499
milligram, 308–309, 499
Metric units of temperature
degrees Celsius, 298, 499
Metric units of volume
cubic centimeter, cubic meter, 311, 499
Metronome, 326–327
Mile, 77, 100, 303, 341, 500
Millennium, 247, 498
Milliliter, 308–310
Mixed numbers. See Fractions and mixed numbers.
Mode, 196–199, 202–205
Money
applications, 267, 277, 281
banking, 277, 281, 372–373
budget, 465
calculating discounts, 407
calculating party costs, 392–393
cost of food items, 317
checking account, 277, 281, 372–373
finding foreign currency exchange rates, 291
finding a money amount when a percent of it is known, 401
finding a percent of a money amount, 387, 401
finding what percent one money amount is of another, 401
in problem-solving, 141, 151, 331
round, compare, and order money, 267
savings account, 372–373
unit price, 190
using consumer skills, 277, 281
Multiples, 117, 128–120. See also least common multiple.
Multiplication
basic facts, 435, 496
with calculator, 83
convert metric measures, 291
cross products, 138–140

Multiplication (continued)
of decimals, 288–289, 291, 301, 315, 318–321, 325
estimating products, 290, 296, 459, 457
finding foreign currency exchange rates, 291
of fractions and mixed numbers, 165, 212–215, 223, 226–228
of integers, 438–440
in magic squares, 99
mental multiplication, 27
of whole numbers, 27, 92–94, 103, 106–108, 229, 315, 325
properties of, 95, 97, 109

N

Napier's bones, 229
Number line, 135, 160, 405, 408–411, 428–431
Number patterns. See Patterns and Functions.
Number skills, 4, 6–7. See Addition, Subtraction, Multiplication, Division, Fractions and mixed numbers, Decimals, Integers, and Whole numbers.
Numeration
ancient numbers, 146–147
applications, 21, 41, 81, 85, 145
base, 38–41
base-two (binary) number system, 41
billions, 18–20, 498
comparing and ordering decimals, 264–267
comparing and ordering fractions, 142–144
comparing and ordering integers, 408–410
comparing and ordering money amounts, 267
comparing whole numbers, 34–36, 135, 193, 257, 405
expanded form, 18–20, 31
exponential notation, 31, 38–41, 45, 82–84
millions, 18–20, 498
periods, 18, 20
place value of decimals, 271
place value of whole numbers, 18–20, 34–35
power, 48–50, 75
powers of ten, 31, 285, 301
Roman numerals, 21
rounding decimals, 260–263, 267, 285
rounding money amounts, 267
rounding whole numbers, 24–26, 59, 257

Numeration (continued)
standard form, 18–21
thousands, 18–20, 498
Numerator, 138–140, 142–144

O

Octagon, 188
Operations, inverse, 45, 52–54
Opposite (inverse) operations, 45, 52-54
Order of operations, 48–50, 89, 312–313
Ordered pairs, 161, 411, 419, 425, 463, 473
Ounce (capacity, weight), 341, 500
Outcomes, 348–355

P

Parallelogram, 165, 172–175, 178, 186–187, 293, 501
Patterns and functions, 5, 10. See also Geometric patterns, and Sequences, number.
applications, 113, 125, 321, 441
divisibility patterns, 113, 125, 203
in division, 113
finding rules describing number patterns, 200–201
Fibonacci sequence, 197
geometric patterns and sequences, 132–133, 261, 331
magic squares, 99
in multiplication, 108, 321
Napier's bones, 229
number patterns and sequences, 93, 99, 108, 111, 125, 129, 197, 200–201, 217, 203, 231, 252, 261, 295, 321, 331, 423, 441, 443
sequences of ordered pairs, 425
tessellations, 132–133
Pentagon, 188
Percent
with calculator, decimals for, 380–381
for decimals, 380–381
discount, 407
finding a number when a percent of it is known, 398–401
finding a percent of a number, 384–387, 401
finding what percent one number is of another, 394–396, 401
fractions for, 378–380, 391
for fractions, 378–381

Percent *(continued)*
  and ratios, 378–379
  in statistics, 259, 381
Perimeter
  of a parallelogram, 501
  of a rectangle, 455, 501
  of a triangle, 501
Periods, 18, 20
Pi (π), 366, 368–370
Pint, 341, 500
Polygons
  decagon, 188
  diagonals of, 188
  hexagon, 188
  irregular, 188
  octagon, 188
  parallelogram, 165, 172–175,
    186–187, 293
  pentagon, 188
  quadrilateral, 186–187, 189
  rectangle, 165, 168–172, 174–
    175, 186, 189, 206–207, 292–
    293, 359, 455
  regular, 188
  square, 186, 189, 234–235
  trapezoid, 186
  triangles, 165, 170–172, 174–175,
    182–185, 189, 293, 470–473
Pound, 341, 500
Power, 48–50, 75
Powers of ten, 31, 285, 301
Prime factorization, 82–84, 117,
  130
Prime numbers, 78–85, 117
  relatively prime numbers, 122–
    123
  twin primes, 85
Probability, 5, 11
  as a fraction, 348, 351, 353–355
  chance and music, 402–403
  combinations, 305
  experiments, 355, 402
  outcomes
    favorable, 348–351
    possible, 348–354
    probable, 355
  predicting, 348–351, 353–355
  sample space, 352–354
  tree diagram, 352–354
Problem Solving
  applications
    with decimals, 247, 253, 263,
      267, 277, 281, 291, 293, 297,
      307, 311, 317, 321, 325, 367,
      407, 465
    with exponents, 41
    with fractions, 141, 145, 155,
      161, 171, 175, 215, 219, 233,
      247, 253, 263, 293, 307, 331,
      355, 371, 460
    with geometry, 161, 168–175,
      185–189, 282–283, 292–293,
      311, 335, 363, 367, 371, 381,
      391, 411, 425, 455, 469, 473

Problem solving *(continued)*
  with integers, 411, 425, 431,
    441, 446, 473
  with measurement, 27, 47, 77,
    150–151, 168–175, 182–189,
    215, 291–293, 297–299, 307,
    311–312, 317, 325, 335, 341,
    363, 367, 436–437, 455, 465,
    469
  with money, 85, 131, 141, 151,
    267, 277, 281, 291, 317, 331,
    387, 393, 397, 407, 445, 465
  with percent, 381, 387, 397,
    401, 407, 460
  with ratio and proportion,
    335, 338–341, 351, 384–387,
    394–396, 398–401
  with statistics and probability,
    37, 47, 77, 199, 205, 351,
    381, 391, 402, 411
  formulating problems. *See also*
    Formulating problems. 16–
    17, 32–33, 46–47, 60–61,
    76–77, 90–91, 104–105,
    120–121, 136–137, 150–151,
    166–167, 180–181, 194–195,
    210–211, 224–225, 242–243,
    258–259, 272–273, 286–287,
    302–303, 316–317, 330–331,
    346–347, 362–363, 376–377,
    392–393, 406–407, 420–421,
    436–437, 450–451, 464–465
Strategies
  choosing an operation, 131,
    219, 325
  choosing an appropriate
    strategy, 426–427
  finding a pattern, 113, 125,
    132, 200–201, 229, 233–235,
    282–283, 321, 331, 441
  identifying extraneous and/or
    missing information, 37, 55,
    66–67, 85
  making a list, 248–249
  solving a simpler related
    problem, 382–383, 401
  using a diagram, 27, 82–84,
    117, 156–157, 171, 175, 352–
    354
  using estimation, 71, 215, 445,
    459
  using an equation, 325, 351,
    384–387, 394–396, 398–401
  using a flowchart, 86–87
  using the five-step problem-
    solving plan, 22–23, 66–67,
    126–127, 155–157, 200–201,
    248–249, 292–293, 336–337,
    382–383, 426–427
  using a formula, 121, 168–
    175, 185–189, 292–293, 311–
    313, 363, 366–370, 455
  using a graph, 37, 161, 199,
    205, 381, 397, 411, 425

Problem solving *(continued)*
  using guess and test, 336–337
  using logic, 99, 382–383
  using a map, 72–73, 307, 388–
    389
  using a table/chart. *See also*
    Formulating problems, 81,
    108, 141, 193, 202–204, 207,
    281, 416, 455
Programs, computer, 86–87, 220,
  268–269, 356, 446–447, 474–475
Projects
  choosing a strategy, 427
  evaluating information, 67
  Finding a pattern, 201
  making a list, 249
  solving multi-step problems, 127
  using a diagram, 157
  using the five-step problem-
    solving plan, 23
  using a formula, 293
  using guess and test, 337
  using logic, 383
Properties of addition
  commutative, 53, 65, 97
  associative, 53, 65
  identity property of zero, 53
Properties of multiplication
  commutative, 95, 97, 109
  associative, 95, 109
  distributive, 109
  property of one, 109
  property of zero, 109
Proportions, 332–335, 338–341,
  345, 391, 394–396, 398–401
Pyramids, 56–57

Q

Quadrilateral, 186–187, 189
Quart, 341, 500

R

Radius, 364–370
Range
  statistics, 196–199, 202–205
  estimation, 96, 98
Ratios and proportions
  cross products in, 334
  equivalent ratios, 332–333, 345
  fractions for, 378–379
  golden ratio, 206–207
  scale drawing, 72–73, 335
  solving proportions, 334, 338–
    341, 345, 391, 394–396, 398–
    401
Ray, 466–468
Reciprocals, 214
Rectangle, 165, 168–172, 174–175,
  178, 186, 189, 206–207, 292–293,
  359, 455, 501

umerals, 21

260–263, 267, 280
mate differences, 71, 83,
445, 497
to estimate products, 93, 215,
290, 296, 459, 497
to estimate quotients, 96, 98,
110–111, 296, 459, 497
to estimate sums, 64, 83, 159,
445, 497
money, 267

S

Sample space, 352–354
Scale drawing, 72–73, 335
Square, 186, 189, 234–235
Square centimeter, 168–175, 499
Square foot, 150–151, 168–175,
210–211, 500
Square inch, 168–175, 500
Square meter, 168–175, 298, 300,
499
Square yard, 168–175, 500
Standard form, 18–21
Statistics, 5, 11
applications, 37, 199, 205, 381,
473
bar graph, 37, 199
circle graph, 381, 397
factor tree, 82–84
flowchart, 87
frequency table, 202–205
grid, 161, 411, 419, 425, 463, 473
line graph, 205
list, 248–249
mean (average), 47, 196–199,
460
median, 196–198
mode, 196–199, 202–205
opinion poll, 259
percent in, 259, 381
range, 196–199, 202–205

Statistics (continued)
table chart, 87, 141, 193, 199,
202–205, 267, 291. See also
Problem-solving strategies.
tallying, 193, 202–204
tree diagram, 352–354
Subtraction
of decimals, 278–281
estimating differences, 71, 445,
497
of fractions and mixed numbers,
158–160
of integers, 428–431
mental subtraction, 27
of whole numbers, 27, 68–71,
271
Symmetry, 371

T

Temperature
Celsius, 298, 499
Fahrenheit, 273, 500
Tessellations, 132–133
Tests
final review/test, 480–481
looking back, 30, 44, 58, 74, 88,
102, 116, 134, 148, 164, 178,
192, 208, 222, 236, 256, 270,
284, 300, 314, 328, 344, 358,
374, 390, 404, 418, 434, 448,
462, 476
midterm review/test, 240–241
quarterly review/test, 118–119,
238–239, 360–361, 478–479
Time
ancient timekeeping, 342–343
calendars, 79, 273
century, 247, 498
decade, 247, 498
hour, 155, 498
leap year, 79
millenium, 247, 498
minute, 47, 421, 498

Time (continued)
schedule, 17, 33, 61, 181
second, 421, 498
year, 79, 225, 247, 498
Ton, 499, 500
Trazezoid, 186
Tree diagram, 352–354
Triangle
acute, 182–184
area of, 170–172, 174–175, 178,
293, 501
equilateral, 184, 189, 501
isosceles, 184, 189, 501
naming, 182
obtuse, 182–184
perimeter of, 501
right, 182–185, 189
scalene, 184, 501
Twin primes, 85

U

Unit price, 190

V

Variable, 51, 454–455, 458
Vertex, of angles, 182
Volume, 311, 341, 363, 499–500

W

Weight, 341, 500

Y

Yard, 341, 500
cubic, 341, 500
square, 168–175, 500
Year, 79, 225, 247, 498

Art Credits

Tom Leonard: pp. 24, 70, 82, 83, 190.
Bradley Clark: p. 79.

Photo Credits

The following abbreviations indicate the position of the photograph on the page: *t*, top; *b*, bottom; *l*, left; *r*, right; *c*, center.

Glyn Cloyd: 80, 109, 235, 332.
Ken Karp/OPC: 308, 310, 326, 353, 406.
Ken Lax: 16, 115, 150, 244, 250, 283, 420.
Victoria Beller-Smith: 4(tl), 177, 224, 316, 392.

2(br), Richard Dunoff/The Stock Market; 2(bl), Gabe Palmer/The Stock Market; 2(tl), D.P. Hershkowitz/Bruce Coleman; 2(tr), David Madison/Bruce Coleman; 4(tr), L.L.T. Rhodes/Taurus Photos; 4(bl,br), Menschenfreund/The Stock Market; 6, Dorothy deLyon/Bruce Coleman; 29, Julian Baum/Bruce Coleman; 32, Don Brewster/Bruce Coleman; 36, S.L. Craig, Jr./Bruce Coleman; 42, Tom McHugh/Photo Researchers; 43, Alvin Uptis/The Image Bank; 46, Richard Choy/Peter Arnold; 57(t,b), Malcolm Kirk/Peter Arnold; 60, Geoffrey Gove/The Image Bank; 71, C. Vergara/Photo Researchers; 76, John Blaustein/Woodfin Camp and Assoc.; 87, Wanda Orlinkowsky; 90, Carl Roessler/Bruce Coleman; 101(t) Frank Whitney/The Image Bank; 101(b), Don Carroll/The Image Bank; 104, Jeff Simon/Wheeler Pictures; 120, Douglas Faulkner/Photo Researchers; 133, Metropolitan Museum of Art, Gift of Arthur Houghton, Jr., 1970; 136, Daniel Mainzer; 147, Borromeo/Art Resource; 163, NASA; 166, Fukuhara/WestLight; 180, Dean Abramson/Stock, Boston; 191, Ted Horowitz/The Stock Market; 195, David Falconer/Bruce Coleman; 207, Norman Tomalin/Bruce Coleman; 211, D.P. Hershkowitz; 221, Tannenbaum/Sygma; 242, Will McIntyre/Photo Researchers; 255, Keith Gunnar/Bruce Coleman; 258, J. Sylvester/FPG; 269, Wanda Orlinkowsky; 272, Ann Hagen Griffith/OPC; 286, John McGrail/Wheeler Pictures; 299(t) Chris Jones/The Stock Market; 199(b) Norman Tomalin/Bruce Coleman; 302, Dan Miller; 327, Cary Wolinsky/Stock, Boston; 330, Dave Johnson/Bruce Coleman; 342, The Granger Collection; 343, Stuart Cohen/The Stock Market; 346, Jim Daniels; 357, Thomas Zimmerman/FPG; 362, Manuel dos Passos/Bruce Coleman; 373, Kim Steele/Black Star; 376, Jane Burton/Bruce Coleman; 403(t), David Burnett/Contact; 403(b), The Granger Collection; 417, David Madison/Bruce Coleman; 433, NASA; 436, George Holton/Photo Researchers; 447, Guy Gillette/Photo Researchers; 450, Clifford Hausner/Leo deWys; 461, Focus on Sports; 464, Michael Gallagher/Bruce Coleman; 475, Wanda Orlinkowsky.